2011243

INSTITUTIONAL CORRUPTION

In this book, Seumas Miller develops distinctive philosophical analyses of corruption, collective responsibility, and integrity systems, and applies them to cases in both the public and the private sectors. Using numerous well-known examples of institutional corruption, he explores a variety of actual and potential anti-corruption measures. The result is a wide-ranging, theoretically sophisticated, and empirically informed work on institutional corruption and how to combat it. Part I defines the key concepts of corruption, power, collective responsibility, bribery, abuse of authority, and nepotism; Part II discusses anti-corruption and integrity systems, corruption investigations, and whistleblowing; and Part III focuses on corruption and anti-corruption in specific institutional settings, namely policing, finance, business, and government. Integrating theory with practical approaches, this book will be important for those interested in the philosophy and ethics of corruption as well as for those who work to combat it.

SEUMAS MILLER has research appointments at Charles Sturt University, Delft University of Technology, and the University of Oxford. His publications include *The Moral Foundations of Social Institutions* (Cambridge University Press, 2010), *Shooting to Kill: The Ethics of Police and Military Use of Lethal Force* (2016), and *Corruption and Anti-Corruption in Policing* (2016).

INSTITUTIONAL CORRUPTION

A Study in Applied Philosophy

SEUMAS MILLER

Charles Sturt University, Delft University of Technology, and the University of Oxford

CAMBRIDGE
UNIVERSITY PRESS

DAMAGED

University Printing House, Cambridge CB2 8BS, United Kingdom

One Liberty Plaza, 20th Floor, New York, NY 10006, USA

477 Williamstown Road, Port Melbourne, VIC 3207, Australia

4843/24, 2nd Floor, Ansari Road, Daryaganj, Delhi – 110002, India

79 Anson Road, #06–04/06, Singapore 079906

Cambridge University Press is part of the University of Cambridge.

It furthers the University's mission by disseminating knowledge in the pursuit of education, learning, and research at the highest international levels of excellence.

www.cambridge.org
Information on this title: www.cambridge.org/9780521869461
DOI: 10.1017/9781139025249

© Seumas Miller 2017

First published 2017

Printed in the United States of America by Sheridan Books, Inc.

A catalogue record for this publication is available from the British Library.

Library of Congress Cataloging-in-Publication Data
NAMES: Miller, Seumas, author.
TITLE: Institutional corruption : a study in applied philosophy / Seumas Miller, Charles Sturt University, Delft University of Technology and the University of Oxford.
DESCRIPTION: Cambridge, United Kingdom ; New York, NY : Cambridge University Press, 2017. | Includes bibliographical references and index.
IDENTIFIERS: LCCN 2017030643| ISBN 9780521869461 (hardback) | ISBN 9780521689632 (paperback)
SUBJECTS: LCSH: Applied ethics. | Corruption. | Moral conditions.
CLASSIFICATION: LCC BJ1031 .M553 2017 | DDC 172–dc23
LC record available at https://lccn.loc.gov/2017030643

ISBN 978-0-521-86946-1 Hardback
ISBN 978-0-521-68963-2 Paperback

Contents

Acknowledgments

I wish to thank the editors of the following academic publications for use of some of the material of mine contained therein: "Joint Action" *Philosophical Papers*, vol. xxi no. 3 (1992); "Freedom of the Press" *Politikon*, 22 (1995); *Ethical Issues in Policing* (1996); *Police Ethics* (with J. Blackler and A. Alexandra) (1997); "Collective Responsibility" *Public Affairs Quarterly*, vol. 15 no. 1 (2001); *Model Code of Principles of Ethics* (2002); "Individual Autonomy and Sociality" in (ed.) F Schmitt *Socialising Metaphysics: Nature of Social Reality* (2003); "Noble Cause Corruption in Politics" in (ed.) I. Primoratz *Politics and Morality* (2007); "Noble Cause Corruption Revisited" in P. Villiers and R. Adlam (eds.), *A Safe, Just and Tolerant Society: Police Virtue Rediscovered* (2004); "Concept of Corruption" in E. Zalta (ed.), *Stanford Encyclopedia of Philosophy*, Fall 2005 edn.; *Ethical Issues in Policing* (with J. Blacker) (2005); (with P. Roberts and E. Spence), *Corruption and Anti-Corruption: A Study in Applied Philosophy* (2005); "Collective Moral Responsibility: An Individualist Account" in P. French (ed.), *Midwest Studies in Philosophy*, vol. XXX (2006); (with A. Alexandra, T. Campbell, D. Cocking, and K. White), *Professionalization, Ethics and Integrity*, Report for the Professional Standards Council (2006); "Institutions, Integrity Systems and Market Actors" in J. O'Brien (ed.), *Private Equity, Corporate Governance and the Dynamics of Capital Market Regulation* (2007); "Against the Moral Autonomy Thesis" *Journal of Social Philosophy*, 38 (2007); (with T. Prenzler), *An Integrity System for Victoria Police: Volume 1* (2008); (with S. Curry, I. Gordon, J. Blackler, and T. Prenzler), *An Integrity System for Victoria Police: Volume 2* (2008); (with A. Alexandra), *Integrity Systems for Occupations* (2010); "What Makes a Good Internal Affairs Investigation?" *Criminal Justice Ethics*, 29 (2010); "Integrity Systems and Professional Reporting in Police Organizations" *Criminal Justice Ethics*, 29 (2010); "Financial Service Providers: Integrity Systems, Reputation and the Triangle of Virtue" in

N. Dobos, C. Barry, and T. Pogge (eds.), *The Global Financial Crisis: Ethical Issues* (2011); (with I. Gordon) *Investigative Ethics: Ethics for Police Detectives and Criminal Investigators* (2014); "Police Detectives, Criminal Investigations and Collective Moral Responsibility" *Criminal Justice Ethics*, vol. 33 no. 1 (2014); "The Corruption of Financial Benchmarks: Financial Markets, Collective Goods and Institutional Purposes" *Law and Financial Markets Review*, 8 (2014); "'Trust me....I'm a (systemically important) bank!': Institutional corruption, market-based industries and financial benchmarks" *Law and Financial Markets Review*, 8 (2014); "Trust, Conflicts of Interest and Fiduciary Duties: Ethical Issues in the Financial Planning Industry in Australia" in N. Morris and D. Vines (eds.), *Capital Failure: Rebuilding Trust in Financial Services* (2014); "The Global Financial Crisis and Collective Moral Responsibility" in Andre Nollkaemper and Dov Jacobs (eds.), *Distribution of Responsibilities in International Law* (2015); (with P. Walsh), "NSA, Snowden and the Ethics and Accountability of Intelligence Gathering" in J. Galliott (ed.), *Ethics and the Future of Spying: Technology, Intelligence Collection and National Security* (2015); *Corruption and Anti-Corruption in Policing: Philosophical and Ethical Issues* (2016).

I would also like to acknowledge support from the Australian Graduate School of Policing and Security Studies at Charles Sturt University, the Department of Values, Technology and Innovation at Delft University of Technology, the Uehiro Centre for Practical Ethics at the University of Oxford and the European Research Council Advanced Grant project on Collective Responsibility and Counterterrorism.

Introduction

The Diversity of Corruption

Corruption is exemplified by a diverse array of phenomena.[1] Here are some paradigmatic cases of corruption. A national leader channels public monies into his personal bank account. The members of a political party secure a majority vote for their candidates by arranging for ballot boxes to be stuffed with false voting papers. The managers of a corporation bribe public officials in order to win lucrative tenders. Traders from a number of leading banks cooperate to manipulate financial benchmarks. The members of a crime syndicate launder money through a legitimate business outlet that they control. A journalist provides unwarranted favorable comment about the banking sector in return for financial rewards from that sector. A group of journalists working for a particular media outlet consistently provide unwarranted unfavorable comment about a political candidate in order to influence the electorate against that candidate. A police officer fabricates evidence in order to secure convictions. Senior members of government pressure the head of an anticorruption unit to abandon a criminal investigation into alleged bribes being paid by a local defense contractor to a foreign government to win a large arms contract. A number of doctors close ranks and refuse to testify against a colleague who they know has been negligent in relation to an unsuccessful surgical operation leading to loss of life. A student provides sexual favors to her teacher in exchange for good grades. An actor provides sexual favors to film directors in exchange for securing acting roles. A respected researcher's success relies on plagiarizing the work of others. A public official in charge of allocating community housing to needy

---

[1] An earlier version of this chapter appeared in Seumas Miller, Peter Roberts, and Edward Spence, *Corruption and Anti-Corruption: A Study in Applied Philosophy* (Saddle River, NJ: Prentice Hall, 2005), chapter 1.

I

citizens unfairly discriminates against a minority group he despises. A manager only promotes those who ingratiate themselves to her. A sports trainer provides the athletes he trains with banned substances in order to enhance their performance.

This is a long list of quite diverse examples of corruption, and it could easily be extended much further. Moreover, the list involves individuals acting alone as well as members of groups acting together. Further, in all of these examples the practice described undermines, or has a tendency to undermine, some legitimate institutional purpose or process, whether it be a political or criminal justice or competitive market process or purpose. In short, institutional corruption is both *causal* and *normative* in character.[2]

Let us now consider the relationship between corruption and illegality. Many of the examples involve unlawful activities. But some do not. Moreover, many of the examples are unlawful in some jurisdictions but not others, or they are now unlawful in a given jurisdiction but were not in earlier times. In short, many of these examples of corruption are not necessarily unlawful. Prior to 1977 it was not unlawful for US companies to offer bribes to secure foreign contracts. Nor apparently was manipulation of the financial benchmark LIBOR (the London interbank offered rate – used in the calculation of interest rates on trillions of dollars of loans throughout the world) unlawful prior to 2012.[3] So corruption is not necessarily unlawful. This is because corruption is not at bottom simply a matter of law. Rather, it is fundamentally a matter of morality, and law and morality are not the same thing, although they are intertwined in various ways.

There is a further distinction to be made in relation to morality and corruption. Corrupt actions are immoral actions, but not all immoral actions are corrupt actions. For corruption is only one species of immorality. Consider an otherwise gentle husband who in a fit of anger strikes his adulterous wife and kills her. The husband has committed an act that is morally wrong; he has killed his wife. But his action is not necessarily an act

---

[2] See Miller et al., *Corruption and Anti-Corruption*, chapter 1; Seumas Miller, "Corruption" in Edward N. Zalta (ed.), *Stanford Encyclopaedia of Philosophy*, www.plato.stanford.edu fall 2005; Dennis Thompson, *Ethics in Congress: From Individual to Institutional Corruption* (Washington DC: Brookings Institution, 1995), "Two Concepts of Corruption: Individual and Institutional," *Edmond J. Safra Working Papers*, 16 (2013) Available at SSRN: http://ssrn.com/abstract=2304419 or http://dx.doi.org/10.2139/ssrn.2304419; Lawrence Lessig, *Republic, Lost: How Money Corrupts Congress – and a Plan to Stop It* (New York: Twelve, 2011).

[3] See HM Treasury, *The Wheatley Review of LIBOR* (Final Report) (London, 2012) available at www.hm-treasury.gov.uk/wheatley_review.htm.

of corruption. An important general distinction in this regard is that between human rights violations and corruption. Genocide is a profound moral wrong, but it is not corruption. This is not to say that there is not an important relationship between human rights violations and corruption; on the contrary, there is often a close and mutually reinforcing nexus between the two.[4] Consider the endemic corruption and large-scale human rights abuse that have taken place under authoritarian regimes such as those of Idi Amin in Uganda, Suharto in Indonesia, Saddam Hussein in Iraq, and Assad in Syria. And it is now generally accepted by economists that there is a (admittedly complex) causal connection between corruption and the infringement of subsistence rights; corruption causes poverty.[5] Indeed, sometimes an act of human rights violation might also be an act of corruption. Thus wrongfully and unlawfully incarcerating one's political opponent is a human rights violation, but it is also a corruption of the political process.[6]

There are many forms of institutional corruption, including many types of economic, political corruption, police corruption, judicial corruption, academic corruption, and so on. Indeed, there are as many forms of institutional corruption as there are types of social institution the institutional purposes and processes of which might be culpably undermined, i.e., that might become corrupted. Moreover, there are a variety of different kinds of attractions that motivate corruption. These include economic gain, status, power, addiction to drugs or gambling, and sexual gratification.

Contemporary societies are typically dominated by organizations and systems of organizations; the forms of activity in question take place for the most part in organizational settings and are undertaken in large part by organizational role occupants. Accordingly, in contemporary settings corrupt activity is in large part institutional corruption.[7] Enron, Arthur Anderson, and Bernard L. Madoff Investment Securities were all economic

---

[4] See Z. Pearson, "An International Human Rights Approach to Corruption" in P. Larmour and N. Wolanin (eds.), *Corruption and Anti-Corruption* (Canberra: Asia-Pacific Press, 2001), pp. 30–61.

[5] J. Stiglitz, *The Great Divide: Unequal Societies and What We Can Do* (New York: W. W. Norton, 2016).

[6] For a useful compendium of work on the multiplicity of forms of political corruption see A. J. Heidenheimer and M. Johnson (eds.), *Political Corruption: Concepts and Contexts*, 3rd edn. (Piscataway, NJ: Transaction Publishers, 2001).

[7] Theorists tend to focus on economic institutions. See S. Rose-Ackerman, *Corruption and Government* (Cambridge University Press, 1999), J. G. Lambsdorff, *The Institutional Economics of Corruption and Reform: Theory, Evidence and Reform* (Cambridge University Press, 2007), and R. B. Reich, *Saving Capitalism: For the Many Not the Few* (New York: Alfred A. Knoff, 2015).

organizations, and capitalism is a system of such organizations, crony capitalism being a corruption of that system. Moreover, contemporary capitalism consists in large part in specific organizational forms, such as multinational corporations, organized into a system and defined in part by laws and regulations, e.g., regulations defining free and fair competition. Likewise, governments and other public sector agencies comprise organizations and systems of organization in the political sphere. Institutions in the sense used in this book are organizations or systems of organizations (albeit, as will become clear, not all organizations are institutions). I provide a detailed account of institutions in Chapter 1.[8] Here I note that whereas all institutions are vulnerable to corruption – institutional corruption tends to undermine institutional purposes and processes – different institutions are vulnerable to different forms of corruption. Thus plagiarism is more likely to be present in universities than in police organizations, and fraud more likely in corporations than in either universities or police organizations. Accordingly, we can distinguish generic forms of corruption by recourse to particular institutions, e.g., academic corruption, police corruption, corporate corruption, and so on. Thus we require not only a definition of institutional corruption per se (see Chapter 3) but also analyses of institutional corruption in different institutions (see Chapters 11–14). We also require analyses of specific types of corruption, such as bribery, nepotism, fraud, and abuse of authority (see Chapter 5).

Moral Environments

Corrupt and/or criminal activities typically take place in a moral environment that might be conducive to, or intolerant of, such activities. The moral environment consists in part of the framework of social norms that are adhered to, or at least, are paid lip-service to within a society or polity and, more narrowly, within an institution. This framework is a more or less coherent structure of social norms.[9] Social norms are regularities in action or omission sustained in part by the moral approval and disapproval of the adherents to those social norms. So the members of

---

[8] Seumas Miller, *The Moral Foundations of Social Institutions: A Philosophical Study* (New York: Cambridge University Press, 2010).

[9] See Seumas Miller, *Social Action: A Teleological Account,* (New York. Cambridge University Press, 2001), chapter 4; Seumas Miller, "Social Norms" in G. Holmstrom-Hintikka and R. Tuomela (eds.), Synthese Library Series, *Contemporary Action Theory* (Dordrecht: Kluwer, 1997), vol. II, pp. 211–229; and Seumas Miller, "On Conventions," *Australasian Journal of Philosophy,* 70 (1992), 435–445.

a social group not only behave in accordance with a structured set of social norms, they believe that they ought to comply with these norms. These beliefs, taken in conjunction with the believed-in goals, ends, or purposes from which many social norms are derived, constitute a structured system of moral beliefs – in short, a worldview about what constitutes morally acceptable, and morally unacceptable, behavior.[10]

Whatever the differences in moral outlook of individual members of a social group, there will inevitably be a high degree of commonality in their moral beliefs and the regularities in action consequent upon those beliefs; in short, social groups require social norms. This is because social norms are necessary for social life beyond a very basic level. For example, social norms against random killing enable cooperative economic and family institutions. Again, social norms of truth-telling and of providing evidence for statements are necessary for institutions of learning.

There is a tendency to confuse social norms with other sorts of closely related conformist behavior, such as conventions and following fashions. Roughly speaking, conventions are regularities in behavior that realize common ends but, unlike social norms in the sense of the term used here, conventions do not necessarily have moral content. Consider, for example, the convention in English to utter "snow" rather than the French word "neige" to refer to snow. In the case of fashions, the individual conforms because she desires to do what others approve of. In the case of social norms, the individual conforms because she believes she morally ought to do what everyone (or most) including the agent herself morally approves of. Hence, in the case of a social norm, but not a fashion, failure to conform produces shame. Consider the corrupt police officers who were brought before the Royal Commission into Corruption in the New South Wales Police Service in Australia in the mid-1990s. Some of these police officers violated social norms by taking bribes, dealing in drugs, and selling child pornography. It was obvious that when many of these men were brought before the Commissioner, and their corruption exposed in video and tape recordings, they experienced deep shame. This indicates that it is not merely a convention or a fashion that they have flouted. So, social norms go hand-in-hand with the social moral emotion of shame. Failure to conform to social norms elicits feelings of shame, and shaming is a powerful form of social control.

There is a distinction between subjectively held social norms and objectively valid moral norms. An objective moral norm is a type of action

---

[10] See M. Boylan, *Basic Ethics* (Upper Saddle River, NJ: Prentice Hall, 1999).

or inaction that is not only widely believed to be morally right, but is, as a matter of objective truth,[11] morally right. It needs to be noted that the concept of an objectively corrupt action is the concept of an action that is objectively corrupt relative to a person, and relative to a set of circumstances. Considered in itself lying is morally wrong; it is *pro tanto* morally wrong. Nevertheless, lying might be morally justified in some circumstances because, for instance, it was the lesser of two evils; it might be morally right all things considered. Police working undercover to expose the activities of the Triads in Hong Kong necessarily deceive and tell lies. Nonetheless, they may be morally justified in doing so since lying to criminals may be a lesser evil than allowing their criminal activities to go unchecked. However, the mere fact that one was a member of a society that had certain social norms, or that the actions of those in the moral environment in which one found oneself were governed by certain social norms, would not in itself make performing the action prescribed by those social norms objectively morally right (even *pro tanto*).

Social norms, on the one hand, and immorality, including corruption, are intimately, if antithetically, related. Robust social norms – at least in the sense of regularities in action that embody ethical or moral attitudes – provide a barrier to corruption; widespread corruption corrodes social norms. This barrier is by no means a sufficient condition for combating immorality, including corruption. But it is a necessary condition. If members of a community or organization do not think there is anything morally wrong with murder, assault, theft, fraud, bribery, and so on, then there is no possibility of these practices being resisted, let alone eliminated; indeed, they will flourish.

So, shared beliefs in the moral unacceptability of these practices are a necessary, but not a sufficient, condition for combating them. Here the role of institutions and sub-institutions is critical and, in particular, anti-corruption institutions or, more broadly, *integrity systems* (see Chapter 7).[12] Such institutions develop, maintain, and promote the internalization of institutional purposes and compliance with social norms, and thus both directly combat corruption and also build resistance to corruption in a community or an organization. Importantly, the members of an

---

[11] For a general defense of objectivity see Thomas Nagel, *The Last Word* (Oxford University Press, 1997).

[12] C. Sampford, R. Smith, and A. J. Brown, "From Greek Temple to Bird's Nest: Towards a Theory of Coherence and Mutual Accountability for National Integrity Systems," *Australian Journal of Public Administration*, 64 (2005), 96–108. See also Andrew Alexandra and Seumas Miller, *Integrity Systems for Occupations* (Aldershot: Ashgate, 2010).

institution who have internalized and value that institution's purposes and its constitutive social norms will tend to possess moral resilience in the face of the temptations of corruption. Of further importance here is the criminal justice system, including the police, the courts, and correctional facilities. These institutions combat corruption as part of their wider anti-crime remit. There are also more specialized anti-corruption institutions, such as independent commissions against corruption and the like. In addition, there are a wide range of educational, awareness raising, and transparency serving institutions and sub-institutional elements, such as the media, churches, professional ethics programs, and fraud and corruption awareness programs at an organization or industry-wide level.

Conditions Conducive to Corruption

Some societies or social groups suffer a breakdown in the framework of social norms, and notably a failure of compliance with, and enforcement of, the moral principles enshrined in the criminal law. Such moral principles include ones not to murder, assault, infringe the freedom of others, steal, defraud, or bribe. There are a number of socio-moral features or conditions that facilitate institutional corruption. If organizations, governments, and communities are to successfully combat (especially) grand or systemic corruption, then I suggest that they need to rectify these conditions.[13]

First, there is the condition of a high level of *conflict and factionalism*. There is good empirical evidence that conflict-ridden societies (involving, for instance, class, caste, and racial factionalism as well as violent conflict), such as apartheid and, for that matter, post-apartheid South Africa, the former Soviet Union (and current nation-states of Ukraine, Russia, and so on), Nigeria, and India provide fertile ground for corruption. Here I note that conflict-ridden societies in this sense include ones with authoritarian governments; the conflict and factionalism in question might obtain between an authoritarian government and its political opposition and, at a deeper level, between an economic elite (supported by the authoritarian government) and a relatively impoverished lower economic class (supported by the political opposition). In conflict-ridden societies there is typically not a robust and sufficiently wide system of social norms that are adhered to by virtually everyone and of common purposes that are pursued

[13] See J. Pope (ed.), *National Integrity Systems: The TI Source Book* (Berlin: Transparency International, 1997); R. Klitgaard *Controlling Corruption* (Los Angeles: University of California Press, 1988).

by virtually everyone. Rather, at most, members of a particular social group
or class pursue only their own narrow collective interests and comply with
social norms in their relations with one another, but not with "outsiders."

A second, and often related, socio-moral condition that is conducive to
corruption is *unjust and unequal systems of wealth and status*. If there are
great disparities of wealth and opportunity, and if differences in wealth and
status are not perceived as fair and as contributing to the common good,
then commitment to institutional roles and conformity to the law and to
social norms will weaken. For example, in many countries the poor and
powerless have turned for assistance to local crime bosses (godfathers) who
provide this assistance, but do so in return for "loyalty," which might take
the form of voting for certain candidates, or turning a blind eye to corrupt
and unlawful activities.

A third socio-moral condition that facilitates corruption is *moral confusion* notably in relation to institutional purposes. Moral confusion has
a number of sources, but typically it involves a combination of a lack of
clarity in relation to moral beliefs about what is right and wrong in the face
of pernicious ideology, and a tempting set of opportunities to do wrong.[14]
In times of rapid social and economic transition, stable moral practices are
upset, and a degree of moral confusion can set in. For example, rapid
economic growth and wealth acquisition can undermine traditional practices of self-restraint, financial prudence, and legal compliance. Moreover,
institutional purposes can be lost sight of. Consider the period immedi-
ately prior to the Global Financial Crisis (GFC) of 2008. During this
period, bankers, traders, and others in the global finance sector came to
possess enormous wealth by engaging in speculative and outright corrupt
practices. In all the excitement many bankers, for instance, evidently lost
sight of a fundamental institutional purpose with which they had been
entrusted, namely, to provide for the security of their depositors' funds.
Moreover, the problematic activities of these financial actors were dependent in part on the gross negligence of legislators, regulators, lawyers,
financial journalists, mortgage holders, and others. The result was quite
literally a global financial crisis.[15]

In relation to so-called victimless crimes, there is often moral confusion
and historically corruption has been fueled by the existence of moral
confusion in relation to gambling, prostitution, drugs, and the like.

---

[14] C. A. J. Coady, *Messy Morality: The Challenge of Politics* (Oxford University Press, 2008).
[15] N. Dobos, C. Barry, and T. Pogge (eds.), *Global Financial Crisis: The Ethical Issues* (London:
Palgrave Macmillan, 2011). Naturally, there were other factors at work. See Ross Garnaut, *The Great
Crash of 2008* (Melbourne: Melbourne University Press, 2009).

Moreover, a restrictive, criminalization approach to these "vices" has failed to work, but has driven these activities underground and enabled the criminal suppliers to make huge profits and to corrupt police and other officials involved in enforcement. This corruption of officials is able to be achieved in part because there is often an understandable feeling that gambling, prostitution, and much drug use is not all that morally reprehensible; accordingly, it is easy to compromise, and thereby set in train a process of compromise and corruption.

A fourth general condition that is conducive to corruption is poorly designed institutional arrangements, including legal and regulatory systems; arrangements that for one reason or another are not fit for their institutional purpose and that therefore, as a by-product, tend to create motives and/or opportunities for corruption. For instance, under-regulation can facilitate the motive and opportunity for corruption; the lack of regulation of economically unsafe financial derivatives is a case in point (see Chapter 12). But over-regulation, notably inappropriate criminalization, can also provide a motive for corruption as well as opportunities. Historically important instances of this have been the above-mentioned creation of victimless crimes, such as gambling and substance abuse. More generally, as I argue throughout this work, institutional design driven by simplistic moralism or an ideology such as market fundamentalism (see Chapter 11) tends to create institutional arrangements that are not fit for purpose and that, as a by-product, provide motives and/or opportunities for corruption.

A fifth, and final, very important general socio-moral condition that is conducive to corruption is *imbalance of power*. What Lord Acton said is now a cliché, but no less true for that: "Power tends to corrupt, and absolute power corrupts absolutely."[16] The massive human rights abuses and corruption perpetrated by autocrats such as Hitler, Mussolini, Suharto, Marcos, Idi Amin, Mobuto, and Pinochet are testimony to the importance of limiting, constraining, diluting, and dividing power. Moreover, as the looting of public funds by dictators, such as Mobutu in Zaire over a thirty-year period from the mid-1960s illustrates, abuse of power and large-scale theft often go hand in hand. Nor is kleptocracy merely a matter of the internal corruption of certain underdeveloped nation-states in, for instance, Africa. Typically, the likes of Mobutu transfer and spend their ill-gotten gains in affluent Western liberal democracies using global banks based in London, New York, Zurich, etc. as their

---

[16] Lord Acton, *Essays on Freedom and Power* (Skyler J. Collins, 2013).

financial intermediaries.[17] Again, Minxin Pei has recently argued that China's authoritarian model of economic modernization is conducive to large-scale corruption.[18] The unleashing of market forces has led to spectacular economic growth, but in the context of the one-party system this has in turn led to widespread corruption and the enrichment of the powerful on a vast scale.

So much for socio-moral features of the moral environment. I need now to turn to a brief consideration of institutional accountability systems, or the lack thereof, as a second generic condition that is conducive to corruption.

Institutional Accountability, Anti-Corruption, and Integrity Systems

I have described the nexus between the power of autocrats and organized crime bosses, on the one hand, and systemic and grand corruption on the other.[19] Corporate collapses, such as the collapse of Enron, illustrate the nexus between power and corruption within a large corporation. The corrupt practices, including the creation of so-called off-the-books Special Purpose Entities (SPEs) designed to mask losses, were the creatures of the CEO, CFO, and other members of the management team. It was their position of authority within the organization that enabled the existence of corruption on such a large scale, and with such devastating consequences.

Naturally, such corruption is not only dependent on the power of the offenders; it is also dependent on their immorality; the Enron CEO and CFO, for example, had few moral scruples, and little concern for the welfare of Enron's shareholders and employees. So the existence of this power/corruption nexus points to the importance of commitment and compliance on the part of individuals both to the moral principles enshrined in social norms and to institutional purposes. However, robust social norms and internalization of institutional purposes by themselves are not enough; they are necessary, but not sufficient. An additional necessary condition for combating corruption is adequate institutional

---

[17] J. C. Sharman, *The Despot's Guide to Wealth Management: On the International Campaign against Grand Corruption* (Ithaca, NY: Cornell University Press, 2017), Introduction: Power and Money.

[18] Minxin Pei, *China's Crony Capitalism: The Dynamics of Regime Decay* (Harvard University Press, 2016).

[19] I use the term "grand corruption" to imply serious systemic corruption that involves corruption on the part of institutional role occupants at the highest levels.

accountability mechanisms. In the case of Enron, such mechanisms included inadequate auditing controls, but let me try to briefly describe the various kinds of institutional accountability mechanisms needed to control corruption. I provide greater detail on anti-corruption systems in Chapters 7–10 and on integrity systems more broadly. Here I note that, roughly speaking, anti-corruption systems are a component of integrity systems, since the former merely focus on corruption, whereas the focus of the latter is on criminality and ethical misconduct more generally. Moreover, accountability systems are but one element in both anti-corruption systems and integrity systems. For example, these latter systems make use of preventative measures that reduce opportunities for corruption or seek to influence motivation by way of ethics education programs.

In relation to the power/corruption nexus, one of the most important accountability mechanisms is *democracy*, and democracy is a key feature of anti-corruption and integrity systems. Democracy limits, constrains, and dilutes power – at least potentially, and often in fact. The past and present existence of autocrats such as those named above underlines the importance of democratic accountability in government, and in public institutions more generally. Again, in the absence of accountability mechanisms to hold the powerful to account, hierarchies based on patronage, rather than merit, tend to develop, and thus benefits, such as promotion, are distributed on the basis of "loyalty" to the powerful, including complicity in corrupt schemes, rather than on the basis of merit, e.g., high-quality performance. Nor does this point pertain only to government. It holds equally for other organizational settings, such as large corporations. Indeed, this claim has been argued persuasively by Robert Jackall[20] in relation to large US corporations in particular. When the notion of democracy is discussed, it is normally done so in the context of government. However, the power/corruption nexus provides good reason for democratizing many other institutions, including corporations.

On the other hand, democratic mechanisms, if inadequately implemented, can facilitate rather than resist corruption. Consider the phenomenon of demagogues who manipulate an uninformed, unreflective, and dissatisfied populace in order to greatly increase their personal power and enable them to undermine, indeed corrupt, central institutions such as an independent judiciary, a free press, and, ultimately, the rule of law. Historically, this phenomenon was well known, including to philosophers such as Plato.

---

[20] Robert Jackall, *Moral Mazes* (New York: Oxford University Press, 1998).

It is evidenced in contemporary settings by leaders such as Vladimir Putin in Russia, Recep Erdogan in Turkey, and perhaps, although it is still early days at the time of writing, Donald Trump in the USA.

A second very important anti-corruption mechanism and a key component of national and organizational integrity systems is that of the *separation of powers*. Institutional separation and institutional independence are of paramount importance in limiting and dividing power, and therefore in controlling corruption. At the extreme end of the spectrum one institution, such as the military, established to perform one kind of function, say defense, overpowers a second institution, say the legislature (parliament), and takes over its function. Military coups in Thailand are a case in point. But other examples are less extreme. Consider the cozy relationship in Japan between politicians, bureaucrats, and business leaders. For example, on retirement former bureaucrats are typically hired and paid large salaries by the very companies who competed for government contracts overseen by these bureaucrats.[21]

A third aspect of accountability mechanisms and anti-corruption and integrity systems pertains to their relationships to the underlying framework of social norms. For instance, corruption is facilitated when *laws, regulations, and institutional roles do not track ethical/moral principles and ends*. One such category involves perverse outcomes in competitive contexts. For instance, nation-states might compete with one another in attracting foreign investment by lowering taxes and loosening compliance requirements, leading, ultimately, to an increase in corruption and a drastic shortfall in public money in many, if not most, of these states. Another category involves conflicts of interest in relation to an institutional role; the role has not been sufficiently circumscribed so as to rule out certain kinds of conflict of interest. Consider the tradition in Thailand whereby tax collectors and police were paid low salaries in the expectation that they would supplement their own salaries from taxes gathered or from fines received.[22] The possibility of justice and probity is greatly reduced by allowing such conflicts of interest in relation to institutional roles. In the Enron corporation, Andrew Fastow's dual role as CFO of Enron and manager of the SPEs involved a clear conflict of interest, and one that greatly facilitated the corruption process at Enron.

---

[21] See, for example, G. McCormack, *The Emptiness of Japanese Affluence* (Sydney: Allen and Unwin, 1996), p. 32f.

[22] P. Phongpaichit and S. Piriyarangsan, *Corruption and Democracy in Thailand* (Chang Mai: Silkworm Books, 1994) (1996 edition), p. 110.

Inadequacies in the investigation of corruption are self-evidently deficiencies in relation to institutional accountability and in anti-corruption and integrity systems. For example, in relation to some categories of fraud in Australia, the UK, the USA, and many other countries there are insufficient police resources to investigate the massive amount of fraudulent activity that is taking place, notably, in recent times, online fraud. One element of this is a traditional police preoccupation with street crime and a tendency not to put resources into investigating white-collar crime.

Another set of deficiencies in institutional accountability and in anti-corruption and integrity systems are *inadequacies in the court system*, or in other systems of adjudication, such as the adjudication of professional negligence by professional bodies. The law courts in most countries often find it difficult to successfully prosecute wealthy fraudsters and crime bosses who employ high-quality, well-paid lawyers. And in some countries, there is a history of bribing or intimidating the judiciary, and thereby perverting the course of justice; consider the Mafia in Sicily.

Relatedly, there are sometimes *inadequacies in the correctional and prison system*, or more generally, in the systems of punishment within organizations; for example, demotion and/or rotation of corrupt police officers within a police service rather than their removal from that service. I note that imprisonment for nonviolent offences, such as fraud, bribery, theft, and the like, may be counterproductive. Prisons may simply serve as expensive, crowded incubators of criminality.

Different institutions and organizations require different accountability systems, different anti-corruption systems, and, more broadly, different integrity systems. A police organization requires an elaborate anti-corruption system in relation to the detection and apprehension of criminal offenders (see Chapter 13) – hardly a priority in, say, a university. On the other hand, universities need to have anti-corruption systems in relation to examinations, plagiarism, and the like. Most organizations require accountability mechanisms and anti-corruption measures in relation to financial transactions. In this connection, consider the absence of accountability and anti-corruption mechanisms in relation to kickbacks to government ministers in return for the awarding of contracts for large infrastructure projects in Japan, or simply the ability of heads of governments, such as former President Suharto in Indonesia, to transfer money from public accounts into ones wholly controlled by themselves, or the inadequacy of auditing controls in the Enron and Worldcom corruption scandals.

Anti-Corruption, Globalization, and Technology

In effect, I have been arguing for the importance of the organizational, social, economic, and so on *context* in the structuring of institutional anti-corruption systems. In this connection, one of the most challenging aspects is dealing with opportunities for corruption arising from changes in technology. Over the last several decades, there have been changes that revolutionized the way in which business is done. Paper-based financial systems have given way to key information being transmitted and stored electronically. Banks and other financial institutions, as well as most business and government enterprises, in developed countries undertake the majority of their business transactions electronically, with billions of dollars' worth of funds transmitted, stored, and analyzed every day. Associated with this is the global communication system of the Internet, whereby governments, businesses, and individuals can communicate with each other not only internationally but also *instantaneously*. All of this fits within a much broader process of globalization. Nation-states no longer serve as the cornerstone for business – transnational corporations straddle the global economy, and the rich and powerful nations of Europe, Japan, and the USA all work together to break down the barriers to business caused by laws and administrative procedures based upon the nation-state.

These changes have had the effect of creating a global marketplace, dominated by the countries mentioned above, albeit less so given the economic rise of China and, more recently, India. This marketplace has created enormous wealth for the players, but has also brought considerable problems, such as cyber-security or, at least, the lack thereof. Importantly, fraud and corruption have been greatly facilitated by the advent of emerging technologies in a globalizing world, and governments have a great deal of difficulty in controlling these changes. For example, it is estimated that more than 10 million Americans a year are victims of identity theft.[23]

Transparency

I have discussed the moral environment and anti-corruption systems, and I have identified a variety of conditions that facilitate corruption. Some of these are elements of the moral environment, such as imbalances of power, and some consist of inadequacies in accountability systems, e.g., auditing

---

[23] Identity Theft Resource Center, *Aftermath Study: What Victims Have to Say about Identity Theft* (The Identity Theft Resource Center, 2015), available at www.idtheftcenter.org.

controls. However, there is a further condition that greatly facilitates corruption that I have not yet elaborated, namely secrecy or lack of transparency (as opposed to confidentiality – see Chapter 10). This condition is one that pertains both to moral environments and to accountability systems. Widespread corruption can flourish in secretive social and institutional environments. Transparency enables existing corruption to be brought to light and discourages incipient corruption. The role of a free and independent media (the Fourth Estate) is important in this regard. Consider, for example, the recent disclosures about the role of the legal firm Mossack Fonseca published in the *Suddeutche Zeitung, Guardian*, and *New York Times* newspapers, in facilitating large-scale tax avoidance, money laundering, etc. by the rich and powerful utilizing offshore tax havens.[24] Transparency is a potent anti-corruption measure, for secrecy is often present in instances of corrupt activity. Secrecy seems to be at least instrumentally desirable, for without secrecy one might not be able to evade detection, and thus escape possible social disapproval and punishment from others, or the State. Secrecy, therefore, is a condition that is highly conducive to corruption. Consider in this connection the CEO and CFO at Enron.

On occasion, agents act in a corrupt manner, but do so openly. Consider, in this connection, some of the activities of Colombian drug lord Pablo Escobar. Many people knew who he was and what he was doing, but many supported him or failed to oppose him. How is this phenomenon to be explained? One kind of explanation concerns social norms. Notice that transparency only succeeds in combating corruption if transparency exists against a background of widely accepted social norms. Only if members of the community find corruption morally unacceptable will its exposure to the harsh light of the public domain bring about the downfall of the corrupt. If the community has a high tolerance for corruption – or at least for specific forms of corruption, such as bribery – then transparency, and the consequent exposure of the corrupt, will not necessarily be a powerful anti-corruption measure.

Accordingly, in the so-called state of nature, conceived of by contract theorists such as the English philosopher Thomas Hobbes (1588–1679), one can openly be corrupt with impunity because there are no legal or moral sanctions. In such a state of nature, there is, as Hobbes tells us in his seminal work, *The Leviathan* (1651), "a war of everyone against everyone" that ultimately benefits no-one, since no-one can efficiently and effectively

[24] B. Obermayer and F. Obermaier, *The Panama Papers* (London: Oneworld, 2016).

maximize their own self-interest under these conditions. In the state of nature, the condition of invisibility becomes redundant as far as social disapproval and legal sanction are concerned. In the state of nature, social-moral attitudes do not matter and legal sanctions do not exist. So social attitudes and legal sanctions are not to be feared, and there is no need to hide one's transgressions on their account. Naturally, the state of nature in its pure form does not typically exist. However, various impure forms in which the powerful dominate the weak in disorderly social and institutional settings, such as Escobar's Colombian "narcocracy," often do exist.

Summary of Chapters

This book on institutional corruption is divided into three parts, and each part consists of a number of chapters. Part I consists of philosophical analyses of the main theoretical notions used throughout the rest of the book. Since my topic is institutional corruption, the philosophical analyses in question consist in large part in what might be referred to as empirically informed, normative *institutional* theory as opposed to normative theory in the sense of theories such as utilitarianism, Kantianism, etc. These latter theories, while prevalent in the philosophical literature, are, I suggest, largely unhelpful in this context.[25] Chapter 1 outlines my normative teleological account of institutions[26]: institutions as organizations or systems of organizations that provide collective goods, e.g., foodstuffs (agribusinesses), security (police), and are constrained by social norms. This chapter is important because an understanding of institutional corruption presupposes some understanding of institutions. A key idea introduced here, and taken from the recently emerged philosophy sub-discipline of social ontology (sometimes referred to as collective intentionality or social philosophy), is that of organizational action as a multi-layered structure of the joint actions of individual human beings. A joint action is a set of individual actions each of which is directed to the same end[27]; such an end being a collective end. Joint actions are, in essence, cooperative actions. Thus two men carrying a safe full of cash is a joint action, as is ten women rowing a boat or one hundred workers building a wall. So my account of

---

[25] For some arguments as to why this might be so see James Griffin, *What Can Philosophy Contribute to Ethics?* (Oxford University Press, 2015).

[26] Miller, *Moral Foundations of Social Institutions.*

[27] So, each agent is aiming at a state of affairs and that state of affairs is the numerically same state of affairs for each agent.

organizational action, and of corruption, is an individualist one, albeit relational individualist. Chapter 2 proffers an account of institutional power and authority; once again, these are notions central to understanding institutions and institutional corruption. Here I marry a broadly Weberian notion of power with my relational individualist account of organizational action. In Chapter 3 I elaborate my definition of institutional corruption: a causal account with normative underpinnings. According to this definition, if an action is an act of institutional corruption then it must involve an institutional actor and it must undermine an institutional purpose (collective good, on my teleological normative account), process, or person (*qua* institutional role occupant). So, institutional corruption is both a moral and a causal notion and, as such, it is tied to the institutional effects of the actions of individual human beings. Chapter 4 consists of a discussion of noble cause corruption; corruption done in order to achieve good. The phenomenon of noble cause corruption is an important counter-example to the prevailing view that corruption must be motivated by private gain, or at least individual or collective self-interest more broadly understood. Chapter 5 consists of philosophical analyses of what I take to be the most salient specific forms of institutional corruption, namely, bribery, nepotism, fraud, and abuse of authority. I argue against the influential view that all forms of corruption are in essence abuses of authority (or, in some versions, abuses of power). In Chapter 6 I elaborate a key notion in relation not only to corruption, but also to anti-corruption and integrity systems, namely, collective responsibility.[28] On my account, collective responsibility is to be understood as joint responsibility. Thus my account of collective responsibility is an extension of my relational individualist account of joint action and of organizational action (as multi-layered structures of joint action). I distinguish, analyze, and display the relationships between individual and collective *moral* responsibility, on the one hand, and individual and collective *institutional* responsibility, on the other.

In Part II of this work I turn from theory to practice and, more specifically, to anti-corruption systems or, more broadly, integrity systems. The emphasis here is on bringing to bear prior philosophical (normative institutional) theory, analyses, and perspectives on the design of anti-corruption systems and some of their key institutional components. Part II has four chapters. In the first of these, Chapter 7, I outline

---

[28] Seumas Miller, "Collective Moral Responsibility: An Individualist Account," *Midwest Studies in Philosophy*, 30 (2006), 176–193.

my general account of integrity systems. A key feature of my account is the emphasis on integrity systems as a matter of collective moral and institutional responsibility. I also reemphasize both the moral and the causal character of corruption and, especially, the need for integrity systems both to embody and to mobilize existing social norms, as well as relying on the more familiar incentive structures favored by economists in particular (e.g., "sticks and carrots"). The criminal justice system is perhaps the most obvious society-wide integrity system (or, at least, component thereof) embodying and mobilizing existing social norms, e.g., laws proscribing murder – even if, in many jurisdictions, it does so inadequately. In Chapter 7 I also discuss types of regulatory frameworks and the relationship between regulatory frameworks and integrity systems. I also distinguish between reactive and preventative integrity systems, and argue for a holistic system that integrates both reactive and preventative elements. In Chapter 8 I discuss corruption investigations. Investigation is a crucial element of any anti-corruption system, yet it gives rise to a raft of ethical issues, including privacy concerns, deception, use of informants, undercover operatives, and entrapment. Here, as elsewhere, both ethics and efficacy need to be accommodated. In Chapter 9 I turn to integrity systems for individual occupations. (In doing so, I bracket the criminal justice system since it is dealt with in earlier chapters.) I construct a model system with standard components, such as codes of ethics, complaints, and discipline systems and the like. However, I also argue for the utility of ethics audits and reputational indexes as a way of mobilizing the individual and collective self-interest in possessing a good reputation. This desire for a good reputation is especially prevalent among certain of the so-called professions. Chapter 9 also includes a discussion of conflicts of interest, one of the main conditions conducive to corruption in occupational and, for that matter, organizational, settings. I distinguish circumstantial from structural conflicts of interest, the latter being especially conducive to corruption. Chapter 10 consists in a discussion of the ethics of whistleblowing. The importance of whistleblowing as an anti-corruption measure in the context of, for example, the above-mentioned Mossack Fonseca disclosures in the "Panama Papers," can hardly be overestimated. However, as the Snowden disclosures in relation to the US National Security Agency's bulk collection of metadata illustrate, there are moral complexities in this area that need to be examined. (I note that whistleblowing in my sense is external disclosure and, as such, is to be distinguished from professional reporting, i.e., internal disclosure.)

In Part III my focus turns to specific institutional contexts. Each chapter focuses on both the nature of corruption in the light of institutional purpose (collective goods) and anti-corruption measures, but does so in relation to a particular kind of institution. The emphasis in Part III is on bringing to bear both prior philosophical (institutional normative) theory, analyses, and perspectives (Part I) and identified features of anti-corruption systems (Part II) on some specific institutions suffering from serious and widespread corruption. Part III consists of four chapters. In Chapter 11 I discuss corruption and anti-corruption in business and corporate settings. I begin with an application of my teleological normative theory to market-based industries. I argue that contrary to prevailing normative accounts, (e.g., the shareholder value theory), market-based industries have an institutional purpose (a collective good), namely, to produce an adequate and sustainable supply of a good or service at a reasonable price and of reasonable quality. Corruption in market-based industries is to be viewed through this lens of institutional purpose, given that corruption ultimately consists in undermining institutional purposes. I go on to discuss corruption and anti-corruption in a specific organization (Enron) and also in monopolistic or oligopolistic markets. In Chapter 12 I discuss corruption and anti-corruption in the global banking and finance sectors. Again, I begin with the question of the institutional purposes that ought to give direction to these market-based industries but which, in point of fact, do not in practice. Thus I outline what I take to be the fundamental institutional purposes of banks – speculative activity using other people's money not being one of them. The chapter also includes a discussion of the recently disclosed widespread practice of financial benchmark manipulation, e.g., LIBOR (London Interbank Borrowing Rate). Here I utilize my theoretical construct of a joint institutional mechanism (introduced in Chapter 1) to illuminate both the institutional nature of financial benchmarks and the damaging character of benchmark manipulation. Chapter 13 concerns integrity systems for police organizations. Police organizations are perhaps the most important anti-corruption institution in contemporary societies. Yet police organizations have themselves been sites of widespread and egregious forms of corruption. A central problem in developing ethical and efficacious anti-corruption systems, or, more broadly, integrity systems, for police organizations has been police culture and, specifically, the so-called blue wall of silence that protects corrupt police officers. In this chapter I analyze police culture and, in particular, its relationship to collective responsibility and professional reporting (as opposed to whistle-blowing). I elaborate a strategy for undermining the "blue wall of silence" by mobilizing collective responsibility in a context of, crucially, effective internal affairs investigations. Chapter 14 is the final chapter in this book and, fittingly, it deals with political corruption. I argue that government is a meta-institution, an institution that gives direction to and regulates other institutions. Accordingly, the members of a government are corrupt if they deliberately enact legislation or put in place policies that undermine the institutional purposes and processes of other institutions, e.g., if they seek to undermine the independence of the judiciary, the Fourth Estate, or the police. The election of political office holders is a process that is perennially subject to corruption intervention. Campaign financing in the US elections is a case in point. I discuss the nature of the latter and do so in the context of influential recent work on the subject by Lawrence Lessig and Dennis Thompson. I also discuss the corruption of the Fourth Estate and of deliberative democracy by market-based media organizations. The latter is important in this context, given the crucial role in a democracy of the citizenry in holding the government to account.

PART I

Corruption: Theory

CHAPTER I

Institutions

To understand institutional corruption it is first necessary to provide an account of that which is suffering corruption: institutions and sub-institutions. It will turn out that institutions are organizations that produce collective goods and that corruption undermines institutional processes and purposes and, thereby, undermines the provision of the collective goods in question.

Social institutions are complex social forms that reproduce themselves such as governments, police organizations, universities, hospitals, business corporations, markets, and legal systems. Moreover, social institutions are among the most important of collective human phenomena; they enable us to feed ourselves (markets and agribusinesses), protect ourselves (police and military services), educate ourselves (schools and universities), and govern ourselves (governments and legal systems). Sometimes the term "institution" is used to refer to complex social forms that are arguably not organizations, such as human languages or kinship systems. However, my concern is only with institutions that are also organizations and/or systems of organizations.

In this chapter, I offer a teleological normative theory of social institutions that is based on an individualist theory of joint action. Put simply, on this account social institutions are organizations or systems of organizations that provide collective goods by means of joint activity. The collective goods in question include the fulfillment of aggregated moral rights, such as needs-based rights for security (police organizations), material well-being (businesses operating in markets), education (universities), governance (governments), and so on. On this teleological conception of institutions, institutional corruption is to be understood fundamentally as a process that undermines legitimate institutional purposes and, thereby, the provision of the collective goods definitive of institutions. Moreover, the organizations

23

and systems of organization constitutive of institutions have sub-institutional components that in some cases may be especially vulnerable to corruption. Important among these are what I refer to as joint institutional mechanisms. An example of a joint institutional mechanism is a voting system within an institution of government. Corruption of a voting system may well be deeply corruptive of the whole institution of government.

1.1   Joint Actions

The central concept in the teleological account of social institutions is that of *joint action*. Joint actions are actions involving a number of agents performing interdependent actions in order to realize some common goal. Examples of joint action are two people dancing together, a number of tradesmen building a house, and a group of robbers burgling a house. Joint action is to be distinguished from individual action on the one hand, and from the "actions" of corporate bodies on the other. Thus an individual walking down the road or shooting at a target are instances of individual action. A nation declaring war or a government taking legal action against a public company are instances of *corporate* action. Insofar as such corporate "actions" are genuine actions involving mental states such as intentions and beliefs, they are, in my view, reducible to the individual and joint actions of human beings.

Over the last decade or two a number of analyses of joint action have emerged. These analyses can be located on a spectrum at one end of which there is so-called (by Frederick Schmitt[1]) strict individualism, and at the other end of which there is so-called (again by Schmitt[2]) supra-individualism. A number of these theorists have developed and applied their favored basic accounts of joint action in order to account for a range of social phenomena, including conventions, social norms, and social institutions. One such theory is my Collective End Theory (CET), elaborated elsewhere.[3] CET is a form of individualism. I will use it throughout this chapter and, indeed, throughout this work.

Individualism, as I see it, is committed to an analysis of joint action such that ultimately a joint action consists of (1) a number of singular actions;

---

[1] F. Schmitt, "Joint Action: From Individualism to Supraindividualism" in F. Schmitt (ed.), *Socializing Metaphysics: The Nature of Social Reality* (Lanham: Rowman and Littlefield, 2003), pp. 129–166.
[2] *Ibid.*
[3] Seumas Miller, "Joint Action," *Philosophical Papers*, 11 (1992) 275–299; Miller, *Social Action*, chapter 2; Miller, *Moral Foundations of Social Institutions*, chapter 1.

(2) relations between these singular actions. Moreover, the constitutive attitudes involved in joint actions are individual attitudes; there are no *sui generis* we-intentions and other like we-attitudes. Here it is important to stress that individualism can be, and in the case of CET certainly is, a form of relationalism. It is relational in two senses. First, as mentioned above, singular actions often stand in relations to one another, e.g., two partners dancing, and the joint action in part consisting of the singular actions, also in part consists of the relations between the singular actions. Second, the agents who perform joint actions can have intersubjective attitudes to one another, e.g., they mutually recognize who one another is; and some (but not all) of these attitudes are *sui generis*. Specifically, some *cognitive* (but not conative) intersubjective attitudes may well be *sui generis*, e.g., mutual consciousness of one another's consciousness.[4] In virtue of such intersubjective attitudes they will also typically have interpersonal relations to one another. Intersubjectivity and interpersonal relations in this sense are not necessarily, or at least are not by definition, social or institutional. To suggest otherwise would be to beg the question against individualism (specifically, relational individualism) in any interesting sense of the term.

By contrast, according to supra-individualists, when a plurality of individual agents perform a joint action the agents necessarily have the relevant propositional attitudes (beliefs, intentions, etc.) in an irreducible "we-form," which is *sui generis*, and as such not analyzable in terms of individual or I-attitudes. Moreover, the individual agents constitute a new entity, a supra-individual entity not reducible to the individual agents and the relations between them.

Basically, CET is the theory that joint actions are actions directed to the realization of a collective end. However, this notion of a collective end is a construction out of the prior notion of an individual end. A collective end is an individual end pursued by more than one agent, and which is such that, if it is realized, it is realized by all, or most, of the actions of the agents involved; the individual action of any given agent is only part of the means by which the end is realized, and each individual action is interdependent with the others in the service of the collective end. Thus when one person dials the phone number of another person and the second person picks up the receiver, then each has performed an action in the service of a collective end: a collective end pursued by each of them, namely, that they communicate with each other.

---

[4] N. Eitan, C. Hoerel, T. McCormack, and J. Roessler, *Joint Attention: Communication and Other Minds* (Oxford University Press, 2005), chapter 14.

On the basis of this individualist notion of a joint action, a number of social notions can be constructed, including the notions of a convention and that of a social norm. Social norms, as we saw in the Introduction, are regularities in action to which adherents have a moral commitment, e.g., the social norm not to tell lies. Some conventions are social norms but many are not. A convention can be understood as being in essence a set of joint actions each of which is performed in a recurring situation. Thus driving on the right-hand side of the road is a convention that each of us adheres to in order to realize a collective end, namely, to avoid collisions. (This convention is also a social norm, given its moral purpose.) Another social action notion that can be derived from our notion of a joint action and is crucial to our understanding of social institutions is that of organizational action.

1.2 Organizational Action

Organizations consist of a (embodied) formal *structure* of interlocking roles.[5] An organizational role can be defined in terms of the agent (whoever it is) who performs certain tasks, the tasks themselves, procedures (in the above sense), and conventions. Moreover, unlike social groups, organizations are individuated by the kind of activity that they undertake, and also by their characteristic *ends*. So we have governments, universities, business corporations, armies, and so on. Perhaps governments have as an end or goal the ordering and leading of societies, universities the end of discovering and disseminating knowledge, and so on. Here it is important to emphasize that these ends are, first, collective ends and, second, often the implicit, latent and/or unconscious (collective) ends of individual institutional actors. An end is implicit if, for example, the agent pursuing it has not expressed this to himself or others. An end is latent if the agent is not pursuing it during a particular period of time because, for example, she is asleep. Naturally, an end is unconscious if the agent pursuing it is not doing so consciously. However, it is important to note that agents pursuing ends must be able, at least in principle, both to become conscious that this is so and to express this fact to themselves or others. In this respect ends, including collective ends, differ from functions. The heart of a fetus has the function of pumping blood but this is presumably not something the fetus could have conscious or explicit knowledge of; nor is this function something that the fetus could decide to pursue or not.

---

[5] Miller, *Social Action*, chapter 5; Miller, *Moral Foundations of Social Institutions*, chapter 1.

A further defining feature of organizations is that organizational action typically consists in what can be termed a *multi-layered structure of joint actions*.[6] One illustration of the notion of a multi-layered structure of joint actions is the organized crime department of a national police organization investigating, say, a drug cartel. (This is also an instance of what I refer to as a chain of institutional collective responsibility. See Chapter 6 Section 6.2.1.) Suppose at an organizational level a number of joint actions ("actions") are severally necessary and jointly sufficient to achieve some collective end, such as the prosecution and imprisonment of its member-ship and, ultimately, the destruction of the cartel. Thus the "action" of a large team of investigators in gathering testimonial evidence from infor-mants and interviews of suspects, the "action" of the members of a forensic team in gathering digital evidence of financial transactions from seized computers, and the "action" of the members of the police prosecutorial unit in putting together a case based on this evidence might be severally necessary and jointly sufficient to achieve the collective end of destroying the drug cartel[7]; as such, these "actions" taken together constitute a joint action. Call each of these "actions" level two "actions," and the joint action that they constitute a level two joint action. From the perspective of the collective end of destroying the drug cartel, each of these level two "actions" is an individual action that is a component of a (level two) joint action: the joint action directed to the collective end of destroying the drug cartel.

However, each of these level two "actions" is already in itself a joint action with component individual actions; and these component indivi-dual actions are severally necessary (let us assume this for purposes of simplification, albeit it is unlikely that every single action would in fact be necessary) and jointly sufficient for the performance of some collective end. Thus the individual members of the team of investigators jointly conduct the investigation in order to realize the collective end of gathering sufficient testimonial evidence for the prosecution case. Accordingly, each investigator, jointly with the other investigators, interviews some subset of the informants/suspects in order to realize the collective end of providing sufficient testimonial evidence for the prosecution case.

---

[6] Miller, *Social Action*, p. 173f; Miller, *Moral Foundations of Social Institutions*, p. 48.
[7] This is, of course, an oversimplification of the joint action that would be required in practice. However, it suffices for present purposes. For a more realistic account see Seumas Miller and Ian Gordon, *Investigative Ethics. Ethics for Police Detectives and Criminal Investigators* (Hoboken, NJ: Wiley Blackwell, 2014).

At level one there are individual actions directed to three distinct collective ends: the collective ends of (respectively) gathering sufficient testimonial evidence, gathering sufficient digital evidence, and developing an adequate prosecutorial case. So at level one there are three joint actions, namely, those (respectively) of the members of the team of investigators, the members of the forensic team, and the members of the prosecutorial unit. However, taken together these three joint actions constitute a single level two joint action. The collective end of this level two joint action is to destroy the drug cartel; and from the perspective of this level two joint action, and its collective end, these constitutive actions are (level two) individual actions.

It is important to note that on this (stipulative) definition of organizations they are, *qua organizations*, non-normative entities (other than in the minimal sense in which an end is normative because successful or unsuccessful, or a belief is normative because true or false). In this respect they are analogous to conventions, as we have defined conventions above. So being an organization is not of itself something that is ethically good or bad, any more than being a convention is in itself ethically good or bad. This can be consistently held while maintaining that organizations, as well as conventions, are a pervasive and necessary feature of human life, being indispensable instruments for realizing collective ends. Collective ends are a species of individual end; but merely being an end is in itself neither morally good nor morally bad, any more than being an intention or a belief are in themselves morally good or morally bad.

While this definition of an organization does not include any reference to a normative dimension, most organizations do as a matter of contingent fact possess a normative dimension. As was the case with conventions, this normative dimension will be possessed (especially, though not exclusively) by virtue of the particular moral/immoral ends (goods) that an organization serves, as well as by virtue of the particular moral (or immoral) activities that it undertakes.

Further, most organizations possess a normative dimension by virtue (in part) of the *social norms* governing the constitutive organizational roles.[8] More specifically, most organizations consist of a hierarchical role structure in which the tasks and procedures that define the individual roles are governed by norms; and in hierarchical organizations some of these norms govern the relations of authority and power within the organization. It is not simply that an employee in fact undertakes a particular set of tasks,

---

[8] Miller, *Social Action*, chapter 4.

or tends to comply with the directives of his employer. Rather the employee undertakes those tasks, and obeys the directives of his employer, by virtue of the social and other norms governing the employee's (and employer's) roles, and the relations of authority and power that exist between these roles (see Chapter 2).

Organizations with the above detailed normative dimension are *social institutions*.[9] So – and as already noted – institutions are often organizations, and many systems of organizations are also institutions.

1.3   Joint Institutional Mechanisms

A feature of many social institutions, whether they be of the organizational or nonorganizational variety, is their use of what I will refer to as *joint institutional mechanisms*.[10] Examples of joint mechanisms are the device of tossing a coin to resolve a dispute, voting to elect a candidate to political office, use of money as a medium of exchange, and, more generally, exchange systems such as markets for goods and services. Importantly, from my theoretical perspective, action in accordance with joint mechanisms – like organizational action – can be understood as derivable from the prior notion of a joint action.

Joint mechanisms consist of (a) a complex of differentiated but interlocking actions (the input to the mechanism); (b) the result of the performance of those actions (the output of the mechanism); and (c) the mechanism itself. Thus a given agent might vote for a candidate. He will do so only if others also vote. But further to this, there is the action of the candidates, namely, that they present themselves as candidates. That they present themselves as candidates is (in part) constitutive of the input to the voting mechanism. Voters vote *for candidates*. So there is interlocking and differentiated action (the input). Further, there is some result (as opposed to consequence) of the joint action; the joint action consisting of the actions of putting oneself forward as a candidate and the actions of voting. The result is that some candidate, say, Barack Obama, is voted in (the output). That there is a result is (in part) constitutive of the mechanism. That to receive the most number of votes is to be voted in is (in part)

---

[9] Anthony Giddens, *The Constitution of Society: Outline of the Theory of Structuration* (Cambridge: Polity Press, 1984); Talcott Parsons, *On Institutions and Social Evolution* (Chicago: Chicago University Press, 1982).

[10] Miller, *Social Action*, p. 174; Miller, *Moral Foundations of Social Institutions*, p. 50; and Seumas Miller, "Joint Epistemic Action: Some Applications," *Journal of Applied Philosophy*, published online February 2016.

constitutive of the voting mechanism. Moreover, that Obama is voted in is not a collective end of all the voters. (Although it is a collective end of those who voted for Obama.) However, that the one who gets the most votes – whoever that happens to be – is voted in is a collective end of all the voters, including those who voted for some candidate other than Obama.

Money, markets, and other systems of exchange are also a species of joint mechanism. Such exchange systems coordinate numerous participants seeking to exchange one thing for another thing, and to do so on a recurring basis with multiple other participants. For participants A, B, C, D, etc. and exchangeable token things w, x, y, z, etc. (possessed by A, B, C, D, etc., respectively), the individual end of each participant, say A, on any single instance of a recurring exchange-enabling situation, e.g., a market-place, is to exchange w for something (x or y or z, etc.) possessed by B or C or D, etc.; similarly for B, C, and D, etc. Moreover, on any such occasion at, or near, the point of exchange two participants, say A and B, will have a collective end; thus A and B each has the collective end that A and B exchange w and x on this occasion. Here the realization of the collective end constitutes a joint action; however, it is a joint action – and its constitutive collective end – in the service of the individual end of each participant.

The set of realized collective ends of these (coordinated) single joint actions of exchange constitutes the output of the joint mechanism, i.e., that A exchanges w for x with B, C exchanges y for z with D, and so on. Naturally, the *particular* configuration of joint actions (individual exchanges) that results on some occasion of the recurring situation is not aimed at by anyone, e.g., it is not a collective end of A or B that C and D exchange y and z. However, that there be *some* coordinated set of exchanges is the point or collective end of the system; certainly, the regulators and designers of the system have or had this as a collective end, and even the participants all have this as a collective end, even if only at an implicit, latent and/or unconscious level. The latter point is evidenced by attempts on the part of participants to remedy defects or problems with the system, for example, by communicating to all participants any change in the location at which the exchanges are to take place.

Since the occasions for exchange are instances of a recurring situation, each participant has a *standing individual* end with respect to a single open-ended set of future-recurring such occasions for exchange, i.e., that on each of these occasions s/he (say, A) will make such an exchange of some relevant thing with B or C, etc. Moreover, each of these standing indivi-dual ends is a standing *collective* end since it is an end possessed interdependently by each (say, A) with each other (say, B or C, etc.) with whom A will make an exchange of some relevant thing on one or more of the future-recurring occasions for exchange in question. Finally, each of the participants has a *standing* collective end with respect to a single open-ended *set of sets of coordinated multiple* future joint actions of exchange, i.e., each has a collective end with respect to the results of the future workings of the joint mechanism, namely, that there be on each future occasion of the recurring situation some coordinated configuration of joint actions of exchange.

Note that an exchange system is institutionalized when it is "regulated" by social norms – and typically by enforceable formal regulations and laws – as a consequence of its constitutive joint actions and/or collective ends having moral significance. This might be as a result of competition between participants for scarce items that provide benefits to their possessors, e.g., social norms of fair competition, promises to hand over the scarce item at the jointly decided exchange rate, and social norms not to "steal" items in the possession of others.

1.4 Acting *Qua* Member of a Group/*Qua* Occupant of an Institutional Role

Some theorists, such as John Searle[11] and Margaret Gilbert,[12] have suggested that actions performed by individuals *qua* members of a group and (relatedly) *qua* occupants of an institutional role constitute a problem for individualist accounts. We shall see shortly that this is not so. In any event, the notion of acting *qua* member of an institutional role is central to understanding institutional action[13].

The notion of acting *qua* member of a group is often quite straightforward since the group can be defined in part in terms of the collective end or ends that the group of individuals is pursuing. Here I am assuming that the members of the group are engaged in interdependent action in the service of this collective end, as described above. Individual agents or numerically different collections of agents who each aim at some common outcome do not necessarily have a collective end in my sense; specifically, there is not necessarily interdependence of action in relation to the aimed-at outcome.

[11] John Searle, *The Construction of Social Reality* (New York: Free Press, 1995).
[12] M. Gilbert, *On Social Facts* (Princeton University Press, 1989).
[13] Miller, *Social Action*, p. 204f; Miller, *Moral Foundations of Social Institutions*, p. 52f.

Consider a group of individuals building an illicit drug production facility in a remote location. Person A is building a wall, person B the roof, person C the equipment, and so on. To say of person A that he is acting *qua* member of this group is in large part to say that his action of building the facility is an action directed toward the collective end that he and the other members of the group are seeking to realize, namely a built drug production facility.

Notice that the same set of individuals could be engaged in different collective projects. Suppose persons A, B, C, etc. in our above example are not only engaged in building a drug production facility but also – during their holidays – building a sailing boat for pleasure. Assume that A is building the masts, B the cabin, C the bow, and so on. To say of A that he is acting *qua* member of this group is just to say that his action of building the masts is an action directed toward the collective end that he and the other members of the group are seeking to realize, namely a built boat. Accordingly, one and the same person, A, is acting both as a member of the "drug facility building group" (G1) and as a member of the "boat building group" (G2). Indeed, since A, B, C, etc. are all and only the members of each of these two groups, the membership of G1 is identical with the membership of G2.

Moreover, when A is building the wall he is acting *qua* member of G1, and when he is building the mast he is acting *qua* member of G2. But this phenomenon of one agent acting as a member of different groups in no way undermines individualism. Indeed, CET is able to illuminate this phenomenon as follows. For A to be acting *qua* member of G1 is for A to be pursuing – jointly with B, C, etc. – the collective end of building the drug facility; for A to be acting *qua* member of G2 is for A to be pursuing – jointly with B, C, etc. – the collective end of building the boat.

Further, let us suppose that G1 and G2 each have to create and comply with a budget; G1 has a drug-dealing funded budget for the drug facility and G2 has a bank loan-based budget for the boat. The members of G1 and G2 know that they must buy materials for the drug facility and the boat (respectively) and do so within the respective budgets. Assume that A, B, C, etc. have allocated $100,000 to pay for bricks for the drug facility. This is a joint action. Moreover, this joint action is one that A, B, C, etc. have performed *qua* members of G1. G1 is individuated by recourse to the collective end of building the drug facility, and the proximate (collective) end of buying bricks is tied to that group, G1, and its ultimate end of building a drug production facility. Accordingly, A, B, C, etc. are not in buying the bricks acting *qua* members of G2, for G2 is individuated by the collective end of building a boat, and A, B, C, etc. do not *qua* members of G2 have any plans to build their boat from bricks!

Thus far I have focused on the notion of acting *qua* member of a group in the sense of a mere set of individuals engaged in joint activity. However, there are other related but more structured collectives whose members act *qua* members of the collective in question. Specifically, there are social groups and institutions.

The notion of a social group is somewhat opaque but it is certainly more than a mere collection of agents who have a collective end. For example, social groups typically conform to a shared set of conventions and social norms.[14] Accordingly, the notion of acting *qua* member of a social group consists in more than simply acting in accordance with a collective end; it also consists in compliance with conventions and social norms. However, acting in accordance with a collective end (or collective ends) is a necessary condition for acting *qua* member of a social group; indeed, it is the central necessary condition.

Given this distinction between mere groups and social groups, it is evident that some members of a group might be members of a given social group, while others might not be. Accordingly, two members of a group might have the same collective end but not be acting *qua* members of a social group (e.g., two voters who vote for Obama but come from different social groups). And the same point can be made in relation to other collectives, such as institutions, e.g., two friends contributing to the building of a house who are not doing so as members of any organization or institution.

Here the notion of acting *qua* occupant of an institutional role is simply that of performing the tasks definitive of the institutional role (including the joint tasks), conforming to the conventions and regulations that constrain the tasks to be undertaken, and pursuing the purposes or ends constitutive of the role (including the collective ends).

Note the relevance here of the above-introduced notion of a *multi-layered structure of joint actions*. As described above, a layered structure of joint actions is a set of joint actions each of which is directed to a further collective end; so it is a macro-joint action composed of a set of constituent micro joint actions. This account of a layered structure of joint actions can be supplemented by recourse to concepts of conventions, social norms, and the like, and especially by recourse to the explicitly normative notions of rights, obligations, and duties that are attached to, and in part definitive of,

---

[14] Miller, *Social Action*, chapter 6.

many organizational roles. It is not simply that organizational role occupants *regularly* jointly act in certain ways in preference to others, or in preference to acting entirely individualistically; rather they have institutional duties to so act and – in the case of hierarchical organizations – institutional rights to instruct others to act in certain ways.

At any rate, the point to be made here is that my account of the notion of acting *qua* member of a group in terms of acting in accordance with collective ends can be, and should be, complicated and supplemented by the normative notions of rights and duties in order to accommodate various different kinds of acting *qua* member of an organized group, including acting in hierarchical roles such as that of President of the USA, for example. So role occupants such as Barack Obama take on the tasks definitive of the role. More specifically, they take on the institutional rights and duties definitive of the role, and some of these institutional rights and duties are also moral rights and obligations. Accordingly, it makes sense to say of Obama that he has this and that moral obligation *qua* President but not necessarily *qua* husband or father.

An important consequence of institutional roles being in part constituted by rights and duties for our purposes in this work is that role occupants can continue to occupy their roles yet deliberately and selectively fail to discharge their duties in ways that undermine the institutional purposes that these roles serve. As our definition of institutional corruption in Chapter 3 will demonstrate, when they do so they are typically or, at least, frequently engaged in corruption. Note that corrupt institutional actors continue to act qua occupants of their institutional role in my sense since they use the opportunities afforded by their continued occupancy of the role – and especially their discretionary rights (see Chapter 5 Section 5.4) – to perform their corrupt actions.

1.5   The Varieties of Social Institution

Self-evidently, social institutions have a multifaceted ethico-normative dimension, including a moral dimension. Moral categories that are deeply implicated in social institutions include human rights and duties, contract-based rights and obligations, and, importantly I suggest, rights and duties derived from the production and "consumption" of collective goods.

Collective goods of the kind I have in mind have three properties: (1) they are produced, maintained, or renewed by means of the *joint activity* of members of organizations or systems of organizations, i.e., by institutional actors; (2) they are *available to the whole community* (at least in principle); and (3) they *ought* to be produced (or maintained or renewed) and made available to the whole community since they are desirable goods and ones to which the members of the community have an (institutional) *joint moral right*.

Such goods are ones that are desirable in the sense that they ought to be desired (objectively speaking), as opposed to simply being desired; moreover, they are either intrinsic goods (good in themselves), or the means to intrinsic goods. They include, but are not restricted to, goods in respect of which there is an institutionally prior moral right, e.g., security.

Note that the scope of a community is relativized to a social institution (or set of interdependent social institutions). Roughly, a community consists in the members of an organization who jointly produced a collective good and/or who have a joint right to that good. In the case of the meta-institution, government, the community will consist in all those who are members of any of the social institutions that are coordinated and otherwise directed by the relevant government. So the citizens of a nation-state will count as a community on this account.

Roughly speaking, on my account, aggregated needs-based rights, aggregated non–needs-based human rights and other desirable goods generate collective moral responsibilities that provide the ethico-normative basis for institutions, e.g., business organizations in competitive markets, welfare institutions, police organizations, universities, etc., which fulfill those rights.

For example, the aggregate need for food generates a collective moral responsibility to establish and maintain social institutions, such as agribusinesses, the members of which jointly produce foodstuffs; once the relevant institutions are established, then the needy have a joint moral right, and ought to have a joint institutional right, to the food products in question. Accordingly, the needy have a right to buy the food products (they cannot be excluded from purchasing them) or, if they are unable to do so, then (other things being equal[15]) the products ought to be provided to the needy free of charge.

I note that in modern economies there is a derived moral right to paid work, i.e., a right to a job (some job or other), since (other things being equal) without a job one cannot provide for one's basic needs (and one's

---

[15] Other things might not be equal if, for example, the needy refuse to make reasonable efforts to contribute to the production of collective goods. See discussion in Section 1.8 on the web of interdependence.

family's needs) and one cannot contribute to the production, maintenance, and renewal of collective goods, e.g., via taxes. Naturally, if no paid job can be made available to some person or group then they have no moral right to one, but if so then (other things being equal) they will have a moral right to welfare.

I also note that some quite fundamental moral rights, values, and principles are logically prior to social institutions; or, to be more precise, logically prior to social institutions that are also organizations, or systems of organizations. Basic human rights, such as the right to life, the right not to be tortured, and the right not to be incarcerated, are logically prior to social institutions. A further important set of rights that are in some cases, at least, logically prior to social institutions are needs-based rights to water, food, and shelter. There are, of course, other needs-based rights that are not logically prior to social institutions, e.g., the need of a business actor for an accountant or of an alleged offender for a lawyer.

Many of these basic human rights provide the *raison d'etre* (by my lights, collective end) for a number of social institutions. Consider, for example, police institutions. The police role consists in large part in protecting persons from being deprived of their human rights to life, bodily security, liberty, and so on; they do so by the use, or threatened use, of coercive force.

Now consider business organizations operating in competitive markets. Many business organizations do not have the protection of human rights or the fulfillment of needs-based rights as a primary purpose; nor should they. On the other hand, human rights are an important *side constraint* on business activity.

1.6 Institutional Moral Rights

Notwithstanding that human rights and some other moral phenomena are logically prior to social institutions, many moral rights, duties, values, principles, and so on are *not* logically prior to social institutions. Consider in this connection the moral right to vote, the moral right to a fair trial, the right to buy and sell land, and the moral right to a paid job; the first right presupposes institutions of government of a certain kind (democratic government), the second criminal justice institutions of a certain kind (e.g., courts of law that adjudicate alleged crimes), and the third and fourth economic institutions of a certain kind. Let us refer to such institution-dependent moral rights as "institutional moral rights" (as opposed to natural moral rights). Evidently, institutional moral rights depend in part on rights-generating properties possessed by human beings *qua* human beings, but also in part on membership of a community or of a morally legitimate institution, or occupancy of a morally legitimate institutional role.

Such institutional moral rights and duties include ones that are (a) derived at least in part from collective goods and (b) constitutive of specific institutional roles, e.g., the rights and duties of a fire officer. They also include moral rights and duties that attach to all members of a community because they are dependent on institutions in which all members of the community participate, e.g., the duty to obey the law of the land, the duty to contribute to one's country's national defense in time of war, the right to vote, the right of access to paid employment in some economy, the right to own land in some territory, and the right to freely buy and sell goods in some economy. These moral rights and duties are institutionally relative in the following sense.

Even if they are in part based on an institutionally prior human right (e.g., a basic human need, the right to freedom), their precise content, strength, context of application (e.g., jurisdiction), and so on can only be determined by reference to the institutional arrangements in which they exist and, specifically, in the light of their contribution to the collective good(s) provided by those institutional arrangements. So, for example, a property regime, if it is to be morally acceptable, must not only reward the producers of goods, e.g., by protecting the ownership rights of the producers of goods to the goods that they produce (e.g., would-be consumers cannot steal their goods), it must also ensure that consumers are benefited and not harmed (e.g., producers are required to meet health and safety standards). More particularly, a property regime, if it is to be morally acceptable, must satisfy the requirements of institutionally prior human rights; specifically, it must ensure that the needs-based rights of consumers are fulfilled (e.g., producers are required to compete under conditions of fair competition, or are otherwise constrained, to ensure that their products are available at prices the needy can afford).

We need to make a further distinction between (a) institutional moral rights; and (b) institutional rights that are not moral rights. The right to vote and the right to stand for office embody the human right to autonomy in the institutional setting of the state; hence to make a law to exclude certain people from having a vote or standing for office, as happened in apartheid South Africa, is to violate a moral right. But the right to make the next move in a game of chess, or to move a pawn one space forward, but not (say) three spaces sideways, is entirely dependent on the rules of chess; if the rules were different (e.g., each player must make two consecutive moves, pawns can move sideways), then the rights that players have would be entirely different. In other words, these rights that chess players have are *mere* institutional rights; they depend entirely on the rules of the "institution" of the game of chess. Likewise, (legally enshrined) parking rights, such as reserved spaces and one hour parking spaces in universities, are *mere* institutional rights, as opposed to institutional *moral* rights.

I will now consider in more detail the moral rights and collective goods that underpin social institutions.

1.7   Joint Rights

As outlined above, social institutions involve the production of collective goods by means of the joint activity of members of organizations. In the case of any given institution there is a collective moral responsibility to produce the collective good in question and there is a joint moral right of access to that good once it is produced. In many instances the collective moral responsibility to produce the collective good is based on an aggregate of individual moral rights, including basic needs-based rights. However, it is only when a certain threshold of aggregate of actual or potential aggregated rights violations (or otherwise unrealized rights) exists that the establishment of an institution takes place; agribusinesses or welfare institutions, for example, are not established because a single person's need for food has not been realized. Only when such a threshold aggregate of unrealized rights exists does the collective moral responsibility arise to engage in joint activity in order to realize the rights in question.

As discussed, a key notion in my account of social institutions is that of a joint moral right.[16] This notion and the role it plays stand in need of elaboration. It will turn out that not only are there joint rights to collective goods once they are produced but also, at least in some cases, joint rights that provide the grounds for the "production" of those goods in the first instance.

Let me now consider one way in which certain human rights, notably the individual human right to autonomy,[17] can underpin social institutions and constitute collective goods. In the kind of case I have in mind, human rights underpin social institutions via joint moral rights, and do so in a particular way. Let me explain.

Consider the right to political secession or abandonment of a common market. Arguably, members of Scotland have a right to secede from the

---

[16] Miller, *Social Action*, chapter 7.
[17] James Griffin, *On Human Rights* (Oxford University Press, 2008).

UK; certainly, members of the UK have a right to abandon the EU. But, if these are rights, they are not rights that some Scottish or UK person has as an individual. After all, an individual person cannot secede. The right of the Scots to secede – if it exists – is a right that attaches to the individual members of Scotland, but does so jointly. Similarly, the related right of UK citizens to exclude others from their territory, if it exists, is a joint right; some English person acting as an individual does not have a right to exclude, for example, would-be immigrants from the EU.

Now consider the right to political participation. Each Canadian citizen (and, perhaps, some noncitizen residents, etc.) has a moral right to participate in political institutions in Canada; non-Canadian citizens do not have a right to such political participation in Canada. Moreover, the right to political participation of each Canadian is dependent on the possession of the right to political participation in Canada of all the other Canadians; Canadians have a joint moral right.

Such joint rights need to be distinguished from universal individual human rights. Take the right to life as an example of a universal individual human right. Each human being has an individual human right to life. However, since one's possession of the right to life is wholly dependent on properties one possesses as an individual, it is not the case that one's possession of the right to life is dependent on someone else's possession of that right.

Notice that joint rights can be based in part on properties individuals possess as individuals. The right to participate in political institutions is based in part on membership of a political and legal community, and in part on possession of the individual human right of autonomy.

Consider the right to vote. This is an individual, institutional moral right. Nevertheless, it is based in part on the prior individual human right to autonomy. In a social or political setting requiring collective or joint decision-making this individual human right is transformed into an individual institutional moral right to vote via a joint right: the joint right to political participation. Indeed, properly speaking, the individual institutional moral right to vote is itself a joint right; each only has a right to vote if each of one's fellow *bona fide* members of the political community in question likewise has a right to vote.

Here there are four related points to be made. First, the institution, (say) representative government, is not directly based on an aggregate of individual human rights, but rather directly on a joint moral right; a joint moral right that is in turn in part based on the individual human right of autonomy. (Note that while many joint moral rights are institutional rights, many are not, e.g., the natural joint right of noninstitutionally based producers to their product.) Second, the exercise of the joint right of political participation is an end in itself; it is not simply a means to some further end (although in fact it is also a means to other ends). Third, the exercise of the joint right to political participation is a collective end; it is an end that is realized by the actions of many, and not by one person acting alone. Finally, it is a collective end that morally ought to be realized (by virtue being the fulfillment of moral rights), and that is enjoyed in being realized; so it is a collective good.

In fact, the institution of representative government is grounded in a number of collective goods. Representative government not only has as a collective end to embody, or give expression to, the joint right to political participation but also to provide various other collective goods, e.g., the coordination and regulation of other social institutions (the education system, the health system, the criminal justice system, the financial system, etc.) to ensure that they realize their (respective) collective ends. Thus governments are meta-institutions; institutions that give direction to and regulate other institutions (see Chapter 14).

In short, political participation is joint activity that morally ought to be performed. Moreover, it is joint activity that is constitutive, both of the collective end-in-itself that it serves and of the collective good that it is; the producers are the consumers, so to speak. In this respect, political institutions differ from, say, welfare institutions. The latter institutions are instruments in the service of prior needs-based rights, rather than an expression or embodiment of those rights. Accordingly, the producers are not necessarily the consumers.

1.8 Aggregated Moral Rights, Joint Rights and Collective Goods

Let me now explain how it is that the realization of aggregated needs-based rights, and other aggregated moral rights, are collective goods in my sense, i.e., jointly produced (or maintained or renewed) goods that ought to be produced (or maintained or renewed), and that are, and ought to be, made available to the whole community since they are desirable goods and ones to which the members of the community have a joint moral right.

As one might expect of something claimed to be a collective good, the fulfillment of aggregated rights is not something that is available to only one person. Of course, the fact that it is *aggregated* rights that are in question makes this trivially true. Moreover, since it is moral rights that are in question then each and every rights-bearer ought to have available to them the good to which he or she has a right; hence the good ought to be made available to the whole community.

However, the enjoyment of rights is typically thought to be an individual affair; and indeed in many respects it is. If, for example, my right to individual freedom is fulfilled then I enjoy the exercise of *my* right and no-one else enjoys the exercise of *my* right (even if they enjoy the exercise of their own). It is also true that the exercise of my right to freedom (at least in part – see later) is logically consistent with the inability of others to exercise their respective rights to freedom, e.g., if I am Robinson Crusoe and everyone else lives in an authoritarian state.

It is, of course, a commonplace of political philosophy that the establishment of government and the rule of law are instrumentally necessary for the preservation of the freedom of each of us, albeit under the restriction not unduly to interfere with others; the alternative, as Hobbes famously said and was noted in the Introduction, is the state of nature, in which life is nasty, brutish, and short. However, I want to make a somewhat different point; there is another reason that most of us rely on the fulfillment of the rights to freedom of others in order to enjoy adequately our own freedom.

Specifically, I cannot engage in freely performed *joint* activity with others if they cannot exercise their rights to freedom. Here the property of being free qualifies the joint activity per se, and not simply the individual action of each considered independently of its contribution to the collective end that is constitutive of that joint activity. Accordingly, a joint action is a freely performed joint action if and only if each freely performed their contributory action *qua* contributory action.

For example, I cannot freely participate in an election, unless others can also freely do so. Of course, I could freely cast a vote in an election in which all the other votes were cast in accordance with (say) the instructions of the dictator of my country. However, such an arrangement is a pseudo-election. It defeats the point of an election, which is to provide a mechanism for participants to jointly arrive at a result acceptable to all – even if not voted for by all – because each participant has had his/her say but none on his/her own can guarantee any particular result. Accordingly, if there are to be elections, as opposed to pseudo-elections, then they will be free (and fair) elections. Moreover, whether or not I can vote, and do so freely, is dependent not only on whether others can vote – elections are a form of joint activity – but on whether others can do so freely. So, one person's freedom to vote is dependent on the freedom to vote of others.

Again, I cannot freely engage in a market, unless others can do likewise. Of course, I could freely offer goods for exchange under a regimented arrangement in which all other participants are required by law to exchange their goods with one another according to some predetermined configuration, but in which I alone can exchange my goods for whatever goods I unilaterally determine. However, such an arrangement is a pseudo-market. It defeats the point of a market, which is to provide an efficient and effective means to coordinate numerous participants seeking to make freely chosen exchanges. Under such an arrangement there are no freely chosen exchanges. Even the exchanges I make are not freely performed *exchanges*. They are not freely performed exchanges since one party in the exchange is not acting freely. Here an exchange is to be understood as a joint action in which the participants A and B have as a collective end that x be exchanged for y. Accordingly, if there are to be markets, as opposed to pseudo-markets, then they will be free markets. Moreover, whether or not I can exchange my goods, and do so freely, is dependent not only on whether others can exchange their goods – markets are a form of joint activity – but on whether others can do so freely. So, one person's freedom to exchange goods is dependent on the freedom to exchange goods of other persons.

So much for aggregated moral rights to freedom. What of aggregated needs-based rights – the right to basic foodstuffs, shelter, and security of one's person and property, for example? In modern economies these aggregated needs are fulfilled by means of joint activity, e.g., foodstuffs by business organizations in competitive markets, security by publicly funded police organizations. So these morally required goods, i.e., fulfilled (aggregated) needs-based rights, are *jointly produced*; so they meet this defining condition for being collective good. What of their enjoyment? In what further respects, if any, does the enjoyment of aggregated needs-based rights meet the defining conditions for being a collective good?

As we saw in the case with aggregated rights to freedom, the fact that the fulfilled needs-based rights in question are *aggregated* makes it trivially true that the members of the community in general enjoy these rights. Likewise, since it is moral rights that are in question then each and every rights-bearer ought to have available to them the good to which he or she has a right. Again, if my right to basic foodstuffs is fulfilled then I enjoy the exercise of *my* right and only I enjoy the exercise of *my* right (even if others also enjoy the exercise of theirs). It is also true that the exercise of my needs-based rights to basic foodstuffs, shelter, and so on is, at least in many cases,[18] logically consistent with the inability of others to exercise their respective rights to

[18] Security is perhaps not one of these since, arguably, if anyone enjoys security under the rule of law in a community then everyone in that community does.

these goods, e.g., if I am a successful subsistence farmer but one living in a failed state in which many are starving. Moreover, others can exercise their needs-based rights without me doing so, e.g., if the needed goods are only available in a market and I cannot afford to pay for them while others can.

Nevertheless, each of us, albeit indirectly, relies on the fulfillment of the needs-based rights of others in order to enjoy adequately our own needs-based rights. The reason for this is twofold. First, in modern societies most individuals rely on social institutions, whether private sector organizations operating in competitive markets (e.g., agribusinesses, manufacturers of building materials) or else publicly funded organizations (e.g., police organizations) to produce the foodstuffs, maintain security, and provide for the various necessities to fulfill their needs-based rights. Indeed, even if they were disposed to do so, few modern individuals are even capable of producing sufficient food, clean water, adequate shelter, medicine, security, etc. for themselves; few of us living in modern societies are, or could easily become, for instance, subsistence farmers. Second, most individuals rely on business organizations operating in competitive markets to provide paid jobs that (a) enable them to pay for the basic necessities of life and (b) generate taxes to fund a variety of other collective goods necessary for the production and distribution of these basic necessities, e.g., transport, communications, research and training, security, and other public infrastructure.

So there is a complex structure of direct, and indirect, interdependence (as opposed to one-way dependence) and overlap between the needy and those who fulfill their needs. For example, there is direct interdependence between agribusinesses and the paying consumers of basic foodstuffs; and there is indirect interdependence between the former and all the other organizations that pay their employees and, thereby, enable them to become paying consumers of basic foodstuffs. Again, there is both economic and functional interdependence between taxpayers and police officers; police protect taxpayers, but taxpayers fund police officers and provide police with information.

Accordingly, there is a complex structure of economic and functional interdependence – a web of interdependence – between members of institutions and the bearers of needs-based rights. As we have seen in relation to joint actions, joint institutional mechanisms and multi-layered structures of joint action, the participants are each aiming at a shared collective end, and the existence of collective ends explains their interdependence of action. However, in the case of webs of interdependence, all or most of the participants do not necessarily have a collective end since many are unaware of the interdependence or are not sufficiently aware of it for it to be action guiding. Nevertheless, *some* participants are, or ought to be, aware, namely those institutional actors whose role is in large part to ensure that the web of interdependence (under some more or less correct description) is maintained. Legislators are perhaps the most obvious category of such participants, given the function of government as a meta-institution. Accordingly, legislators have as one of their collective ends the collective good of the maintenance of various morally and institutionally required webs of interdependence. I return to this issue in Chapter 14.

Let us focus only on economic interdependence, since it is perhaps less obvious. For our purposes here, an important feature of this complex structure of economic interdependence and overlap is the indirect interdependence between the bearers of needs-based rights themselves, i.e., the consumers of basic necessities; they rely on one another economically to maintain the agribusinesses, etc., which provide their basic necessities. Accordingly, in modern economies, speaking generally, if one person's needs-based right to food, shelter, etc. is fulfilled then so are the relevant needs-based rights of many other persons.

This *de facto* indirect web of economic interdependence between the bearers of needs-based rights does not, of course, necessarily encompass *all* the members of a community, e.g., there might not be any dependence of the employed on the unemployed. Nevertheless, under conditions of full employment (or near full employment in conjunction with welfare payments to the unemployed) and sufficient production of basic necessities to meet the needs of all, then this *de facto* indirect *web of economic interdependence* will encompass all members of the community; the web of economic interdependence will be complete.

This web of economic interdependence is, of course, not of such a kind that the meeting of the needs of a single person is a necessary or sufficient condition for the meeting of the needs of any other single person, let alone of all other persons taken in aggregate. Rather, the interdependence between individuals, between small subsets of the whole community, and between individuals and small subsets is partial and incremental. Roughly speaking, the larger the subset, the greater the dependence on it of its members (taken individually), and of individuals and subsets outside it; and the less dependent it is on any particular subset outside it (or on any small subset of itself).

Each and every member of the community has a needs-based right to the basic necessities of life. Accordingly, if the *de facto* web of economic interdependence is complete – and there are adequate production levels – then the needs-based rights of all will be fulfilled. Moreover, such a completed web of economic interdependence will parallel a deontic structure of interdependent (aggregated) needs-based rights. The (aggregated) needs-based rights in question are interdependent by virtue of being joint rights. Let me explain.

As mentioned above, a needs-based right is not *per se* a jointly held right; it follows that an aggregate of needs-based rights is not necessarily a set of jointly held rights. However, a needs-based right and, likewise, an aggregate of needs-based rights are such only in the context of the possibility of their fulfillment (either by the rights bearers themselves or by others); one cannot have a right to something if it is impossible (logically or practically) for it to be provided.

The context in question, i.e., a well-functioning modern economy, is one in which aggregated needs-based rights are fulfilled (and realistically can only be fulfilled) by economic institutions characterized by a completed web of economic interdependence among the consumers of basic necessities, i.e., the bearers of the needs-based rights in question. But in that case – given that rights exist only if it is possible for them to be fulfilled – then the needs-based rights in question are *joint* rights. One member of the community in question only has a right to basic necessities if others do, and vice versa. The institutional arrangements in question are not such that they could provide for one person, or even a small group of persons; they are designed to provide for aggregate needs, i.e., for large groups of consumers. Since it is not possible to provide for one person (or even a small group), that person cannot have a right to the basic necessities independent of others having this right. That is, the right of any one person to the basic necessities is a jointly held right; the needs-based rights in question are joint rights.

I have defined collective goods as jointly produced goods that ought to be produced and made available to the whole community since they are desirable goods and ones to which the members of the community have joint moral rights. The fulfillment of aggregated needs-based rights is a collective good in this sense.

1.9 Conclusion

In this chapter, as a precursor to defining institutional corruption, I have elaborated a teleological normative account of institutions and some key sub-institutional components of institutions, notably joint institutional mechanisms. On this view, institutions are organizations and/or systems of organizations that provide collective goods by means of joint activity, specifically, multi-layered structures of joint action. Moreover, this joint activity is constrained by social norms and performed by institutional actors whose institutional roles are defined in part by institutional rights and duties that are often also moral rights and duties. The collective goods in question include the fulfillment of aggregated moral rights, such as needs-based rights for security (police organizations), material well-being (businesses operating in markets), education (universities), governance (governments), and so on. Accordingly, on this view institutional corruption is to be understood fundamentally as a process that compromises the provision of the collective good definitive of the institution in question. I have also introduced the notion of a web of interdependence that obtains between members of institutions and those with needs-based rights, and which is such that the "consumers" of institutionally produced collective goods are also, ultimately, the "producers" of those goods and, as such, have joint rights to those goods.

CHAPTER 2

Social Power

As stated in the Introduction, imbalances in power are highly conducive to corruption. Indeed, power and corruption have a symbiotic relationship, albeit corruption can exist independently of power relationships. To reiterate Lord Acton's dictum: Power tends to corrupt, and absolute power corrupts absolutely. Moreover, power and, relatedly, authority are in part constitutive of most, if not all, institutions in contemporary settings. Accordingly, it is critical that an understanding of power, in the sense of social power, be provided. However, the concept of power has proven to be a difficult one to explicate adequately.[1] In this chapter I examine the concept of power and social power, in particular.

2.1 Definition of Power

My concern here is with power in the sense of one human agent or collection thereof having power over another human agent or collection thereof. The collections in question include organizations and systems of organizations, i.e., social institutions in the sense defined in Chapter 1. Moreover, the *social* power of institutions resides, I suggest, ultimately in the individual human beings who occupy the institutional roles in part constitutive of these institutions. Indeed, the exercise of this power is not to be understood in narrow, mechanical, causal terms. Rather the powerful have at least some degree of *rationally informed* control over those in respect of whom they exercise that power. For example, the powerful might use the powerless as means to their ends. Instances of social power include the

---

[1] The most detailed philosophical analysis of power to date is Peter Morriss, *Power: A Philosophical Analysis* (Manchester University Press, 2002). Earlier analyses were provided by Steven Lukes, *Power: A Radical View*, 2nd edn. (London: Palgrave Macmillan, 2005); P. Bachrach and M. S. Baratz, *Power and Poverty: Theory and Practice* (Oxford University Press, 1970).

military power of the members of the US armed forces in relation to the members of the armed forces of Saddam Hussein during the US led invasion of Iraq, the economic power of a large corporation in relation to a small supplier firm, the power an employer might have over an employee, the power a police officer might have over an offender. This is not to dispute that collective entities, such as populations or organizations, can have nonrationally informed *causal* powers that attach to those entities as such, and that are potentially beyond the control of the individual human agents constitutive of those entities. For instance, increasing or decreasing birthrates in a human population can have profound economic effects. However, absent the means to acquire knowledge of these birth rates, and absent an authoritarian government to forcibly intervene, the birthrates of such populations may well be beyond the control of the members of these populations.

Some forms of power are natural, as opposed to institutional. For example, there is the physically strong man's power over a weak one or a woman's psychological power over a submissive man. Our concern in this work is primarily with a central species of social power, namely, institutional power. Nevertheless, institutional power relies in part on both physical and psychological power. Consider the commander of an army, whose institutional power relies in part on the physical and psychological power of his individual combatants; physical power that in part depends on their bodily strength and in part on their weaponry, and psychological power that in part depends on their training and mental resilience. Indeed, natural power and institutional power are intertwined in manifold ways, albeit they can be conceptually demarcated. I will focus on natural power only to the extent that it is relevant to social power and, in particular, to institutional power. Social power is a somewhat wider notion than institutional power since unstructured social groups might have social power without the power in question being institutional in character. Noninstitutional social power is an important phenomenon but it is relevant to this work only to the extent that it connects with institutional power and, ultimately, to institutional corruption.

It is important to distinguish power from ability.[2] Social power (at least in the sense being used in this work) is not simply the "power" to do something, e.g., the ability to lift a heavy load or to drive a car. Social power involves a *relationship* between one or more human beings and especially

---

[2] Theorists such as Morriss (in his *Power*) and Giddens (in his *The Constitution of Society*) tend to conflate the notions of ability and power.

between one or more institutional actors. Therefore, it is not merely an ability, although it does involve an ability. It is also important to distinguish the *possession* of power from the actual exercise of that power. One can have power without exercising it, e.g., the strong man might never seek to cause the weak one to do anything against the latter's will, even though he could do so if he chose.

The exercise of power involves one agent A having as an end that another agent B perform an action, x (or refrain from doing so), and thereby realize A's end; if A's exercise of power in relation to B is successful then B x's. A presupposition of A's exercise of power over B is that there is an initial conflict of ends, e.g., pursued interests, values, and A is seeking to get B to do (or refrain from doing) something, x, that B is resistant to do (or refrain from doing). Accordingly, exercises of power typically contrast with cooperative or joint action. As we saw in Chapter 1, joint actions involve a shared or collective end. On the other hand, if an exercise of power is successful then the agent who is the "victim" of the exercise of power comes to have the end that the agent exercising the power wants that agent to have. Here the end in question is that definitive of the action to be performed by the victim, e.g., handing over one's wallet in order that the robber will have one's money. Naturally, the victim does not desire the end, but desiring an end is not the same thing as having an end. Moreover, a single agent or group may exercise his/her/their power over another group of agents, causing the latter to perform a joint action, albeit a joint action they do not desire to perform. In the latter case, the victims of the exercise of power come to have the collective end constitutive of the joint action in question; however, they do not desire to have it. Consider a group of slaves engaged in building a house for their master on pain of being beaten. They are performing a joint action: building the house. Moreover, they have the built house as a collective end. However, they do not desire to build the house; rather they have been coerced into building it.

It may be that in some instances the process of enslavement is so deep that the slave does not simply pursue an end that he or she does not desire because coerced into doing so, but actually desires to realize the end in question. However, even in these cases I suggest that at a deeper level still there is a conflicting desire not to obey the slave-owner, albeit a desire that has been repressed under massive ongoing physical and psychological duress. For my purposes here this second kind of case simply provides an additional complication rather than a counter-example (see later).

As is illustrated by our first slave example, the exercise of power by A over B necessarily involves the use or threat of the use of sanctions, e.g., the infliction of harms. Here a sanction is to be understood as a harm or deprivation that B finds it very difficult to endure and that renders the action A seeks to get B to perform one that B finds it very difficult to resist performing.

We have seen that the exercise of power involves a degree of conflict, at least at the level of interests, desires, or values. The end of the agent exercising the power, A, is in conflict with the victim's end, interest, or desire, at least initially. Note that the conflict in question is not simply or necessarily rule-governed competition between consenting agents, albeit such competition typically involves a struggle between wills, and a process involving gains and losses that terminates in a winner and a loser. The exercise of power is not necessarily rule-governed and the victims of power have not necessarily consented to anything. And while competition may involve the use of sanctions, it does not necessarily do so. Note also that if A overpowers B to the point that B ceases to have any agency whatsoever, e.g., if A kills B, then A ceases to have power over B. Specifically, A can only have power over B if A can get *B to act*. Importantly, however, A's power over B can reach the point where B (in effect) has his/her *desired* end to realize whatever ends A wants B to realize. This is an extremely high level of domination of B by A. Indeed, B might be said to have radically diminished autonomy. Nevertheless, B is still engaged in action in the sense of forming intentions that cause his or her actions. Moreover, B's autonomy is, at least in principle, retrievable, and retrievable, in particular, in the absence of A's application of sanctions. Thus, as mentioned above, at some deeper level, B has a conflicting desire: a desire not to do what A wants B to do. If, on the other hand, B has reached the point where s/he is literally the instrument of A's desires absent any sanctions, then B is no longer an agent and, as such, is not the victim of power any more than an inanimate object is.

If A has power over B in our favored sense then A has this power by virtue of some resource, R, such as physical strength/armaments, psychological strength, wealth, status, and especially, given our concerns in this work, institutional position. This resource is one A can utilize as a sanction in the service of getting B to do what A wants B to do. The sanctions in question include the use or the threat of the use of physical, psychological, financial, and reputational harms or deprivations. They also include the threat of the loss of power. Thus A might exercise power in relation to B by virtue of the threat of removing B's power over C. Consider a high-level manager, A, who exercises power over a middle-level manager, B, by threatening to remove or suspend B's authority (and, therefore, power) to discipline a recalcitrant employee, C, who is currently under B's authority.

Some further points to note in respect of social power are as follows. First, the extent of one's power is not necessarily equivalent to the extent of one's resources. A might have great power over B by virtue of A's having one million dollars but very little power over C, since whereas B is impoverished C is wealthy. So A's power over B is partly dependent on properties possessed or, in some cases, not possessed by B.

Second, the existence of a sanction distinguishes power from influence. One can influence another person or persons without recourse to sanctions; one cannot exercise power without sanctions.

Third, the use of force is not necessarily the exercise of power. The exercise of power might involve the use of force, but the use of force (e.g., shooting someone) is not necessarily the exercise of power since force might not be used to make the agent perform an *action* (or refrain from performing an action) but merely cause the agent to engage in involuntary behavior. On the other hand, the actual use of force (or some other sanction), as opposed to the mere threat to use it, does not entail that power has *not* been successfully exercised, albeit this might in fact be so. In particular, if by the use of force A gets B to intentionally act to realize A's end, then this is an exercise of power. Suppose A tells B to stop or he will shoot but B continues to flee. Suppose A shoots B in the leg and while B could continue to try to flee he can only do so with great pain; so B abandons his attempt to flee. This is a case of A exercising power over B. If, on the other hand, the use of force by A prevents B from acting at all (including intentionally refraining from acting), e.g., if A shoots B dead when B refused to hand over his wallet, then A has not exercised power over B although he has certainly used force.

Fourth, A's exercise of power over B can be implicit (e.g., an abusive husband, A, makes implicit, but not explicit, threats against his abused wife, B), and perhaps even unconscious (e.g., the self-image of abused wife, B, prevents her from seeing that she is actually acting out of fear of her husband rather than, say, for the good of the family).

2.2 Institutional Power

There are a number of different sorts of social power that might be distinguished. In this work I discuss two of the main ones, namely, institutional power and the power of social norms. In this section my focus is on institutional power. Please bear in mind that social institutions also involve the power of social norms since, as stated in Chapter 1, social institutions are in part constituted by social norms, albeit social norms also operate outside social institutions.

I note at the outset the well-known distinction between power and authority and, in particular, between institutional power and institutional authority. Roughly speaking, authority is legitimate power.[3] Here as elsewhere, however, we need to distinguish between moral and institutional legitimacy. Institutionally legitimate authorities are frequently also morally legitimate authorities. However, this is not necessarily the case. For example, a lawfully and appropriately democratically appointed political leader – an institutionally legitimate political authority – might in actual fact be a demagogue bereft of workable public policy prescriptions and, as such, morally illegitimate.[4] Moreover, we also need to keep in mind the distinction between institutions and organizations. By the lights of my teleological *normative* account elaborated in Chapter 1, social institutions are organizations or systems of organizations; as such they have collective ends. However, in the case of institutions, but not necessarily organizations, their constitutive collective ends are also collective goods. Accordingly, there are organizations the constitutive collective ends of which are not also collective goods; for instance, organizations the core business of which is both unlawful and immoral, such as the mafia. The leader of an organization such as the mafia does not have *moral* legitimacy, given this kind of organization is inherently immoral. On the other hand, a mafia leader might have assumed his leadership in strict accordance with that organization's procedures; moreover, he might enjoy the support of mafia members. Accordingly, this leader might have very considerable organizational power. Nevertheless, in the light of our distinction between organizations and institutions, the mafia leader in question would not be a legitimate *institutional* authority, for a mafia organization is not an institution (in our favored sense) let alone an institutionally (or morally) legitimate organization.[5]

---

[3] Max Weber, *Economy and Society: An Outline of Interpretive Sociology* (New York: Bedminster Press, 1968); Joseph Raz (ed.), *Authority* (New York University Press, 1990); L. Green, *The Authority of the State* (Oxford University Press, 1989).

[4] Arguably, such a leader is only morally illegitimate *all things considered*.

[5] Conceivably there might be institutions which were, nevertheless, not institutionally legitimate because, for instance, their legitimacy relies on institutional procedures that have not been adequately adhered to, e.g., a public school of reasonable general educational quality but which does not meet higher government-based educational standards and, as a result, is under the threat of being defunded.

Social power is often *jointly* possessed and exercised, including, in the case of organizational and sub-organizational, action via multi-layered structures of joint action (see Chapter 1). Assume that A and B are two sets of agents and that the members of A jointly have the power to get one or more of the members of B to perform an action or actions that they would not otherwise perform. For example, the members of a gang of extortionists (set of agents, A) acting jointly, but not singly, have the power to get regular payoffs from the terrified shopkeepers in a neighborhood (set of agents, B). Here a joint action is to be understood in the sense elaborated in Chapter 1, namely, as a set of individual actions performed to realize a collective end. A collective end is an end that each agent has but no one agent can realize on his or her own (or could realize it only with difficulty). As we also saw, joint action involves *interdependence of action*; each acts only if the others do, since otherwise the end will not be achieved and each acts if the others do, since in that case the end will be achieved. By virtue of being interdependent action in the service of a collective end, joint action is a species of social *action* but not necessarily of social power. The joint action of extortion is an act of power because it relies on sanctions; it is the threat of, say, violence by the extortionists that makes their joint action an exercise of power, notwithstanding that a single agent acting on his own could not exercise power over the shopkeepers because, let us assume, he could not make a *credible* threat.

Perhaps the most salient form of social power is the power of large hierarchical organizations, such as governments, military organizations, and corporations. How are such organizations to be understood for the purposes of ascribing social power to them? In Chapter 1, I argued that organizational action consists of multi-layered structures of joint actions. Consider, for example, members of a mortar squad and members of an infantry platoon in a battle. The members of the mortar squad jointly fire mortar shells on enemy soldiers, members of infantry move forward and hold ground formerly occupied by enemy soldiers; members of the mortar squad and of infantry have jointly won the battle. This might simply be an example of the use of military force, as opposed to an exercise of power; it would be an example of the exercise of power if the battle in question was (say) in the service of causing the enemy to surrender in the war in question. Again, a large monopoly retailer, such as Walmart, comprising a structure of organizational roles occupied by thousands of individuals engaged in multi-layered structures of joint action might exercise market power over some of its small individual suppliers who are economically dependent on Walmart to buy their products, and Walmart managers might do so by threatening not to sell their suppliers' products unless they supply them to Walmart at rock bottom prices.

Within hierarchical organizations some individuals have great power by virtue of their occupancy of a position of authority in the organization; their possession and exercise of power is not joint in our above senses. The power attached to a position of authority, i.e., the power attaching to the office (as opposed to the particular person who might occupy the office at a certain time) in a hierarchical organization depends in the first instance on some resource, such as control of an organization's finances, or physical force applied by subordinates that is utilizable as a sanction.

However, while institutional authorities often wield individual (as opposed to joint) power, they are also dependent on the collective acceptance of others. Consider Peter Sellars in the movie, *Being There*. Sellars plays the role of a gardener who for various reasons begins to be treated by the staff of the President of the USA, and ultimately by everyone, as if he is in fact the President. Eventually, he could even have run for office and been elected. Unfortunately, he has no under-standing of the political system, or of relevant policies, and has no leadership qualities whatsoever. Nevertheless, it seems to be the case that the gardener can become the President by virtue of widespread collective acceptance.

The power of institutional authorities in the sense of those who occupy positions of authority in hierarchical organizations should not be confused with the power of occupants of hierarches of status, albeit the two are related. Status hierarchies do not necessarily rely on organizational power, or on authority more generally. Certainly, status hierarchies, like organiza-tional hierarchies, are dependent on widespread collective acceptance. However, the collective acceptance in question tends to be different in nature. Specifically, status hierarchies, but not necessarily organizational hierarchies, essentially depend on mobilizing the desire to be approved. The notion of approval here used is a generic one embracing the desire to be admired, to be respected, and even to be envied; it is not simply the narrower notion of moral approval. This (generic) desire for social approval is at the core of status hierarchies. Importantly, the power of the occupants of organizational hierarchies can be buttressed by, or even partly depend on, social approval and, likewise, occupancy of a position in the upper levels of an organizational hierarchy can confer status and, therefore, social approval. Consider Donald Trump prior to his becoming President. He had high status among many voters and this may well have been what led to his being elected to high political office, President of the USA; certainly his prior celebrity status was a key part of his electoral strategy.

Notwithstanding the power of institutional *authorities*, they are, nevertheless, inherently vulnerable from within. As Searle points out, the communist government of Russia turned out to have clay feet.[6] Once people chose not to obey its directives, it was finished; it simply ceased to function or exist as a government. There is a particular reason for the vulnerability of institutional authorities. The moral and institutional right of institutional authorities to possess and exercise institutional power is dependent on collective acceptance. The point here is not simply that (say) rulers cannot *exercise* their (moral and institutional) right to rule, if their right to rule is not collectively accepted; though this is in fact the case. Rather, a ruler does not even *possess* a right to rule unless she is able to exercise authority over her subjects. This seems to be a general feature of the institutional and moral rights and duties of those occupying positions of institutional authority.

Accordingly, the rights possessed by institutional authorities are not only rights to exercise powers in the narrow sense of a right that might not actually be able to be exercised; rather, speaking generally, these rights are ones that, if not able to be exercised, are not possessed.[7] In short, these rights are *de facto powers*, albeit they are not merely *de facto* powers. Indeed, the actions of those in authority constitute in large part the *exercise of power*, e.g., with respect to their subordinates. As such, these actions of authorities are an *in-principle* threat to individual autonomy. Naturally, this in-principle threat might cease to exist under certain conditions, e.g., if the institutional authority is subject to consensual democracy.

As we have seen, the power of institutional authorities is dependent on collective acceptance. To this extent, institutional power is potentially constrained by autonomous individuals acting collectively. Perhaps the collective acceptance in question consists in large part in compliance with social norms, e.g., merit-based procedures for determining leadership positions. Such social norms may themselves involve the exercise of social power. (I return to this issue below.) However, collective acceptance might be passive in a sense of passivity consistent with the nonexistence of autonomy. This might be so if the collective acceptance in question

---

[6] Searle, *The Social Construction of Reality*, p. 91.

[7] There might be some circumstances in which the right to rule is possessed but not able to be exercised, e.g., during a brief period of instability.

consists in large part in unmotivated habitual behavior. Moreover, even if the members of some majority actively accept some authority – that is, they exercise their autonomy in accepting the authority – it might still be the case that the members of a relevant minority do not. If so, then the autonomy of the members of that minority may well be compromised by the exercise of power over them by the authority in question.

As is well-known, institutional mechanisms have been developed to deal with this problem of respect for individual autonomy in the context of hierarchical organizations. Democratic processes are perhaps the most important category of such institutional mechanisms. The basic idea is a very familiar one. It involves each individual autonomously participating in the democratic process, and deciding to abide by the outcome of that democratic process, e.g., voting for a particular leader and accepting the outcome of the vote.

Insofar as individuals autonomously choose to participate in organizational hierarchies, or insofar as individuals autonomously accept (say) democratic decision procedures, and those democratic decision procedures permeate organizational hierarchies, then organizational hierarchies are not necessarily inconsistent with individual autonomy. However, in contemporary societies, at least, organizational hierarchies, such as large public and private sector bureaucracies are unavoidable, and in many cases are not subject to mean-ingful democratic decision-making procedures. Accordingly, to this extent individual autonomy is compromised. Moreover, individual autonomy is also compromised in nondemocratic nation-states, and perhaps even in many or all democratic nation-states – since in the contemporary world, at least, there is no real option but to live in a nation-state, and thereby to be subject to governmental control.

The loss of power of political institutions and, specifically, of those occupying positions of governmental power often results from a power struggle involving joint action and the use of sanctions by those mobilizing against the government in question. These joint actions and the joint action responses to them on the part of government's supporters (including members of the security agencies) constitute a (social) power struggle. The sanctions deployed include the use of physical force, such as forcible entry and occupancy of strategic locations (e.g., government offices), harassment of public officials, destruction of property, and so on.

The power attaching to positions of authority in *some* corporations, indeed the existence of the corporations themselves, is not merely depen-dent on economic resources and physical force provided by security agencies. For example, the power attaching to positions of authority in financial institutions, such as banks, is ultimately dependent on investors and savers (depositors). The loss of power does not necessarily involve a power struggle; there is no *joint* action or use of sanctions by those who withdraw their investments/savings. The Global Financial Crisis involved the collapse of a number of financial institutions, notably Lehman Brothers, and the most immediate cause of many of these banking collapses was a lack of confidence and trust on the part of investors and depositors in those institutions. In short, collective acceptance of, including participation in, hierarchical institutions is not simply dependent on economic resources and brute physical power; it also relies on less tangible collective attitudes, such as collective confidence, collective trust and, more generally, reputation. By the lights of the form of relational individualism favored in this work, such collective attitudes are to be understood as relational properties. Thus depositor A1 trusts bank B and does not withdraw her funds from B, in part because A1 believes depositors A2, A3, etc. trust B and, therefore, will not withdraw their funds from B.

Naturally, the power attaching to positions of authority in corporations is ultimately dependent on the legal system and its enforceability and, therefore, on other hierarchical organizations, e.g., police organizations possessed of power in part based on physical force. However, as the example of communist Russia mentioned above demonstrates, the legal system (including police organizations, courts, prisons, etc.) is itself in turn ultimately dependent on collective acceptance by members of the relevant community.

A critical component underpinning the power of hierarchical organizations, including governments and corporations, are the moral attitudes of members of a social group, i.e., the social norms of the members of a social group, whether it be collectively held beliefs in relation to general values such as democracy, individual freedoms, and private property rights, or in relation to specific offences such as fraud, bribery, and insider trading. It also has to be said that hierarchical organizations are in a position to influence these moral attitudes and thereby the shape, strength, and even existence of social norms, e.g., to promote consumerism (contemporary corporations), to undermine commitment to individual rights (governments engaged in over-zealous counter-terrorism activities), to generate support to outlaw usury (medieval church). Moreover, some authoritarian governments have sought to exercise power over the moral attitudes of their citizens by the use of "brainwashing," reeducation camps, and so on, i.e., methods involving recourse to physical, psychological, and other sanctions.

2.3   The Power of Social Norms

The second kind of social power to be discussed in this chapter is the power of social norms.[8] Conformity with social norms might be freely undertaken or it might be the consequence of an exercise of social power. However, it might be argued individuals who comply with social norms are necessarily being subjected to a form of power, presumably the power of the social group constituted in part by these norms. Let us get clearer on the nature of social norms.

In Chapter 1 we distinguished between social norms and conventions. Both social norms and conventions are regularities in actions involving interdependence between participants. However, social norms, but not necessarily conventions, involve moral attitudes. Moreover, whereas conventions are defined directly in terms of interdependence of action, social norms are to be defined in terms of an *interdependence of attitude* that sustains a commonality of attitude and of action. Consider the social norm against incest in a community. Each disapproves of incest and thus refrains from incest; however, this disapproval of each is at least *in part* sustained by the disapproval of the others. Hence social norms are a species of social action (but not necessarily of social power).

Assume that whereas most but not all the members of a social group rightly believe that fraud is wrong, all members of the group refrain from committing fraud, i.e., there is complete compliance with the objectively correct moral principle and social norm, Thou Shalt Not Commit Fraud. Accordingly, there are various motivating factors in relation to compliance. The members of the social group do not commit fraud because one or more of the following conditions obtains: (a) Most believe that it is morally wrong to engage in fraud; (b) Most desire to be morally approved of by others and to avoid their moral disapproval, and they know that they will be disapproved of if they commit fraud (disapproval bringing with it *informal* sanctions, such as expressions of contempt, verbal condemnation, and social ostracism); (c) If anyone is caught committing fraud they will be subjected to *formal* sanctions, i.e., they will be charged, convicted, and imprisoned.

There are a small minority who do not believe that fraud is morally wrong and do not care whether others morally dis/approve of them.

---

[8] Earlier versions of the material in this section appeared in Miller, *Social Action*, chapter 6; Miller, *Moral Foundations of Social Institutions*, chapter 2; and Seumas Miller, "Individual Autonomy and Sociality" in F. Schmitt (ed.), *Socialising Metaphysics: Nature of Social Reality* (Lanham: Rowman & Littlefield, 2003), pp. 269–300.

However, members of this group do care about being subjected to formal sanctions; indeed, for these individuals the threat of imprisonment is both a necessary and a sufficient condition for them to refrain from committing fraud. For the members of this minority, enforcement of the law prohibiting fraud is an exercise of social power. It is an exercise of social (specifically, institutional) power by virtue of the fact that they are only refraining from doing what they would otherwise do on the basis of the threat of formal sanctions – in this case formal sanctions emanating from organizations, e.g., the police, the courts, and the prisons.

There is a second small minority, each of whom refrains from committing fraud simply because each believes that it is morally wrong to defraud; their compliance with the moral principle is not dependent either on formal or informal sanctions. Accordingly, each member of this minority acts (refrains) independently of the behavior (e.g., formal sanctions) or attitudes (specifically approval and disapproval) of others. For members of this minority neither the law nor the social norm *qua* social norm are exercises of social power. Rather, the moral belief of any given member of this group is both a necessary and a sufficient condition for that person refraining from committing fraud.

Let us now turn to the majority membership of the social group. Assume that for most members of the social group the belief that fraud is wrong taken together with the desire to be approved of (and not to be disapproved of) are jointly sufficient for conformity, but neither is sufficient on its own.[9]

With respect to this majority of agents who are motivated to comply with the anti-fraud principle in part by their desire to avoid disapproval (as well as in part by their moral beliefs), we must distinguish between two groups: (a) those agents who would commit fraud if they believed that their transgression would go undetected, since they are only concerned with *actual* disapproval and its associated informal sanctions (taken in conjunction with their belief that fraud is wrong), and (b) those agents who would not commit fraud, even if they believed that their transgression would go undetected and believed; therefore, that they would not in fact suffer informal sanctions (or, of course, formal sanctions).

The agents motivated by avoidance of *actual* social disapproval (and its associated informal sanctions), i.e., group (a), are subject to social power,

---

[9] Doubtless, there are another group for whom all three motivating factors are operative (moral belief, informal sanctions, formal sanctions), and each of which is necessary. However, I do not need to pursue this complication here.

although not necessarily the power of hierarchical organizations (and, there-fore, of formal sanctions), but rather the power of members of the social group *qua* sources of approval and disapproval. The threat of socially based sanctions, e.g., strong disapproval, displays of contempt, verbal condemna-tion, and social ostracism, are required to prevent members of group (a) from doing what they know to be morally wrong. Insofar as sanctions, albeit informal sanctions, are required to motivate their compliance with moral principles, they are in the same boat as those deterred by formal sanctions, e.g., by the threat of imprisonment. That is, their compliance with social norms relies on the exercise of social power.

By contrast with the members of group (a), the members of group (b) are motivated by the thought that others would disapprove of their noncompliance with moral principles, if these others knew of their transgression; that is, members of group (b) are sensitive to the fact that others would be *justified* in disapproving of them (including justified in their condemnation, social ostracism, etc.) if their transgressions became known. Moreover, members of (b), but not (a), are sensitive to the fact that if they have transgressed and yet continue to be approved of, then this approval is unjustified.

The whole point of moral disapproval is that if a person does what is morally wrong then there is a good and decisive reason that the person be disapproved of (and subjected to moral condemnation, displays of con-tempt, etc.) and if he does what is right then there is a good and decisive reason that he be approved of. So, if A is rational, then A's *operative* desire will be the desire that he not be *unjustifiably* disapproved of or *unjustifiably* approved of (but rather justifiably dis/approved of). In this respect, mem-bers of group (b), but not members of group (a), are rational.

Moreover, unlike the members of group (a), the members of group (b) are not subject to the exercise of social power since they are not motivated by the fear of informal sanctions per se, but rather by the desire to be justifiably dis/approved of and not to be unjustifiably dis/approved of. To be motivated by the latter desire is not to be subjected to the exercise of social power (i.e., fear of informal sanctions per se), but rather to be sensitive to the voice of the morally informed reason of social creatures, i.e., the voice of rational human beings living in a moral community.

Accordingly, unlike the members of group (a), the members of group (b) have an aversion to informal sanctions unjustifiably applied; albeit this is not directly relevant to the case in question, since no sanctions are going to be applied. However, in addition, the members of group (b) – but not the members of group (a) – have an aversion to being unjustifiably approved of. This is directly relevant since this will be the case if the agents transgress (in the context of their continuing to be approved of because their transgressions have not been found out). Members of group (a) would transgress if they knew that their transgressions would not be found out since they would not suffer actual disapproval (or formal sanctions). By contrast, members of group (b) would not transgress even in these circumstances, since they desire to avoid being *unjustifiably* approved of (and transgressors ought to be disapproved of).

Thus far we have been concerned with social norms proscribing behavior that is morally wrong and generally believed to be such. Let us now consider an example of a social norm proscribing behavior that is *falsely* believed to be morally wrong: the social norm that was in place in apartheid South Africa that blacks and whites ought not to form sexual relationships.

Assume that this moral belief that it is wrong for blacks and whites to form sexual relationships is false; nevertheless, in South Africa under apartheid it is widely believed by both blacks and whites to be morally wrong for blacks and whites to form sexual relationships, and such relationships are strongly disapproved of. This disapproval takes the form, let us assume, of informal sanctions, e.g., displays of contempt, verbal condemnation, or social ostracism.

Insofar as these informal sanctions have the effect of causing a black man and a white woman who desire to form a sexual relationship, see nothing wrong with so doing, and who would otherwise form this relationship, nevertheless, to choose not to form this relationship, then it is an exercise of social power; the fear of informal sanctions is governing their behavior. In this respect, the black and the white woman are akin to members of group (a) in our above fraud example. In this situation the members of the community in question have an interdependent attitude of disapproval of interracial sexual relationships, and apply informal sanctions, including by virtue of a jointly held resource (e.g., the ability to ostracize).

Other blacks and whites might desire to form interracial sexual relationships and might believe at a conscious level that there is nothing morally wrong in so doing but, nevertheless, might experience feelings of shame in so acting and this might be sufficient to cause them to refrain, even when their inter-racial sexual acts would escape the notice of others. In this respect, they are akin to members of group (b) in our above fraud example. These blacks and whites have not been able to completely dissociate themselves from the attitudes of the social group to which they belong; perhaps at an unconscious level they believe what they want to do is somehow wrong or contemptible. Unlike members of (b), they are victims of an effective use of social power operating at a subliminal level.

This raises the question of what sustains this social norm governing interracial sexual relationships, given that it has no objective basis in morality; it is false that blacks and whites morally ought not to engage in interracial sexual relationships. Doubtless, in the racist community in question the false belief of each that interracial sexual relationships are morally wrong is sustained in part by the social norm and its associated informal sanctions, i.e., the social norm is a necessary condition for the false belief. However, social power is at its strongest when it deploys both organizational power, notably of the state, and the power of social norms, i.e., the two forms of social power are mutually reinforcing. Assume that the moral belief that it is wrong for blacks and whites to form sexual relationships is not only false, but that it exists to serve the interest of the white ruling class. The latter maintain their position of power and privilege in part by means of an ideology and its constitutive social norms. Central among these social norms are ones expressing the racial superiority of whites and the consequent undesirability of interracial sexual relationships. The structure of social norms goes hand in glove with a racially based hierarchical organizational structure. The members of the white ruling class maintain their position of power and privilege in part by a racially based system of hierarchical organizations that functions in all spheres of activity, i.e., government, the economic system, and the education system. The structure of social norms brings with it informal sanctions and the hierarchical organizational structure brings with it formal sanctions. Moreover, if the society were relatively free and open then presumably most of its members, whether black or white, would believe the claim that it is morally wrong for blacks and whites to form sexual relationships to be false; that is, this false moral belief requires the exercise of social power in order to be widely held.

2.4   Conclusion

Social power is constitutive in part of most, if not all, institutions in contemporary settings and imbalances in power are highly conducive to corruption. Hence there is a need for an understanding of social power. In this chapter I have outlined a conception of social power that is broadly Weberian in inspiration, but which helps itself to notions of joint action put forward in Chapter 1. On this account, social power is relational; if A has power then A has power over some other agent, B. Moreover, social power is jointly possessed and exercised (so A is a plurality of agents) on the basis of sanctions. The application of sanctions requires a resource, such as physical force. Such resources could also be psychological or social in character, e.g., the ability to confer social status by virtue of oneself possessing social status. I have distinguished power from ability, and also from influence and force. I have also distinguished between power and authority, and between institutional power and the power of social norms. Institutional power is most evident in large hierarchical organizations and is wielded by those in positions of organizational authority. While institutional power relies heavily on the use of formal sanctions, ultimately this form of institutional power is based on collective acceptance and, given collective acceptance typically involves social norms, on the power of social norms. The power of social norms is jointly possessed by members of a social group (including economic and social classes) and its exercise consists in large part in securing compliance with a regularity based on the informal sanction of joint disapproval.

CHAPTER 3

Defining Corruption

Thus far in this book, corrupt actions have been distinguished from some other types of immoral action and accounts have been provided of two of the main theoretical notions presupposed by institutional corruption, namely, institutions and social power. Institutional corruption presupposes both the notion of an institution and that of institutional authorities exercising institutional and, therefore, social power. I now turn directly to the concept of institutional corruption itself.[1] I proceed by discussing five constitutive features of institutional corruption.[2] The first of these pertains to institutional role occupants, i.e., persons who occupy such positions.

3.1   The Personal Character of Corruption

There are at least two general forms of corruption, namely institutional corruption and noninstitutional personal corruption. Noninstitutional personal corruption is corruption of persons outside institutional settings. Such corruption pertains to the moral character of persons, and consists in the despoiling of their moral character. If an action has a corrupting effect on a person's character, it will typically be corrosive of one or more of a

---

[1] See Heidenheimer and Johnston, *Political Corruption*, Part 1: Terms, Concepts and Definitions. Robert Klitgaard, Ronald Maclean-Abaroa, and H. Lindsey Parris define corruption as "misuse of office for personal gain" (in R. Klitgaard, R. Maclean-Abaroa, and H. Lindsey Parris, *Corrupt Cities: A Practical Guide to Cure and Prevention* (Oakland, CA: ICS Press, 2000), p. 2). An important exception here is the more sophisticated analytical account offered by Dennis Thompson of political corruption in his *Ethics in Congress* and "Two Concepts of Corruption." For one of the most influential statements of the abuse of public office for private gain definitions see Joseph Nye, "Corruption and Political Development: A Cost-Benefit Analysis," *American Political Science Review*, 61 (1967), 417–427.

[2] Earlier version of the material in this chapter appeared in Seumas Miller, "Concept of Corruption" in E. N. Zalta (ed.), *Stanford Encyclopedia of Philosophy*, Fall 2005 edn., available at http://plato.stanford.edu. Parts also appeared in Miller, Roberts, and Spence, *Corruption and Anti-Corruption*, chapter 1.

person's virtues. These virtues might be virtues that attach to the person *qua* human being, e.g., the virtues of compassion and fairness in one's dealings with other human beings. Alternatively – or, at least, additionally – these virtues might attach to persons *qua* occupants of specific institutional roles, e.g., impartiality in a judge or objectivity in a journalist.

There is a distinction to be made between possession of a virtue and possession of a disposition to behave in certain ways. Virtues consist in part in dispositions, but are not wholly constituted by dispositions. A compassionate person, for example, is disposed to help people. But such a person also experiences certain emotional states, and understands other people in a certain light; compassion involves nondispositional states. Moreover, a compassionate person has actually performed compassionate acts; he or she is not simply disposed to do so. Accordingly, while personal corruption may consist in part in the development or suppression of certain dispositions, e.g., in developing the disposition to accept bribes or in suppressing the disposition to accept them, the production of such dispositions would not normally be fully constitutive of the corruption of persons. Thus a person who has a disposition to accept bribes but who is never offered any is not corrupt, except perhaps in an attenuated sense.

My concern in this work is only with institutional corruption. Nevertheless, it is plausible that corruption in general, including institutional corruption, typically involves the despoiling of the moral character of persons and in particular, in the case of institutional corruption, the despoiling of the moral character of institutional role occupants *qua* institutional role occupants. To this extent, institutional corruption involves personal corruption.

Note that personal corruption, i.e., being corrupted, is not the same thing as performing a corrupt action, i.e., being a corruptor. Typically, corruptors are corrupted, but this is not necessarily the case. Note also that corruptors are not simply persons who perform actions that corrupt, they are also morally responsible for this corruption. (As we shall see, there is one important category of corruptors that is an exception to this, namely corruptors who are not morally responsible for being corrupted, yet whose actions are both an expression of their corrupt characters and also have a corrupting effect.) The precise nature of corruptors and their relationship to the corrupted is discussed in more detail below.

Naturally, in the case of institutional corruption, typically institutional damage is being done above and beyond the despoiling of the moral character of the institutional role occupants. Specifically, institutional processes are being undermined and/or institutional purposes subverted.

Here I note that one important way in which institutional processes, in particular, are undermined is by institutional actors failing to meet the moral standards that are enshrined in these processes, e.g. when a rule or law is unfairly applied.

However, the undermining of institutional processes and/or purposes is not a sufficient condition for institutional corruption. Acts of institutional damage that are not performed by a corruptor and also do not corrupt persons are better characterized as acts of institutional *corrosion*. Consider, for example, funding decisions that gradually reduce public monies allocated to the court system in some large jurisdiction. As a consequence, magistrates might be progressively less well trained and there might be fewer and fewer of them to deal with the gradually increasing workload of cases. This may well lead to a diminution over many years in the quality of the adjudications of these magistrates, and so the judicial processes are to an extent undermined. However, given the size of the jurisdiction and the incremental nature of these changes, neither the magistrates nor anyone else might be aware of this process of judicial corrosion, or even able to become aware of it (given heavy workloads, absence of statistical information, etc.). Moreover, even if they did become aware of it, given the scarcity of public funds, there might not be anything that they or their political masters could do about it; the corrosion might be unavoidable in these straitened circumstances. These judges have not undergone a process of personal corruption (qua institutional role occupants) and may well simply be making the best of a bad situation; accordingly, we are disinclined to view this situation as one of institutional corruption.

One residual question here is whether or not institutional role corruption could exist in the absence of the undermining of institutional processes and/or institutional purposes. Perhaps it could not for the reason that an institutional role is defined in large part in terms of the institutional purposes that the role serves as well as the institutional processes in which the role occupant participates in the service of those institutional purposes. A possible counter-example might be that of a "sleeper": an official who accepts regular pay from a foreign spy agency but has not and perhaps never will be asked for any reciprocal service.[3] If the official in question actually accepts the payments and will in fact provide the reciprocal service if called upon to do so, then the official has a disposition to perform a corrupt action but has yet to act on that disposition. (Here I am assuming

---

[3] I owe this example to Thomas Pogge.

that the acts of offering and accepting the payments stop short of actually undermining either the processes or purposes of the institution in question.) At any rate, the close relationship between institutional roles on the one hand, and institutional processes and purposes on the other explains why institutional corruption typically involves both the despoiling of institutional role occupants *qua* institutional role occupants and the undermining of institutional processes and purposes.

A second residual matter concerns the structure of a corrupt action considered in itself. Some, perhaps most, corrupt actions are joint actions (see Chapter 1 Section 1.1). At any rate, most corrupt actions involve conditional individual actions, and conditional individual actions are not necessarily joint actions since conditional individual actions do not involve a collective end; as such, they are not inherently cooperative. Bribery, for instance, involves conditional individual actions since the briber pays the bribe on condition the bribee provides a benefit to the briber and the bribee provides this benefit on condition the briber pays the bribe (see Chapter 5 Section 5.1).

Finally, we need to formulate precisely the first defining feature of institutional corruption and, specifically, acts of institutional corruption: To be corrupt, an action must involve a corruptor who performs the action or a person who is corrupted by it. Of course, corruptor and corrupted need not necessarily be the same person, and indeed there need not be both a corruptor and a corrupted; all that is required is that there be a corruptor or a corrupted person. This feature is a necessary condition for an action being an instance of institutional corruption and, indeed, for its being an instance of corruption at all. I refer to this feature as the personal nature of corruption. Let us now turn to the second defining feature of institutional corruption.

3.2   The Causal Character of Corruption

If a serviceable definition of the concept of a corrupt action is to be found – and specifically, one that does not collapse into the more general notion of an immoral action – then attention needs to be focused on the moral *effects* that some actions have on persons and institutions. An action is corrupt only if it corrupts something or someone – so corruption is not only a moral concept, but also a *causal* or quasi-causal concept.[4] That is, an action

---

[4] This kind of account has ancient origins, e.g., in Aristotle. See B. Hindess, "Good Government and Corruption," in P. Larmour and N. Wolanin (eds.) *Corruption and Anti-corruption* (Asia-Pacific Press, 2001) pp. 1–10.

is corrupt by virtue of having a *corrupting effect* on a person's moral character or on an institutional process or purpose. If an action has a corrupting effect on an institution by virtue of undermining institutional processes or purposes, then typically – but perhaps not necessarily – it has a corrupting effect also on persons *qua* role occupants in the affected institutions. Likewise, if an action has a corrupting effect on a person *qua* role occupant then typically – but again perhaps not necessarily, as we saw above in relation to the 'sleeper' – it will undermine institutional processes or purposes.

Thus in relation to the concept of *institutional* corruption, the second defining feature and, therefore, necessary condition of an act of institutional corruption is its causal character; specifically, an action is corrupt only if it has the effect of undermining an institutional process or of subverting an institutional purpose or of despoiling the character of some role occupant *qua* role occupant. In light of the possibility that some acts of corruption have negligible effects, such as a very small, one-off, bribe paid for a minor service, this defining feature needs to be qualified so as to include acts that are of a kind that tend to undermine institutional processes, purposes, or persons (*qua* institutional role occupant) or, at least, tend to do so[5], if they are performed frequently, by many institutional role occupants or by those in the upper echelons of institutions. Here it is important to stress the possibility of various structures of interdependence between corruptors. In some cases corruptors perform joint actions in the service of a common goal (collective end), as in the case of the members of a single hierarchical criminal organization who launder money through one of their own "legitimate" businesses or, in a looser arrangement, the members of an economic cartel who have an unstated "policy" of fixing prices. In other cases, corruptors might only engage in corruption because they feel that they cannot afford *not* to do so, given others are doing so, as in the case of a firm that reluctantly pays a bribe to an official in a competitive tendering process in the knowledge that others are doing so and that the firm's bid will be excluded if it does not do likewise. In still other cases, an institutional actor does not perform his corrupt action in cooperation with others or in competitive circumstances; rather the action is performed independently of the actions of other corruptors, at least in the first instance, albeit it eventually contributes to a culture of corruption that undermines institutional processes, purposes or persons

---

[5] Dennis Thompson has defined corruption in terms of a tendency. See his "Two Concepts of Corruption."

(qua institutional role occupants). Consider a university in which many academics engage in the unchecked practice of failing or giving unwarranted low grades to students who do not curry favor with them or who they otherwise dislike, and giving unwarranted high grades to students who do curry favor with them or who they otherwise like.[6] Indeed, in some cases of independently performed corrupt actions, the action type in question might not even constitute corruption if only one person performed one token of it since in that case its institutional effect would be negligible. However, when most or all perform actions of the type in question and do so on a recurring basis then the aggregate effect can be institutionally damaging and in these circumstances each single action may constitute corruption. Consider, for instance, the proverbial free cup of coffee and doughnuts given by a single café owner to all police officers at a particular police station in a high crime area that the café owner rightly calculates will result in his café getting, in effect, unwarranted round the clock police protection because of frequent police presence.

Accordingly, the concept of institutional corruption can be defined in part in terms of a causal role and, therefore, the property of being corrupt supervenes (so to speak) on logically prior action types, notably acts of bribery, nepotism, abuse of authority, and the like. This is why attempts to define the notion of institutional corruption in terms of one or more species of moral/legal offence, e.g., bribery, breach of a fiduciary duty, are ultimately unsatisfactory. Corruption is a causal concept, whereas breach of fiduciary duty, for example, is not. Conceivably, a single instance of breach of fiduciary duty (or, for that matter as we saw above, a single instance of bribery) might not undermine an institutional process or purpose. Moreover, whether or not such breaches tend to undermine institutional processes or purposes is a matter of contingent fact and not of logical necessity. Therefore, it cannot be *definitive* of an action being a breach of fiduciary duty (or of bribery, abuse of authority, etc.) that it is an act of corruption; so breaches of fiduciary duty (or of bribery, abuse of authority, etc.) are not species of corruption *by definition* and, therefore, it is not a trivial logical truth that such breaches are acts of corruption. Rather, if breaches of fiduciary duty are also acts of corruption then they are so by virtue of their effects; they tend to undermine institutional processes or purposes. Accordingly, if breaches of duty do in fact tend to

---

[6] The individual acts of corruption of the academics might or might not be conditional individual actions, i.e., performed on condition the students curry favor or, indeed, provide favors, e.g., sexual favors.

undermine institutional processes or purposes then not only are they acts of corruption, but their property of being corrupt supervenes (causally) on those properties definitive of them as breaches of fiduciary duty, e.g., supervenes on the trust element definitive of a fiduciary relationship.

In this regard, note that an infringement of a specific law or institutional rule does not in and of itself constitute an act of institutional corruption. In order to do so, any such infringement needs to have an institutional *effect*, e.g., to defeat the institutional purpose of the rule, to subvert the institutional process governed by the rule, or to contribute to the despoiling of the moral character of a role occupant *qua* role occupant. In short, we need to distinguish between the offence considered in itself and the institutional effect of committing that offence. Considered in itself the offence of, say, lying is an infringement of a law, rule, and/or a moral principle. However, the offence is only an act of institutional corruption if it has some effect, e.g., it is performed in a courtroom setting and thereby subverts the judicial process.

An additional point to be made here is that an act that has a corrupting effect might not be a moral offence considered in itself. For example, the provision of information by a corporate officer to an investor that will enable the investor to buy shares cheaply before they rise in value might not be a moral offence considered in itself; in general, providing information is an innocuous activity. However, in this corporate setting it might constitute insider trading, and do institutional damage; as such, it may well be an act of corruption.

I also note that acts performed by noninstitutional actors that undermine institutional processes or purposes yet do not involve the participation of institutional actors are not acts of institutional corruption. Thus someone who robs a bank is not engaged in corruption. On the other hand, if the bank robber had relied on "inside information" from a bank employee then the robbery would have involved corruption. A further point to be made here concerns the alleged responsibility for corruption of external noninstitutional actors in contexts in which there are mediating internal institutional actors. In general, an act performed by an external noninstitutional actor is not an act of institutional corruption if there is a mediating institutional actor who is fully responsible for the institutional damage in question. (In the bank robbery involving an insider the bank-robber and his insider accomplice have joint moral responsibility.) Consider an accountant who is besotted with a woman with expensive tastes. His obsession with the woman causes him to spend money on her that he does not have. Accordingly, he embezzles money from the company he works for. There is a causal chain of sorts from her expensive tastes to his act of embezzlement and the consequent institutional harm that his act in turn causes. However, she is not an institutional corruptor; rather, he is, for he is fully responsible for his act of embezzlement, and it is this act – and this act alone – that constitutes an act of institutional corruption. It does so by virtue of the institutional damage that it does.

It might be argued that while she did not corrupt any institutional process or purpose, she nevertheless corrupted him *qua* role occupant, e.g., by undermining his disposition to act honestly. But in the example as described *she* has done no such thing. Rather, his disposition to act honestly has been undermined by himself, and specifically by his desire to please her coupled with his lack of commitment to the ethical and institutional requirements of his institutional role as an accountant.

Another point regarding institutional corruption pertains to the priority of undermining institutional purposes, as opposed to institutional processes and persons (*qua* role occupants). As was argued in Chapter 1, the ultimate institutional purposes in question are collective ends the realization of which constitutes the provision of collective goods. Moreover, institutional processes and roles are in large part simply means to these collective ends. (Of course, these processes and roles are also subject to side-constraints and in some cases ought themselves to embody moral principles, such as principles of procedural fairness.) Accordingly, institutional purposes (understood as collective goods)have a certain moral priority over institutional processes and roles. Note that some institutional purposes may merely be means to other institutional purposes in which case these proximate purposes might not themselves be collective goods. Notwithstanding the moral priority of ultimate institutional purposes understood as collective goods, institutional processes and roles are in part constitutive of institutions and, therefore, if they are undermined then, other things being equal, the institution is undermined.[7] Accordingly, a deliberate act of undermining an institutional process or person (*qua* role occupant) may well be an act of corruption even if it has a negligible impact on the realization of institutional purpose.

In response to my claim that corrupt actions have a causal character the following alleged counter-example might be provided. Suppose Q is responsible for counting votes in a precinct. He cheats and records more votes for candidate A than A actually received, but this does not affect the election result – A wins, but A would have won anyway. Assume also that

---

[7] Things might not equal if, say, role of the process in question is extremely minor or the process is flawed in some important respect. See Section 3.5 and Chapter 14 Section 14.2.

this action has no effect on Q, as he is a very corrupt person to begin with. On the causal account of corruption, Q has cheated, but has there been corruption? There are two salient kinds of case. Suppose there are only two candidates, A and B, in the precinct and the vote count without cheating would have been *heavily* in favor of A anyway, i.e., the false recording of votes made no significant difference either in terms of the substantive outcome (A winning) or in terms of the margin of the win (A winning by a landslide). According to the unqualified causal account there has not been corruption – even if there was attempted corruption and the infringement of an institutional rule. On the other hand, according to the qualified account, the act in question is of a kind, namely cheating, that tends to undermine the electoral process. Accordingly, it is an act of corruption notwithstanding its negligible effect. This seems correct. On the other hand, if A would have won anyway, but only by a wafer thin margin absent the false count – then the false vote counting has made a significant difference to the outcome, albeit only in terms of the relative number of votes for A and the electorate's consequent false belief that A was supported by an overwhelming majority. According to the causal account in both its qualified and unqualified forms there has been corruption. Again, this seems to be correct.

A final point regarding institutional corruption concerns the intentions of corruptors. Clearly, the corruptor deliberately performs the act, such as an act of bribery, which undermines the institutional process, purpose, or person (*qua* institutional actor) in question. Moreover, the corruptor intends or knows or should know that his or her action will have this undermining effect. Nevertheless, those who engage in corruption do not typically intend to *destroy* the institution that their actions are undermining. So corruptors are typically not saboteurs or revolutionaries. The reason that corruptors do not seek to destroy the institutions that they corrupt is that, speaking generally, corruptors benefit or otherwise gain from the continued existence of an institution, even as they undermine it. So institutional corruption is parasitic on institutions and, as is the case with parasites more generally, corruptors can only continue to enjoy the fruits of their corrupt activity if the host survives. In short, corruptors are institutional parasites.

To sum up this section: A necessary condition for an action being an instance of institutional corruption is that the action undermines to some non-negligible degree an institutional purpose (understood as a collective good), process or person (*qua* institutional role occupant) or, at least, that it an instance of a kind of act which tends to undermine institutional purposes, processes, or persons (*qua* institutional role occupants) but do so without, in all likelihood, destroying the institution in question. This feature is the *causal character of corruption*.

3.3   The Moral Responsibility of Corruptors

As already noted, an action is corrupt only if the person who performs it either intends, foresees, or ought to have foreseen the institutional harm that it will cause. (Here I am assuming that the person who performs the corrupt action could have done otherwise; the act of corruption, and hence the institutional harm or damage it caused, was avoidable.) This is the third necessary condition for corruption. Let us say that this condition expresses *the moral responsibility of corruptors*.

As noted above, there is one important exception to the moral responsibility of corruptors condition. The exception is that sub-class of corruptors who are (a) corrupt, but not morally responsible for being so, and (b) whose actions are an expression of their corrupted characters and also have a corrupting effect.

We need to invoke our earlier distinction between acts of institutional corruption and acts of institutional *corrosion*. An act might undermine an institutional process or purpose without the person who performed it intending this effect, foreseeing this effect, or indeed even being in a position such that they could or should have foreseen this effect. Such an act may well be an act of corrosion, but it would not necessarily be an act of corruption. Consider our magistrates example involving a diminution over time in the quality of the adjudications of these magistrates. Neither the government and other officials responsible for resourcing and training the magistracy nor the magistrates themselves intend or foresee this institutional harm; indeed, perhaps no-one could reasonably have foreseen the harmful effects of these shortcomings in training and failure to respond to increased workloads. This is judicial corrosion, but not judicial corruption.

On the other hand, if the magistrates became aware of the diminution in the quality of their adjudications and chose to do nothing about it, then arguably the process of corrosion might have become a process of corruption by virtue of the corrupting effect it is having on the character of the magistrates *qua* magistrates. This example shows that there can be corruption of a person (the magistrate(s)) without a corruptor (assume the government and other officials are unaware of the problem of educating and resourcing the magistracy). Naturally, as was pointed out above, if the resources were simply unavailable then there would not be corruption on anyone's part, notwithstanding their knowledge of the harm being done. For if an outcome is unavoidable then presumably even those who causally contributed to the outcome are not morally responsible for it; for they could not have done otherwise than cause it.

A further point in relation to institutional corruption and institutional corrosion is that they may exist side by side and reinforce one another. Returning to a version of our judicial scenario, let us assume that a lack of resources over a long period of time is undermining the quality of the adjudications, as was the case in the other versions of the scenario. But now let us assume that although this lack of resources is to a considerable extent unavoidable, since resources are indeed quite scarce, nevertheless, it is also to a considerable extent due to the magistrates themselves; they use the lack of resources (e.g., understaffing of courts) as an excuse not to prepare themselves adequately, to allow a large backlog of cases to build up, and so on.

Because persons who perform corrupt actions (corruptors) intend or foresee – or at least should have foreseen – the corrupting effect their actions have, these persons typically are blameworthy, but this is not *necessarily* so. For there are cases in which someone knowingly performs a corrupt action but is, for instance, coerced into so doing, and therefore is not blameworthy. So prima facie it is possible to perform an act of corruption, be morally responsible for performing it, and yet not be blameworthy.

Moreover, we earlier distinguished between two species of corruptor. There are those corruptors who are morally responsible for their corrupt actions. And there are those corruptors who are not responsible for their corrupt character, but whose actions are (a) an expression of their corrupted character and (b) actions that have a corrupting effect.

Accordingly, we now have a threefold distinction in relation to corruptors: (1) corruptors who are morally responsible for their corrupt actions and blameworthy; (2) corruptors who are morally responsible for their corrupt actions but not blameworthy; (3) corruptors who are not morally responsible for having a corrupt character but whose actions are (a) expressive of their corrupt character and (b) actions that have a corrupting effect. The existence of the third category of corruptors demonstrates that moral responsibility is not, strictly speaking, a necessary condition for institutional corruption. On the other hand, presumably most, if not all, rational, morally sensitive adults can reasonably be expected to take steps to renovate their corrupt character, even if they were not morally responsible for its initial development. Accordingly, it is likely that there are only a small number of corruptors who are not morally responsible for their corrupt actions, namely, those meeting the following two conditions: (i) they were not morally responsible for the development of their own corrupt character (e.g., they were children reared by corrupt parents); and (ii) they have not had sufficient time or opportunity to renovate their corrupt character (e.g., they are young adults struggling to renovate their corrupt character in a corrupt environment).

A final point regarding the blameworthiness of those who are morally responsible for corruption is as follows. If a person is coerced into performing an action that definitely would otherwise be corrupt then he or she may, nevertheless, be morally responsible for performing the corrupt action. Consider, for example, a junior police officer who is coerced by senior fellow officers into signing a false statement about a suspect. Whether or not the officer is morally responsible for their action depends on whether the officer performed an action in an appropriately strong sense of that term, and this in turn depends on the nature of the coercion used. If, for example, the fear-inducing coercion was such that the person literally could not have done otherwise than comply then, arguably, the person has not performed an action for which the person is morally responsible (and therefore, of course, cannot be blameworthy). Perhaps, for example, the junior officer signed only because he was being tortured. On the other hand, in some cases the level of coercion might be such that the person could have done otherwise and so was morally responsible for their action. Perhaps, for example, the junior officer signed because he did not wish to be beaten. Typically, in such cases the persons in question while morally responsible for their action will, nevertheless, not be blameworthy. Accordingly, if an action is coerced then it might or might not be an act of corruption. If the person is morally responsible, but not blameworthy, for an otherwise corrupt action then, arguably, the action remains a corrupt action. On the other hand, if the person is not even morally responsible for an otherwise corrupt action then the action is not a corrupt action.

3.4 The Asymmetry between Corruptors and Those Corrupted

The fourth feature of institutional corruption concerns persons – in the sense of institutional role occupants – who are corrupted. The contrast here is twofold. In the first place, persons are being contrasted with *institutional processes and purposes* that might be subverted. In the second place, those who are *corrupted* are being contrasted with those who *corrupt* (the corruptors).

Those who are corrupted typically have to some extent, or in some sense, allowed themselves to be corrupted; they are *participants* in the process of their corruption. Specifically, they have *chosen* to perform the actions that ultimately had the corrupting effect on them, and they could have chosen otherwise. In this respect, the corrupted are no different from the corruptors. Note that from this it does not follow that the corrupted are necessarily morally responsible for being so since, for instance, they may lack the requisite moral maturity. I return to this issue below. Note also that this ability of those being corrupted to choose otherwise is consistent with their being corrupted through coercion, so long as they could have chosen to resist the coercion.[8]

Doubtless, many individuals become corrupt politicians, or corrupt business persons or corrupt academics as a consequence of aspects of their personality, or financial or other circumstances, that have little or nothing to do with the institutional setting in which they are operating. Consider an accountant who becomes addicted to gambling and as a consequence engages in acts of corporate corruption. However, the process by means of which an individual person is corrupted *qua* institutional role occupant is often one that has become part of the fabric of the institution in question, and as such makes the individual vulnerable in that institutional setting. Such processes are by no means necessarily dependent on the individual being corrupt or lacking in resilience to corruption prior to his or her participation in that institution. Rather, it is a case of a person of average moral character (so to speak) being placed in an institutional environment in which there are (initially subtle) incremental, undue inducements to engage in legal or moral offences and, as a consequence, gradually and imperceptibly becoming corrupted. Consider a young police officer who has just started working in the narcotics area. Keen to "fit in," he foolishly accepts a minor "gift" of money from a senior police officer without knowing what it is for; he has committed a relatively minor legal, or at least regulatory, infraction. Later on at a drunken party he reluctantly agrees to smoke a cannabis joint with some of his new colleagues (another minor legal infraction). Still later he is informed that the payment was his "cut" of an unlawful drug deal. This is done in the context of his being

---

[8] Note finally, however, that if the putative actions of those being corrupted were, for example, drug induced or otherwise not under their control, then they cannot be said to have chosen to perform them and these putative actions are not acts of corruption since they are not even actions in the required sense. Moreover, such "actions" could conceivably over time have the effect of undermining the moral character of the persons in question in which case we have instances of corrupt persons who may not be able to resist the process of their corruption during this period of (in effect, involuntary) corruption inducing "action." If this is so then there is an asymmetry between the corruptors and the corrupted. Whereas all corruptors can *do* otherwise than corrupt perhaps some of the corrupted cannot *be* otherwise than corrupt.

enthusiastically welcomed as "one of them," albeit the dire consequences of "ratting" on one's fellow police officers are also made clear. Confused and scared he fails to report this unlawful payment; now he has committed a serious offence. The police officer is compromised, and compromised in a corrupt and intimidating police environment. He is on the proverbial slippery slope.

Accordingly, those who are corrupted and those who corrupt may be different in respect of their intentions and beliefs concerning the corrupting effect of their actions. Specifically, it may not be true of those who allow themselves to be corrupted that they intended or foresaw or even should have foreseen this outcome, notwithstanding that they could have foreseen it. This is especially likely in the case of the young and other vulnerable groups who allow themselves to be corrupted, but lacking the necessary moral maturity cannot necessarily be expected to realize that their actions, or more likely omissions, would have this consequence. The above-mentioned young police officer is an example. Consider also the case of children recruited into Hitler's Youth Movement (Hitler Jugend) who were inducted into the practice of spying on their classmates, teachers, and even parents, and reporting to the Nazis any supposedly suspicious or deviant activities. Arguably, these children were not morally responsible for their moral character, let alone morally blameworthy for it. If so, then whereas agents are necessarily morally responsible for their corrupt actions (although they are not necessarily blameworthy for their corrupt actions), they are not necessarily morally responsible for being corrupted. So there is at least this asymmetry between corruptors and the corrupted.

Naturally, a corruptor of other persons or institutional processes can in performing these corrupt actions also and simultaneously be producing corrupting effects on him or herself. That is, acts of corruption can have, and typically do have, a side effect in relation to the corruptor. They corrupt the corruptor, albeit usually unintentionally. Consider bribery in relation to a tendering process. The bribe corrupts the tendering process, and it will probably have a corrupting effect on the moral character of the bribe-*taker*. However, in addition, it might well have a corrupting effect on the moral character of the bribe-*giver*.

Here we need to distinguish between a corrupt action that contributes to the corruption of the moral character of the would-be corruptor but has no corruptive effect on any institutional process or on the moral character of any other person, and an apparently *non-corrupt* action that is a mere *expression* of a corrupt moral character but has no corruptive effect on any institutional process or on the moral character either of the person who performs it or on that of anyone else. In this connection consider two sorts of would-be bribe-givers whose bribes are rejected. Suppose that in both cases their action has no corrupting effect on an institutional process or other person. Now suppose that in the first case the bribe-giver's action of offering the bribe weakens his disposition not to offer bribes; so the offer has a corrupting effect on his character. However, suppose that in the case of the second bribe-giver his failed attempt to bribe generates in him a feeling of shame and a disposition not to offer bribes. So his action has no corrupting effect, either on himself or externally on an institutional process or other person. In both cases, the action is the expression of a partially corrupt moral character. However, in the first case, but not the second, the bribe-giver's action is corrupt by virtue of having a corrupt effect on himself. Nevertheless, even in the second case the action is an act of corruption according to our qualified definition of corruption since it is an instance of a kind of action that tends to undermine institutional process, purposes, or persons (*qua* institutional actors).

I have argued that the corrupted are not necessarily morally responsible for being corrupted. I have also argued that corruptors are morally responsible for performing their corrupt actions. Accordingly, I have offered the hypothesis of an asymmetry between the corruptors and the corrupted. But what of those corruptors who are not morally responsible for their corrupt characters? They are not morally responsible for their moral characters but they are morally responsible for their corrupt actions, notwithstanding that their actions are an expression of their characters. How can this be? Presumably, in some cases, such as young children who have been corrupted, they are not morally responsible for those actions that express their corrupt moral characters, notwithstanding the harmful institutional effects that these actions have. Perhaps some very young members of the above-mentioned Hitler Youth were not morally responsible for their institutionally harmful actions; so their actions were not corrupt actions (other than being corrupt in the sense of being actions of a kind that tend to corrupt). However, these very young members of the Hitler Youth do not demonstrate the alleged asymmetry between corruptors and the corrupted. Whereas they are not morally responsible for their corrupt characters, nor are they morally responsible for performing any corrupt actions. What of the corrupted who are not responsible for being corrupted but whose actions are corrupt and who are, therefore (by my lights), morally responsible for their corrupt actions?

As mentioned above, many of those who are not morally responsible for initially having been corrupted (e.g., in their youth) are, nevertheless, morally responsible for not now (e.g., in their adulthood) trying to renovate their corrupt characters. To that extent they might be held, at least indirectly, morally responsible for the corrupt actions that are the freely performed expression of their corrupt characters, even if not for initially having been corrupted.[9] Further, there is a difference between an action that is the *freely performed* expression of a corrupt character[10] and an action that has an institutionally harmful effect but which is not under the control of the person who performed it or the person is not otherwise morally responsible for it, e.g., the person did not intend to perform it or the person's intention to perform it was caused by some agent external to the person or the person is not a morally responsible adult (as in the case of the very young members of the Hitler Youth). Even if a person has a corrupt character and can do little about this in the short term, it does not follow that they have no control over or are not otherwise morally responsible for the actions that are the freely performed expression of that character. Consider, for instance, a corrupt official who finds it very hard to refuse bribes but who is, nevertheless, aware of his corrupt character and tries to avoid opportunities in which he will be offered bribes. The upshot of this is that the proposition that there is an asymmetry between corruptors and the corrupted evidently holds up, although in a qualified form. Specifically, corruptors are always *to some degree* morally responsible for their corrupt actions, whereas the corrupted (e.g., vulnerable youths) are not necessarily morally responsible for their corrupt characters. Even corruptors who are not responsible for their corrupt characters and have not had sufficient opportunity to renovate their moral characters are, nevertheless, to some degree morally responsible for the corrupt actions that are the freely performed expression of their moral characters. This asymmetry is the fourth feature of institutional corruption.

3.5 Corrupting and Corrupted Institutional Actors

The fifth and final feature of institutional corruption to be discussed concerns noninstitutional agents who culpably perform actions that undermine institutional processes or purposes. As concluded above, corruption,

[9] Of course, against this it might be argued that they were not morally responsible for the putatively corrupt actions that they performed during the period when they were being corrupted.
[10] Here I am assuming that there is a distinction between those actions that are a "mechanistic" causal expression of moral character (and, as such, unmediated by morally informed judgment) and those that are a freely performed expression of moral character (and, therefore, mediated by morally informed judgment, however, flawed).

even if it involves the abuse of public office, is not necessarily pursued for private gain.[11] Moreover, I have argued that acts of institutional corruption are sometimes actions performed by persons who do not hold public office but rather, for example, occupy positions in the private sector. Thus those who offer or accept bribes in relation to purely private sector business transactions are engaged in corrupt activity.

More generally, as noted in Chapter 1 and elaborated in Chapter 5 Section 5.4, institutional role occupants who engage in corruption typically use the opportunities afforded by their position, and especially their discretionary rights, to breach their duties; in short, they abuse their institutional position. Here we need to distinguish between abusing one's institutional position and abusing one's authority. After all, many institutional role occupants are not institutional authorities. Lower echelon employees, such as cleaners, are a case in point. From this it follows that definitions of institutional corruption in terms of abuse of authority are flawed; abuse of authority is but one species of corruption (see Chapter 5 Section 5.4).

We also need to invoke a distinction between persons who hold a public office or private sector position, on the one hand, and persons who have an institutional role. Citizens are not necessarily holders of public offices or occupants of private sector positions, but they do have an institutional role *qua* citizens, e.g., as voters.

Consider the case of a citizen and voter who holds no public office or private sector positions but who, nevertheless, breaks into his local electoral office and falsifies the electoral role in order to assist his favored candidate to get elected. This is an act of corruption; specifically, it is corruption of the electoral process. However, it involves no public office holder (let alone private sector position holder), either as corruptor or as corrupted. By contrast, consider a fundamentalist Muslim from Saudi Arabia who is opposed to democracy and who breaks into an electoral office in an impoverished African state and falsifies the electoral roll in order to facilitate the election of an extremist right-wing candidate who is likely, if elected, to polarize the already deeply divided community and thereby undermine the fledgling democracy. Let us further assume that the fundamentalist does so without the knowledge of the candidate, or indeed of anyone else. We are disinclined to view this as a case of corruption for two reasons: First, there is no corruptor or corrupted who is the occupant of an

---

[11] Dennis Thompson also makes this point in relation to political corruption. Thompson, *Ethics in Congress*, p. 29.

institutional role. The offender is not an occupant of a relevant institutional role; he is not a citizen or even a resident of the state in question. And, while the offender undermined a legitimate institutional process, viz. the electoral process, he did not corrupt or undermine the character of the occupant of an institutional role. Second, the offender is ultimately trying to destroy the institution of democracy rather than undermine one of its processes in the service of political gain within the context of a continuing institution.

Accordingly, we can conclude that acts of institutional corruption necessarily involve a corruptor who performs the corrupt action *qua occupant of an institutional role* and/or someone who is corrupted *qua occupant of an institutional role*.

This enables us to distinguish not only acts of corruption from acts of corrosion, but also from moral offences that undermine institutional processes and purposes but are, nevertheless, not acts of corruption. The latter are not acts of corruption because no person in their capacity as institutional role occupant either performs an act of corruption or suffers a diminution in their character. There are many legal and moral offences in this latter category. Consider individuals not employed by, or otherwise institutionally connected to, a large corporation who steal from or defraud the corporation. These offences may undermine the institutional processes and purposes of the corporation, but given the noninvolvement of any officer, manager, or employee of the corporation, these acts are not acts of corruption.

A final point to be made before we turn to our explicit definition of corruption concerns the possibility that a corruptor might perform a corrupt action, but do so without breach of their explicitly specified, or otherwise formal, institutional duties. Accordingly, an action might be corrupt by virtue of its self-evidently undermining institutional purpose, yet because of a flawed or incomplete institutional process the institutional actor in question might not be in breach of his or her formal institutional duty. Instances of such corruption include some actions that exploit loopholes in laws and regulations. Consider some lawyers whose main activity is facilitating large-scale tax avoidance on the part of wealthy companies by devising legally compliant, complex structures of shell companies that only pay tax in off-shore tax havens and, thereby, deprive countries of billions of revenue owed by these companies by virtue of them having conducted their business activity, and hence in fact made their profits, in these countries. These lawyers may well not be in breach of the law or their institutional duties narrowly specified; but their actions self-evidently undermine legitimate institutional purposes. Accordingly, by the lights of my account their actions are corrupt (see definition below and Chapter 14 Section 14.2).

3.6   The Concept of Institutional Corruption

In light of the discussion of the five defining features of the concept of institutional corruption, the following summary definitional account of institutional corruption is available:[12]

An act x (whether a single or joint action) performed by an agent A (or set of agents)[13] is an act of institutional corruption if and only if:

(1)   x has an effect, or is an instance of a kind of act that has a tendency to have an effect, not in all likelihood of destroying some institution, I, but rather of undermining, or contributing to the undermining of, some institutional process and/or purpose (understood as a collective good or as a direct or indirect means to the realization of a collective good) of I, and/or has an effect, or is an instance of a kind of act that has a tendency to have an effect, of contributing to the despoiling of the moral character of some role occupant(s) of I, agent(s) B, *qua* role occupant(s) of I;

(2)   At least one of (a) or (b) is true:

    (a)   A is a role occupant(s) of I, A used the opportunities afforded by his role – and especially A's discretionary rights – to perform x, and in performing x, A intended or foresaw the untoward effects in question, or A should have foreseen these effects;

    (b)   is a role occupant of B (or set of agents, B1, B2, B3, etc.) I, and B (or B1, etc.) could have avoided the untoward effects, if B (B1, etc.) had chosen to do so.[14]

Note that some cases of corruption involve a joint action performed by a set of institutional actors who are corruptors and some joint acts of

---

[12]   Regarding the definition, note that agent B could in fact be agent A. Regarding clause (1), note that agent A is not necessarily fully morally responsible or morally blameworthy for the untoward effect that his or her action x produces. Recall also that we are assuming some acceptable definition of moral responsibility without having provided and defended a detailed account.

[13]   I am assuming that the action is intentionally performed, the intention is under the agent's control, and that the agent could have done otherwise.

[14]   Here I am not admitting the possibility countenanced in note 9 above of a corrupt person who could not have resisted the process of their corruption. If this possibility is admitted then the definition would need to be adjusted accordingly.

corruption involve an institutional actor and a noninstitutional actor (e.g., a citizen (the briber) who bribes an official (the bribee)). Note also that (2)(a) tells us that A is a corruptor and is, therefore, either (straightforwardly) morally responsible for the corrupt action, or A is not morally responsible for A's corrupt character and the corrupt action is an expression of A's corrupt character. Note further that A does not necessarily breach A's institutional duties in performing a corrupt action, although typically A would do so.

According to the above account, an act of institutional corruption brings about, or contributes to bringing about, a corrupt condition of some institution (or is of a kind that has a tendency to do so). But this condition of corruption exists only relative to an uncorrupted condition, which is the condition of being a morally legitimate institution or sub-element thereof. Aside from specific institutional processes and purposes, such sub-elements also include institutional roles and the morally worthy character traits that are associated with the proper acting out of these institutional roles.

Consider the uncorrupted judicial process. It consists of the presentation of objective evidence that has been gathered lawfully, of testimony in court being presented truthfully, of the rights of the accused being respected, and so on. This otherwise morally legitimate judicial process may be corrupted, if one or more of its constitutive actions are not performed in accordance with the process as it ought to be. Thus to present fabricated evidence, to lie under oath, and so on, are all corrupt actions. In relation to moral character, consider an honest accountant who begins to "doctor the books" under the twin pressures of a corrupt senior management and a desire to maintain a lifestyle that is only possible if he is funded by the very high salary he receives for doctoring the books. By engaging in such a practice he risks the erosion of his moral character; he is undermining his disposition to act honestly.

On this view, the corrupt condition of the institution exists only relative to some moral standards, which are definitional of the uncorrupted condition of that institution, including the moral characters of the persons in institutional roles. The moral standards in question might be minimum moral standards, or they might be moral ideals. Corruption in relation to a tendering process is a matter of a failure in relation to minimum moral standards enshrined in laws or regulations. On the other hand, gradual loss of innocence might be regarded as a process of corruption in relation to an ideal moral state.

If the process of corruption proceeds far enough then we no longer have a corrupt official or corruption of an institutional process or institution; we cease to have a person who can properly be described as, say, a judge, or a process that can properly be described as, say, a judicial process – as opposed to proceedings in a kangaroo court. Like a coin that has been bent and defaced beyond recognition, it is no longer a coin; rather it is a piece of scrap metal that can no longer be exchanged for goods.

The corruption of an institution does not assume that the institution in fact existed at some past time in a pristine or uncorrupted condition. Rather, an action, or set of actions, is corruptive of an institution insofar as the action, or actions, have a negative moral effect on the institution. This notion of a negative moral effect is determined by recourse to the moral standards constitutive of the processes, roles, and purposes of the institution as that institution morally ought to be in the sociohistorical context in question. Consider a police officer who fabricates evidence but who is a member of a police service whose members have always fabricated evidence. It remains true that the officer is performing a corrupt action. His action is corrupt by virtue of the negative moral effect it has on the institutional process of evidence gathering and evidence presentation. To be sure, in general in this institution this process is not what it ought to be, given the corrupt actions of the other police in that particular police force. But the point is his action contributes to the further undermining of the institutional process; it has a negative moral effect as judged by the yardstick of what that process ought to be in that institution at that time.

In relation to institutions, and institutional processes, roles, and purposes, I have insisted that if they are to have the potential to be corrupted then they must be *morally* legitimate, and not merely legitimate in some weaker sense, e.g., lawful. Perhaps there are non-moral senses of the term "corruption." For example, it is sometimes said that some term in use in a linguistic community is a corrupted form of a given word, or that some modern art is a corruption of traditional aesthetic forms. However, the central meaning of the term "corruption" carries strong moral connotations; to describe someone as a corrupt person, or an action as corrupt, is to ascribe a moral deficiency and to express moral disapproval. Accordingly, if an institutional process is to be corrupted it must suffer some form of moral diminution, and therefore in its uncorrupted state it must be at least morally legitimate. So although marriage across the color bar was unlawful in apartheid South Africa, a priest, Priest A, who married a black man and a white woman was not engaged in an act of corruption. On the other hand, if another priest, Priest B, married a man and a woman, knowing the man to be already married, the priest may well be engaged in an act of corruption. Why was Priest B's act corrupt? Because it served to undermine a lawful, and morally legitimate, institutional process, viz. marriage between two consenting adults who are not already married. But Priest A's act was not corrupt. Why? Because a legally required, but morally unacceptable, institutional procedure – refusing to marry two consenting adults because they are from different race groups – cannot be corrupted. It cannot be corrupted because it was not morally legitimate to start with. Indeed, the legal prohibition on marriage across the color bar is in itself a corruption of the institution of marriage. So Priest A's act of marrying the black man and the white woman was not corrupt.

A further point arising from this example pertains to the possibility of one institution (the apartheid South African government) corrupting another institution (the church in apartheid South Africa). Other things being equal, insofar as the priests (and other relevant institutional actors) in the church acted as Priest A did, i.e., resisted the apartheid laws, the church as an institution would not have been corrupted. Moreover, the apartheid government's undermining of the institutional processes of the church did not in itself constitute corruption, since the government and its leaders are not per se – at least in a secular state – role occupants of the institution of the church. What of those priests who complied with the apartheid laws and did not marry mixed-race couples? Here we need to distinguish mere compliance with the apartheid laws from embracing the laws. A priest might have complied with the apartheid law but only because no mixed-race couple ever approached him to marry them. Presumably, such a priest was neither a corruptor nor a person corrupted. What of a priest who actively supported the apartheid law by condemning such mixed-race marriages as not legitimate in the eyes of God, denouncing the priests who performed them, and so forth? Presumably, this priest has been corrupted and – insofar as he is successful in his endeavors – he is a corruptor of the institution of marriage.

A related point arising from the example concerns the possibility of the corruption of one component of an institution as opposed to the institution in its totality. Naturally many, perhaps most, actions that damage a sub-institution, or even a single institutional process, thereby damage the institution as a whole; after all, an institution consists of its parts. Nevertheless, in the case of some large institutions at least the damage to the institution as a whole might be negligible, notwithstanding that the damage to the sub-institutional element or institutional process was sufficiently serious to warrant the offending action being described as an act of corruption. Naturally, the offending action might be an action of a kind that tends to undermine the institution, especially if performed frequently, by many institutional role occupants or by those in the upper echelons, e.g., bribes. However, there might be actions that are of a kind that only undermines a single institutional process and the process in question is not of much importance to the institution as a whole. Perhaps an academic failing to wear his or her academic gown on the relevant formal occasions would undermine this particular ritual yet have negligible impact on the university as a whole and, in particular, on the realization of its ultimate academic purposes. Evidently, the correct response to this kind of example is to deny that the offence in question is in fact a species of corruption and do so on the grounds that the institutional process in question (the academic ritual) is in itself not sufficiently institutionally important in terms of its contribution to ultimate institutional purposes, i.e., to the collective goods definitive of the institution.

There are three residual points to be made in conclusion. First, the despoiling of the moral character of a role occupant, or the undermining of institutional processes and purposes, would typically require a pattern of actions – and not merely a single one-off action. We saw this above in relation to police officers receiving free coffee and doughnuts. Note here the pivotal role of habits. We have just seen that the corruption of persons and institutions typically requires a pattern of corrupt actions. More specifically, corrupt actions are typically habitual. Yet, as noted in the Introduction, one's habits are in large part constitutive of one's moral character. Accordingly, morally bad *habits* – including corrupt actions – are extremely corrosive of moral character, and therefore of institutional roles and ultimately institutions.

However, there are some cases in which a single, one-off action would be sufficient to corrupt an instance of an institutional process. Consider a specific tender. Suppose that one bribe is offered and accepted, and the tendering process is thereby undermined. Suppose that this is the first and only time that the person offering the bribe and the person receiving the bribe are involved in bribery. Is this one-off bribe an instance of corruption? Surely it is, since it corrupted that particular instance of a tendering process. On the other hand, we can imagine a one-off very small bribe that has a negligible effect on institutional purposes, processes, and persons (*qua* institutional role occupants). Nevertheless, as mentioned above, since it is a bribe we are inclined to view it as an instance of corruption. Hence I have added the qualification in the above account of institutional corruption, namely, that such a one-off action is of a kind (namely, being a bribe) that has a tendency to undermine, or contribute to the undermining of, institutional purposes, processes, or persons (*qua* role occupants).

The second residual point is that among instances of corruption there are ones in which corruptors are culpably *negligent*; they do, or allow to be done, what they reasonably ought to have known should not be done, or should not have been allowed to be done. For example, a safety inspector within an industrial plant who is negligent with respect to his duty to ensure that safety protocols are being complied with might be guilty of corruption by virtue of contributing to the undermining of those safety protocols.

There are complexities in relation to corruption involving culpable negligence that are not necessarily to be found in other forms of corruption. Consider a company official who has a habit of allowing industrial waste products to be discharged into a river because this is the cheapest way to get rid of the unwanted products. But now assume that the official does so prior to the availability of any relevant scientific knowledge concerning the pollution that results from such discharges, and prior to the existence of any institutional arrangement for monitoring and controlling pollution. It seems that the official is not necessarily acting in a corrupt manner. However, the same action might well be a case of corporate corruption in a contemporary setting in which this sort of pollution is well and widely understood, and anti-pollution arrangements are known to be in place in many organizations. While those who actively corrupt institutional processes, roles, and purposes are not necessarily themselves the occupants of institutional roles, those who are culpably negligent tend to the occupants of institutional roles who have failed to discharge their institutional obligations.

The third and final residual point pertains to the cooperative nature of many of the more serious cases of institutional corruption and, especially, organizational, systemic and grand corruption (see Introduction). These latter forms of corruption involve joint action, indeed often multi-layered structures of joint action. Accordingly, the corruptors and the corrupted typically have collective moral responsibility, and not merely individual moral responsibility for the undermining of institutional purposes, processes, and persons (*qua* institutional role occupants). I provide an analysis of collective moral responsibility in Chapter 6.

Moreover, corruption of a person *qua* role occupant may involve undermining a role occupant's commitment to moral principles embodied in social norms, such as honesty. Whereas those institutional duties of role occupants that are also moral duties are not necessarily embodied in social norms, many are; honesty being a case in point. Accordingly, society-wide processes that undermine (objectively valid) social norms are frequently conducive to institutional corruption. Further, these untoward processes themselves may well be a matter of collective moral responsibility. For example, if telling lies or engaging in dishonest financial dealings are widely accepted practices, then there is a collective moral responsibility to do something about this. Indeed, an important reason for doing something about these practices is the negative effect that they might be having on institutions; widespread acceptance of violations of such social norms may well contribute to institutional corruption, even if indirectly. A corollary of this pertains to social norms that are objectively morally wrong, e.g., class-based discrimination. As we saw in the Introduction, as with all social norms, such norms are sustained by interdependent attitudes of disapproval of noncompliance. Accordingly, there is a collective moral responsibility, both on the part of those possessed of these attitudes (to reverse them) and on the part of those who do not (to confront and contest these attitudes when they come across them in others).

3.7 Conclusion

My principal task in this chapter has been to elaborate the defining features of institutional corruption. I have argued that institutional corruption has five main defining features: (1) corrupt actions involve a person who is a corruptor and/or a person who is corrupted (the personal character of corruption); (2) an action is corrupt only if it undermines or is of a kind that tends to undermine an institutional purpose, process, or person (*qua* role occupant) (the causal character of corruption); (3) persons who perform corrupt actions are morally responsible for so doing (the moral responsibility of corruptors), albeit they are not necessarily blameworthy if, for example, they were coerced; (4) unlike persons who corrupt, persons who are corrupted are not necessarily morally responsible for being corrupted (the asymmetry of corruptors and corrupted); (5) acts of institutional corruption necessarily involve a corruptor who performs the corrupt action *qua* occupant of an institutional role – and, therefore, uses the opportunities afforded by his or her position – and/or a person who is corrupted *qua* occupant of an institutional role (institutional corruption requires the active participation of institutional role occupants).

CHAPTER 4

Noble Cause Corruption

As we have seen in earlier chapters, there are many forms of generic corruption, such as political corruption, financial corruption, police corruption, judicial corruption, academic corruption, and many specific types of corruption, such as vote-rigging, bribery, evidence-tampering, and plagiarism. My concern in this chapter is with so-called noble cause corruption. Noble cause corruption is a particular feature of those occupations and institutions that have an important collective good as their *raison d'etre* yet rely on morally problematic means, notably the use of violence. The most salient of these are political, military, and policing institutions. In the first section of the chapter, I consider noble cause corruption in relation to police institutions, and in the second section noble cause corruption in relation to political institutions.

4.1 Noble Cause Corruption in Policing

As we have seen in the Introduction and in Chapter 3, in the paradigm cases corrupt actions are a species of morally wrong, habitual, actions performed by institutional role occupants who use the opportunities afforded by their role. What of the motive for corrupt actions? We have also seen in the Introduction and in Chapter 3 that there are many motives for corrupt actions, including desires for wealth, status, and power. However, there is apparently at least one motive that we might think ought not to be associated with corruption, namely, acting for the sake of good. Here we need to be careful, for sometimes actions that are done for the sake of good are, nevertheless, morally wrong actions. Indeed, some actions that are done out of a desire to achieve good are corrupt actions, namely, acts of so-called noble cause corruption.[1]

---

[1] An earlier version of the material in this section appeared in Seumas Miller and John Blackler, *Ethical Issues in Policing* (Aldershot: Ashgate, 2005). See also Seumas Miller, *Corruption and Anti-Corruption in Policing: Philosophical and Ethical Issues* (Dordrecht: Springer, 2016), chapter 3.

The notion of noble cause corruption receives classic expression in the film *Dirty Harry*.[2] Detective Harry Callaghan is trying to achieve a morally good end. He is trying to find a kidnapped girl whose life is in imminent danger. In the circumstances, the only way he can determine where the girl is in order to save her is by inflicting significant pain on the kidnapper who is refusing to reveal her whereabouts. The image of Harry Callaghan inflicting excruciating pain on a murderous psychopath is emotionally, and indeed ethically, compelling. However, the question that needs to be asked is whether in general fabricating evidence, beating up suspects, "verballing" suspects, committing perjury, and so on to obtain convictions is in the same moral category as Harry's action. The answer is in the negative.

For one thing, Harry Callaghan's predicament is a romantic fiction or, at best, a highly unusual combination of circumstances. Most instances of police fabrication of evidence, and even excessive use of force, have not been used to save the life of someone in imminent danger, nor have they been the only means available to secure a conviction. For another thing, the ongoing recourse to such methods not only violates the rights of suspects but also tends to have the effect of corrupting police officers and, ultimately, undermining the institutional purposes that ironically may well have motivated it. The dangers attendant upon noble cause corruption demand that we provide a principled account of the difference between justifiable use of normally immoral methods and noble cause corruption. We can do so as follows. When police officers act in accordance with the legally enshrined moral principles governing the use of harmful methods, they achieve three things at one and the same time. They do what is morally right; their actions are lawful; and they act in accordance with the will of the community.

It might be argued – and seems to have been argued by Andrew Alexandra[3] – that recourse to the notion of the use of harmful methods in accordance with communally sanctioned objective moral principles does not remove the theoretical problem posed by noble cause corruption, and specifically the alleged (by Alexandra) immorality of even the lawful use of harmful methods by police. To be sure, a suspect who is guilty of a serious crime has not been treated immorally if he is lawfully – and not

---

[2] See C. B. Klockars, "The Dirty Harry Problem," reprinted in A. S. Blumberg and E. Niederhoffer (eds.), *The Ambivalent Force: Perspectives on the Police* (New York: Holt, Rinehart and Winston, 1976). See also John Kleinig, "Rethinking Noble Cause Corruption," *International Journal of Police Science and Management*, 4 (2002), 287–314.

[3] Andrew Alexandra, "Dirty Harry and Dirty Hands" in Tony Coady, Steve James, Seumas Miller, and Michael O'Keefe (eds.), *Violence and Police Culture* (Melbourne: Melbourne University Press, 2000), pp. 235–248.

unreasonably – harmed by being coerced, deceived, or surveilled.[4] But Alexandra asks: What if he is innocent? In *that* case, harmful methods have been lawfully used, but their use is immoral – suggests Alexandra. Let us respond to this argument. First, the person harmed needs to be a suspect, i.e., there is, or should be, some form of evidence that he is guilty. Nevertheless, sometimes persons reasonably suspected of committing crimes are in fact innocent. However, innocent persons wrongly suspected of crimes are not harmed by the police *in the knowledge* that they are innocent. So we do not have intentional harming of persons known to be innocent. Rather we have intentional harming of persons thought likely to be guilty, and we have unintended harming of the innocent as a by-product of police work. Troublesome as this is, it does not put immorality at the core of the police function, as Alexandra seems to suggest. If there are some police methods that do involve intentional harming of those known to be innocent, e.g., intrusive surveillance of a criminal engaged in sexual activity with a woman known not to be a criminal, then perhaps these methods ought not to be deployed. Moreover, in the case of persons only suspected of committing crimes, the degree of harm inflicted upon them by police as part of their investigative process ought to be minimal (e.g., not involve prolonged detention) and calibrated not only by reference to the seriousness of the crime that they are suspected of committing or about to commit, but also by reference to the nature and extent of the evidence generating the suspicion on the part of the police; good evidence (albeit not sufficient to warrant laying a charge) that the suspect has committed a serious crime, such as armed robbery, might justify intrusive surveillance, but not weak evidence that the suspect has committed a minor offence, such as car theft.

The moral problem of noble cause corruption arises in policing when moral considerations pull in two different directions, and especially when the law thwarts, rather than facilitates, morally desirable outcomes and institutional purposes in particular. But here we need to distinguish types of case. Assume that a police officer breaks a morally unacceptable law, but acts in accordance with the law as it ought to be. For example, suppose a police officer refuses to arrest a black person who is infringing the infamous "pass laws" in apartheid South Africa. Such a police officer is not necessarily engaged in noble cause corruption; for breaking a morally unacceptable law is not necessarily engaging in corruption, and therefore not necessarily engaging in noble cause corruption. For such

---

[4] I am assuming here that the law appropriately tracks reason-based ethical principles.

laws not only violate natural rights they may actually undermine institutional purposes, such as the collective good of an orderly community under the rule of law.

A second kind of case involves a police officer breaking a law, which, although not morally unacceptable, is flawed in that it does not adequately reflect the ethical balance that needs to be struck between the rights of suspects and the rights of victims. For example, assume that a law only allows a suspect to be detained for questioning for a limited period of time; a period that is wholly inadequate for certain kinds of criminal investigations. The law is not necessarily immoral, but it ought to be changed. A police officer who detains a suspect for slightly longer than this period has technically breached the law, but the officer has not violated a suspect's rights in any profound sense. Once again, the term "corruption" is too strong. This is not a case of noble cause corruption; though it is a case of unlawful, and perhaps unethical, conduct.

A third kind of case involves a police officer violating a suspect's legally enshrined moral rights by, for example, using the third degree or fabricating evidence or committing perjury. The point about these kinds of case is that the police officer has not only acted illegally, but also immorally. Moreover, the (*pro tanto*) moral wrongdoing in question is serious in nature. If a police officer engages in this kind of corrupt activity, and does so in order to achieve morally desirable outcomes including, but not restricted to, institutional purposes such as the conviction of known perpetrators of serious crimes, then the officer is engaged in noble cause corruption. Let us examine this kind of case further.

4.2   Justifying Noble Cause Corruption

Noble cause corruption is obviously not morally justified if there is some lawful means to achieve the morally desirable outcome. But are there cases in which the only way to achieve a morally obligatory outcome is to act immorally? In order to enable us to explore the philosophical issues associated with noble cause corruption further, and to focus our discussion, let us consider the following case study.[5]

---

[5] The discussion in this section relies heavily on Seumas Miller, "Corruption and Anti-Corruption in the Profession of Policing," *Professional Ethics*, 6 (1998), 83–107. Other versions of this material appeared in Seumas Miller, "Noble Cause Corruption in Policing Revisited" in R. Adlam and P. Villiers (eds.), *A Safe, Just and Tolerant Society: Police Virtue Rediscovered* (Waterside Press, 2004) and Miller, Roberts, and Spence, *Corruption and Anti-Corruption*, chapter 5.

CASE STUDY 1 – NOBLE CAUSE CORRUPTION

A young officer, Joe, seeks advice from the police chaplain. Joe is working with an experienced detective, Mick, who is also Joe's brother-in-law, and looked up to by Joe as a good detective who gets results. Joe and Mick are working on a case involving a known drug-dealer and pedophile. Joe describes his problem as follows:

> Father – he has got a mile of form, including getting kids hooked on drugs, physical and sexual assault on minors, and more. Anyway, surveillance informed Mick that the drug-dealer had just made a buy. As me and Mick approached the drug-dealer's penthouse flat, we noticed a parcel come flying out the window of the flat onto the street. It was full of heroin. The drug-dealer was in the house, but we found no drugs inside. Mick thought it would be more of a sure thing if we found the evidence in the flat rather than on the street – especially given the number of windows in the building. The defence would find it more difficult to deny possession. Last night, Mick tells me that he was interviewed and signed a statement that we both found the parcel of heroin under the sink in the flat. He said all I had to do was to go along with the story in court and everything will be sweet, no worries. What should I do Father? – perjury is a serious criminal offence.[6]

In this scenario, there are two putative instances of noble cause corruption. The first one is Mick intentionally unlawfully loading up the evidence and committing perjury in order to secure a conviction. As it is described above, this instance of noble cause corruption is not morally sustainable, for there is a presumption against breaking communally sanctioned ethical principles enshrined in the law, and this presumption has not been offset by the moral considerations in play here. Indeed, it is by no means clear that in this situation Mick's unlawful acts are even necessary in order for the drug-dealer to be convicted. Moreover, achieving the good end of securing the conviction of the drug-dealer is outweighed by the moral and institutional harm being done by undermining other important institutionally enshrined moral ends, namely due process of law and respect for a suspect's moral rights.[7]

Nor is there anything to suggest that this is a one-off unlawful act by Mick, and that he had provided himself with what he took to be a specific and overriding moral justification for committing it on this particular occasion. Indeed, the impression is that Mick loads up suspects and

---

[6] The above case study was provided in a suitably disguised form by Father Jim Boland, Chaplain to the NSW Police.

[7] Howerd Cohen, "Overstepping Police Authority," *Criminal Justice Ethics*, 6 (1987), 52–60, p. 57.

commits perjury as a matter of routine practice. Further, there is nothing to suggest that police powers in this area – at least in Australia – are hopelessly inadequate, that police and others have failed in their endeavors to reform the law, and that therefore police officers have no option but to violate due process law, if they are to uphold so-called substantive law. Of course, it is a different matter whether or not current Australian anti-drug policies are adequate to the task. Evidently they are not. But this in itself does not justify an increase in police powers in particular. Arguably the problem is that the policy of criminalization is inadequate. Accordingly, Mick and like-minded detectives do not have available to them the argument that noble cause corruption is justifiable because there is a discrepancy between what police powers ought to be, by the lights of objective ethical principles, and what they in fact are. In the first place, there is no such discrepancy, although current anti-drug policies are evidently failing. In the second place, loading up suspects, perjury, and the like could never be lawful procedures grounded in objective ethical principles. Lastly, if in fact an increase in police powers were morally justified, then the appropriate response of the police ought to be to argue and lobby for this increase, not engage in unlawful conduct.

There is a second possible example of noble cause corruption in our scenario that is more difficult to resolve. This is Joe committing perjury in order to prevent a host of harmful consequences to Mick, Joe, and their families. If Joe does not commit perjury, Mick will be convicted of a criminal act, and their careers will be ruined. Moreover, the friendship of Mick and Joe will be at an end, and their respective families will suffer great unhappiness. The second example is a candidate for justified, or at least excusable, unlawful behavior on the grounds of extenuating circumstances. Let us assume that were Joe to commit perjury, his action would be morally justified, or at least morally excusable. The question to be asked now is whether it is an act of noble cause corruption.

Certainly, such an act of perjury is unlawful. But here we need to distinguish a number of different categories. Some acts are unlawful, but their commission does not harm any innocent person. Arguably, such unlawful acts are not necessarily immoral. The drug-dealer will be harmed in that he will go to prison, but he is not innocent; he is a known drug-dealer and pedophile who deserves to go to prison.

But the fact that the drug-dealer is guilty of serious crimes does not settle the issue. Consider Joe's actions. Some acts are unlawful, but their commission does not infringe anyone's moral rights. Joe's act will certainly infringe the drug-dealer's moral rights, including the right to a fair trial based on admissible evidence. Moreover, perjury undermines a central plank of due process law. Without truthful testimony, the whole system of criminal justice would founder; perjury is a species of institutional corruption. Considered in itself, the act of perjury is a serious moral wrong, and an act of corruption. Unfortunately, as we have already seen, the moral costs of Joe not committing perjury are also very high – perhaps higher than those resulting from the single act of perjury.

We can conclude that Joe faces a genuine moral dilemma; he will do moral harm whatever he does. Does it follow that we have found an instance in which noble cause corruption is justified? Here there are really two questions. First, is Joe's action an instance of noble cause corruption? Second, is his action morally justified? The distinction between corruption – including noble cause corruption – on the one hand, and immorality on the other is a fine distinction in this context, but it is no less real for that.

As we have seen in earlier chapters, corruption is a species of immorality, and corrupt actions are a species of immoral actions; nevertheless, not all immorality is corruption, and not all immoral actions are corrupt ones. Most corrupt actions have a number of properties that other immoral actions do not necessarily possess. First, corrupt actions are typically not one-off actions. For an action to be properly labeled as corrupt, it has to in fact corrupt, or be of a kind that tends to corrupt. Corrupt actions are, therefore, typically the expression of a disposition or habit on the part of a corrupt agent. Indeed, one of the reasons most acts of noble cause corruption are so problematic in policing is that they typically involve a disposition or habit. Acts of noble cause corruption are typically not simply one-off actions; they are habitual. Now Joe's action is not habitual. However, as we saw in Chapter 3, some acts of corruption are one-off. So the fact that Joe's action is a one-off, non-habitual action does not settle the question as to whether it is corrupt or not.

Secondly, most corrupt actions – involving as they do a habit to act in a certain way – are not performed because of a specific, non-recurring eventuality. Rather, they are performed because of an ongoing condition or recurring situation. In the case of noble cause corruption in policing, the ostensible ongoing condition is the belief that the law is not fit for institutional purpose, not only because it fails to provide police with sufficient powers to enable offenders to be apprehended and convicted, but also because it fails to provide sufficiently harsh punishments for offenders. Accordingly, so the (somewhat paradoxical) argument runs, police need to engage in noble cause corruption in order to achieve the institutional purposes of the law; that is, they need to develop a habit of bending and breaking the law in the service of the greater moral good of justice, given the inadequate features of the criminal justice system.

Now although Joe is motivated to do wrong to achieve good, or at least to avoid evil, he is responding to a highly specific – indeed extraordinary – circumstance he finds himself in and one which is highly unlikely to recur.[8] He has not developed a disposition or habit in response to a felt ongoing condition or recurring situation. However, again the point has to be made is that some corrupt actions are one-off, non-habitual actions that are responses to a highly specific, nonrecurring circumstance. Accordingly, we cannot conclude from the nonrecurring nature of these circumstances that Joe's action is not a corrupt act.

Third, corrupt actions are typically motivated at least in part by individual or narrow collective self-interest. In the case of policing, the interest can be individual self-interest, such as personal financial gain or career advancement. Or it can be the narrow collective self-interest of the group, such as in the case of a clique of corrupt detectives. Certainly, Joe's action is not motivated by his own self-interest. However, it is a defining feature of acts of noble cause corruption that they are motivated by a desire to do good and, therefore, *not* simply motivated by self-interest (or narrow collective self-interest insofar as such collective self-interest is not to be equated with the good in the context in question), and so this feature of Joe's action does not prevent it being an act of corruption – and specifically, an act of noble cause corruption. Here I note that the good in this context could refer to the collective good definitive of the institution or to the good in some more general sense, e.g., the morally best outcome all things considered. I note further that institutional actors who perform actions in accordance with the latter good (consequentialists, let us say) at the expense of the former are typically guilty of a form of institutional overreach and, as such, are not only likely to undermine the institution to which they belong but also in danger of failing to achieve the best outcome all things considered. As philosophers have frequently noted, all things considered long-term best outcome is often achieved not by everyone aiming at it, but by each complying with the rules (or, in this case, rule-governed institutional role) that have been designed in a manner such that if everyone complies with these rules then the best outcome will be achieved.

---

[8] See E. Delattre, *Character and Cops*, 2nd edn. (Washington, DC: AEI Press, 1994), chapter 11, for a discussion of such extraordinary situations, and the need – as he sees it – for consultation with senior experienced police officers.

Let us take stock and do so in the light of our definition of institutional corruption proffered in Chapter 3. Joe's act of perjury undermines a legitimate institutional process, and the fact that is a one-off act of noble cause corruption does not prevent it being an instance of corruption. Moreover, Joe is morally responsible for his action. Joe is aware that his act of perjury will undermine a legitimate institutional process; it is not as if he is ignorant of the institutional damage that he is doing. Accordingly, it seems that Joe is morally responsible for performing a *pro tanto* morally wrong action.

Is this *pro tanto* morally wrong action an act of corruption? In order for his action to be an act of noble cause corruption it has to be corrupt, and in order for it to be corrupt it is sufficient that the following three conditions identified in Chapter 3 are met. First, the action corrupts something or someone. Joe's action, as we have seen, undermines a legitimate institutional process, namely, the process of providing testimonial evidence. Second, there is a corruptor who is morally responsible for the act. Joe is morally responsible for his act of perjury and he knew it would have the effect of undermining the testimonial process. Third, the corruptor is an institutional actor acting qua institutional actor (and, therefore, uses the opportunity afforded by his institutional role). Joe is a police officer acting qua police officer. Since all three conditions are met we can conclude that Joe performs an act of corruption, albeit – given his motivation – an act of noble cause corruption. Note that it is possible for the action to be corrupt, and yet for the agent not to be culpable in the sense of blameworthy. (Here, as elsewhere, I am distinguishing between moral responsibility and blameworthiness/praiseworthiness.) For example, in the circumstance in question, it may well be that although the action was corrupt (and, therefore, morally wrong) *pro tanto*, it was not morally wrong, all things considered. So Joe's action was corrupt, but the question remains as to whether Joe's action was morally wrong from an "all things considered" standpoint and, in particular, in the light of the good consequences (including avoidance of harm) that it is likely to have.

Joe faces a genuine moral dilemma. Perhaps it would be morally wrong for him to commit perjury even taking all relevant matters into consideration. Moreover, he is morally responsible for his action. However, even if this is so, it may well be that Joe is not morally blameworthy if he committed perjury in these circumstances. Specifically, Joe has a moral excuse, even if not a legal one, for committing perjury in these circumstances. The dilemma is such that we cannot confidently claim that Joe ought to have known that committing perjury *in these circumstances* would be morally wrong all things considered. I conclude that whether or not Joe's act of perjury in these circumstances would be morally wrong (both *pro tanto* and all things considered), it is unclear whether Joe would be morally blameworthy for performing it.

Before summing up our discussion of noble cause corruption in policing, I would like to present another example of noble cause corruption in which the corruptor appears to be morally justified. Consider a police officer in India whose meager wages are insufficient to enable him to feed, clothe, and educate his family, and who is prohibited by law from having a second job. Accordingly, he supplements his income by accepting bribes from certain households in a wealthy area in return for providing additional surveillance and thus greater protection from theft; this has the consequence that other wealthy households tend to suffer a somewhat higher level of theft than otherwise would be the case. The police officer is engaged in corruption, and his corruption has a noble cause (albeit not that of serving the institutional purposes of policing), namely, to provide for the minimal well-being of his family. Moreover, arguably his noble cause corruption is morally justified by virtue of the moral obligations he has to provide for the basic needs of his family.

We have seen that corrupt actions, including acts of noble cause corruption, are typically – but not necessarily or invariably – habitual actions; typically, they are not one-off actions performed in accordance with moral principles that have been applied to a particular nonrecurring situation. So in most cases of noble cause corruption, the motivating force is in part that of habit, and there is no attempt to perform a rational calculation of the morality of means and ends on a case-by-case basis. Accordingly, there is an inherent possibility, and perhaps tendency, for such acts of noble cause corruption not to be morally justified when individually considered. After all, the police officer who has performed such an individual act of noble cause corruption has acted in large part from habit, and has not taken the time to consider whether or not the means really do justify the ends in the particular case. Moreover, given a presumption against infringing communally sanctioned and legally enshrined ethical principles, this failure to engage in moral decision-making on a case-by-case basis is surely not only morally wrong but blameworthy by virtue of being – at the very least – morally negligent.

What we have said thus far points to the morally problematic nature of doing wrong to achieve good as a matter of unthinking routine. This does not show that noble cause corruption is after all motivated by individual (or narrow collective) *self-interest*. Rather, noble cause corruption remains noble in the sense that it is motivated by the desire to do good. However, there is a weaker claim to be made here, namely that most acts of noble cause corruption are motivated, or at least in part sustained, by a degree of moral negligence.

The officer who habitually performs acts of noble cause corruption does not feel the need to examine the rights and wrongs of his (allegedly) ends-justified immoral actions on a case-by-case basis. Yet given the presumption against infringing communally sanctioned ethical principles enshrined in the law, surely decision-making on a case-by-case basis is typically morally required. Moreover, as we saw above, acts of noble cause corruption have not been communally sanctioned; they are actions only justified – if they are justified at all – by some set of moral principles held to by the individual police officer or group of officers. Further, this set of alleged ethical principles is typically not objectively valid; it is not a set that ought to be enshrined in the law. Rather, these allegedly ethical principles are in fact typically spurious; they are the kind of principle used to justify actions of the sort that Mick commits, such as loading up suspects and committing perjury.

Accordingly, inherent in noble cause corruption there is a strong possibility of, and perhaps tendency toward, moral arrogance, moral insularity and the application of unethical principles. Accordingly, noble cause corruption is both dangerous in its own right, and likely to be at least in part self-serving.

In short, while acts of noble cause corruption are by definition not motivated by individual (or narrow collective) self-interest, insofar as they are habitual actions they are likely to be indirectly linked to, and in part sustained by, self-interest. Indeed, this claim of an indirect connection between noble cause corruption and self-interest seems to be supported by empirical studies. It appears to be an empirical fact that police who start off engaging in noble cause corruption often end up engaging in common or garden, out-and-out corruption.[9]

4.3   Noble Cause Corruption in Politics

From the perspective on offer in this chapter, acts of noble cause corruption in politics are actions that corrupt morally legitimate political institutions, but actions that are nevertheless motivated by good ends, including

---

[9]   See Justice J. Wood, *Final Report: Royal Commission into Corruption in the New South Wales Police Service* (Sydney: NSW Government, 1998).

legitimate institutional purposes.[10] Such actions might be one-off actions or consist of a pattern of actions. On this account, the Watergate break-in was an act of corruption, and – assuming Nixon, Gordon Liddy et al. were motivated by a desire to further the national interest – perhaps an act of noble cause corruption. Moreover, since on my general account of noble cause corruption there is room for morally justified acts of noble cause corruption, so there will be room for morally justified acts of noble cause corruption in politics.

Recall that my account of political corruption presupposes that the political institution thus corrupted is in some sense and to some consider-able extent morally legitimate. As is well-known, the question of what counts as a morally legitimate state is inherently problematic. For example, different political theories will deliver different verdicts on the question of the moral legitimacy of a given government.

Notice that in some states agreed by all hands to be illegitimate, e.g., totalitarian states such as the Soviet Union under Stalin, acts that might otherwise count as acts of corruption, such as destroying voting slips cast in favor of Stalin, might not count as acts of corruption. However, when it comes to political institutions, moral legitimacy admits of degrees and in some cases slides into indeterminacy. Moreover, in a given state, some political institutions or sub-elements thereof might have a degree of moral legitimacy and others not. Within China, perhaps the subnational govern-ment of Hong Kong has a degree of legitimacy that the Chinese-installed government of Tibet does not have.

As we saw in the Introduction, some theorists of political corruption, such as Joseph Nye, have claimed that all corruption, including political corruption, involves the abuse of public office for private gain.[11] In earlier chapters I rejected this claim. In the context of this chapter it is self-evident that I must reject it; it is inconsistent with the possibility of noble cause corruption. A more plausible variant of this claim is that political corrup-tion involves at least the abuse of public office, though not necessarily for private gain. As we saw in Chapter 3, contra this view, acts of political corruption might be actions performed by institutional actors who do not hold a public office, e.g., citizens who do not hold a public office, as opposed to (say) politicians.

---

[10] An earlier version of the material in this section appeared in Miller et al. *Corruption, and Anti-Corruption*, and Seumas Miller "Noble Cause Corruption in Politics," in I. Primoratz (ed.), *Politics and Morality* (Basingstroke: Palgrave Macmillan, 2007), pp. 92–112.

[11] Nye, "Corruption and Political Development," 417–427.

Thus far I have been motivating the view that political corruption can be accommodated within my overall theory, or quasi-theory, of corruption and of noble cause corruption. In what remains of this chapter, I want to address the claim associated with Machiavelli, Max Weber, Michael Walzer and others that there is something special about the role of political leaders such that engaging in noble cause corruption is somehow a defining feature of the political role.[12] Here I am assuming that these theorists are making a stronger claim than the one that I am committed to. You recall that I am committed to the claim that in politics, as elsewhere, there may well be morally justified acts of noble cause corruption. However, I reject the claim that engaging in noble cause corruption is a defining feature of the political role.[13]

This kind of claim is sometimes made in the context of a discussion of the so-called problem of dirty hands. Here it is important to first note some conceptual differences between the concept of dirty hands and the concept of noble cause corruption. The idea of dirty hands is that political leaders, and perhaps the members of some other occupations such as soldiers and police officers, necessarily perform actions that infringe central or important principles of common morality, and that this is because of some inherent feature of these occupations. Such "dirty" actions include lying, betrayal, and especially the use of violence.

The first point to be made here is that by my lights it is not self-evident that such acts are necessarily acts of corruption, and hence necessarily acts of noble cause corruption. In particular, it is not self-evident that all such acts undermine to any degree institutional processes, purposes, or role occupants (*qua* role occupants). (This is compatible with such acts having a corrupting effect on the moral character of the persons who perform them, albeit not on those traits of their moral character necessary for the discharging of their institutional role responsibilities as (say) politicians, police, or soldiers.) On the other hand, it might be argued that such acts are instances of corruption since they are of a kind that has a tendency to undermine institutional processes, purposes or role occupants *qua* role occupants. To this it can be replied that this would not be so if the performance of the type

---

[12] N. Machiavelli, *The Prince*, any edition, Max Weber "Politics as a Vocation" in H. Gerth and C. Wright Mills (eds.), *From Max Weber: Essays in Sociology* (London: Routledge, 1991); Michael Walzer, "Political Action: The Problem of Dirty Hands," *Philosophy and Public Affairs*, 2 (1973), 160–180.

[13] This view in relation to dirty hands is espoused by C. A. J. Coady in his "Dirty Hands," *Encyclopaedia of Ethics*, 2nd edn. (London: Routledge, 2001), p. 407f. On the other hand, Coady seems also to be endorsing a version of moral absolutism, and if so, he would not want to accept a range of what I would regard as morally justified acts of noble cause corruption.

of acts in question are justified in terms of institutional purpose, and appropriately constrained and subjected to stringent accountability mechanisms.

The second and related point is that some putatively "dirty" actions are indeed definitive of political roles, as they are of police and military roles. For example, earlier I argued that a defining feature of police work is its use of harmful and normally immoral methods, such as deceit and violence, in the service of the protection of (among other things) human rights.[14] Clearly, a similar definition is required for the role of soldier. And since political leaders necessarily exercise power and – among other things – lead and direct police and soldiers, they too will participate in "dirty" actions in this sense. However, such use of deceit, violence, and so on can be, and typically is, morally justified in terms of the publicly sanctioned, legally enshrined, ethical principles underlying police and military use of harmful and normally immoral methods, including the use of deadly force. In short, some putatively "dirty" actions are publicly endorsed, morally legitimate, defining practices of what I, and most people, take to be morally legitimate institutions, viz. government, and police and military institutions. I take it that the advocates of "dirty hands" intend to draw our attention to a phenomenon above and beyond such publicly endorsed, legally enshrined, and morally legitimate practices. But what is this alleged phenomenon?[15]

According to Walzer, politicians necessarily get their hands dirty, and in his influential article on the topic he offers two examples.[16] The first is of a politician who in order to get reelected must make a crooked deal and award contracts to a ward boss. The second is of a political leader who must order the torture of a terrorist leader if he is to discover the whereabouts of bombs planted by the leader and set to go off, killing innocent people. I take it that these examples consist of scenarios in which politicians are not acting in accordance with publicly endorsed, legally enshrined, morally legitimate practices; indeed, they are infringing moral and legal requirements.

The first example presupposes a corrupt political environment of a kind that in a liberal democracy ought to be opposed and cleansed rather than complied with. Moreover, it is far from clear why the politician's reelection

---

[14] Miller and Blackler, *Ethical Issues in Policing*, chapter 1.

[15] Max Weber (in Weber, *Politics as Vocation*, pp. 77–78) seems to want to avoid the whole problem by defining political leadership purely in terms of one of its distinctive means, namely the exercise of physical force. This seems to me to be an unjustifiably narrow and negative view of political leadership and politics more generally.

[16] Walzer, "Political Action," pp. 164–167.

is an overriding moral imperative. The second example is hardly an example of what politicians in well-ordered, liberal democracies routinely face; indeed, it is evident that even in the context of the so-called war on terror such cases only arise very occasionally, if at all. I conclude that Walzer's examples go nowhere close to demonstrating the necessity for politicians to "dirty" their hands in the sense of infringing central or important moral principles. At best, the second illustrates the requirement to infringe moral principles for the sake of the greater good in some highly unusual emergencies.[17]

4.4 Noble Cause Corruption, Dirty Hands, and Institutional Emergencies

There might in fact be *some* political contexts in which central or important moral principles do need to be infringed on a *routine* basis, albeit for a limited time period. Such contexts might include ones in which fundamental political institutions had themselves collapsed or were under threat of collapse. Consider the Colombian drug baron Pablo Escobar.[18]

CASE STUDY 2: PABLO ESCOBAR

After one of the biggest manhunts in recent history, Pablo Escobar, the notorious drug baron from Colombia, was cornered and shot dead on the roof of his hideout in his home town, Medellin, on December 2, 1993. There is some evidence to suggest that the precision shot to the head that killed him was delivered from close range after Escobar's escape was thwarted by a debilitating initial shot to the leg.[19] In short, he was very possibly executed. He was a man who from the time of his rise to power in the early 1980s had terrorized a whole nation. The hunt that lasted over four years and cost the US and Colombian governments hundreds of millions of dollars and several thousand lives involved members of the Colombian Search Bloc, a special police unit set up to capture Pablo Escobar, and special intelligence and anti-terrorist units from the United States, including elite units of the CIA, Centra Spike, Delta Force, as well as the DEA, the FBI, and the Bureau of Alcohol, Tobacco, and Firearms (ATF). This was not merely a hunt for the capture of a criminal – albeit an

[17] I argue this in detail in Seumas Miller, "Is Torture Ever Morally Justifiable?" *International Journal of Applied Philosophy*, 19 (2005), 179–192.

[18] This case study is taken from Miller, Roberts, Spence, *Corruption and Anti-Corruption*, p. 27f.

[19] See M. Bowden, *Killing Pablo* (London: Atlantic Books, 2001).

international criminal who headed the largest cocaine cartel in Colombia, accounting for up to 80 percent of the multi-billion dollar export of Colombian cocaine to the United States – but all-out war. Indeed, the Colombian state, with the technical, military, and intelligence support of the United States, was fighting this war for the sake of its very own survival.

The means to combat Escobar included the "dirty means" of an unofficial alliance of the Colombian special police unit, Search Bloc, with a vigilante group or "civilian militia," *Los Pepes* (People Persecuted by Pablo Escobar), which comprised known drug criminals from other drug cartels and some disaffected ex-associates of Escobar. In their willingness to use the same unlawful and violent means to destroy Escobar as those used by Escobar himself against his enemies, Los Pepes wreaked havoc against Escobar's operations, killing many of his associates and members of his family, and destroying many of his estates.

Now the above situation is one of emergency, albeit institutional emergency. So even if one wanted to support all or some of the methods used by the Colombian authorities one would not be entitled to generalize to other nonemergency political contexts. Moreover, there are reasons to think that many of the above-described dirty methods, e.g., execution and use of criminals to combat criminals – or at least the extent of their usage – were in fact counter-productive. For example, use of other criminal groups against Escobar tended to empower those groups. Further, such methods, although "dirty," are not as dirty as can be. In particular, methods such as execution of drug lords are directed at morally culpable persons, as opposed to innocent persons. I take it that at the dirty end of the spectrum of dirty methods that might be used in politics are those methods that involve the intentional harming of innocent persons.

However, the main point to be made here is that even if such dirty methods are morally justified, it is in the context of an argument to the effect that their use was necessary in order to reestablish political and other institutions in which the use of such dirty methods would presumably not be permitted. Accordingly, such scenarios do not demonstrate that the use of dirty methods is a necessary feature of political leadership in circumstances other than those of institutional emergency.

4.5   Conclusion

In this chapter I have discussed noble cause corruption: corruption motivated by the desire to do good. Noble cause corruption is a particular feature of those occupations and institutions that rely on morally problematic means, such as the use of deceit and violence. The most salient of these are political, military, and policing institutions. I have first considered noble cause corruption in policing, and then noble cause corruption in relation to political institutions. While noble cause corruption might be prevalent in these occupations and institutions, I have argued that it is not definitive of them. Since noble cause corruption is, after all, corruption and corruption is *pro tanto* morally wrong, it follows that noble cause corruption is *pro tanto* morally wrong. Nevertheless, some acts of noble cause corruption might be morally right all things considered. For instance, in circumstances of an institutional emergency, an act of corruption might be morally right all things considered. Moreover, some acts of noble cause corruption that are morally wrong all things considered might, nevertheless, be morally excusable.

CHAPTER 5

Bribery, Nepotism, Fraud and Abuse of Authority

On my teleological normative account of social institutions (Chapter 1), institutional purposes are collective ends and, specifically, collective ends the realization of which consists in the provision of collective goods. These realized collective ends are collective goods by virtue of their possession of the following three properties: (1) they are produced, maintained, or renewed by means of the *joint activity* of members of organizations, i.e., by institutional role occupants; (2) they are *available to the whole community*; and (3) they *ought* to be produced (or maintained or renewed) and made available to the whole community since they are desirable (as opposed to merely desired) and such that the members of the community have an *(institutional) joint moral right* to them.

Moreover, on the teleological account, institutional structure and culture are in large part means to an end: the realization of institutional purpose and, specifically, the production, maintenance, or renewal of the collective good that is the *raison d'etre* of the institution in question. As we have seen (Chapter 3), institutional corruption consists in the undermining of institutional purposes, processes, or persons (*qua* institutional role occupants). Further, the undermining of institutional processes and persons (*qua* institutional role occupants) is morally problematic in large part because such processes and role occupants exist, or ought to exist, in large part to serve institutional purposes, i.e., as means to the collective end/collective good definitive of the particular institution in question.

Accordingly, institutional corruption is fundamentally morally problematic because it undermines the production, maintenance, or renewal of the collective goods definitive of institutions. That said, a good deal of institutional corruption consists in the first instance in the undermining of institutional processes and persons (*qua* institutional role occupants). Moreover, the undermining of institutional processes and role occupants directly impacts on institutional structure (and, therefore, indirectly on institutional purposes (collective goods)), since such processes and roles are in part constitutive of structure. Further, the corruption of institutional role occupants, in particular, directly impacts on institutional culture and, therefore, indirectly on institutional purposes (collective goods).

As we have seen, there are numerous different types of institutional corruption and many different ways of categorizing them. Moreover, we cannot address all of these types and categorizations here. However, there are a smaller number of species of corruption that are especially salient and these warrant more detailed analysis. They are bribery, nepotism, fraud, and abuse of authority. I note that sometimes abuse of authority is used as an umbrella term to include the other categories. However, as we will see later, abuse of authority is a distinct category. Further, sometimes fraud is contrasted with corruption. Again, as I argue below, this is a mistake, depending on the kind of fraud in question.

5.1   Bribery

Bribery is widely regarded as the quintessential form of corruption. So much so that some have taken bribery and corruption to be synonymous. As I have already argued, there are many forms of corruption other than bribery. However, bribery does seem to be necessarily corruption unlike, for instance, fraud.

Maybe so, but providing an adequate definition of bribery, and even establishing agreement on the immorality of bribery, have proved to be difficult to attain. Many have argued, for example, that bribery "oils the wheels of industry." And some have claimed that bribes are simply gifts, and that therefore the distinction between bribes and gifts cannot be made.

Prima facie, bribery involves a briber providing a benefit (the bribe) to the bribee in order to get the bribee to do something the bribee *ought not* do (a "favor") and which is in the briber's interest. As mentioned above (Chapter 3 Section 1) the briber and the bribee perform conditional individual actions; the bribe is offered on condition the favor is done and the favor is done on condition the bribe is paid.[1] Bribery is thus

---

[1] Note that the briber and/or the bribee could be a single person or a group of persons (including an organized group such as a commercial company); if the briber is a group then the act of bribery could be a species of joint action (see Chapter 1 Sections 1 and 3). However, it would complicate matters unnecessarily to continually refer to the possibility of acts of bribery that are joint actions. Thus, for the sake of simplicity my discussion is couched in terms of the case of individual acts of bribery. However, my definition is generalizable to the various types of joint action. The same point holds for

distinguished from gifts, since gifts are not necessarily conditional on a favor in return and the purpose of gifts is not necessarily to get the recipient to do something they ought not to do. Moreover bribery is, thereby, also distinguished from extortion. First, a benefit is offered by a briber, whereas a threat is made by an extortionist. Second, therefore, the "favor" provided by the bribee is voluntary rather than coerced, whereas it is coerced rather than voluntary in the case of the victim of extortion.

There are a number of definitions of bribery in the literature. John Noonan has offered an exhaustive account of bribery. He defines the core of the concept of a bribe as: "an inducement improperly influencing the performance of a public function meant to be gratuitously exercised."[2] Thomas Carson offers the following definition: "an individual (the briber) pays another individual (the bribee) something of value in exchange for the bribee's doing something that violates a special duty or special obligation that attaches to an office occupied, or a role or practice participated in, by the bribee."[3] However, the most sophisticated definition of bribery that I am aware of is that provided by Stuart Green. According to Green: "X (a bribee) is bribed by Y (a briber) if and only if: (1) X accepts, or agrees to accept, something of value from Y; (2) in exchange for X's acting, or agreeing to act, in furtherance of some interest of Y's; (3) by violating some duty of loyalty owed by X arising out of X's office, position, or involvement in some practice."[4]

One immediate problem with the prima facie definition – but not with Noonan's, Carson's, or Green's definitions – is that it does not restrict bribees to office holders or others with special duties. If Y pays X to murder Z this is not bribery. This point is crucial for our purposes in this work. Bribery strikes at the heart of institutions since it typically involves institutional role occupants violating their institutional (i.e., special) duties. Incidentally, this is a further distinction between extortion and bribery; extortion does not necessarily involve the violation of a special duty by the victim of extortion.

A second potential problem with the above prima facie definition of bribery (and perhaps also with Carson's and Green's definitions) arises

my discussions of acts of fraud and abuse of authority in the sections following this one. Nepotism is often somewhat different, as will become clear.

[2] J. T. Noonan, *Bribes* (New York: Macmillan, 1984), chapter 1.

[3] T. L. Carson, "Bribery," in L. C. Becker and C. B. Becker (eds.), *Encyclopaedia of Ethics*, 2nd edn. (London: Routledge, 2001), p. 158. See also M. S. Pritchard "Bribery: The Concept," *Science and Engineering Ethics*, 4 (1998), 281–286.

[4] Stuart P. Green, *Lying, Cheating and Stealing: A Moral Theory of White Collar Crime* (Oxford University Press, 2006), p. 194.

from omissions – as opposed to commissions – on the part of officials to perform their duties unless they are bribed. Briber, Y, might have to pay a bribe to bribee, X, to get X to discharge X's special duty.[5] For example, Y might be entitled to a permit to sell goods but X will not give Y the permit, or will greatly delay Y getting the permit, unless Y pays X a bribe. On the other hand, it might be argued that Carson's and Green's definitions can be read so as to include the receipt of the bribe as a violation of the bribee's special duty. However, arguably such receipt is not a violation of a *special* duty.

A third problem concerns the use of the notion of the briber's *interest* in both the prima facie definition and in Green's definition (and, perhaps, Carson's depending on how the term "value" in his definition is understood). Surely a briber might desire the bribee to do something that is actually not in the briber's interest, albeit the briber desires that the bribee do it. Consider a bribe paid to a correctional officer by a drug-addicted jail inmate in order to cause the officer to allow the drug addict to continue to use illegal and impure drugs likely to cause the inmate's death. Again, consider a bribe paid to a corrupt border official of an authoritarian regime by a foreign benefactor of humanitarian causes seeking to enable a human rights activist to (illegally) leave the country. It may not be in the benefactor's interest to pay the bribe but she might feel under a moral obligation to do so. Accordingly, the weaker notion of a briber's desire, or even merely intention, rather than interest seems required.

A fourth potential problem with these definitions arises from secrecy. According to Richard DeGeorge, concealment is a necessary condition for bribery.[6] The idea here is that if bribery were out in the open then it would lose its point since it could not induce favorable treatment. However, as Pritchard points out, this is overstated.[7] For even if everyone paid a bribe, and this was mutually known to be the case, it would not follow that the payments were not unlawful and institutionally harmful. Consider a bribe paid to an official by everyone who wants a license to operate in a market. At the very least, this drives up the cost of doing business and may result in licenses being issued to those who ought not to receive them because, for example, they produce harmful goods. On the other hand, bribery frequently involves secrecy since in many, if not most, institutional settings if bribes are offered and accepted openly the likelihood of the briber and

---

[5] Pritchard, "Bribery," p. 285 makes this point.
[6] R. DeGeorge, *Competing with Integrity* (New York: Oxford University Press, 1993), p. 198.
[7] Pritchard, "Bribery," p. 283.

bribee being caught and punished is greatly increased. Accordingly, here, as in other instances of corruption, secrecy or concealment is a pervasive, although not a defining, feature.

A fifth issue arises in relation to bribes offered as part of integrity tests. Consider an undercover police officer who offers a payment to another police officer to commit an offence. Here the officer being "bribed" (the bribee) is not intended to receive the payment and the briber does not intend the bribee to commit the offence. Accordingly, a question arises as to whether this is an instance of bribery. Let us set aside integrity tests for the moment and focus instead on a standard instance of bribery. If a bribe is refused then it is a case of attempted bribery. If the bribe is accepted, yet the action the bribe was paid for is not performed (for whatever reason), then it is an unsuccessful bribe but, nevertheless, a bribe. Let us now return to our integrity tests. In the case of these integrity tests, the police officer offering the payment does so having as an end that the bribee accept the bribe (which the bribee does, let us assume) and that the bribee forms the intention to commit the offence (again, let us assume this). However, the briber does not have as an end that the bribee actually commit the offence. Here I am assuming that police officers ought not to be engaged in criminal actions, or inducing others to commit criminal actions, and assuming also that the (successful) act of bribing someone to commit a criminal offence is itself a criminal offence. If this is correct then evidently the "briber" (the undercover police officer) does not intend to offer a bribe since he does not have as an end that the bribee (the target of the integrity test) actually commit the offence, but merely intends that the bribee (the target) form the intention to do so.

5.2   Nepotism

Roughly speaking, nepotism is favoritism based on kinship. Thus, hiring or promoting one's own sons or daughters over others are paradigms of nepotism. Nepotism also refers to favoritism based on kinship once removed. Thus George W. Bush appointed the son of Senator Thurmond to the position of US attorney for South Carolina and did so at the Senator's request. Indeed, nepotism in the US government has been a subject of severe criticism.[8] While nepotism in the context of small private family businesses is widely regarded as acceptable, nepotism in the context of public institutions, such as government, is typically regarded

---

[8] Helen Thomas, UPI Washington correspondent.

as a form of corruption, e.g. President Trump's hiring of family members. It is regarded as corruption since it flies in the face of principles of merit. The best applicant ought to get the job, both because she or he deserves it, and because the institution will be best served if hiring is based on merit. However some have offered arguments in qualified support of nepotism. See, for example, Adam Bellow's *In Praise of Nepotism*.[9] Qualified support for nepotism often takes the form of an argument to the effect that it is morally acceptable to hire, promote, and so on one's relatives if they are suitably qualified, but not if they are not. This is an attempt to balance one's institutional (and moral) duties with one's moral obligations to one's nearest and dearest.

While an act of nepotism is not necessarily a joint action, other than perhaps in a weak sense, since the beneficiary may not perform any action other than that of merely accepting the benefit, nepotism typically takes place in the context of a structure of joint enterprises, e.g., a family business, and, therefore, of joint actions and, indeed, collective self-interest. I return to this issue below.

The narrow notion of nepotism in terms of favoritism based on kinship needs to be broadened in the context of our discussion of salient forms of institutional corruption. For example, favoritism based on personal friendship rather than merit is potentially corruptive of institutions. Moreover, commentators such as Bellow frequently use the term "nepotism" in an extended sense that includes favoritism based not only on kinship and friendship but also on class membership (e.g., membership of an elite) or, even more broadly, on membership of a particular racial or gender group. Here there is a danger of extending the notion of nepotism too far and, thereby, undermining its status as a salient species of institutional corruption by viewing it simply as a form of social injustice. Doubtless, nepotism is unjust and, as noted in the Introduction, injustice is one of the conditions that are conducive to corruption. But we need to maintain the distinction between salient species of institutional corruption, on the one hand, and conditions conducive to corruption, on the other. Moreover, the extension of the meaning of "nepotism" to include favoritism based on social, economic, and so on class membership is implausible on other grounds.

Suppose Reginald is born into a wealthy family and, as a consequence, enjoys the benefit of a good formal education; a benefit not available to Mick who was born into a poor family. Now suppose that in a hiring

[9] A. Below, *In Praise of Nepotism: A Natural History* (New York: Doubleday, 2003).

process for a teaching job, Reginald is preferred to Mick wholly on the basis of merit, although it is only Reginald's superior formal education that makes the difference. Arguably, all things considered, this outcome is unfair to Mick. However, surely this is not a case of nepotism. Here we need to distinguish structural features of a society, notably economic class, that advantage some and disadvantage others from deliberate acts or practices of favoritism based on kinship or personal friendship. Again, suppose that there are two applicants for a job, one of greater merit than the other, but the employer is a racist and chooses the applicant of lesser merit because he is white and the other black. This not a case of nepotism, but rather of racism. So favoritism based on race (or, indeed, gender and other such broad categories) is not nepotism. Accordingly, we should restrict the meaning of nepotism to favoritism based on kinship or friendship (or similar interpersonal relationships): the favors in question being bestowed or received by institutional role occupants. More precisely, since such favoritism might at times be compatible with institutional duties, nepotism is favoritism based on kinship or friendship (or similar interpersonal relationships) in breach of institutional duties. Perhaps this is not quite right, given that institutional duties might not be as they should be, as in the case of an absence of meritocratic hiring principles in an organization. Accordingly, let us define nepotism as favoritism based on kinship or friendship (or similar interpersonal relationships) in breach of institutional duties as they ought to be.

Edward Banfield's notion of amoral familism introduced in his classic book, *The Moral Basis of a Backward Society*,[10] provides one account of what is wrong with over-reliance or exclusive reliance on members of one's immediate family and with an unwillingness to trust others. According to Banfield, corruption is to a large measure an expression of particularism – the felt obligation to help and give resources to members of one's family above all, but also to friends and members of the social group to which one belongs. This solidarity with members of one's family and social group can produce a self-interested culture that is hostile to the interests of outsiders. To this extent, it is analogous to excessive, indeed immoral, individual self-interest; it is excessive and immoral collective self-interest. Nepotism is one of the clearest examples of such collective self-interest. I note that Banfield's use of the term "amoral" implies that there is a lack of any moral sense. I prefer, therefore, the term "immoral," which does not have this implication. However, I will continue to use the term "amoral familism"

---

[10] E. Banfield, *The Moral Basis of a Backward Society* (New York: Free Press, 1958).

since this is Banfield's terminology, albeit I do so with the meaning of "immoral familism."

Banfield argues that in a society of amoral families there is little or no loyalty to the larger community and only weak acceptance of social norms of behavior. Accordingly, amoral familism tends to facilitate corruption. An extreme form of amoral familism is the Mafia.[11] Although Banfield's research concerns specifically the people of Southern Italy, Francis Fukuyama, in his book *Trust*,[12] makes similar observations about various other cultures and subcultures outside Europe, including in Asia. Of particular interest here is the Confucian notion of guanxi. Guanxi and amoral familism are evidently related concepts.

Roughly speaking, Guanxi refers to a reciprocal, particularist, and partialist relationship in which parties to the relationship exchange favors (e.g., gifts, information) in order to serve a mutually beneficial purpose. The parties to a guanxi relationship typically have some shared preexisting base upon which to maintain or develop the relationship, such as membership of the same family or social group.[13] According to Thomas Dunfee and Danielle Warren a relationship of guanxi is developed through "invitations to visit one's home or place of business, entertainment, gifts, use of supportive intermediaries and such things as hiring the offspring of the subject party."[14] It is more difficult and time-consuming, but quite possible, for a guanxi relationship to develop between strangers.[15] In business dealings within China, by both Chinese and foreigners, guanxi is important, for it provides those within a given guanxi network greater access than outsiders to opportunities and resources, e.g., finance.

The concepts of amoral familism and guanxi can be extended to some close-knit professional groups such as the police, where references to police corruption have often been related to perceptions of police solidarity and a police culture.

A culture of amoral familism, whether in business or in other institutional settings, is conducive to corruption. Moreover, the *invisibility* of forms of corrupt practices within close-knit families creates problems for the detection and deterrence of such corruption. It also creates problems

---

[11] *Ibid.*, pp. 119–120.
[12] F. Fukuyama, *Trust: The Social Virtues and the Creation of Prosperity* (London: Penguin, 1996).
[13] T. W. Dunfee and D. E. Warren, "Is Guanxi Ethical? A Normative Analysis of Doing Business in China," *Journal of Business Ethics*, 32 (2001), 191–204.
[14] *Ibid.*, p. 192.
[15] Y. Fan, "Guanxi's Consequences: Personal Gains at Social Cost," *Journal of Business Ethics*, 38 (2002), 371–380.

for anti-corruption measures that seek to exploit the lack of trust that typically obtains between corrupt institutional actors motivated only by individual self-interest, e.g., promises of immunity if one "rats" on one's corrupt colleagues.[16] The problem is exacerbated by weak criminal justice institutions. Likewise, guanxi is conducive to institutional corruption since networks of guanxi relationships often exist in order to acquire wealth, power, and status for members of the network at the expense of outsiders and to the detriment of the impartialist principles and collective goods definitive of social institutions.

Both familial amoralism and guanxi privilege the essentially private interests of particular families and social groups over public values and institutions. Interestingly, in these familial-based forms of corruption, a morally misguided understanding of the fiduciary relationship between members of a family can motivate corrupt practices. In many forms of corruption, the violation of a well-understood fiduciary relationship is driven by individual self-interest, e.g., financial gain. However, in the case of corruption arising from amoral familism, a morally misguided understanding of one's fiduciary duty to other members of the family drives the corruption.

The explanation for such morally misguided understanding of fiduciary duties to members of one's family (or professional group) lies in the strength of group loyalty in solidaristic groups with a deeply felt, indeed excessive, commitment to collective self-interest. Misplaced, particularist fiduciary "duties" to family, friends, or professional colleagues override any commitment to universal moral principles or to actual fiduciary duties. The Watergate scandal is a clear illustration of one kind of amoral familism, namely, the political clique prepared to go to extreme lengths, including immoral and unlawful actions, to achieve its collective political ambitions. Members of such a clique act in part out of a misplaced loyalty and sense of obligation, both to their professional colleagues in the clique, and to the leader of the clique. Consequently, their actual fiduciary duties to, say, the American people are downplayed or ignored, sometimes with the assistance of rationalizations, e.g., that the end (a Nixon-led US government – since this is allegedly in the public interest) justifies the means (unlawful break-ins and a cover-up).

While amoral familism is not to be identified with nepotism, the two notions are connected.

---

[16] Lambsdorff's favored anti-corruption strategy is vulnerable to this kind of point (Lambsdorff, *Institutional Economics of Corruption and Reform*).

Amoral familism and nepotism are connected insofar as they both involve particularism and partialism – the felt obligation to help and give resources to members of one's family above all, and also to one's friends and members of the interpersonal group to which one belongs. As already mentioned, this solidarity with members of one's family and with members of the interpersonal group to which one belongs can produce excessive and immoral collective self-interest. Nepotism is a clear example of this. That said, appropriate collective self-interest, e.g., our employing organization's interest, our national interest, is often something that we praise individuals for pursuing, especially in contexts in which there is unwarranted pursuit of individual self-interest.

Institutional role occupants have institutional rights and duties that are also moral rights and duties. However, they are also members of interpersonal networks within institutional settings. As argued in Chapter 1, these institutional rights and duties derive in large part from institutional purposes (collective goods). Often institutional rights and duties, on the one hand, and interpersonal obligations on the other, do not conflict and, indeed, are mutually supportive. For example, friendship may facilitate organizational teamwork. However, institutional duties and interpersonal obligations can come into conflict. Indeed, the pursuit of the latter may be regarded as paramount; or, even worse, an institutional actor may simply regard his or her institutional role occupancy as a means to facilitate self-aggrandizement and/or to further the interests of the family or other interpersonal group to which he or she belongs. If so, then there is the potential for, perhaps even inevitability of, nepotism and, therefore, institutional corruption.

5.3 Fraud

In monetary terms, fraud is without question one of the most costly of crimes in the contemporary world and fraud has been greatly facilitated by the advent of emerging technologies. For example, fraud is estimated to have cost the UK economy more than £30 billion in 2011. Moreover, there is now an extremely wide range of frauds and, in the case of cyber fraud, new forms are constantly evolving.[17] Further, it turns out that an enormous

---

[17] I note that there are definitional issues arising from the use of the term "cyber-crime." Specifically, some so-called cyber-crimes are simply traditional crimes, e.g., theft, fraud, involving the use of computers and the like. However, the recent developments in communication and information technology have arguably given rise to new forms of crime not adequately described by traditional definitions, e.g., computer hacking.

amount of cyber-crime, including cyber theft, is actually conducted by governments or with the collusion of governments, notably the Chinese government.[18] In some authoritarian regimes, such as China, the boundaries between private and public sector agencies, and between commercial and law enforcement, are porous or even nonexistent.

Cyber criminals are invading homes and offices across the world, not by burglary, but by breaking into laptops, personal computers, and wireless devices.[19] This is computer hacking, the use of malicious software inserted into computer systems that undertake activity inside the system to corrupt it, to extract personal data, or to rob the individual or company, e.g., by transferring funds out of the individual or company accounts into the hacker's account. Many of these acts of cyber theft involve deception and, therefore, are instances of cyber fraud. This activity has an enormous impact on personal, corporate, and even national finances – costing billions of dollars/pounds in stolen information, money, disruption, and repairing systems. It can also be life threatening since the disruption can disable hospitals and emergency services. Moreover, identifying and prosecuting cyber criminals can be extremely difficult, given that they are often operating in cyberspace and based overseas.

Nor is the problem simply one of the fraudsters themselves; for those who are defrauded are also often implicated. When investigating frauds, investigators can find that financial institutions (banks, credit unions, mortgage providers, insurance companies, etc.) are reluctant to disclose fraudulent activities. The financial cost to these institutions is enormous and only a fraction is investigated to a conclusion by their own investigators or other agencies such as the police, the FBI in the USA, the Serious Fraud Office (SFO) in the UK, and the Australian Crime Commission (ACC) in Australia.

There are various different definitions of fraud.[20] However, typically or, at least, historically, acts of fraud are said to possess the following defining features[21]: first, fraud involves providing oneself with a financial benefit,

---

[18] See Mandiant Intelligence Centre, *APT1: Exposing One of China's Cyber Espionage Units* (Washington, DC: Mandiant Intelligence Centre, 2013), available at http://intelreport.mandi ant.com.

[19] Grabosky, Smith, and Dempsey, *Electronic Theft*.

[20] For a general introduction to fraud and its investigation see, G. Smith, M. Button, L. Johnson, and K. Frimpong (eds.), *Studying Fraud as White Collar Crime* (London: Palgrave Macmillan, 2011). For analysis of the crime of fraud see Green, *Lying, Cheating and Stealing*, chapter 13. For an elaboration of the practicalities of fraud investigation see J. T. Wells, *Fraud Examination: Investigation and Audit Procedures* (New York: Quorum Book, 1992).

[21] My definition of fraud relies on Stuart Green's discussion and general view of fraud as theft by deception. See Green, *Lying, Cheating and Stealing*, chapter 13.

including by failing to provide someone with a service for which they have paid; second, the financial benefit in question is one that the fraudster is not entitled to; and third, the means by which the benefit is secured involves deception. The deception consists of communicating with the intention to cause the hearer to have a false belief. So the communicator might explicitly assert what he knows to be false or he might merely imply it. Indeed, the communicator might not rely on linguistic communication to cause the false belief. He might, for example, use a faulty weighing machine. Moreover, there are a diverse range of types of fraud, including credit card fraud, computer fraud, tax fraud, false accounting, forgery, and so on.

In recent times, the definition of fraud has come under close scrutiny. In particular, the view that fraud necessarily involves deceit has been challenged.[22] Nondeceptive fraud is held to involve dishonesty. Aside from the problem of defining the somewhat vague term, "dishonesty," this has the effect of greatly extending the range of types of fraud to include such offences as breaches of trust and nonperformance of contractual obligations.

As we have seen, fraud can be loosely defined as theft involving deception; as such it involves not only the violation of individual property rights but also the breach of the basic moral principle not to deceive. However, the scale of fraud, nationally and globally, is such that it has a further untoward moral consequence; it does great damage to economic and other institutions. Importantly, fraud is not necessarily corruption, although it frequently is. Fraud is corruption when it meets our definition of institutional corruption proffered in Chapter 3. Roughly speaking, if an act of fraud undermines an institutional purpose, process, or person (*qua* role occupant) and is performed by an institutional role occupant acting *qua* role occupant (and, therefore, using the opportunity afforded by his or her position), then the fraud is an act of corruption. Thus if a bank trader defrauds the bank he works for or the bank's clients in the course of doing his job then his act of fraud is also an act of institutional corruption.

On the other hand, if a private citizen, A, acting as a private citizen defrauds another private citizen, B, of B's own property, then this instance of fraud is not also an instance of institutional corruption. As we saw in Chapter 3, in order for an act to be an instance of institutional corruption there must be a corruptor who performs the corrupt action *qua occupant of an institutional role* and/or someone who is corrupted *qua occupant of an institutional role*. Notice that even if the victim of fraud, B, is acting in his or her capacity as an institutional role occupant it may not be an instance of

---

[22] *Ibid.*, p. 149.

institutional corruption, since B may have been deceived by A and, as such, is neither a corruptor nor someone who is necessarily corrupted.

5.4 Abuse of Authority

Abuse of authority is one of the most pervasive and institutionally damaging forms of corruption. Consider, for example, the damage that senior politicians can do to democratic structures when they abuse their authority by incarcerating opponents on trumped up charges or police officers can do to criminal justice processes when they beat up suspects to obtain confessions. Not only are these particular types of abuse of authority directly corruptive of institutions, they are also human rights violations; specifically, violations of the human right to freedom and to personal security (respectively). Moreover, such abuses of authority are corrosive of public trust in institutional authorities and, therefore, also *indirectly* corruptive of institutions. The legitimacy and, therefore, efficacy (see Chapter 1) of especially public authorities relies in part on public trust.

Many definitions of corruption in effect identify corruption with abuse of authority (or, relatedly, abuse of power) and, indeed, abuse of authority for private gain. For example, Transparency International defines corruption as "Corruption is the abuse of entrusted power for private gain."[23] As we have already seen, institutional corruption is not necessarily motivated by private gain; noble cause corruption, for example, is motivated by the desire to do good (see Chapter 4). Certainly, there is a close connection between abuse of authority and institutional corruption. Nevertheless, the two are not conceptually equivalent. Rather, as we saw in Chapter 3, abuse of authority, like bribery and nepotism, is a particular institutional and moral offence upon which institutional corruption supervenes. Therefore, as one would expect, there are counter-examples to the claim that instances of the abuse of authority are necessarily instances of institutional corruption and, especially, counter-examples to the claim that instances of institutional corruption are necessarily instances of abuse of authority. Regarding the former claim, an overstressed parent can abuse their parental authority by unfairly castigating their child, but this is not necessarily an instance of corruption, even corruption of the "institution" of the family.[24] Regarding the latter claim, a low-level administrative assistant in a police

---

[23] See the homepage of the Transparency International website: www.transparency.org/what-is-corruption/.

[24] Families are not institutions in my sense since they are not organizations or systems of organizations.

force might accept a bribe to provide information to a criminal and, thereby, potentially compromise a criminal investigation. The administrative assistant has certainly breached his institutional duty of confidentiality and engaged in unauthorized disclosure. However, the assistant does not occupy a position of authority, for he has no subordinates (let us assume). It might be responded that the assistant has also abused his authority in making this unauthorized disclosure. This response is implausible since if accepted, it would have the effect of requiring *all* breaches of institutional duties by *all* institutional actors to be instances of the abuse of authority. But now the distinction between a mere institutional actor and an institutional authority has been jettisoned and, as a consequence, the notion of authority has been stripped of its substantial defining element of power (see Chapter 2[25]), e.g., the (legitimate) power of a superior police officer vis-à-vis a subordinate or a member of the public. In addition, all breaches of institutional duties by authorities are now abuses of their authority. But a senior public servant who steals a computer from her office is not abusing her power, albeit her workplace location has afforded her this opportunity for theft and she is in breach of her institutional (including legal) duty not to steal government-owned equipment.

Abuses of authority are, in the first instance, abuses by institutional authorities. Moreover, they involve institutional authorities exercising their power (or failing to do so) in breach of their duties; so an abuse of authority is not *merely* a breach of institutional duty by an institutional authority (although it is a breach of institutional duty). Since an abuse of authority involves an abuse of *power* on the part of an institutional authority – and power is a relation – there must be some subordinate, member of the citizenry or the citizenry at large who is on the receiving end of this exercise of power (or failure to exercise power). Naturally, many abuses of power involve an institutional authority instructing a subordinate to perform some action that is itself an exercise of power, e.g., a head of state who instructs his subordinate police officers to fire on peaceful protesters. However, this is not necessarily the case. Consider, for instance, a superior who refuses to promote a subordinate who is worthy of promotion on grounds of personal dislike.

Abuses of authority can be distinguished from abuses of office. Any institutional actor can abuse their office in the sense that they can use the *opportunities* afforded by the institutional *rights* constitutive of their institutional role to breach their institutional *duties* in the service of

---

[25] See, for example, R. DeGeorge, *Nature and Limits of Authority* (University of Kansas Press, 2000).

(typically) individual or collective interests (see Section 5.2 on nepotism) other than the collective goods definitive of the institution in question. By virtue of the rights constitutive of an institutional role, institutional role occupants are often afforded opportunities to engage in corrupt behavior – opportunities not afforded to others. For example, a head of state might have the institutional right to select the members of his cabinet, a middle-manager might have the right to authorize payments up to a certain amount, and a barman (but not the bar cleaner) the right to use the cash register. Moreover, institutional actors and, especially, institutional authorities often have a sphere of *discretionary* action. It may well be that an institutional actor in exercising her discretion does not *formally* breach any of her institutional duties; she adheres to the letter, but not the spirit, of the law, so to speak. Nevertheless, she might consistently perform her discretionary actions in the service of individual and collective ends other than the collective good(s) constitutive of the institution. Such discretionary actions are an abuse of her office, albeit an abuse it may well be hard to detect and even harder to demonstrate. Presumably, depending on the nature, frequency, and spread (in terms of the numbers of institutional actors involved) of the actions in question, abuses of office might undermine institutional processes, purposes, and/or institutional actors (*qua* institutional actors); if so, they would constitute institutional corruption, notwithstanding that they might not be unlawful. However, an abuse of office in this general sense, unlike an abuse of authority, might not be a species of institutional corruption since the relationship between abuses of office and the undermining of institutional purposes, processes, and persons (*qua* role occupants) might be relatively weak. That is, abuses of office, as a general category, might not sufficiently undermine, and might not have a tendency to sufficiently undermine, institutional processes, purposes, or persons in order to qualify as a species of institutional corruption. On the other hand, some specific instances of abuse of office (that are not also abuses of authority) will by virtue of their damaging institutional effects be instances of institutional corruption. Moreover, some *kinds* of abuse of office that are not also abuses of authority are clearly species of corruption; specifically, abuses of office that exploit fiduciary relationships are a species of corruption. I return to this issue below.

As argued above, abuse of authority is conceptually distinct from institutional corruption (as well as from breach of institutional duty). Nevertheless, abuse of authority typically undermines institutional processes and purposes, and therefore typically constitutes a form of institutional corruption. Moreover, abuse of authority also corrupts institutions by, at least in some cases, (directly) undermining the institutional relationships between superiors and subordinates and, more generally, by undermining the relationships between, on the one hand, institutional authorities (those abusing their authority) and, on the other hand, fellow institutional actors and the citizenry whom they serve (or, at least, are supposed to serve). Importantly, as already noted, abuse of authority undermines public trust.[26]

5.4.1 Trust

This raises the question of how trust is to be understood. In institutional contexts, perhaps especially in financial contexts, trust is often conflated with confidence. However, while confidence is related to trust, the two notions are conceptually distinct. Like confidence, trust pertains to future actions and outruns the evidence in favor of those action occurring. However, unlike confidence, trust involves a moral obligation on the part of the person trusted to the one doing the trusting.[27] Let me explain.

If person A trusts person B then A is dependent on B in some respect – and, therefore, to some extent vulnerable to B – and dependent on B to perform some action x. Moreover, B is under a moral obligation to perform x, or at least A believes that B is under this obligation, and believes also that B believes this.[28] So it is not just that A is dependent on B to perform x, or even that A has brought it about that he is dependent on B to perform x, although both of these conditions obtain when A trusts B; rather this dependence is such that B has a moral obligation to perform x (or, at least, A believes that B has an obligation to perform x and A also believes that B believes that B has this obligation).

In the case of confidence, matters are somewhat different. Perhaps person A forms the belief that company B will perform well and buys shares in B in order to make a good return; A has confidence in B. Indeed, A may well be, albeit perhaps unwisely, depending on B to perform well. However, it does not follow that B is under a moral

---

[26] See, for example, O. O'Neill, *A Question of Trust: Reith Lectures for 2002* (Cambridge University Press, 2002); F. Fukuyama, *Trust: The Social Virtues and the Creation of Prosperity* (London: Penguin Books, 1996).

[27] I am here concerned with trust relationships between institutional actors; I am not concerned with trust in personal relationships, e.g., between friends.

[28] This is a *pro tanto* moral obligation; it can, at least in principle, be overridden by other more stringent moral obligations.

obligation to A (nor that A believes B is under such an obligation and believes, also, that B believes this) such that B will have failed to discharge B's(believed) obligation if in fact B does not do well financially; the relationship is one of confidence, but not necessarily of trust. Naturally, it is consistent with the above relationship of confidence that there is *in addition* a relationship of trust. For example, A trusts that B is a *bona fide* company that is competing in a given market, as opposed to a sham company set up to fail after an asset-stripping exercise. In the latter case, B has failed to discharge its moral obligations to A; A has breached the relationship of trust (among other moral infractions).

We should further distinguish between breaches of trust between A and B, and other breaches of moral principles on the part of B that may negatively impact on A. In particular, there are various universal, or at least very general, moral principles that each of us is obliged to comply with and that each of us relies on others to comply with. Thus there is a moral principle not to kill, assault, steal from, and so on. However, the failure to comply with these principles is not necessarily a breach of trust. If B is unknown to A and B steals A's car, then B has committed a moral and legal offence. However, B has not breached A's trust in B, for there was no relationship of trust between A and B to breach.

Trust is a relationship between specific individuals or between groups of individuals,[29] e.g., the citizenry and government (the public trust), and one from which other individuals (or groups) are excluded. To say that A trusts B is not to say that A trusts C, even if in fact A *also* trusts C. Moreover, trust is a contingent relationship that is created and can cease to exist, notwithstanding the continued existence of the former trustee and truster.

The paradigmatic relationships of trust are between promisors and promisees (and, relatedly, parties to agreement, contracts, etc.). Without trust, promises are unlikely to be believed or even made. Moreover, broken promises betray trust and, indeed, often destroy trust. Here one needs to keep in mind that promises can be implicit as well as explicit.

Notwithstanding that the relationship between promisors and promises is a paradigm of trust, trust relationships do not necessarily involve promises. Take assertions, for example. Hearers trust speakers to speak the truth (as opposed to performing some future action, as in the case of

---

[29] Typically, such individuals are individual human beings. Perhaps trusting collective entities such as corporations is (or should be) in the last analysis trusting individual human beings. See Miller, "Collective Moral Responsibility," 176–193.

promises). However, the social practice of promising presupposes that of assertion; so presumably, assertions do not necessarily involve promises.

The notion of trust relevant to institutional corruption is an ongoing relationship involving at least one institutional actor and in which that actor is trusted in our above sense by some other actor or actors to perform her institutional duties. So there is a relationship of dependence and also one of obligation (and not merely believed obligation). I note that many institutional relationships involving obligations do not involve dependence in any strong sense and the obligation does not arise in part from this dependence. Thus the relationship between buyers and sellers in a market in which the principle of "buyer beware" is operative is not a relationship of trust in our sense. There are two paradigmatic kinds of trust relationship in institutional settings. One of these is the above-mentioned public trust that attaches to public officials and especially to public officials in positions of authority. The other is the so-called fiduciary relationship that obtains, or ought to obtain, between professionals and clients, e.g., lawyers and clients, doctors and patients, and bankers and depositors. Professionals have moral obligations to their clients and clients are typically in a relation of dependence vis-à-vis professionals. Hence there is a need for trust.

As noted above, in the case of public officials in positions of authority, such as politicians, judges, and police officers, abuse of authority undermines public trust; undermines, that is, the relationship of trust between the citizenry and these officials. Since this relationship of public trust is critical to the realization of the purposes of these institutions, abuse of authority is profoundly (albeit indirectly) corruptive of these institutions. Moreover, as we saw above and leaving aside the problem of undermining public trust, abuse of authority directly undermines institutional purposes, processes, and persons. So abuse of authority is a species of institutional corruption that is doubly problematic.

What of the related notion of abuse of office? Clearly not all instances of abuse of office involve corruption; nor, arguably, are all kinds of abuse of office instances of corruption by virtue of a tendency for instances of the kind in question to undermine institutional processes, purposes, or persons. However, some instances and kinds of abuse of office do have this tendency, such as embezzlement of trust funds. I suggest that institutional office holders with fiduciary relationships, e.g., bankers and lawyers, who exploit those relationships in order to, for example, defraud their clients are engaged in institutional corruption. The reason for this is the importance of the fiduciary relationship to those institutions; when the fiduciary relationship is seriously compromised, the institutional purposes are undermined. Consider in this connection the auditing firm Arthur Anderson; when it's illegal activity became known, trust evaporated and the firm collapsed.

5.5 Conclusion

Bribery, nepotism, fraud and abuse of authority are salient species of institutional corruption. As such, they undermine institutional purposes, processes, and/or persons (*qua* institutional actors). In this chapter, I have provided analyses of each of these species of institutional corruption. I have argued that fraud is a species of corruption when it involves an institutional actor acting in his or her capacity as an institutional actor, either as corruptor or corrupted, but not otherwise. I have also argued against the widely held view that all forms of institutional corruption are instances of abuse of authority. In doing so, I differentiated between breaches of institutional duty, abuses of one's office, and abuse of one's institutional authority. The latter is always a form of corruption but not necessarily the former two kinds of transgression. On the other hand, abuses of office that exploit fiduciary relationships are invariably instances of corruption. In the context of the discussion of fiduciary relationships I distinguished trust from confidence and defined the former notion.

CHAPTER 6

Institutional Responsibility:
Individual and Collective

In this chapter our primary concern is with institutional responsibility and its relation to moral responsibility. Moreover, the responsibility in question is both individual and collective in character. Understanding responsibility in institutional settings is critical both for understanding institutional corruption (the moral responsibility of corruptors for their corrupt actions – see Chapter 3) and, relatedly, for designing effective means to combat it (the moral responsibility of institutional actors for anti-corruption measures).

6.1 Responsibility

We need first to distinguish some different senses of responsibility.[1] Sometimes to say that someone is responsible for an action is to say that the person had a reason, or reasons, to perform some action, then formed an intention to perform that action (or not to perform it), and finally acted (or refrained from acting) on that intention, and did so on the basis of that reason(s). Note that an important category of reasons for actions are ends, goals, or purposes; an agent's reason for performing an action is often that the action realizes a goal the agent has. Moreover, it is assumed that in the course of all this the agent brought about or caused the action, at least in the sense that the mental state or states that constituted his reason for performing the action was causally efficacious (in the right way), and that his resulting intention was causally efficacious (in the right way).[2] Further, it is assumed that the agent chooses the ends, goals or purposes in question

---

[1] Much of the content of this section was drawn from earlier versions published in S. Miller, "Collective Responsibility," *Public Affairs Quarterly*, 15 (2001), 65–82; and S. Miller, *Social Action*, chapter 8.

[2] See D. Davidson, "Freedom to Act" in T. Honderich (ed.), *Essays on Freedom of Action* (London: Routledge and Kegan Paul, 1973), and J. R. Searle, *Intentionality* (Cambridge University Press, 1983), chapter 3.

(and could have chosen otherwise, but see later). Here I note that an action could be chosen in this sense and yet be coerced, albeit this might not be the case if the coercion used was extreme, as in some cases of torture. For in the latter cases, the agent no longer has control of his or her actions.

There are omissions or, at least acts of refraining, that are analogous to actions in the above described sense. In such cases one intentionally refrains from performing some action having some end in mind and the intention is causally efficacious in the right way and so on. In what follows I use the term "action" to include such intentional omissions, unless I indicate otherwise.

This sense of being responsible for an action is different from other well-known cognate senses of responsibility. These latter include what might be termed, "bare responsibility." An agent has bare responsibility for an action if and only if he intentionally performs the action (and the intention causes the action). I note that an agent in such cases might not be responsible for his intention and to that extent not responsible for his action. These cognate senses also include the notion of a responsible agent – as distinct from someone being responsible for an action. An agent is a responsible agent if he or she is not insane, is not under the influence of drugs, and so on. Finally, there is being responsible for an action in the sense of freely perform the action. This notion of a freely performed action is notoriously difficult to pin down. Presumably it does not include actions that are coerced and according to one popular line of thought, a freely performed action is at least an action such that the agent could have done otherwise. But this latter line of thought has been heavily criticized.[3]

At any rate, I will dub the very first of these above-mentioned senses of being responsible for an action "natural responsibility," viz. intentionally performing an action and doing so for a reason. Here, as elsewhere in this work, there is a contrast to be made between the natural and the institutional; the latter presupposes the former.

A second sense of "being responsible for an action" is being institutionally responsible. What is meant is that the person in question occupies a certain institutional role, and that the occupant of that role is the person who has the institutionally determined right or duty to decide what is to be done in relation to certain matters. For example, the police officer may have

---

[3] See J. M. Fischer (ed.), *Moral Responsibility* (London: Cornell University Press, 1986), p. 14f. For attempts to analyze free action, and related notions of autonomy, by recourse to higher order attitudes see H. G. Frankfurt, "Three Concepts of Free Action" in Fischer (ed.), *Moral Responsibility*; G. Dworkin, *The Theory and Practice of Autonomy* (Cambridge University Press, 1988). For accounts of one's responsibility for one's character see F. Schoeman, *Responsibility, Character and the Emotions* (Cambridge University Press, 1987).

the responsibility to arrest the fraudster, irrespective of whether or not he does so, or even contemplates doing so.

A third sense of "being responsible" for an action is a species of our second sense. If the matters in respect of which the occupant of an institutional role has an institutionally determined duty to decide what is to be done include ordering other agents to perform, or not perform, certain actions, then the occupant of the role is responsible for those actions performed by those other agents. We say of such a person that he is responsible for the actions of others persons in virtue of being in charge of them, or of being the person with authority over them.

The fourth sense of responsibility is moral responsibility. Roughly speaking,[4] an agent is held to be morally responsible for an action if the agent was responsible for that action in one of our first three senses of responsible, and that action is morally significant (and the agent knows this or, at least, ought to have known this). The ways in which an action can be morally significant are too many and varied to be detailed here. They include instances of infringing or conforming to a moral principle or right and causing good or evil.

I note that responsibility in its moral and institutional senses can be used in a backward-looking (retrospective responsibility) or forward-looking (prospective responsibility) sense. An example of the former sense is: "Madoff is morally responsible for defrauding his clients." An example of the latter sense is: "The members of the Securities and Exchange Commission are institutionally responsible for enforcing financial regulations."

Responsibility needs to be distinguished from blameworthiness/praiseworthiness,[5] on the one hand, and accountability,[6] on the other. If a cleaner does his job of cleaning the office to an acceptable standard, but not to a high standard, then he is responsible for having cleaned the office; but he is presumably neither praiseworthy nor blameworthy. Evidently, therefore, praiseworthiness and blameworthiness presuppose responsibility, but should not be equated with it. Again, responsibility should not be confused with accountability. The cleaner is responsible for cleaning the office, but accountable for his performance as a cleaner to (say) his supervisor. That is, the supervisor might be tasked with monitoring and assessing the cleaner's performance and, if necessary, intervening in the case of poor performance by retraining, disciplining, or perhaps even firing him.

---

[4] This rough definition needs to be subject to "an other things being equal" clause. See definition of collective moral responsibility below (Section 6.2).

[5] P. F. Strawson, "Freedom and Resentment," *Proceedings of the British Academy*, 48 (1962), 187–211.

[6] M. Bovens, "Analysing and Assessing Accountability," *European Law Journal*, 13 (2007), 447–468.

The notion of institutional responsibility,[7] including but not restricted to legal responsibility,[8] presupposes some notion of an institution.[9] In this work, of course, we are taking institutions to be organizations and/or systems of organizations. Institutions in this sense are among the most important of collective human phenomena; they enable us to feed ourselves (markets and agribusinesses), to protect ourselves (police and military services), to educate ourselves (schools and universities), and to govern ourselves (governments and legal systems). In short, institutions have purposes (collective goods, normatively speaking). Institutions consist in part of institutional roles defined in terms of tasks and these roles are structured in terms of relationships of authority. Institutional role structures vary greatly. Compare, for example, the hierarchical top-down structure of military organizations with the flat democratic structures typical of amateur sporting clubs. The third main dimension of institutions is culture[10]; the "spirit" or informal set of attitudes that pervades an organization and which might reinforce or negate the more formal requirements of the organization. An example of the latter is the culture in certain police organizations that protects those engaged in corruption rather than exposing them.

Among other things, a normative theory of institutions specifies what the purpose of particular types of institution *ought to be*, as opposed to what in fact it is. Enron, for example, apparently had the *de facto* institutional purpose of enriching its CEO and other senior officers, but this was surely not what its institutional purpose ought to have been.

As outlined in Chapter 1, my normative theory of social institutions is based on an individualist theory of joint action.[11] Put simply, on this account the organizations or systems of organizations are ones that provide collective goods by means of joint activity. The collective goods in question include the fulfillment of aggregated moral rights, such as needs-based rights for security (police organizations), material well-being (businesses operating in markets), education (universities), governance (governments), and so on.[12]

Whether one accepts this normative theory or some other, establishing, maintaining, or redesigning the institutional responsibilities of institutional

---

[7] J. Ladd, "Philosophical Remarks on Professional Responsibility in Organizations," *International Journal of Applied Philosophy*, 1 (1982), 58–70.

[8] R. A. Duff, *Answering for Crime: Responsibility and Liability in the Criminal Law* (Oxford: Hart Publishing, 2007).

[9] J. R. Searle, *Making the Social World* (Oxford University Press, 2011); Miller, *Moral Foundations*.

[10] R. Harre, *Social Being*, 2nd edn. (Oxford: Blackwell, 1993).

[11] Miller, *Moral Foundations of Social Institutions*.

[12] So collective goods in this sense are not public goods in the economists' sense of public goods, i.e., non-excludable, non-rival goods.

role occupants ought to be done in the context of some normative account of the institutional purpose of the institution in question. To some extent, this purpose will determine what is an appropriate structure and culture and, therefore, what the tasks to be performed by the institutional role occupants ought to be and the manner in which they ought to be performed. That is, institutional role structure and associated culture ought to facilitate institutional purpose. This is most obvious in relation to the tasks definitive of a role; tax accountants ought to know the tax laws, how to prepare tax returns, and so on. It is less obvious in relation to authority relationships. Perhaps a hierarchical structure is necessary if military organizations are to realize their institutional purposes of successfully waging war. On the other hand, top-down hierarchical structures may not be conducive to academic work and, therefore, ought not to be imposed on universities.

In the light of the above, we can distinguish three possible ways of understanding institutional responsibility. First, there is the responsibility *to institutions*. This is the responsibility (possibly moral responsibility) that an individual or, more likely, group might have to establish, maintain, or redesign an institution. Here the property "institutional" does not qualify the notion of responsibility; rather, it is part of the content of the responsibility. This sense of institutional responsibility is not our direct or principal concern here.[13] Second, there is responsibility *of institutions*. For example, corporations are ascribed *legal* responsibilities (in some weak sense of that term).[14] However, some theorists have wanted to ascribe *moral* responsibility to institutions. This is the notional possibility that institutional *and* moral responsibility might attach to collective entities (specifically, institutions) *per se*. This possibility could only obtain if institutions (and like collective entities) were *minded* agents: agents possessed of mental states, such as desires, intentions, and beliefs.[15] For only minded agents perform actions in the appropriate sense of action, and only minded agents can sensibly be held morally responsible for their actions. However, the idea that institutions per se, as opposed to their human members (institutional role occupants), have minds is problematic or, at the very least, controversial.[16] At any rate, in this

---

[13] Although it is indirectly relevant. See final point in Section 6.3.

[14] Michael S. Moore, *Causation and Responsibility: An Essay in Law, Morals and Metaphysics* (Oxford University Press, 2009).

[15] Peter French, "The Corporation as a Moral Person," *American Philosophical Quarterly*, 16 (1979), 207–215; Toni Erskine, "Assigning Responsibilities to Institutional Moral Agents," *Ethics and International Affairs*, 15 (2001), 67–85.

[16] David Copp, "Collective Moral Autonomy Thesis," *Journal of Social Philosophy*, 38 (2007), 369–388; Seumas Miller, "Against the Moral Autonomy Thesis," *Journal of Social Philosophy*, 38 (2007), 389–409.

work I set aside any further consideration of this way of understanding institutional responsibility. I do so while acknowledging that for heuristic reasons institutional responsibility (in some weak sense) can be ascribed to institutions per se. Third, there is the responsibility *of institutional role occupants*. This is the institutional responsibility of the human beings who occupy institutional roles: responsibility *qua* institutional role occupant. It is this third sense of institutional responsibility and its relationship to moral responsibility that is our principal concern here.

6.2 Individual and Collective Responsibility

As we saw above, individual role occupants are *individually* institutionally responsible for at least some of their actions and omissions. Again, an institutional role occupant in a position of authority over another might have an *individual* institutional responsibility (forward-looking sense) to see to it that her subordinate performs the tasks definitive of the subordinate's role. Moreover, if the subordinate consistently fails to perform the tasks in question, and his superior (the supervisor) fails to intervene, then the supervisor is individually responsible (backward-looking sense) for failing to see to it that the subordinate does his job and this failure attaches to the supervisor *qua* institutional role occupant.

On the other hand, a number of institutional role occupants might be *collectively* institutionally responsible for some outcome.[17] The paradigmatic cases here are ones of joint action: actions involving cooperation between institutional actors to achieve some outcome.

As we saw in Chapter 1, roughly speaking, a joint action[18] can be understood thus: two or more individuals perform a joint action if each of them intentionally performs an individual action (or omission), but does so with the (true) belief that in so doing they will jointly realize an end that each of them has. So joint actions are interdependent actions directed toward a common goal or end. However, as we also saw in Chapter 1, the notion of a joint action (analyzed in terms of the collective end theory or CET) can be used to provide an analysis of organizational

---

[17] Dennis F. Thompson, "Moral Responsibility and Public Officials: The Problem of Many Hands," *American Political Science Review*, 74 (1980), 259–273; Larry May, *Sharing Responsibility* (University of Chicago Press, 1992); Michael Zimmerman, "Sharing Responsibility," *American Philosophical Quarterly*, 22 (1985), 115–122.

[18] Michael Bratman, *Shared Agency* (Oxford University Press, 2014); Seumas Miller, "Joint Action," *Philosophical Papers*, 11 (1992), 275–299; Kaarlo Miller and Raimo Tuomela, "We-intentions," *Philosophical Studies*, 53 (1988), 115–137.

action (multi-layered structures of joint action) and joint institutional mechanisms, e.g., voting mechanisms.

Collective responsibility of the kind in question here is the responsibility that attaches to the participants of a joint action (including, at least in principle, in the sense of a multi-layered structure of joint action and of a joint action performed by means of a joint institutional mechanism) for the performance of the joint action in question and, in particular, for the realization of the collective end of the joint action. There are different accounts of collective responsibility, some of which pertain to the responsibility of groups and organizations per se for their group or "corporate" (so to speak) actions. Here our concern is only with collective responsibility for joint actions of human beings in their capacity as institutional role occupants. One such salient account conceptualizes collective moral responsibility for joint action as *joint responsibility*.[19]

On this view of collective responsibility as joint responsibility, collective responsibility is ascribed to individual human beings only, albeit jointly.[20] As in the case of individual responsibility, in the case of collective responsibility we can distinguish between natural, institutional, and moral responsibility. Moreover, we can relate collective natural and institutional responsibility, on the one hand, to collective moral responsibility, on the other.

Agents who perform a joint action are responsible for that action in the first sense of collective responsibility: collective natural responsibility. Accordingly, to say that they are collectively responsible for the action is just to say that they performed the joint action. That is, they each had a collective end, each intentionally performed their contributory action, and each did so because each believed the other would perform his contributory action, and that therefore the collective end would be realized. Moreover, each chose to perform their individual action and to pursue the collective end, and each could have done otherwise.

Here it is important to note that each agent is individually (naturally) responsible for performing his contributory action, and responsible by

---

[19] Gregory Mellema, "Collective Responsibility and Qualifying Actions," *Midwest Studies in Philosophy*, 30 (2006), 168–175; Seumas Miller, "Collective Moral Responsibility."

[20] Accordingly, there is no need to maintain that collective responsibility attaches to collective entities per se, as collectivist theorists such as Gilbert (in her *On Social Facts*) and (in a somewhat different vein) Christian List and Philip Pettit, in *Group Agency* (Oxford University Press, 2011), have done. For criticisms of these collectivist accounts see Seumas Miller and Pekka Makela, "The Collectivist Approach to Collective Moral Responsibility," *Metaphilosophy*, 36 (2005), 634–651; Andras Szigeti, "Are Individualist Accounts of Collective Moral Responsibility Morally Deficient?" in A. Konzelmann-Ziv and H. B. Schmid (eds.), *Institutions, Emotions and Group Agents: Contribution to Social Ontology*, *Studies in the Philosophy of Sociality* 2 (Dordrecht: Springer, 2014).

virtue of the fact that he intentionally performed this action, and the action was not intentionally performed by anyone else. Of course, the other agents (or agent) *believe* that the first agent is performing, or is going to perform, the contributory action in question. But mere possession of such a belief is not sufficient for the ascription of responsibility to *the believer* for performing the individual action in question. So what are the agents *collectively* (naturally) responsible for? The agents are *collectively* (naturally) responsible for the realization of the (collective) *end* that results from their contributory actions.

Further, on this account, to say that they are collectively (naturally) responsible for the realization of the collective end of a joint action is to say that they are *jointly* responsible for the realization of that end. They are jointly responsible because (1) each relied on the other to bring about the state of affairs aimed at by both (the collective end); (2) each intentionally contributed causally to the realization of the collective end (by performing his or her individual contributory action); and (3) each performed their contributory action on condition, and only on condition, that the other(s) performed theirs. Here condition (3) expresses the *interdependence* of action involved in joint action. There is also interdependence at the level of ends. Each only has the (collective) end in question if the others have it since no agent can realize the end by acting on his or her own; therefore, there would be no point to a single agent possessing the end if the others did not.

Let us now consider collective institutional responsibility. If the occupants of an institutional role (or roles) have an institutionally determined obligation to perform some joint action then those individuals are collectively responsible for its performance, in our second sense of collectively responsibility. Consider the collective institutional responsibility of the members of a team of auditors to ensure that the financial reports of a large company are true and fair. Here there is a *joint* institutional obligation to realize the collective end of the joint action in question. In addition, there is a set of derived *individual* obligations; each of the participating individuals has an individual obligation to perform his/her contributory action. (The derivation of these individual obligations relies on the fact that if each performs his/her contributory action then it is almost certain, or at least probable, that the collective end will be realized.)

The *joint* institutional obligation is a composite obligation consisting of the obligation each of us has to perform a certain specified action in order to realize that end. More precisely, an agent A has the obligation to realize a collective end by means of doing some action, believing agent B to have performed some other action for that self-same end. The point about joint obligations is that they are not to be discharged by one person acting alone.

Notice that, typically, agents involved in an institutional joint action will discharge their respective individual institutional obligations and their joint institutional obligation by the performance of one and the same set of individual actions. For example, if each of the members of an anti-corruption task force performs his individual duties having as an end the exposure and conviction of the members of a money laundering operation then, given favorable conditions, the task force will achieve its end. But one can imagine an investigating agent who is prepared to discharge his individual institutional obligation, but not his jointly held obligation to realize the collective end in question. This investigator might have an overriding individual end to get himself promoted, but the head of the task force might be ahead of him in the queue of those to be promoted. So the investigator does not have exposing and convicting the members of the money laundering operation as a collective end. Accordingly, while he ensures that he discharges his individual obligation to, say, interview a particular suspect, the investigator is less assiduous than he might other-wise be because he wants the task force to fail in its overall enterprise and, therefore, he cannot be said to have fully discharged his jointly held obligation to realize the collective end.

As already mentioned, there is another sense of institutional responsibility. This sense concerns those in authority. Here we need to distinguish two kinds of case. If the occupant of an institutional role has an institutionally deter-mined right or obligation to order other agents to perform certain actions, and the actions in question are joint actions, then the occupant of the role is *individually* (institutionally) responsible for those joint actions performed by those other agents. This is our first kind of case, but it should be set aside, since it is not an instance of *collective* responsibility. In the second kind of case, it is of no consequence whether the actions performed by those under the direction of the person in authority were joint actions or not. Rather, the issue concerns the actions of the ones in authority. In what sense are they collective? Suppose the members of the Cabinet of the UK government (consisting of the Prime Minister and her Cabinet Ministers) collectively decide to exercise their institutionally determined right to establish an anti-corruption agency in relation to the government and its bureaucracy. Accordingly, a budget is allocated, the anti-corruption agency is established, law enforcement agencies are briefed, and so on. The anti-corruption agency, relevant law enforcement agencies, and others do what they have been instructed to do, and the Cabinet is collectively responsible for establishing the anti-corruption program, in some sense of collective responsibility. There are a couple of things to keep in mind here. First, the notion of responsibility in question here is, at least in the first instance, institutional – as opposed to moral – responsibility. Second, the "decisions" of committees, as opposed to the individual decisions of the members of committees, need to be analyzed in terms of the notion of a joint institutional mechanism (see Chapter 1 Section 1.3).[21] So the "decision" of the Cabinet – supposing it to be the Cabinet's decision, and not simply the Prime Minister's – can be analyzed as follows. At one level, each member of the Cabinet voted for or against the establishment of the anti-corruption agency, and let us assume that some voted in the affirmative and others in the negative. But at another level, each member of the Cabinet agreed to abide by the outcome of the vote; that is, each voted having as a (collective) end that the outcome with a majority of the votes in its favor would be the one adopted.[22] Accordingly, the members of the Cabinet were jointly institutionally responsible for the decision to establish this anti-corruption agency. So the Cabinet was collectively institutionally responsible for establishing the agency, and the sense of collective responsibility in question is *joint* (institutional) responsibility.[23]

What of the fourth sense of collective responsibility, collective *moral* responsibility? Collective moral responsibility is a species of joint responsibility. Accordingly, each agent is individually morally responsible, but conditionally on the others being individually morally responsible; there is interdependence in respect of moral responsibility. This account of collective moral responsibility arises naturally out of the account of joint actions. It also parallels the account given of individual moral responsibility.

Thus, we can make the following claim about moral responsibility. If agents are collectively (i.e., jointly) responsible for the successful performance of a joint action, in the first or second or third senses of collective responsibility, and if the joint action is morally significant then – other things being equal – the agents are collectively (i.e., jointly) morally responsible for that

---

[21] Miller "Joint Epistemic Action: Some Applications."

[22] Or at least all those who voted in good faith had this collective end and even those who did not were institutionally bound to accept the outcome of the vote and were institutionally responsible for it (jointly with the others).

[23] This mode of analysis is also available to handle examples in which an institutional entity has a representative who makes an individual decision, but it is an individual decision that has the joint backing of the members of the institutional entity, e.g., an industrial union's representative in relation to wage negotiations with a company. It can also handle examples such as the firing squad in which only one real bullet is used, and it is not known which member is firing the real bullet and which merely blanks. The soldier with the real bullet is (albeit unknown to him) *individually* responsible for shooting the person dead. However, the members of the firing squad are *jointly* responsible for its being the case that the person has been shot dead.

joint action, and can reasonably attract moral praise or blame, and (possibly) punishment or reward for performing it and, in particular, for the realization of its collective end.

Here we need to be more precise about what agents who perform morally significant joint actions are collectively morally responsible for. Other things being equal, each agent who intentionally performs a morally significant *individual* action has *individual* moral responsibility for the action. So in the case of a morally significant joint action, each agent is *individually* morally responsible for performing *his contributory* action, and the *other* agents are *not* morally responsible for his individual contributory action. But, in addition, the contributing agents are *collectively* morally responsible for the outcome that constitutes the realization of the *collective end* of their various contributory actions. To say that they are collectively morally responsible for bringing about this outcome is just to say that they are *jointly* morally responsible for it. So each agent is individually morally responsible for bringing about this outcome, but conditionally on the others being individually morally responsible for bringing it about as well.

Note the following residual points. First, it is not definitive of joint action that each performs his/her contributory action on the condition, and only on the condition, that *all* of the others perform theirs. Rather, it is sufficient that each perform his/her contributory action on the condition, and only on the condition, that *most* of the others perform theirs. So the interdependence involved in joint action is not necessarily *complete* interdependence.

Second, an agent has moral responsibility if his action was intentionally performed in order to realize a morally significant collective end, and the action causally contributed to the end. The action does not have to be a necessary condition, or even a necessary part of a sufficient condition, for the realization of the end.

Third, agents who intentionally make a causal contribution in order to realize a morally significant collective end are not necessarily fully morally responsible for the end realized. This is especially so in cases of joint action in which there are very large numbers of contributors, e.g., the thousands of small contributors to a charity. Moreover, in some cases of joint action some participants have a greater responsibility than others, either by virtue of their greater contribution or by virtue of their position of authority over others.

Fourth, according to the definition participants in a morally significant joint action are collectively morally responsible for that action *other things being equal*. Naturally, other things might not be equal if, for instance, the participants were not morally sentient or were coerced into performing the joint action. Moreover, as discussed in Section 6.3, there are some morally significant, institutional omissions, in particular, that agents failed to perform and yet could not reasonably have been expected to perform. In some of these cases things are not equal and, as a consequence, although there is institutional responsibility and moral significance, nevertheless, there is not moral responsibility.

A problem arises for the in relation to collective moral responsibility for the actions of large groups and organizations. Consider the Mafia. The actions of the members of the Mafia are interdependent in virtue of the collective end – say, to profit from the sale of heroin in Southern Italy. Naturally, this interdependence is far more complex than simple cases of joint action, given the existence of a hierarchical organization, and its more loosely structured extensions. Moreover, the contribution of each individual to the outcome is far more various, and in general quite insignificant, given the large numbers of people involved. At this point, the notion of a multi-layered structure of joint actions[24] (introduced in Chapter 1 Section 1.2) needs to be invoked and applied to the Mafia organization in question. The team of Mafia "soldiers," drivers, and others ensures that a given heroin shipment is procured and transported safely to the distribution point in a large city – this is a level one joint action; a Mafia "sales" team distributes smaller quantities of the heroin to individual dealers – this is a level one joint action, and finally the money received back from individual dealers is laundered by members of the organization's money laundering arm, e.g., by being deposited in small amounts in numerous bank accounts – this is level one joint action. However, each of these level one joint actions are elements of a larger level two joint action directed to the collective end of making money from the sale of heroin, i.e., running a heroin business. Each of these individual actions – procuring, selling, and laundering – is part of the larger "business" plan of the Mafia leadership.

Accordingly, if all, or most, of the individual actions of the members of the Mafia organization were performed in accordance with collective ends, and the performance of each of the resulting level one joint actions were themselves performed in accordance with the collective end of making money for the Mafia organization from the sale of heroin, then, at least in principle, we could ascribe joint moral responsibility for the realization of this collective end to the individual members of the Mafia organization.

At any rate, we are now entitled to conclude that agents involved in complex cooperative enterprises can, *at least in principle*, be ascribed collective or *joint natural* responsibility for the outcomes aimed at by

---

[24] Miller, *Moral Foundations of Social Institutions*, chapter 1.

those enterprises, and in cases of morally significant enterprises they can be ascribed collective or *joint moral* responsibility for those outcomes. This conclusion depends on the possibility of analyzing these enterprises in terms of layered structures of joint action. Such structures involve (1) a possibly indirect and minor causal contribution from each of the individuals jointly being ascribed responsibility; (2) each individual having an intention to perform his or her contributory (causally efficacious) action; and (3) each individual having as an ultimate end or goal the outcome causally produced by their jointly performed actions.

The upshot of the discussion in this section is that the undoubted existence of the phenomenon of collective moral responsibility for actions is entirely consistent with individualism in relation to moral responsibility. An acceptable individualist account of collective moral responsibility is available.

I have argued that collective institutional responsibility and collective moral responsibility (understood as joint institutional responsibility and joint moral responsibility, respectively) are involved not only in joint (institutional) actions but also in the related phenomena of organizational action understood as *multi-layered structures of joint action* and of *joint institutional mechanisms*. However, there is yet another central kind of case of collective institutional responsibility (and collective moral responsibility). It is an extension of joint institutional mechanisms in the above sense. I refer to these as *chains of institutional responsibility*.[25] Let me explain.

6.2.1 Chains of Institutional Responsibility

Consider a team of detectives investigating a major crime. Let us assume that the team is engaging in a joint institutional action, namely, that of determining who is the Yorkshire Ripper. So members of the team gather physical evidence, interview witnesses, and, in particular, the main suspect, Peter Sutcliffe. Moreover, they do so having as a collective end to determine the *factual* guilt or innocence of this and other suspects. At some point, the detectives complete this process and provide a brief of evidence to the prosecutors according to which, and based on all the evidence, Sutcliffe is the Yorkshire Ripper. So far so good, but the criminal justice processes do not terminate in the work of the detectives, for there is now the matter of the trial; that is, the determining by the members of a jury of

[25] Seumas Miller, "Police Detectives, Criminal Investigations and Collective Moral Responsibility," *Criminal Justice Ethics*, 33 (2014), 21–39.

the legal guilt or innocence of Sutcliffe. Let us assume that the members of the jury perform the joint action of deliberating on *legal* guilt or innocence of Sutcliffe, and jointly reach the verdict of guilty (as in fact happened). The question that now arises concerns the institutional relationship between the joint institutional action of the detectives and the joint institutional action of the members of the jury. It is here that the notion of a chain of institutional responsibility is illuminating.

Let us assume in what follows that the collective end of the criminal justice process comprising both the investigating detectives *and* the members of the jury (as well as others, but here I simplify) is that the factually guilty be found legally guilty (and the factually innocent not be found legally guilty). Note that from the perspective of this larger institutional process the collective end of the detectives (that of determining the factual guilt or innocence of a suspect) is merely *proximate*, whereas that of the members of the jury is *ultimate*. (It is, of course, only penultimate from the perspective of the criminal justice system more broadly conceived, given the need for sentencing and incarceration.)

Moreover, in all this there is an institutional division of labor and segregation of roles that involves each type of institutional actor, e.g., investigator, prosecutor, judge, jury, making a contribution to the further (collective) end of identifying and appropriately punishing the guilty and exonerating the innocent. However, unlike many institutional arrangements, the criminal justice process is predicated on strict adherence on the part of institutional actors to the segregation of roles on pain of compromising this further end. I emphasize that this segregation of roles is consistent with all of these actors, each with their own different and segregated role, having a common further aim; agents can have a common aim and yet it be a requirement that each is to make a different and distinct contribution to that aim, and not perform the tasks assigned to the others, and do all this in the service of that common aim.

In respect of this segregation of roles, the relationship between the institutional actors, including investigators, in the criminal justice process is *unlike* that which holds between (say) a manager, a waiter, and a barman in a small pub. There is no reason why, for example, the manager and the waiter might not assist the barman in doing his job of pouring beers during a rush period or even stand in his place when he is called away. But there is good reason why the prosecutor should not also be the judge or the investigator the jury; in an adversarial system any such conflation of roles would constitute a structural conflict of interest and, as such, would be likely to undermine the administration of justice.

Institutional arrangements, such as this, in which there is a segregation of roles (and associated responsibilities) but, nevertheless, a common further end involve a chain of institutional responsibility.

In chains of institutional responsibility all the participants aim (or should be aiming) at the further end in addition to undertaking their own roles (and, therefore, aiming at the end definitive of their own particular role). Moreover, all the participants (at least, in principle) share in the *collective responsibility* for achieving that further end (or for failing to do so). Let us work with our example of Peter Sutcliffe, the Yorkshire Ripper, who was ultimately convicted of thirteen counts of murder (the victims being prostitutes working in Yorkshire in the UK).

The detectives involved were (collectively in the sense of jointly) institutionally responsible for gathering and analyzing the evidence that identified Peter Sutcliffe as the Yorkshire Ripper; they acquired the required knowledge of Sutcliffe's *factual* guilt and, thereby, realized the collective end of their institutional role as detectives. On the other hand, members of the court and, in particular, the members of the jury were (collectively) institutionally responsible for finding Sutcliffe *legally* guilty and, thereby, realized the (collective) end of their institutional roles as jury members. So far so good, but what was the ultimate end that was realized by the detectives *and* the members of the jury (as well as the other actors involved in the institutional process, e.g., the judge)?

Presumably, the end in question is for the factually guilty to be found legally guilty (and the factually innocent not to be found legally guilty[26]) and this is an end (a collective end) that is realized by the detectives working jointly with the members of the jury (and the other relevant institutional actors). It is not an end that the detectives could achieve on their own; they can only arrive at knowledge of factual guilt. But equally it is not an end that the members of the jury could realize on their own, for they rely on the knowledge provided by the detectives.[27] Moreover, it is a morally significant end. Accordingly, other things being equal, the members of the detective team and the members of the jury are collectively (i.e., jointly) morally responsible for the realization of this end (the factually guilty being found legally guilty and the factually innocent not being found legally guilty).

[26] Assuming there are only two possible verdicts, guilty and innocent, which is not the case in some jurisdictions, e.g., Scotland.

[27] Chains of institutional and moral responsibility consist of a process in which the completion of one stage institutionally triggers the commencement of the next stage, e.g., arrest is followed either by the suspect being charged or released within a specified timeframe.

Notwithstanding this above-described mandatory segregation of roles (in the context of a chain of institutional responsibility), detectives have been known to try to preempt the outcome of the criminal justice process, e.g., by "loading up" suspects they believe are guilty and deserving of severe punishment, rather than remaining within the confines of their designated role of evidence gathering in the service of truth and being content to rely on prosecutors, judges, and juries to undertake their different (albeit, ultimately interlocking) roles in relation to assessing the case against suspects, determining guilt, passing sentence, and so on.

6.3   Institutional and Moral Responsibility

The relationship between institutional responsibility and moral responsibility is a difficult one to unravel, not least because the notion of moral responsibility is itself theoretically complex and a matter of controversy. Moreover, I cannot here elaborate on these complexities and controversies. However, there are some general points that can be raised. In raising them I assume that, as argued above (roughly speaking), an agent, A, is morally responsible for an action (or omission), x, or the foreseeable and avoidable outcome of x, if x is morally significant (and A is aware, or should be aware, of this moral significance), A intentionally performed x, A's intention to x caused x, and A chose to perform x, and so on.

We saw above that some institutional actions – actions performed by the human occupants of institutional roles in their capacity as institutional actors – are not morally significant and some morally significant actions are not institutional. On the other hand, many institutional actions are morally significant.

Let us henceforth consider only institutional actions that are morally significant in some general sense and known to be so by the relevant institutional actor – or, at least, the institutional actors should know that the actions in question are morally significant. A question now arises as to whether or not with respect to these actions at least, moral responsibility necessarily tracks institutional responsibility. If so, then an institutional actor who is institutionally responsible for performing a (morally significant) institutional action, or for failing to do so, is necessarily morally responsible for the performance of that action or omission.[28] However, this appears not to be the case. Consider, for example, a senior

---

[28] I note that this is not entailed by our definitions of individual and collective moral responsibility since those definitions have an "other things being equal" clause.

government official, such as a cabinet minister, a number of whose subordinates engage in serious and ongoing acts of fraud. Such acts are morally significant and the subordinates are morally responsibility for perpetrating them. What of the senior government official? Under some institutional arrangements, the senior official might be held institutionally responsible for failing to ensure that such fraud as this did not take place and, consequently, might be forced to resign. Nevertheless, the senior official might not be morally responsible for failing to prevent this fraud. Let us assume that the senior official could have prevented these frauds, if he knew about them and he could have known about them if he had spent a good deal of his time focused on fraud prevention. However, he did not; he had other legitimate and more pressing priorities. Perhaps the senior official took all the steps that might reasonably be expected of him to prevent these frauds but his job is an onerous one, the fraudsters were exceptionally clever, and so on. In short, whereas he is institutionally responsible for failing to prevent these frauds he is, arguably, not morally responsible. So apparently, institutional responsibility does not necessarily track moral responsibility. Specifically, it does not track it in certain cases in which the untoward institutional action is not one that the institutional actor in question actually performed (e.g., the acts of fraud) or could reasonably have been expected to perform (e.g., the act of fraud prevention).Nor is it obvious that such an institutional arrangement, supposing it exists, is necessarily deficient *qua* institutional arrangement. I note that Schauer, for example, has argued in detail[29] that institutional arrangements, including laws, are necessarily blunt instruments and, as such, cannot be sensitive to all the requirements of morality.

A second claim concerning the relationships between moral responsibility and institutional responsibility is that institutional arrangements can sometimes make a difference with respect to whether moral responsibility is full or partial.[30] Thus, as a consequence of institutional arrangements put in place to deal with some collective action problem, each agent might, it is claimed, have full moral responsibility (jointly with others) for some adverse outcome O – notwithstanding the fact that each only made a very small causal contribution to the outcome. Suppose the impoverished members of sailing ships' crews in the eighteenth century are informed of a law to the effect that anyone stealing one or more of the (somewhat expensive) screws inserted into their ship's woodwork to hold its wooden

---

[29] Frederick Schauer, *Profiles, Probabilities and Stereotypes* (Cambridge: Harvard University Press, 2003).

[30] Seumas Miller, "Joint Epistemic Action and Collective Moral Responsibility," *Social Epistemology*, 29, 3, 2015, pp. 280–302.

planks together will be flogged and, further, if the ship sinks as a consequence of multiple screws being removed in this manner then anyone who has removed at least one of these screws will be held to be *fully* legally responsible for any deaths resulting from the ship sinking and to be legally liable to the death penalty. Let us assume that this admittedly harsh criminal law is morally justified in the circumstances, perhaps in part because of the difficulty of identifying which sailors removed screws. At any rate, this apparently harsh law is the only means to prevent these wooden ships frequently sinking and, therefore, the only means to prevent great loss of life. In that case, it might be thought to be morally justified for each screw-thief who contributed to causing a ship to sink be held *fully legally responsible* for the loss of life, notwithstanding that his causal contribution to the sinking might be minute. This being so, it might be further argued that each such screw-thief is also *fully morally responsible* for any loss of life. If so, then the establishment of institutional arrangements can evidently transform prior *partial* moral responsibility for an adverse outcome (e.g., prior to the existence of a relevant law) into *full* moral responsibility (post the enactment of the law). Moreover, it can do so notwithstanding that the underlying causal responsibility is unchanged and is only *partial causal* responsibility for the adverse outcome.

A final claim concerning the relationships between moral responsibility and institutional responsibility is that institutional arrangements assign moral responsibilities to agents that those agents did not previously have and, indeed, in some cases that no agent previously had.[31] In the case of the institutional role of police officer, for example, the moral basis appears to be aggregate human security. Each member of a community has an individual human right to, say, some minimum level of security, if he or she needs it. It is only when a certain threshold of aggregate need exists, however, that the establishment of an institution takes place. For example, a police organization with its constitutive institutional role occupants – police officers – is not established because a single person's right to security is not being realized. When such a threshold of aggregate need exists, what is required is collective or joint action on the part of many persons. Accordingly, a cooperative enterprise or institution is established that has as a collective end the provision of security to the needy many by means of the joint activity of the police officer members of the police institution. In

---

[31] Miller, *Moral Foundations of Social Institutions*; and Miller, "Joint Epistemic Action and Collective Moral Responsibility." For a contrary view, see Bernard Gert, *Common Morality* (Oxford University Press, 2007).

such cases a collective good is, in effect, *institutionally embodied* as a means to discharge a prior collective moral responsibility to ensure the availability of that good.

The (collective) duty to assist may, then, in certain cases, imply the duty to establish and support institutions to achieve the object of the duty. Once such institutions with their specialized role occupants are in place it may be that we generally have no further duty to assist within the area of the institutions' operations. Indeed, it may be that generally we should not even *try* to assist, given our relative lack of expertise and the likelihood that we will get in the way of the role occupants. Moreover, these specialized role occupants have duties that they did not have before and, indeed, that no-one had before the establishment of the institutional role with its specific duties. For example, police officers may have an institutional and, indeed now, *moral* duty to put themselves in harm's way in a manner and to an extent that is not morally required of ordinary citizens and, indeed, that was never morally required of anyone prior to the establishment of police organizations.

Once institutions and their constitutive roles have been established on some adequate moral basis, such as the duty to aid, then those who undertake these roles necessarily put themselves under obligations of various kinds – obligations that attach to, and are in part constitutive of, those roles. To understand the specific content of institutional role morality, then, we need to examine the purposes – to meet aggregate security needs, in the case of police officers – that the various institutions and their constitutive roles have been formed to serve, and the way in which roles must be constructed in order to achieve those purposes. Of course, one only comes to have an institutional role through voluntary action, but the morality that comes with that role is not itself ultimately grounded in the individual's choice but rather in the larger purposes (collective ends) of the role, or so the argument goes.

6.4 Conclusion

In this chapter I have distinguished between natural, institutional, and moral responsibility, and between individual and collective responsibility. I have argued that collective responsibility can be understood as joint responsibility. I have distinguished institutional responsibility in the context of joint action, joint institutional mechanisms, multi-layered structures of joint action, and chains of institutional responsibility. I have argued that the individual human agents who perform the institutional actions involved in these various institutional forms can be held individually and collectively (i.e., jointly) morally responsible for the (morally significant) collective ends realized by these institutional actions. I have further argued that even in the case of morally significant institutional actions, moral responsibility does not precisely track institutional responsibility.

PART II

Anti-Corruption: Practice

CHAPTER 7

Integrity Systems

Part I of this book, i.e., Chapters 1–6, has consisted of philosophical analyses of the key theoretical notions to be utilized throughout this work, namely, institutions, institutional corruption, institutional power, salient specific forms of corruption (bribery, nepotism, fraud and abuse of authority), and collective institutional and moral responsibility. It is now time to turn from theory to practice and, in particular, to the elaboration of anti-corruption systems or, more broadly, integrity systems. The emphasis in Part II (Chapters 7–10) is on integrating the philosophical (normative institutional) theory, analyses, and perspectives provided in Part I with broad brush empirical description in the service of outlining the general features of efficacious and ethical accountability mechanisms, and anti-corruption and integrity systems, and key institutional components thereof. I begin with an account of the general features of integrity systems; this is the content of this chapter. In Chapter 8 I focus on a central feature of any anti-corruption or integrity system that is fit for purpose, namely, investigations. In Chapter 9 I elaborate an integrity system for occupational groups and, especially, the professions. In Chapter 10 I discuss a critical feature of anti-corruption and integrity systems, namely, whistleblowing: individuals that investigators and, more generally, anti-corruption systems heavily rely on.

7.1 Integrity Systems

Integrity systems can be contrasted with structures of laws and regulations, albeit they overlap and, indeed, the latter are in part constitutive of integrity systems. Legal and regulatory structures obviously consist in part of explicit laws and regulations governing morally significant behavior; criminal laws are an obvious example. Moreover, these laws and regulations are issued by some institutional authority and backed by sanctions. Such structures serve to ensure compliance with minimum moral or ethical standards (namely those embodied in a law, rule, or regulation), but this is only one of their purposes. There are numerous laws, rules, and regulations that have little or nothing to do with morality or ethics. An integrity system, by contrast, is an assemblage of institutional entities, mechanisms, and procedures, the fundamental purpose (collective end) of which is to ensure compliance with minimum *moral* standards, and to promote the pursuit of *ethical* ideals, among members of occupations, organizations, and industries, i.e., among institutional role occupants. Given that, as we have seen, corruption is at bottom a matter of immorality, combating corruption is a central feature of integrity systems; indeed, it is a core component of the collective end of an integrity system.

Given the significant differences between occupations, organizations, and industries with respect to the nature of the constitutive activity and purposes of their respective members, there are, and ought to be, corresponding differences in integrity systems; when it comes to integrity systems, it is not a matter of "one size fits all." For example, integrity systems for nonmarket-based occupations, such as doctors and lawyers, will need to go beyond the ethical norms and ideals of good commercial practice. Specifically, they will need to address the requirement that the professions in question are realizing their defining collective end, e.g., serving the ends of good health or justice. Moreover, they will also need to ensure that professional rights are protected, professional duties discharged, and professional virtues promoted and exercised. For example, an adequate integrity system will protect professional autonomy while ensuring professional accountability.

But we need to get clearer about integrity systems.[1] The term "integrity system" has recently come into vogue in relation to what is in fact a very ancient problem for organizations, occupational groups, and, indeed, whole polities and communities, namely the problem of promoting ethical behavior and eliminating or reducing crime, corruption and other immoral behavior.

Here the term "system" is somewhat misleading in that it implies a clear and distinct set of integrated institutional mechanisms operating in unison and in accordance with determinate mechanical, or at least quasi-mechanical, principles. However, in practice integrity "systems" are a messy assemblage of formal and informal devices and processes, and they operate in often indeterminate, unpredictable, and sometimes even conflicting ways. That said, it is necessary that this assemblage has

---

[1] See Miller, Roberts, and Spence, *Corruption and Anti-Corruption*, chapter 7; Miller, *Moral Foundations of Social Institutions*, chapter 5; Alexandra and Miller, *Integrity Systems for Occupations*.

some structure so that its elements are not in conflict but rather reinforce one another. Accordingly, this assemblage ought to constitute a web of institutional interdependence (see Chapter 1 Section 1.8) and one that is given direction and shape by governments in their role as meta-institutions. Naturally, the individual institutional components of integrity systems are typically subject to analysis in terms of our theoretical notions of organizational action (multi-layered structures of joint action) and joint institutional mechanisms and their particular defining collective ends (which are collective goods) (see Chapter 1). For example, an integrity system for a police organization ought to have as one of its collective ends to reduce police corruption in that organization (see Chapter 13). Moreover, the relevant individual institutional actors in such specialized anti-corruption or integrity systems can be held, at least in principle, collectively, i.e., jointly, morally responsible for its successes and failures in the manner outlined in Chapter 6.

The term "integrity," as used in the expression "integrity system," is also problematic in that it appropriates a moral notion normally used to describe individual human agents and applies it to organizations and other large groups of individuals. By contrast with the notion of an individual person's integrity, integrity used in the context that we are employing it here is of an integrity system for an occupation, organization, or industry. As such, the notion of an integrity system applies to institutional arrangements such as relevant fragments of legal and regulatory frameworks, criminal justice agencies (e.g., the police), oversight bodies (e.g., independent commissions against corruption), and representative bodies, (e.g., American Medical Association), as well as sub-institutional components of institutions (e.g., complaints and discipline committees, whistleblower protection processes, anti-fraud and anti-corruption units within corporations).

The integrity of an occupational or organizational group is in large part dependent on the individual integrity of its members, and therefore an integrity system is in large part focused on developing and maintaining the individual integrity of these members. Nevertheless, these groups are not simply the sum of its members, and so determining the integrity level for any of these groups is not simply a matter of summing the levels of integrity of the individuals who happen to be its members.

In the first place, the individuals who comprise the occupations and organizations in question are institutional role occupants, and the responsibilities and virtues required of them are somewhat different from, and often in some respects greater than, those required of ordinary individual persons not occupying such roles. So, for instance, scrupulous attention to numerical detail might be a constitutive virtue of the role of an accountant and suspiciousness a virtue for detectives, but neither of these are virtues in the role of a wife, husband, or friend. And, of course, the responsibilities and attendant competencies required of the senior manager, farmer, lawyer, police officer, medical doctor, or engineer are not typically required of ordinary individual persons not occupying such roles.

Moreover, what counts as an institutional responsibility or virtue, both in terms of technical and ethical competencies, varies greatly across different occupational and organizational groups. The technical competencies for which the banker, trader, chemist, academic, lawyer, medical doctor, or engineer are each responsible are not common *across* these groups. Similarly, the virtues are often role specific.

While, arguably, the "zealous advocacy of one's client's interests" is a critical virtue to the role of a lawyer or barrister in adversarial legal systems, it is clearly not a critical virtue for the car salesperson or financial trader. So what counts as integrity in an individual institutional role occupant is neither wholly captured by what counts as integrity in an ordinary person or what counts as integrity in some other occupational or organizational role. One important task then, for specific institutional roles is to determine what precisely the constitutive virtues of the individual role-occupant are, and devise strategies to ensure that these virtues are developed and maintained in the members of that occupation, organization, or industry.

In the second place, the integrity of an occupational or organizational group is not simply a matter of the integrity of the individual role occupants who comprise these groups. The integrity of an institution is partly a matter of the structure, purpose (collective end), and culture of the occupation or organization *qua* institution. Consider structure, both legal and administrative. In an occupation or organization possessed of integrity, the administrative processes and procedures in relation to, for example, promotion or complaints and discipline, would embody relevant ethical principles of fairness, procedural justice, transparency, and the like.

Now consider purpose (collective ends that are also collective goods). In an occupational or organizational group possessed of integrity, the occupational or organizational goals actually being pursued would align closely with the collective ends, i.e., collective goods, of the occupation or organization, such as, for example, the promotion of security of depositors' funds for bankers or of human health for doctors, rather than merely with purely commercial considerations. Finally, consider culture. In an occupation or organization possessed of integrity, the pervasive *ethos* or spirit, i.e., the culture, would be one that was, for example, conducive to high performance, both technically and ethically, and supportive in times of need, but intolerant of serious incompetence, corruption, or other unethical conduct.

In looking at options to promote integrity and combat ethical failures it is very easy to leap to a particular single "magic bullet" solution, like increasing penalties or giving more intrusive powers to investigative agencies or giving immunity to those offenders prepared to testify against their fellow offenders[2], and doing so without considering the full array of implications, including the demonstrable (as opposed to "hoped for") benefits (which of these measures has been tested and, as a consequence, is *known* to work?), and the costs in terms of resources, damage to occupational or organizational trust, and so on.

"Magic bullet" solutions are often offered in relative ignorance of both the actual nature and causes of the problems that they are supposed to address. The truth is often in the detail. Moreover, the question should always be asked: solution for who and over what time-frame? Perhaps the alleged solution is merely a short term fix for a single organization rather than a long-term solution for an industry. For instance many organizations are accused of quietly "letting go" persons who have engaged in corrupt or criminal behavior, rather than seeking to have them prosecuted, and doing so to protect the organization's reputation, notwithstanding that the offender in question is now a threat to other organizations. Moreover, such self-interested 'solutions' come at the expense of the legitimate interests of consumers or the public at large.

There are at least two other significant factors commonly in play. First, there is the difficulty of making reliable judgments (as opposed to merely harboring suspicions) or, relatedly, of gathering sufficient evidence for a prosecution. Second and, again, relatedly, there is the highly litigious nature of some of the areas in question, e.g., lawsuits in relation to alleged professional incompetence.

In short, promoting integrity and combating ethical failures, notably corruption, is far from straightforward. However, it is critical that the nature of these corruption (and other ethical) problems, and in particular their causes, are first identified prior to rushing to implement any putative solution, "magic bullet" or otherwise.

In attempting to determine the causes of corrupt practices, there are a number of preliminary questions that need to be addressed. One set of questions pertains to the precise nature of the practice at issue, and the

---

[2] This is a species of a more general strategy of exploiting the immoral characters of, and lack of trust between, offenders. See Lambsdorf, *Institutional Economics of Corruption and Reform*.

context in which it occurs. What is the structure of the corrupt practice, e.g., what is the "favor" asked by the briber or the bribe and what is the benefit going to the bribe? What is the motivation of the parties to the corrupt transaction, e.g., personal gain in the form of money, collective organizational gain in terms of market advantage? Are there powerful corruption drivers present, e.g., those who refuse to pay bribes are refused tender contracts? What opportunities might there be to engage in this corrupt practice, e.g., wide discretionary powers in relation to allocation of resources. What are the relations of interdependence between corrupt actors engaged in corrupt activity? What opportunities do these relations of dependence afford anti-corruption officers in their efforts to combat corrupt activity? What are the accountability mechanisms or lack thereof, e.g., lack of a well-resourced, independent, oversight agency with intrusive powers of investigation in relation to politicians and senior bureaucrats? Another set of questions concerns the extent of the corruption or unethical practice: Is it sporadic or continuing, restricted to a few "rotten apples" or systemic? Does it reach up into the upper echelons? Is it grand corruption? Here, as elsewhere, rhetoric is no substitute for evidence-based conclusions.

Even when the answers to these questions have been provided there will arise further questions in relation to any remedies proposed. For example, any contemplation of mechanisms to redress corruption and other forms of misconduct that will require the expenditure of energy and resources – and may well impinge on individual freedom – needs to be justified in terms of the seriousness and extent of the corruption or other misconduct in question as well as the efficacy of these mechanisms.

Understanding the causes of corruption and other misconduct and designing remedies to address them will involve distinguishing between, and taking into account, at least the three sorts of motivation for compliance with moral principles that have already been noted in this work. One reason for compliance is the fear of punishment, including as a result of betrayal by co-offenders: "sticks." A second reason for compliance arises from the benefit to oneself: "carrots." These two reasons are essentially appeals to self-interest; taken together they constitute the "stick-carrot" approach. However, there is a third reason for compliance: one's belief that the corrupt action is morally wrong and one's desire to do what is morally right.

Here we need first to note the contrast between appeals to moral beliefs and appeals to self-interest. What is right or good is not conceptually equivalent to what is in one's interest; indeed, the problem of devising anti-corruption systems stems in large part from the fact that morality and self-interest are often in conflict. Relatedly, the motive of acting from a concern to do what is right or good is not the same thing as acting out of self-interest and does not depend on it. Indeed, moral motives can and often do trump the motive of individual self-interest. This is perhaps most obvious in the case of individual who are motivated by collective self-interest at the expense of their individual self-interest, e.g., soldiers who sacrifice their lives for their comrades, parents who make sacrifices for their children, workers who work long hours on behalf of the firm without commensurate individual reward.

Here we need to distinguish between individual self-interest and collective self-interest, and also between collective self-interest and collective goods. The former is obvious enough, the latter perhaps less so. Consider, therefore, the collective self-interest of members of a group of corrupt police officers, and the collective good of the institution (the police organization) to which the members of the group belong. Speaking generally, morality is on the side of the police officers who act in the service of the collective good of the institution rather than in the collective self-interest of some of its members. (It is also true that the collective self-interest of the members of a group may well be at odds with the individual self-interest of some of the members of the group, e.g., a single ambitious police officer.)

Notwithstanding these conceptual differences between individual self-interest, collective self-interest, and the moral motive to do what is right, there are also important connections to be highlighted and promoted. Self-interest and morality are, at least potentially, in considerable harmony. First, of course, the appeal to morality must be balanced by the appeal to self-interest. If, for instance, it is at great cost to one's self to be, say, honest or fair, then one may have sufficient reason to not be honest or fair. Second, self-interest can be shaped by moral considerations. Consider in this connection the induction processes of the professions involving the internalization of the collective goods definitive of those professions. If successful, the individual self-interest of (say) a doctor consists in part in saving the lives, and otherwise promoting the health, of his or her patients.

It is evident that widespread and ongoing compliance typically requires appeals to self-interest (sticks and carrots) but also appeals to moral beliefs. Ideally, integrity systems should have penalties for those who do not comply, should enable benefits to flow to those who do comply, and should resonate with the moral beliefs of the people thus regulated; for instance, laws and regulations should be widely thought to be fair and reasonable.

Thus, institutional design that proceeds on the assumption that self-interest, individual or collective, is the only human motivation worth considering fails. It fails because it overlooks the centrality of moral beliefs in human life, and therefore does not mobilize moral sentiment. On the other hand, institutional design that proceeds on the assumption that self-interest can be ignored, and that a sense of moral duty on its own will suffice, also fails; it fails because self-interest is an ineradicable and pervasive feature of all human groups. In this connection I note the importance of reputation to self-interest; reputational loss can have a devastating impact on members of the profession, notably in financial terms. In Section 9.5 I provide a detailed discussion of reputation and role that the mobilization of reputation can play in enhancing integrity systems.

7.2   Reactive Integrity Systems

Integrity systems can be thought of as being either predominantly reactive or predominantly preventive.[3] Naturally, the distinction is somewhat artificial, since there is a need for both reactive elements, e.g., criminal investigations, a complaints and discipline system, as well as preventive elements, e.g., ethics training and transparency of processes, in any adequate integrity system. Nevertheless, integrity systems can be considered under the two broad headings, reactive and preventive.

Reactive mechanisms for dealing with corrupt behavior are fundamentally linear: setting out a series of offences (usually in legislation or regulations), waiting for an individual to transgress, then investigating, adjudicating, and finally taking punitive action. Criminal investigations and adjudications, and complaints and discipline systems are basically reactive institutional mechanisms. Naturally, these systems are also preventative mechanisms by virtue of their deterrence role; however, the adequacy of this deterrence role is typically dependent on their effectiveness *qua* reactive mechanisms, i.e., their success in detecting, investigating, and prosecuting offenders.

Reactive integrity mechanisms are a necessary part of any feasible integrity system. Sometimes, however, too much reliance is placed on them, and the weaknesses of the reactive approach are made manifest. One obvious weakness is the passivity of the approach; by the time the investigators swing into action, the damage has been already done. Another problem stems from the fact that corrupt behavior is often secretive, e.g., a bribe might be known only to the briber and bribee (both of whom have an

---

[3] An earlier version of the material in this section and the following two sections appeared in Miller, Roberts, and Spence, *Corruption and Anti-Corruption*, chapter 7.

interest in keeping the transaction secret); professional associations may "close ranks" to protect the reputation of the group.

Yet a further problem stems from the inadequacy of the resources to investigate and successfully prosecute the huge volume of corrupt activity; investigation and prosecution are resource intensive. Consider fraud in this connection. Fraud is widespread in modern economies, yet police and other agencies simply do not have the resources to investigate adequately all the reports of fraud brought to their attention. Yet if the chances of being caught or complained about are relatively slight due to under-resourcing, the deterrent effect is undermined, which in turn means there are an even larger number of offences and offenders for investigators to deal with.

Of course, the effectiveness of a reactive approach requires that significant detection mechanisms are available. Those who engage in corruption, crime, and other serious misconduct have at least two good reasons to fear exposure: first, detection may lead to legal or associational sanctions, such as imprisonment, fines, suspension, or expulsion from the industry, and second, it may lead to moral sanctions emanating from work colleagues, community, and from significant others, e.g., friends and relatives. Nevertheless, there are a number of sources of intelligence in relation to most forms of corruption. One of the most important is fellow-workers who may report such conduct or suspicious activity to superiors, or even blow the whistle.

Having considered the general nature of the reactive approach to dealing with ethical misconduct, it is now necessary to examine two central planks of the linear and logical progression that proceeds from the offences that are set down in legislation and in regulations, moves to the detection of the offence and its investigation, and finally to prosecution and the imposition of punishment – namely, the legal and regulatory framework and the investigative process. It is clear that corruption embraces a wide variety of activities ranging from serious criminal offences, e.g., major embezzlement, through to noncriminal professional misconduct that may warrant disciplinary measures, e.g., a relatively minor conflict of interest. For the purposes of this analysis, I will concentrate upon corruption that is identified in criminal codes and is subject to criminal investigation processes; I do so on the understanding that the criminal justice system represents the most salient and sophisticated, reactive institutional response to combating serious forms of corruption. Note that in Chapter 8 I provide a detailed examination of investigations, and in Section 9.4 an examination of complaints and discipline systems and, therefore, of the reactive response to noncriminal corruption (and other forms of misconduct).

7.2.1 Legislative and Regulatory Frameworks

Almost every jurisdiction has criminal laws against self-evident forms of serious corruption by institutional actors in organizational and occupational settings, such as offering or soliciting bribes, fraud, and abusing the authority of a public office. While it is common for anti-corruption laws and other criminal laws to be consolidated into a criminal code, it is almost universal that legislation dealing with particular areas of activity, like the regulation of companies and corporations, will also contain criminal offence provisions. In essence, these provisions will be dealing with the same issues of abuse of office, bribery, fraud, and so on, but in a more specific context.

At the core of dealing with serious ethical misconduct using reactive mechanisms is the codification of the community's moral attitudes into statutes, regulations, or other such instruments. These are enacted by a legislature and embody a fragment of the basic social norms of the community. By virtue of embodying social norms in a community, anti-corruption laws and the like reflect the moral beliefs of the community; by virtue of being laws passed by the duly elected representatives of the community, criminal law reflects the will of the community.

The creation and maintenance of a legislative regime to deal with corruption and other serious ethical misconduct involves a number of difficulties. As the Global Financial Crisis and its aftermath have served to underline yet again, in the sphere of commercial activity there is an ever-present financial incentive to find ways to avoid compliance with laws and regulations. As a consequence, there is a constant need to monitor compliance with the regulatory system in order either to ensure that new forms of corruption have not been found, or if they have, to enable legislative changes to be made to defeat them. This is presumably so in the case of the so-called toxic financial products that were part of the cause of the GFC, i.e., non-transparent packaged bundles of mortgages (including sub-prime mortgages) incorrectly assessed by ratings agencies as high quality on the spurious grounds that the investment banks that packaged them allegedly had good risk assessment processes. Given its infamy and the availability of detailed analyses, consider the case of Enron. Here an array of techniques was used to undermine the regulatory framework existing at that time, including so-called Special Purpose Entities (SPEs).

SPEs, which were a specialty of Andrew Fastow (Enron's Chief Financial Officer), were initially introduced by banks and law firms as "structured finance" – complex financial deals intended to enable companies to generate tax deductions and move assets off a company's books.[4] With names such as Cactus, Braveheart, Whitewing, JEDI, Chewco, Raptors, LJM I, and LJM II (named after Fastow's wife Lea and his two children), Enron used SPEs for various purposes. The primary purpose was for financing new projects in Enron's ever-expanding trading business, which continuously needed new injections of cash funds to sustain that expansion, as well as providing insurance hedging for those projects whilst managing – sometimes legally, but mostly not – to keep debt related to those projects off its balance sheet, whilst taking up earnings relating to those projects in its income statements. For his role in those SPEs, Andrew Fastow reportedly made more than US$45 million. In the wake of the revelations concerning Fastow's key role in the Enron SPEs, especially Chewco and LJM – and just one month prior to Enron's final collapse and bankruptcy on 2 December 2001 – the company was forced to restate its earnings from 1997 through to 2002, which required a US$1.2 billion equity write-down.

The Enron collapse and the damage wrought on the international financial system by toxic financial products have highlighted the difficulty that legislatures face in establishing and maintaining a regulatory regime in such complex and rapidly changing fields. Moreover, there is a range of often-competing regulatory models on offer, e.g., "light touch" self-regularity models less in vogue post the GFC. Let us turn to a brief consideration of some of these.

7.2.2 Regulatory Models

As we have already noted, regulatory frameworks are simply one element of the overall integrity system. However, they are an increasingly important element in the architecture of integrity systems and there are a variety of models on offer. Here it needs to be kept in mind that the term "regulation" as used in regulatory frameworks, regimes, etc. has come to have an expanded and vague meaning.[5] I want to resist what I regard as an expansion into unclarity; however, it is not always possible to do so when discussing the work of others. This is the case in the following section. Specifically, some of what is referred to below as regulation is by my lights either not the process of regulation properly understood but some other

---

[4] See Peter Behr and April Witt, "Visionary's Dream Led to Risky Business," *Washington Post*, July 28, 2002.
[5] See Arie Freiberg, *The Tools of Regulation* (Sydney: Federation Press, 2010).

process, e.g., influencing behavior, or it is not the process of regulation per se but rather the institutional entity or entities thus regulated, e.g., the regulatory state. Moreover, there is some degree of dispute and confusion among occupations/industry bodies and commentators/analysts as to how the regulatory spectrum should be broken up and classified into distinct regulatory models or modes. However, there are a number of more or less distinct regulatory models. These include self-regulation, meta-regulation, and "black-letter law" explicit government regulation. Of these, self-regulation implies minimal government intervention and, therefore, stands in contrast with "black-letter law" explicit government regulation at the other end of the spectrum.

These models of regulation are, of course, also different from particular integrity mechanisms that might be subject to regulation, such as codes of conduct, disciplinary procedures, entry restrictions (e.g., minimum qualifications, licensing, registration). Many of these integrity mechanisms can be subject to regulation in the context of a number of different regulatory models, although some integrity mechanisms will be more commodious with some regulatory models than others.

In *self- regulatory* models, obligations to comply with codes of conduct and other regulating requirements are voluntarily adopted by members of an occupational group or industry. Members' obligations are contractual in the sense that they are based on a voluntary agreement, usually with their industry body or occupational group. The occupational or industry group undertakes to provide members with certain benefits in exchange for them abiding by the group's membership requirements.

The occupational group is solely responsible for regulating the conduct of its members, and for applying sanctions for breaches of conduct (e.g., disciplinary measures such as letters of warning or fines). Neither the occupational group's conduct requirements nor the sanctions it imposes are legislatively underpinned, and the government does not directly intervene by way of ensuring members' conduct, applying sanctions, monitoring the group's practices, or by assisting the occupational group to do any of these.

Evidently, self-regulatory models are appropriate for minor ethical misconduct, including relatively minor forms of corruption. Moreover, they can have the virtue of limiting the burden and costs of over-regulation. However, they tend to under-regulate and can be ineffective in relation to serious forms of corruption, including corruption that might not constitute criminality. For example, self-regulatory models often tolerate structural conflicts of interest that are highly conducive to corruption. Consider, in this connection, financial advisors who are employed by the very financial institutions who manufacture the financial products that they sell. On the other hand, self-regulatory models may be appropriate for certain occupational groups such as journalists. In the case of journalists, government intervention is arguably problematic, given the role of the so-called Fourth Estate in holding governments to account. Arguably, government intervention will result in a free press being muzzled.

In the case of "*black-letter" explicit government regulatory models* there are no self-developed, voluntarily adopted, or self-administered codes or standards by occupational/industry bodies. Whatever codes or standards or requirements apply to occupations/industries, these are all generated by government through explicit legislation, and enforced by the government through legal sanctions. Explicit "black letter law" government regulation is typified by legislatively imposed occupational standards, codes of conduct, and practice requirements; government inspection and monitoring to detect non-compliance; and punitive sanctions. This model is open to the charge of creating the unnecessary burden of overregulation. On the other hand, this model may be appropriate for some industries, such as the nuclear industry, where safety concerns are paramount.

The "meta" in *meta-regulatory models* refers to government regulation of occupational and industry groups' self-regulation arrangements. Rather than the government seeking to regulate occupations and organizations directly through statutes and other coercively backed measures, it allows representative groups to directly regulate themselves (self-regulate), but adopts a monitoring and accountability role, and seeks to ensure that the self-regulatory procedures the occupational group adopts are applied and adhered to appropriately. This procedural oversighting by the government is expressly specified in the relevant statutory or legislative provisions as a condition of an occupational group or industry being allowed to self-regulate. Accordingly, meta-regulatory models seek to have the best of both worlds. On the one hand, they allow self-regulation and hence avoid over-regulation. On the other hand, they provide for accountability mechanisms and, therefore, arguably prevent the worst excesses of under-regulation. Meta-regulatory models seem appropriate for many occupational groups and industries; however, as the examples of the journalists and the nuclear industry seem to indicate, perhaps not for all.

In conclusion: what goes for integrity systems in general goes for regulatory models in particular. It is a matter of "horses for courses" rather than "one size fits all."

7.3 Preventative Integrity Systems

A preventive integrity system will typically embrace, or act in tandem with, a reactive integrity system. However, we can consider preventive mechanisms for dealing with ethico-professional misconduct independent of any reactive elements. If we do so, we see that they can be divided into four categories:

- Institutional mechanisms for promoting an environment in which integrity is rewarded and, as a consequence, unethical behavior is discouraged; this is an attempt to reduce the desire or *motivation* to act unethically, so that opportunities for unethical behavior are not pursued or taken, even when they arise.
- Institutional mechanisms for reducing the *capacity* of those who might otherwise have the motivation to engage in corruption, e.g., legislation to downsize oligopolists in order to prevent cartels;
- An array of institutional mechanisms that limit (or eliminate) the *opportunity* for unethical behavior. Such mechanisms include corporate governance mechanisms, such as separating the roles of receiving accounts and paying accounts to reduce the opportunity for fraud.
- Those institutional mechanisms that act to expose unethical behavior, so that the organization or community can deal with them. The term "*transparency*" may be used to characterize these mechanisms.

I accept that this fourfold distinction is somewhat artificial, and that some institutional mechanisms will in fact come under more than one heading, and indeed that some, e.g., regulations, have both a reactive and a preventive role.

The first category in our breakdown of prevention mechanisms are those institutional processes that exist to promote ethical behavior. This category is made up of those components of an integrity system that engage with the individual's desire to do what is morally right and avoid what is morally wrong, and to be morally approved of by others for so acting (see Chapter 2 Section 2.3). These institutional instruments include codes of ethics and professional development programs. I discuss codes of ethics in Chapter 9 Section 9.3. The second category consists in large part of macro-structural reforms that limit the power of organizations or industries or government relative to other institutions or to the community as a whole. I discuss a number of such reforms in Chapters 11, 12, and 14. Let me turn to the third category.

7.3.1   Reducing Opportunities for Unethical Behavior

An important aspect of integrity systems is in the reduction of opportunities for individuals and organizations to engage in unethical behavior. There are multifarious institutional mechanisms devised to reduce such opportunities ranging from physical security (e.g., safes, locks and keys, computer passwords, firewalls), and personnel security (e.g., background checks, surveillance and monitoring of employees), through to role specifications (e.g., investigators not being subject to the authority of those who they investigate), and the design of mechanisms to deal with known sources of ethical misconduct (e.g., conflicts of interest).

Some mechanisms in this regard are:

- Separation of financial functions, e.g., accounts payable divided from accounts receivable.
- Conflict of interest prohibitions for individuals, e.g., conflicting financial interests, outside employment (see Chapter 9 Section 9.6).
- Elimination of structural conflicts of interest (see Chapter 9 Section 9.6). For example, Arthur Andersen was Enron's auditor and yet earned US $52m in fees in 2000 from Enron – indeed, Enron was AA's largest client, and acted as Enron's management consultant.
- "Revolving door" restrictions on public officials leaving their positions to work for companies whose business it is to lobby governments, or that have significant business dealings with governments. The concern arises from the suspicion that prior to leaving, the officials will set up (in secret) highly lucrative deals so as to attract high salaries from their future employers, and/or use their extensive social contacts within government to give their new employer an unfair advantage.
- Eliminate excessive payments to management. Consider the recent widespread media reports post the GFC relating to huge payments to executives, in some cases 100s of times that of employees.[6]
- Limit executive stock options so as to reduce the interest executives might have in ignoring suspect deals that if terminated would negatively impact on the share price.
- Stringent accountability mechanisms to deal with power imbalances between superiors and subordinates in relation to, for example, promotion within an organization.
- Independent auditing; the knowledge that an independent body will be examining the financial records of an organization acts to inhibit unethical

---

[6] Reich, *Saving Capitalism*, chapters 10–12.

activity. For example, Enron staff deliberately ignored accepted accounting practice in the valuing of assets when they conspired with the banks to represent loans as profits.

- Tendering and contracting procedures, including requirements to advertise tenders, to make clear specification of the work to be done and of the criteria for success in the tender process, to establish systems to guarantee that tenders are not accessed by persons other than the designated authorities.

7.3.2   Transparency

Let us now turn to the last of the salient types of preventative mechanisms for dealing with serious unethical behavior, namely transparency mechanisms. One of the most important conditions conducive to corruption and many other forms of unethical behavior is secretiveness. Hence the importance of transparency mechanisms – mechanisms that ensure that transactions are conducted openly, and/or are subject to appropriate scrutiny.

At a national level a fully functioning parliamentary system plays a central role in deterring ethical misconduct in the public sector, for public sector officials are required to go through a detailed and rigorous process in relation to their expenditure of public monies and their exercise of the powers vested in the public offices that they occupy. Congressional committees in the United States, and parliamentary committees in the United Kingdom and Australia, play a crucial role in making officials accountable for their actions by using powers to require those officials to explain their actions. At a less dramatic level, there are a variety of public institutions that operate to enable the community to be assured that officials are acting in accordance with the detailed accounting requirements that are in place in the public sector. One of these is the Auditor-General (or the General Accounting Office in the United States). Reports of these bodies make transparent the details of expenditure of public monies.

Operating at yet another level are those mechanisms of transparency that enable citizens to access reasons for decisions that affect them (Administrative Appeals Tribunal Act, Administrative Decisions (Judicial Review) Act) and information (Freedom of Information Act, Privacy Act, Archives Act). All the mechanisms described above operate to open the workings of government to scrutiny and therefore enable the community to assess whether they are being governed in a way that meets their expectations of integrity.

A parallel, though typically less onerous, set of transparency mechanisms operate in the commercial sphere. Companies are required to file certain reports about their activities and these are made public. The intent behind these processes is to make key decisions transparent, and to assist the community in making judgments about investments. These transparency mechanisms have the force of law, and failure to comply with them is a criminal offence.

Before leaving the role of transparency, it is necessary to note the crucial role the media plays in the exposure of serious ethical misconduct, and therefore, if the other mechanisms are operating effectively, in reducing unethical behavior. A vibrant and free media is essential in bringing to the community's attention corruption and other serious forms of unethical behavior – whether they occur in the corporate sector, like Enron, or in the public sector. I return to this issue in Chapter 14 Section 14.3.

7.4 Holistic Integrity Systems

Thus far in the analysis of integrity systems, I have looked at integrity systems and mechanisms under the headings of reactive systems and preventive systems. It is evident that in most societies, jurisdictions, and indeed organizations, the attempt to combat unethical behavior involves both of the above. That is, integrity-building strategies involve reactive systems as well as preventive systems, and within preventive systems there are mechanisms that promote ethical behavior, there are corporate governance mechanisms with, e.g., anti-corruption functions, and there are various transparency mechanisms.

Moreover, it seems clear that an adequate integrity system cannot afford to do without reactive as well as preventive systems, and that preventive systems need to have all the elements detailed above. This suggests that there are two important issues. The first is the adequacy of each of the elements of the above systems. For example, how adequate are the complaints and discipline processes including the investigative capacity thereof?; how effective are the mechanisms of transparency? The second issue pertains to the level of integration and congruence between the reactive and the preventive systems; to what extent do they act together to mutually reinforce one another?

In this connection, it is worth noting that many jurisdictions have "watchdog" agencies. Such bodies are established by statutes that also define a range of offences and have powers to investigate and refer matters to the courts for prosecution. However, it is notable that these watchdog agencies also involve themselves in prevention programs involving the development of preventive mechanisms; many no longer see their role as merely that of a reactive agency. We should think of effective integrity systems, therefore, as holistic in character, and conceive of specific integrity building mechanisms as elements of a holistic integrity system. In looking at the set of integrity building processes as a holistic system, we need first to remind ourselves what is presupposed by an integrity system.

First, and most obviously, there must be some shared moral values in relation to the moral unacceptability of specific forms of behavior, and a disapproval of those who engage in such behavior. That is, there needs to be a framework of accepted social norms (see Chapter 2 Section 2.3). Second, there needs to be a broadly shared conception in relation to what needs to be done (the institutional means) to minimize it (the collective end), e.g., should it be simply criminalized or should the response include restorative elements to enable offenders to be reintegrated into the relevant community having renounced their past wrongdoing (and perhaps paid some price for it)?[7] Third, there needs to be present some capacity to create and implement institutional mechanisms that deal with the issue of unethical behavior and corruption, and this presumes some form of legal or regulatory system and organizational structure. Here considerations of efficiency and effectiveness are important.

Finally, there needs to be some source of authority whereby sanctions can be applied to individuals who engage in unethical behavior. However, this needs to be done in the context of an understanding that, and a holistic integrity system in which, reducing unethical behavior is a *collective* moral responsibility and a collective responsibility that has been appropriately institutionally embedded (see Chapter 6 Section 6.3).

7.5 Conclusion

In this chapter I have outlined the notion of an integrity system, an institutional arrangement that has as one of its central purposes (collective good) to combat corruption. Accordingly, many of the institutional actors within the organizational and sub-organizational components of such systems have collective institutional and moral responsibilities derived in large part from those institutional purposes. We need to distinguish between

---

[7] See Seumas Miller and John Blackler, "Restorative Justice: Retribution, Confession and Shame" in J. Braithwaite and H. Strang (eds.), *Restorative Justice: From Philosophy to Practice* (Aldershot: Ashgate Press, 2000), pp. 77–93.

structures of laws and regulation, on the one hand, and integrity systems on the other (and between integrity systems and the narrower notion of an anti-corruption system). These overlap, but should not be confused. Moreover, we can distinguish between self-regulatory, black letter explicit government, and meta-regulatory models. As is the case with integrity systems in general, when it comes to regulatory models it is a matter of "horses for courses"; some regulatory models are more appropriate than others for particular occupational and industry groups. We can also usefully distinguish reactive integrity systems from preventative ones. I have argued that appropriately integrated blends of reactive and preventative integrity systems are, in general, to be preferred. I refer to these as holistic integrity systems. Finally, I have suggested that the effective implementation of holistic integrity systems requires the institutional embedding of the underlying collective moral responsibility for combating corruption.

CHAPTER 8

Investigations

In this chapter the focus is on a key feature of any anti-corruption or integrity system that is fit for purpose: investigations. I begin with a general account of investigations and some of the ethical problems that arise for investigators. In the next section I discuss a critical institutional feature of the investigative role: investigative independence. In ensuing sections I discuss some important investigative tools, namely, informants and traps (stings) and the ethical problems that they give rise to. Here, as elsewhere, the problem is to integrate ethics with efficacy.

Unlike, for example, murder, the victim of a crime of corruption is available, at least in principle, to provide evidence in relation to the crime, e.g., the nature of the goods stolen or the failed tender awarded to an undeserving competitor who paid a bribe. Such evidence might pertain to the who, what, where, when, and/or how of the crime. Unfortunately, crimes of corruption are typically done in secrecy, and so unlike, say, assaults, the victim is not able to identify the offender and, indeed, might not even be aware of the crime; moreover, there are often no witnesses to the crime. On the other hand, there is often *some* evidence of the crime and the offender, e.g., written, including emailed communications, depleted or inflated bank accounts. If, for example, the stolen goods or bribe-money are found to be in the possession of person A, then this is (prima facie) evidence that A stole it (or at least that A knows who stole it since A presumably received it from this person) or received the money as a bribe.

The direct victim of institutional corruption is sometimes an organization, e.g., a defrauded corporation, a systemically corrupt police force. However, even in these cases the indirect victim – the ultimate victim, so to speak – is a person or persons, e.g., the shareholder or the customers (corporate fraud), the bank's depositors (banking corruption and collapse), the community at large (tax evasion), victims of crime (compromised police investigations). This is so even if the precise amount of the financial or other loss suffered by any individual person as a consequence of the corruption cannot be specified because the impact of the crime is too indirect and diffuse, e.g., when a corporation passes on the loss to its customers by way of increased charges.

For a number of reasons, many crimes of corruption that are committed are not actually reported to the police or other investigative agencies. These reasons include the following ones.

(1) The crimes of corruption go undetected by the victims, e.g., bribes paid to officials for favors.

(2) There is a belief, on the part of the victim, that the police would or could do nothing about it, even if it was reported. This attitude often prevails in areas where there is a high level of corruption, including among police, politicians, and other public officials, and the population has lost faith in the police being able or willing to prevent crimes of corruption.

(3) Non-reporting may occur in areas in which there are minority ethnic populations who have an "us versus them" attitude to the majority population, are distrustful of police, and of the criminal justice system more generally.

(4) The victim is insured and simply makes a claim on their insurance policy.

(5) A major area of non-reporting of crimes of corruption is by financial institutions that are concerned about the reputational risk and, in any case, may protect themselves against losses from crime by, in effect, building in such losses as a business cost and, thereby, passing on the costs to their customers.

The morally problematic outcomes of not reporting crimes, including corruption, are multiple and include the following ones: (1) the harm done to the victim, e.g., the financial loss, might go unaddressed – bearing in mind that the failure to report might not be a failure on the part of the ultimate victim(s), as in the case of an organization that fails to report corruption and simply passes on the loss to its customers or shareholders; (2) the offender might escape justice; (3) other would-be offenders might be emboldened to commit corruption; (4) the criminal recording system might not be a (reasonably) accurate portrayal of corrupt activity in a jurisdiction, which in turn may impede the efforts of the police to combat corruption, e.g., due to misallocation of police resources; (5) as we have seen, corruption, by definition, undermines institutions by undermining institutional processes, persons (*qua* institutional actors), and institutional purposes (i.e., impedes the production of the collective goods that are the *raison d'etre* for institutions); and (6) the community might come to have the belief that the type of corruption in question can be committed with impunity, which in turn may cause the members of the community to lose faith in the ability of the police and anti-corruption agencies to protect them and themselves and their institutions from corruption.

8.1   Investigation of Crimes of Corruption

In cases where victims do contact the police, or crimes otherwise come to the attention of the police, an investigation typically takes place.[1] Traditional means of investigation involve an officer visiting the crime scene to take a detailed report of the crime and assess the scene to determine if a forensic specialist should examine it for fingerprints, forensic samples (e.g., saliva), physical evidence (e.g., tools), or computers left by the offender. Speed of enquiry is of the essence in order to ensure the recovery of any scientific evidence such as trace materials on the offender's body, on clothing, in vehicles, etc.

Enquiries would be made in the vicinity to find potential witnesses to the offence and, where available, local informants may be contacted for information. It is, however, not uncommon to find potential witnesses who are reluctant to speak to the police and even hold back or destroy important information to protect family, friends, and colleagues. There are a number of reasons for this lack of a willingness to be involved, but it can arise as a result of a previous personal experience as a witness or the reports of others who have come forward as witnesses. The court system in most countries is bureaucratic and typically regarded by those who come into contact with it, whether as offenders, victims, or witnesses, as insensitive to their needs and entitlements. For example, witnesses are often required to put themselves out by taking time off work and travelling to courts at some distance from their homes or workplaces, and yet the time taken off and the travel, meals, and other expenses incurred in being a witness are not adequately remunerated or, if they are, not in a timely fashion.

---

[1] An earlier more detailed version of the material in this section is to be found in Miller and Gordon, *Investigative Ethics: Ethics for Police Detectives and Criminal Investigators* chapter 6. For elaboration on the practicalities of property investigation, see Michael F. Brown, *Criminal Investigation: Law and Practice*, 2nd edn. (Boston: Butterworth-Heineman, 2001), chapter 10. On business investigations see Iain MacNeil, Keith Wotherspoon, and Kathryn Taylor, *Business Investigations* (Bristol: Jordan Publishing, 1998).

On occasion, the method by which a crime was committed (its modus operandi – MO) may be so unusual that it points to an offender who habitually uses that MO, for example, a Ponzi scheme in the financial sector. If the investigator has such knowledge of MO or recovers it by interrogating an intelligence database or from an informant, then a path to a suspect could open up. If the various lines of enquiry proved negative, it is usual for the crime to be quickly filed as undetected or unsolved. This decision would be made by the investigator then generally endorsed by a supervisor. The crime report would be filed pending any further development in the future. Investigation of property crimes, including many, but by no means all, crimes of corruption, are typically subjected to a triage process with respect to the extent of the investigation. Factors in play here include solvability in the light of the available evidence and of witnesses, type and location of offence, value of item stolen/damaged, harm done to victim, and so on.

Ideally, this process of prioritization should be unbiased and based on objective factors. However, in practice there will be occasions when public interest, media pressure, and, in some jurisdictions, political pressure may be brought to bear on decision-making in this regard and sometimes this will be difficult, if not impossible, to ignore. Such influences might need to be accommodated to a degree insofar as the allocation of resources is concerned, for example. However, they need to be resisted insofar as they are attempts to interfere with the investigative process itself, e.g., determination of suspects, evidence-gathering, and evaluation. Naturally, the ability to resist depends in large part on the institutional independence of both the police organization and the investigator.

With the advent of computer databases and intelligence-based policing, there is the opportunity to use bulk metadata and to deploy sophisticated new methods, such as machine learning, to help investigators conduct their investigation. Covert methods, such as intrusive surveillance, use of informants, and undercover operatives are also used in relation to organized crime and corruption. The availability of forensic technology to investigators has greatly improved the evidential link between crime scenes and offenders. DNA evidence has been used to solve property crimes in those countries with a database. It has been found that the collection and analysis of physical evidence, including DNA evidence, at crime scenes, not only improves the ability of investigators to identify, arrest, and prosecute offenders in crimes against the person, such as murder and rape, but also in property crimes.

Here, as elsewhere, investigators need to gather as much and as good evidence as possible. The weight of the totality of the available evidence (including both exculpatory and inculpatory evidence) is important and is (obviously) a function of the amounts of and kinds of evidence, e.g., fingerprints, DNA, eye-witness reports, expert evidence. Indeed, it is only when an investigator has a sufficiently weighty quantum of evidence (again, including inculpatory and exculpatory evidence) that s/he can with confidence begin the process of weighing that evidence in the different sense of weighing the inculpatory against the exculpatory, and doing so by the appropriate standard, e.g., the standard of beyond reasonable doubt.

In recent times, the police services in most countries have had a focus on improving procedures and practices in relation to evidence gathering. In the UK, for example, interviews of both suspects and witnesses are conducted using structured interview techniques such as cognitive interview techniques. Investigators in many jurisdictions in the USA, UK, and Australia now use audio and/or video to tape interviews of suspects.

If the development of new technologies, the availability of new forms of evidence, and the more widespread use of best practice investigative techniques by corruption investigators has assisted the process of combating corruption, the digital revolution and the process of globalization, in particular, have greatly facilitated institutional corruption and highlighted the importance of institutional integrity systems and the integrity of individual human institutional actors. Take, for example, the fraudster, Bernard L. Madoff. Madoff recently ran the biggest Ponzi scheme in history, operating it for thirty years and causing cash losses of $19.5 billion. Shortly after the scheme collapsed and Madoff confessed in 2008, evidence began to surface that for years major banks had suspected he was a fraud. None of them reported their suspicions to the authorities, and several banks decided to make money from him without, of course, risking any of their own funds.[2] Of course, as is well known, criminal organizations, notably drug cartels, now operate on a global scale, are in many cases more or less out of control, and have a profoundly corruptive effect on institutions. By one estimate, the illegal narcotics industry has annual revenues of over $300 billion.[3] Now consider the recent Mandiant revelations regarding state-based cybercrime.

[2] Charles Ferguson, "Heist of the century: Wall Street's role in the financial crisis," *The Guardian*, May 20, 2012.
[3] Tom Wainwright, *Narconomics* (London: Ebury Press, 2016), p. 3.

"On the outskirts of Shanghai, in a run-down neighborhood dominated by a 12-story white office tower, sits a People's Liberation Army base for China's growing corps of cyber-warriors. The building off Datong Road, surrounded by restaurants, massage parlors and a wine importer, is the headquarters of P.L.A. Unit 61398. A growing body of digital forensic evidence – confirmed by American intelligence officials who say they have tapped into the activity of the army unit for years – leaves little doubt that an overwhelming percentage of the attacks on American corporations, organizations and government agencies originate in and around the white tower."[4]

The upshot of this situation is that there is now a moral imperative on the part of governments and law enforcement agencies to mobilize resources and develop strategies and tactics to combat what amounts to a serious national and global criminal threat (including, as we saw above, from other governments). Naturally, these strategies include political, social, and economic ones. In the case of corruption arising from drug cartels and international drug trafficking, examples include ones such as providing cocaine- and opium-growing farmers with alternative sources of income. However, the threat is such that there is a need to engage in a degree of institutional design in respect of investigative agencies, including by (1) accelerating the process of embedding the intelligence-based policing model and extending it to new and emerging areas of corruption, including cybercrime/corruption; (2) establishing wider and deeper national and international inter-agency links with police and non-police agencies alike; (3) developing and funding specialist technical units (e.g., forensic computer accountants); (4) rethinking regulatory arrangements in the financial and other sectors in the light of the failure of "victim" organizations to adequately respond to corruption, including by assisting investigative agencies; and (5) introducing corruption awareness-raising programs for police, financial, and other institutions, and the public at large.

8.2 Investigative Independence and Accountability

As interference by the Blair UK government in the UK's Serious Fraud Office's investigation of BAE[5] and, at the time of writing, the furor over President Trump's firing of FBI Director, James Comey, in the midst of

---

[4] Extract from David Sanger, D. Barboza, and N. Perlroth, "Chinese Army Unit Is Seen as Tied to Hacking against US," *New York Times*, February 18, 2013.
[5] Miller and Gordon, *Investigative Ethics*, pp. 109–110.

the latter's investigation into potentially inappropriate relations between Trump and senior Russian officials graphically illustrate, liberal democracies, let alone authoritarian regimes, are not immune to political interference in criminal investigations to the point at which important criminal investigations can be shut down. Here we need to invoke the distinction between the independence of the investigative agency and the independence of the particular investigator. The former is largely a matter of institutional design. The latter is more an issue of the particular qualities of individual investigators.[6]

Self-evidently, individual investigators need to be highly competent; they need to be experts. This is both a presupposition and a justification of their being granted investigative independence. Clearly, they will not have high levels of competence if they have not done the necessary training, e.g., have successfully undertaken an investigator's course, do not have experience, e.g., have undertaken a reasonable number of relevant investigations, do not show aptitude, e.g., have displayed the necessary capacity for logical thinking and open mindedness, and have not demonstrated expertise, e.g., have *successfully* completed previous investigations. Accordingly, competence and performance indicators, e.g., audits of the investigator's past investigator reports, briefs of evidence, ratios of successful to unsuccessful prosecutions, and so on, need to be developed to determine what counts as a competent investigator, and these should be applied to investigators in a systematic and objective manner.

It should also be noted that competence is to some extent relative to the *person* to be investigated. Presumably, other things being equal, a novice investigator should not be assigned the task of, for example, undertaking the investigation of a serious complaint made against a police officer who is him/herself a highly experienced investigator. Again competence, or at least standards of investigative competence, is to some extent relative to investigative competence elsewhere within the organization and outside the organization: What processes are in place to attract high-quality investigators from other parts of the organization or from other organizations?

As I have stressed, the investigator needs to be, and to be seen to be, independent. There are at least three respects in which the independence of the investigator might be compromised: (1) Institutional independence

---

[6] An earlier version of the material in this section and the following one appeared in Seumas Miller, "What Makes a Good Internal Affairs Investigation?" *Criminal Justice Ethics*, 29 (2010), 30–41. See also Miller, *Corruption and Anti-Corruption in Policing*, chapter 6.

both from government and other agencies and from a given police organization. Concerning the latter point, police from a given police organization may investigate large numbers of complaints of *systemic* police corruption in that organization. Some have argued that in relation to serious police corruption (whether allegedly systemic or not) and other serious forms of criminality the investigators should not be members of the police organization whose members are under investigation.

(2) Conflict of interest. Consider, for example, an investigator investigating an allegation against his relative. The notion of a conflict of interest involves one person, P1, being required to exercise judgment in relation to another person, P2, (e.g., P1 is investigating an allegation made by P3 against P2) and P1 has a special interest tending to interfere with P1's proper exercise of his/her judgment in relation to P2.[7] The special interest in question can be a personal interest, e.g., P2 is a relative, or a conflicting role interest, e.g., P2 is P1's immediate superior. (For further discussion see Chapter 9 Section 9.6.)

(3) Bias. Consider, for example, an investigator investigating an allegation of corruption by a non-police complainant against another police officer. Strictly speaking, this is not necessarily a conflict of interest since the investigating officer might not have a *special interest* in the required sense. Indeed, one might reasonably expect police to resist any temptation to be unduly influenced by the fact that the person being investigated is merely a police officer in the same organization and not, for example, friends. On the other hand, there might be a tendency for bias or, at least, the appearance thereof.

In relation to each of the above, performance indicators might be developed, e.g., existence of requirement to make conflicts of interest disclosure (and to avoid conflicts of interest), case audits of police investigations in relation to conflicts of interest.

Investigators need to be held accountable for the investigations, including processes undertaken and the results delivered. Accordingly, they need to be able to withstand scrutiny from both internal and external agencies. A variety of such forms of scrutiny have been mentioned above, including audits and the like. An important dimension of accountability, indeed presupposition of accountability, is transparency; what procedures are in place to ensure that investigative processes are transparent, including not only to internal and external oversight agencies but also to victims,

---

[7] Definition taken from Michael Davis, "Conflicts of Interest" in R. Chadwick (ed.), *Encyclopedia of Applied Ethics* (London: Academic Press, 1998), Volume 1 (A–D), p. 590.

witnesses, and suspects. (Naturally, the nature and level of transparency needs to be consistent with security and confidentiality requirements.)

A further point here is that the decisions and recommendations made by the investigator need to be justified in terms of reasons, and these reasons need to adequately documented.

Accountability is operative at two levels (at least): (i) there is the accountability of the investigator in relation to a particular investigation considered in itself; and (ii) there is the accountability of the investigator in relation to his/her investigative performance over a period of time. The latter is susceptible to performance indicators not necessarily applicable to the former, e.g., the number and ratio of corruption complaints investigations in which the investigator's recommendation is that the complaint in question is sustained.

Investigation is a dynamic mode of activity, in part because those investigated seek to avoid investigation and/or subvert investigative techniques. Hence, the need to identify and implement best practice, including using the latest investigative tools, e.g., tools made available by forensic science, and to innovatively apply such practices and tools to the specific internal affairs context in which the investigators are operating, e.g., in the design of integrity tests. Hence a criterion of the quality of investigations is the extent to which they not only deploy best practice but are monitored with a view to improvement in light of new developments.

In addition, data need to be collected in relation to investigations undertaken, including the number of investigations undertaken and finalized per annum, time take to finalize investigations, the outcome in terms of decisions such as conviction rates, and the levels of satisfaction of victims, witnesses, etc. since these provide an important picture of agency work and can be used to indicate areas of underperformance by investigators.

8.3   Informants

Informants are an important source of information for law enforcement agencies, especially in areas such as drug-dealing and corruption where there is no direct victim as such, e.g., drugs and corruption, or in relation to other hard to reach groups where it is difficult to find voluntary information, e.g., terrorist groups.[8] Following the Twin Towers attack in 2001, the

---

[8] Earlier versions of the material in this section appeared in Miller and Blackler, *Ethical Issues in Policing*, chapter 4; Miller and Gordon, *Investigative Ethics*, chapter 9.

subsequent enquiry was critical of the CIA and its lack of informants. According to Skolnick (1994), "without a network of informants – usually victims, sometimes police – narcotics police cannot operate."[9] On the other hand, informants are something of a double-edged sword. Some researchers have questioned the benefits of informants in terms of crime reduction,[10] and they can have a corrupting effect on police.[11]

Following a surge of organized crime, in the 1970s, the term "supergrass" began to appear in newspaper reports on criminal trials. It reflected the change within the UK police service to engage with informants, mainly criminals themselves, who were prepared to give information and then testify in court against high-level criminals and gangs.[12]

Typically, informants are members or associates of the criminal element. And they inform on other criminals, or provide information to police, for a multiplicity of reasons; though primarily for their own advantage. Accordingly, the information provided is not necessarily accurate.

Such advantages might be thought – at least by the informant – to include the police refraining from investigating offences already committed by the informant, or even turning a blind eye to present and future offences of the informant, e.g., the so-called license to deal given to informants who are themselves drug dealers in order to catch "bigger fish."[13] Sometimes the informant, in effect, might be coerced by the police officer; noncooperation might lead to arrest and conviction for past offences hitherto ignored. This is morally undesirable from the perspective of the moral rights of the informant. At other times, the relationship between (say) a detective and his informant can become one in which the detective is manipulated by the informant. In some extreme cases the informants have become *de facto* handlers and the police handler the informant. Organized crime, for example, has a vested interest in corrupting police officers, and one favored way of doing so is for a criminal to become a police informant, and for the police officer to begin to feed

---

[9] J. H. Skolnick, *Justice without Trial: Law Enforcement in a Democratic Society* (New York: Macmillan, 1994), p. 117.

[10] C. Dunnighan and C. Norris, "The Detective, the Snout and the Audit Commission: The Real Costs in Using Informants," *Howard Journal of Criminal Justice*, 38 (2005), 67–86.

[11] For a useful discussion of the ethical issues that the use of informers gives rise to, see Clive Harfield, "Police Informers and Professional Ethics," *Criminal Justice Ethics*, 31 (2012), 73–95.

[12] For a UK-focused discussion of informants and informant management practices and legal requirements see Clive Harfield and Karen Harfield, *Covert Investigation*, 3rd edn. (Oxford University Press, 2012), Chapter 9.

[13] R. Billingsley, T. Nemitz, and P. Bean (eds.), *Informers: Policing, Policy and Practice* (Cullompton, Devon, 2001), chapter 1.

information to his "informant" in return for financial rewards made available by the organized crime bosses.[14]

As with surveillance and undercover operations, the use of informants gives rise to privacy concerns, albeit these might be at one remove from the police themselves. Accordingly, if an informant infringes (as opposed to violates) the privacy rights of a suspect then there should be a reasonable suspicion of serious wrongdoing and the infringement should be otherwise justified.[15] There is also the potential risk to the life and/or limb of the informant, if the suspect discovers that they are an informant. Additional risks that attach to the use of informants in the absence of an appropriate accountability system are as follows.

- There is no management or official documentation of meetings and, therefore, what transpires, e.g., what was promised by the officer and by the informant, is open to challenge.
- There is no corroboration that the actual payment to the informant was made or in what form, e.g., drugs, reciprocal information, and, as a consequence, the arrangement is open to abuse by officers, e.g., some officers have taken a share of the payment intended for the informant.
- There is no control over the venue and timing of the meetings and, therefore, there is a physical risk to both officer and informant.
- The secrecy of the identity of the informant means that general tasking of informants by and behalf of other officers cannot easily be done.
- In the pressure to get to the target of an investigation, officers may be tempted to promise large money payments or favorable prosecutorial or judicial outcomes to informants. Unfortunately, in some instances they have been unable to keep these promises. Informants may indeed receive a reduced sentence for substantial assistance, but what qualifies as substantial assistance is determined subjectively by a judge, not the investigator. Oftentimes, this subjectivity can lead to too much leniency, or not enough.
- There is the risk of compromise in a court case where the informant makes allegations against an officer to protect him or herself.

It follows that if the relationship between police handler and informant is secretive – the police organization has no knowledge of it – then such problems are unlikely to be resolved, and the relationship likely to be very damaging, not only to the detective but also to police operations.

---

[14] *Ibid.*, chapter 2.   [15] See Harfield, "Police Informers and Professional Ethics."

Some informants might not be prepared to provide information unless confidentiality is guaranteed. On one view, the relationship between investigators and their informants is one of trust on a par with that between professionals and their clients. Even if this is so, the requirements for confidentiality between investigators and informants are obviously different. For one thing, the reason for confidentiality in the case of informants might have more to do with the possible harm that might come to the informant from those he or she is informing about, rather than from the informant's basic right to privacy.

In this context, there is obviously a need for stringent accountability mechanisms, including the following ones: the informant is named in documentation; an investigator with an informant has a supervisor who meets with the investigator and the informant; the supervisor monitors the investigator's dealings with the informant; all payments are recorded (including electronic transfers to prevent theft).

The first consideration that ought to inform informant management systems is that informants realize their essentially epistemic or knowledge-based purpose in relation to the provision of intelligence and evidence. So there needs to be active identification of informants and their opportunities, and informants need to be regularly assessed in relation to their actual or potential contribution to intelligence/evidence requirements.

Informants encompass a broad range of persons who may provide intelligence and/or evidence; persons giving it for personal rewards of some sort, but also undercover officers and those who act as test purchasers, e.g., in drugs investigations. It can apply to a police officer who has confidentially reported corrupt or unethical behavior by a colleague and is then asked to get more information from that colleague. In many jurisdictions, the police officer must be registered as an informant otherwise the intrusion may be unlawful. The use of the source should be proportionate, with detailed records being kept and available for scrutiny by an oversight body.

Investigations involving covert operations typically generate large amounts of information that ought to be recorded on the intelligence system of the relevant police service. The information in question includes the tactics used and the people involved in any given covert operation. So there is a risk that this information becomes available to persons who ought not to have access to it. Accordingly, systems must be in place to minimize this risk, while ensuring that the information remains accessible to those authorized to access it.

Investigations involving covert operational teams may acquire information that is not related to the operation or the investigation of which the operation is a part – collateral information. An important moral question arises here as to limits that ought to be placed on the recording, storage, and accessing of such "collateral" information. On the one hand, some of this information may be potentially useful intelligence in relation to other investigations. On the other hand, such potentially useful information may infringe the privacy and/or confidentially rights of individuals or organizations.

Let us assume that acquiring, or at least retaining, the potentially useful information in question does infringe the privacy and/or confidentiality rights of some individual or organization and, therefore, that prima facie it ought not to be recorded and stored for future access. By assumption, the acquisition and retention of the information in question is not morally justified by virtue of serving the purposes of the (presumably morally legitimate) investigation during the course of which it was acquired. However, its retention might be morally justified if it demonstrably served the purposes of some other *extant* investigation, or if it otherwise pertained to a person or organization with respect to which there was reasonable suspicion of criminal activity (and if its acquisition/retention met the other moral constraints on information acquisition/retention in that investigation or in respect of that person/organization, e.g., proportionality). On the other hand, the retention of the information would not be morally justified by the mere fact that it was judged to be potentially useful in relation to some unspecified future investigation of an individual or organization in relation to which there was no reasonable suspicion of criminal activity.

The management of informants ideally involves the use of trained staff tasked for recruitment of informants in line with the intelligence priorities for the organization rather than the motives of would-be informants seeking personal benefits (e.g., sentence reduction, revenge). The use of informants for anti-corruption work requires some additional expertise over and above that for standard criminal investigation.

8.4   Undercover Operations and Traps (Stings)

Many undercover operations might be considered to be entrapment in the ordinary common sense meaning of that term, i.e., to *trap* or "sting" someone.[16] This sense of entrapment is to be distinguished from legal definitions of the term, especially US definitions, in which entrapment is a

---

[16] Earlier versions of the material in this section appeared in Miller, *Corruption and Anti-Corruption in Policing*, chapter 7; Miller and Gordon, *Investigative Ethics*, chapter 11; Miller and Blackler, *Ethical Issues in Policing*, chapter 6; and Seumas Miller (ed.), *Ethical Issues in Policing* (Wagga Wagga: Keon, 1997).

legal defense.[17] I am using the term "trap" to refer to a proactive law enforcement strategy used in many jurisdictions in preference to reactive strategies, such as complaints investigations. Traps make use of undercover operatives posing as drug buyers, bribers, or criminals. It can involve the building of lengthy interpersonal relationships. Instances of successful traps are to be found in the 1990s in Australia.[18] Corruption in the NSW Police was systemic, and evidently the only way to bring corrupt police to justice was by way of a trap involving "turned" corrupt police officers operating undercover. Only such officers would be trusted by corrupt fellow officers, and only a managed trap scenario would enable reliable evidence, such as videotapes, to be obtained.

Traps can be random or targeted. Targeted traps focus on a specific person (or persons) who is/are reasonably believed to be involved in crime. Random traps are not directed at any specific person. For example, a police officer posing as a prostitute on a street corner in order to trap clients is engaged in random entrapment.

Traps or stings raise a number of ethical issues, including (a) deception; (b) the infringement of privacy; (c) uncertainty in relation to the moral culpability of the offender, i.e., the offender was "tricked" into doing what he or she otherwise would not have done; and (d) impropriety of law enforcement agents, since they might be creating crimes that otherwise would not exist.

Infringements of privacy by law enforcement officials are morally justifiable if certain conditions are met. These conditions include the following ones: (a) there is reasonable suspicion that the person whose privacy is to be infringed intends to commit a serious crime; (b) the methods in question are effective; and (c) there is no alternative nonintrusive, or less intrusive, method of investigation.

Arguably, trapping is required – or is far more effective than reactive methods, such as investigating complaints – in relation to certain crimes. The crimes in question include ones that do not necessarily involve a complainant, e.g., corruption, drug-dealing, or areas such as organized crime, where offences might be difficult to prove because offenders are well-organized, well-funded, and/or highly secretive. But in relation to

---

[17] For a useful overview of the legal and ethical issues raised by current forms of entrapment and the application of contemporary republican normative theory to these issues, see Simon Bronitt and Declan Roche, "Between Rhetoric and Reality: Socio-Legal and Republican Perspectives on Entrapment," *International Journal of Evidence and Proof*, 4 (2000), 77–106.

[18] James Wood, *Royal Commission into Corruption in the NSW Police Service: Final Report (Vol. 2)* (Sydney: NSW Government, 1997).

certain kinds of offence and offender, arguably traps do better on a cost/benefit analysis than reliance on informers, or on undercover operatives who observe but do not trap. Informers often provide unreliable information, and often fail to provide evidence of the guilt of those they implicate in crimes. Undercover operations are resource intensive and their outcomes uncertain. This is especially so when undercover operatives simply wait for a suspect to create the opportunity to commit a crime, and then hope to gather evidence in relation to the crime when it does happen. By contrast, traps involve stage-managing a crime at a time and place chosen by investigators; so there is an assurance that the crime will be recorded and the offender convicted.

If persons who have been trapped are justifiably to be convicted, then they must have committed a crime. However, even if they have performed a criminal act, there might be important reasons not to convict them. Specifically, they might have been the victims of morally unjustified traps. What tests ought to be applied to determine whether someone was the victim of a morally unjustified trap (entrapment in the legal sense in the USA)? In the USA, two legal tests to determine whether someone has been entrapped have been proposed; the subjective test and the objective test. Arguably, however, elements of both of these tests ought to be used.[19] Note that in the sense of "entrapment" in question in the legal environment of the USA, entrapment is necessarily unlawful; in the USA, entrapment, by definition, involves proactive policing practices that fail (in particular) the subjective test. While our concerns in this book are not with the law, let alone specific jurisdictions, the subjective and objective tests raise important ethical and philosophical issues that are of interest in their own right. Accordingly, I discuss these tests, and the conditions associated with them, at some length.

The subjective test asks whether the suspect has a disposition to commit crimes of the kind in question. Theoretically, but not necessarily, or indeed actually, in law, we might establish the existence of a disposition on the basis of his/her past behavior, e.g., past criminal convictions. Evidently, the point of this test is to ensure that the person trapped has the requisite degree of culpability; an important motivating reason for using this test is the concern that without it the police might induce an intention or inclination to commit a crime that was otherwise absent.[20]

---

[19] For useful discussions of these tests and the issues that they raise, see Gerald Dworkin, *The Theory and Practice of Autonomy* (Cambridge University Press, 1988), chapter 9; John Kleinig, *Ethics in Policing* (Cambridge: Cambridge University Press, 1996), chapter 8.

[20] Dworkin, *Theory and Practice of Autonomy*, p. 134, and Kleinig, *Ethics in Policing*, p. 153.

The objective test asks whether or not the State has acted improperly by virtue of instigating the crime. This resolves itself into two issues. The first issue is whether or not the contribution of the police or other investigators to the creation of the opportunity to commit the crime is excessive. For example, suppose an undercover police officer supplies a person with the raw materials and the equipment to manufacture heroin, and suppose that the raw materials and equipment are not available to the person from any other source(s). The second issue is whether or not the inducement offered to commit the crime was unreasonable (too strong), e.g., offering someone a bribe of one million dollars to avoid loss of one's driving license for three months or to engage in illicit sex.[21]

One problem for the subjective test is how to provide evidence of a disposition. This problem is heightened in legal contexts in which knowledge of past crimes and convictions is not normally allowed to be used in determining guilt in relation to a current crime. A further possible problem for the subjective test is that it does not rule out strong inducements. Police officers might abuse the system by offering inducements that are too strong, and yet conviction would follow if the suspects had strong dispositions to commit the crime.[22] A related problem arises from the fact that a disposition to commit a crime is not equivalent to an intention to commit that crime. Suppose someone has a disposition to commit a crime. However, knowing that he has this disposition, he puts himself in a context in which there is no opportunity to commit the crime. Consider a heroin addict who wants to avoid taking heroin and decides to live in a heroin-free area, avoid contact with other addicts, and so on. Now assume a police officer seeks out the addict and persistently offers heroin to the addict. Again consider a formerly corrupt official who is trying to continue to "go straight" notwithstanding his financial problems; he has joined the local church community; he avoids his corrupt colleagues; and so on. Now assume an undercover operative seeks out this official and persistently offers him substantial bribes. Examples such as these show that the mere presence of a disposition is not sufficient for morally justified trapping; so the subjective test – at least as described above – would have to be strengthened.

A possible problem for the objective test is that it protects some people who should be found guilty.[23] Suppose strong inducements are used in

---

[21] Dworkin, *Theory and Practice of Autonomy*, p. 135, and Kleinig, *Ethics in Policing*, p. 154.
[22] W. Sinnott-Armstrong, "Entrapment in the Net," *Ethics and Information Technology*, no. 1, 1999, p. 99.
[23] *Ibid.*

cases of suspects with strong dispositions to commit the crime, and suppose these suspects are in fact guilty of this kind of crime. Such inducements will be ruled out by the objective test, and yet the guilty persons in question will go free. On the other hand, it is far more preferable that some of the guilty go free than that some of the innocent are convicted. So this objection is relatively weak. A stronger objection is that the objective test – insofar as it involves random testing – amounts to the government engaging in integrity testing of its citizens. This is surely unacceptable; governments have no right to convict a citizen merely because the citizen fails to resist an inducement to commit a crime, even if it is an inducement that they ought to have resisted. As Dworkin points out, "To encourage the commission of a crime in the absence of any reason to believe the individual is already engaged in a course of action is to be a tester of virtue, not a detector of crime."[24] Moreover, the objective test is not a particularly effective test of virtue. Someone who lacked the disposition to commit that kind of crime, or indeed crimes in general, might nevertheless fail the objective test on a single occasion.

What might be acceptable is targeted integrity testing of individuals reasonably suspected of committing the crime that is the subject of the test. Moreover, random integrity testing of certain categories of public servants, such as police or politicians, in relation to a circumscribed set of crimes might be acceptable under certain conditions. For example, suppose bribe-taking is rife in a specific government department, and all other measures have failed to curtail it; perhaps random integrity testing is now warranted. The general moral justification for this is that such public servants need to have a certain standard of integrity in relation to specific kinds of inducement, and they voluntarily accept a public office on the basis that they meet that standard. Accordingly, their integrity might reasonably be open to testing, especially if it is made clear to them before they accept the public office that their integrity might be subjected to a test.

There is a general objection to trapping, and this objection apparently stands irrespective of whether the subjective test or the objective test is applied. This is the objection that traps involve the creation of crime and corruption, rather than the detecting or preventing of crime and corruption that would have existed independently of trapping.[25] If this objection is sustained then evidently trapping should be abandoned. But is this objection sustained?

---

[24] Dworkin, *Theory and Practice of Autonomy*, p. 144.   [25] *Ibid.*, p. 136.

In order to assist our deliberations, consider the following.[26] Suppose a low level junior administrative official, A, whose contract of employment is about to expire is given the task of counting a large amount of drug money confiscated by investigators (approximately $100,000). She forms an intention to commit the one-off crime of fraud by the device of stealing $5,000 from this amount of cash and understating the amount in her count by that amount. Official A believes that the stolen money will not be missed since she knows the camera monitoring the room is not working at the time. Now suppose that unknown to A, corruption investigator, B, intentionally omitted to require that some other person be present in the room for monitoring purposes, notwithstanding the failure of the monitoring camera, and did so in order to perform a random integrity test with a view to trapping A, for A might be one of those employees who opportunistically commit acts of theft and fraud. As it happens, although A has always complied with the law, A will shortly be unemployed and very short of money. At any rate, A hides the $5,000 on her person, is searched and caught red-handed.

Notice that if the objective test is applied, the police and other investigators are entitled to engage in this kind of trapping. In the first place, the inducement, e.g., $5,000, is of a kind that the normal employee could reasonably be expected to resist. In the second place, it was the breakdown of the monitoring equipment that created the opportunity for fraud. What the corruption investigator did was fail to remove this opportunity; something that admittedly he should have done and would have done, if he had not wanted to set his trap. On the other hand, this kind of trap is ruled out by the subjective test; for A, I have assumed, does not have a disposition to commit fraud.

Given the nature of this one-off opportunity, and A's general disposition to comply with the law, A would probably not have committed any crime if the corruption investigator had not trapped her. The reason is that she would never have been afforded the opportunity to commit the only sort of opportunistic crime that she is capable of committing. Yet given that she believed that the opportunity had arisen, she formed the intention to commit the crime. I suggest that the mere possession of an intention – in a context of crime or corruption investigator provision of opportunity – is not sufficient to justify trapping. The reason is not that A is not culpable; clearly A is guilty of an act of fraud. Rather, the reason is that trapping under these conditions involves the creation of crime, rather than the

[26] See *ibid.*, p. 140, for a contrary view.

detecting or preventing of crime that would have existed independently of the trap.

Let us take another look at another version of our scenario. This time let us assume that, unbeknown to the investigator, B, A1 has a disposition to commit opportunistic acts of fraud of large amounts of money, if they are available and A1 believes he will escape detection. But let us further assume that there are no such opportunities. While A1 hopes for such opportunities, and boasts to his friends he is waiting for such opportunities, none have been or are ever likely to be forthcoming. However, investigator B has set the same trap for A1 as he did in the scenario involving A. Given A1's disposition, A1 readily falls into B's trap. Obviously, the subjective test does not rule out this kind of trap, for A1 has a disposition to engage in opportunistic fraud of this kind. Moreover, we saw above that the objective test did not rule out this kind of trap either.

Notwithstanding the existence of A1's disposition to engage in opportunistic defrauding of large amounts of money, it still remains the case that A1 would not have committed any crime if the investigator had not trapped him. The reason is that he would never have been afforded the opportunity to commit the only sort of opportunistic crime that he is disposed to commit. Accordingly, I suggest that the possession of a disposition and an intention – in a context of provision of opportunity by the state (e.g., by a police officer) consistent with the requirements of the objective test – is not sufficient to justify trapping. The reason is that trapping under these conditions involves the creation of crime and corruption, rather than the detecting or preventing of crime and corruption that would have existed independently of the trap.

As a corollary to this, I conclude that neither passing the subjective test nor passing the objective test nor passing both tests is sufficient to justify trapping. Needless to say, this does not show that trapping is not justified under certain circumstances.

Walter Sinnott Armstrong[27] argues that trapping on the Internet is dissimilar to other forms of traps by virtue of being (a) less intrusive, since there are not so many innocent people involved as there are in, for example, posing as a drug-dealer at a university campus; (b) less dangerous to investigators/undercover operatives; and (c) less abuse-prone, since the evidence is there for all to see.

However, the general problems with trapping also afflict trapping on the Internet. Traps, whether on the Internet or not, face the general objection

---

[27] Sinnott-Armstrong "Entrapment in the Net".

that they involve the creation of crime. Moreover, the above-mentioned objections to the objective and subjective tests remain. On the other hand, specific forms of trapping, e.g., targeted traps and random traps of certain categories of public officials, might well be justifiable.

Let us bring this chapter to a close by attempting to detail the general conditions under which the trapping of ordinary citizens might be morally permissible.[28] In so doing, I try to accommodate the various objections made above to traps, and to the subjective and objective tests.

First, there are a number of such general conditions, such as the condition that the method of trapping is the only feasible method available to law enforcement and anti-corruption agencies in relation to a certain type of offence, and that the offence type is a serious one. This condition reflects the general presumption against trapping.

Second, the trap should be a targeted trapping of a person (or group) who is/are reasonably suspected of engaging in crimes of the relevant kind. This condition rules out testing the virtue of citizens.

Third, the suspect is ordinarily presented with, or typically creates, the kind of opportunity that they are to be afforded in the entrapment scenario. This condition in large part rules out police creation of crime.

Fourth, the inducement offered to the suspect is (a) of a kind that is typically available to the suspect and (b) such that an ordinary citizen would reasonably be expected to resist it.[29] This condition rules out excessive inducements, and therefore one way in which crime might be created by the police.

Fifth, the person not only has a disposition[30] to commit the type of crime in relation to which they are to be trapped, but also a standing intention to commit that type of crime. This condition not only protects those with inoperative inclinations to crime, but also those with a fleeting intention to commit a one-off crime – an intention not underpinned by any disposition to criminal activity. Evidence of a disposition to commit a type of crime might consist of an uninterrupted pattern of past crimes of that type, and no evidence of any change in attitude or circumstance. Evidence of a standing intention to commit that type of crime might be

---

[28] See Dworkin, *Theory and Practice of Autonomy*, p. 144, for a reasonably similar set of conditions to this. See also Kleinig, *Ethics in Policing*, p. 158.

[29] Or – in the case of tests for personnel in high-risk occupations – "such that a person in that role would reasonably be expected to resist it."

[30] The existence of such a disposition might be established by recourse to evidence such as an uninterrupted pattern of past crimes, and no evidence of a change in attitude or circumstances.

verbal and/or evidence of current detailed planning activities, and/or attempts to provide the means to commit such crimes.

8.5 Conclusion

As we have seen, investigations are a central component of anti-corruption and integrity systems and, indeed, of the criminal justice system itself. In this chapter I have focused on criminal investigations, and investigations of serious corruption, in particular. Issues discussed include investigator independence, infringements of privacy, use of informants, and use of undercover operatives to trap suspects. In relation to the latter, I have discussed the so-called subjective and objective tests and set out the conditions under which traps by crime and corruption investigators might be morally justified.

CHAPTER 9

Integrity Systems for Occupations

In Chapter 7 I outlined the general features of integrity systems for institutions, including the appropriate relationship between such systems and institutional purpose, structure, and culture. Moreover, different regulatory models were discussed. In Chapter 8 I focused on a very fundamental aspect of integrity systems, namely, criminal and corruption investigations. In this chapter I discuss integrity systems for occupations in more detail, and in doing so I take the more general features of integrity systems, including criminal and corruption investigations, as given.

9.1 Occupations and Professions

An occupation is defined by its occupational role.[1] According to my teleological normative account of social institutions, institutional roles, including occupational roles, are teleological; they are distinguished from one another according to the collective ends that they serve, and these collective ends are, normatively speaking, collective goods. While necessary to differentiate roles, the collective end of a role is not sufficient to distinguish one role from another. Perhaps the end of lawyers, like that of police, is to ensure that the law is complied with and, in doing so, that the principles of justice that underpin the law (or which ought to) are not breached. Accordingly, we also need to attend to the means or type of action or activity by which the end of some occupational role is realized. Police, but not lawyers, uphold the law by means of their own use, or their own threatened use, of coercive force. So occupational roles are defined in part by the end or ends that they serve, and in part by the types of action or activities that they perform that are the means to that end(s). Thus all financial advisors provide financial advice (the means)

---

[1] Alexandra and Miller, *Integrity Systems for Occupations*, chapter 1.

but what is the end? Is it to sell a product or to serve the financial interests of their client?

In addition, some roles are evidently in part defined by the moral beliefs, commitments, and associated attitudes that practitioners ought to have. For example, a commitment to the physical and mental well-being of "clients" is a feature of the so-called caring occupations, e.g., nurses, social workers, psychologists. Likewise, accountants and auditors ought to have moral commitments to accuracy, truthfulness, and so on. Such moral attitudes, if widespread and interdependently held, are constitutive in part of the culture of an organization or occupational group. So what is the culture of financial advisors in a given industry? What are their prevailing commitments? Evidently, members of many contemporary financial planning businesses have the culture of a sales-team, e.g., success is measured in terms of the financial value of commissions earned.

Historically, a further distinction has been made between occupations and professions. All professional roles are occupational roles, but not all occupational roles are professional roles. This distinction is important because the process of professionalization is a key feature of the strategy to deal with ethical issues among members of many occupations, such as that of financial advisor, e.g., in Australia and the UK.[2]

Notwithstanding attempts to collapse the distinction, there is a large degree of consensus in the sociological and philosophical literature as to the characteristic features of professional occupations – features that serve to distinguish them from other occupations.[3] Three such marks are especially salient. An occupational group counts as a profession in virtue of its having the following features: the work of its members is oriented to the provision of some good (as opposed to mere desire or preference), e.g., health (doctors), justice (lawyers); members of the group possess and exercise creative expertise in the provision of this good; and they possess a high degree of autonomy in the exercise of their expertise. The good or goods in question are typically goods in part constitutive of the interests of the clients of the professional, e.g., the doctor has as his end the good health of the patient and the good health of the patient is in the patient's interest. However, the good served by the profession and the client's interest can diverge in particular cases. Thus the lawyer serves the interest of her client

---

[2] Seumas Miller, "Trust, Conflicts of Interest and Fiduciary Duties: Ethical Issues in the Financial Planning Industry in Australia" in Nicholas Morris and David Vines (eds.), *Capital Failure: Rebuilding Trust in Financial Services* (Oxford: Oxford University Press, 2014), pp. 305–331.

[3] Other marks, such as self-regulation, are more controversial. See, for example, Michael D. Bayles, "Professional Power and Self-Regulation," *Business and Professional Ethics Journal*, 5 (1986), 27.

and that interest, if served, will often coincide with the requirements of justice. However, the requirements of justice might not coincide with the interests of the client, e.g., if the client is rightly found to be guilty and sentenced to a term in jail.

The basic conception of the professions is necessarily different from other more market-based occupations.[4] As already noted, on one view the salient features of the professions can be understood and assessed by seeing the role of the professional as the provider of ethical goods, including catering for fundamental needs, as opposed to mere desires and preferences, e.g., desire for an ice-cream, a fashionable address, or a Porsche motor car. Unlike desires, needs are objective, limited, and typically – given the harm caused by unmet needs – generate moral obligations.[5] Accordingly, professionals have a duty to provide these goods and satisfy these needs. Moreover, the members of a profession have collective obligations (i.e., joint obligations) to provide aggregates of these goods and services; that is, the goods and services in question are collective goods viewed from the perspective of the profession as a whole. Moreover, the standards of professional practice are institutional standards and, as we saw in Chapter 1, such standards are often themselves moral standards.

Given this, the relation between professionals and their client group should not be assimilated to that which holds between buyers and sellers in a market. In the idealized (and by no means uncontested) picture of the market with which we are familiar from the writings of contemporary economists, market actors – buyers and sellers alike – are driven by selfish motivations, the desire to satisfy their own desires. A transaction is rational when, and only when, each of the parties to the transaction believes, with good reason, that their desires will be more satisfied after the transaction than they were before. In my view, as will become clear below, this picture overstates the motive of self-interest and, as a consequence, oversimplifies the motives in play in markets. Nevertheless, the motives and obligations of market actors (*qua* market actors) stand in some contrast with those of professionals (*qua* professionals).[6] For

---

[4] See Andrew Alexandra and Seumas Miller, "Needs, Moral Self-Consciousness and Professional Roles" in *Professional Ethics* (co-author – A. Alexandra) vol. 5 no. 1–2 (1996), pp. 43–61; Miller, *Moral Foundations of Social Institutions*, chapters 6 and 10, for discussions of some of these issues.

[5] David Wiggins, "Claims of Need" in David Wiggins (ed.), *Needs, Values, Truth: Essays in the Philosophy of Value*, 2nd edn. (Oxford: Blackwell, 1991), pp. 6–11.

[6] Many professionals are, of course, also market actors. However, historically, as mentioned, a professional role in the market was constrained. This is much less so now.

example, there is no obligation on the owner of a product to sell it if he prefers to use it, or if he judges that he will not be better off after the transaction than before. Matters are somewhat different for professionals, since they do have an obligation to provide certain kinds of goods to those in need of them. This general obligation helps explain restrictions on the contractual freedom in dealings between clients and professionals. A professional is obliged to do what is necessary for the satisfaction of a client's needs, so they are not free to enter into agreements that would prevent them from so acting. More generally, unlike market actors, when the interests of professionals and their clients conflict, professionals are obliged to act in their clients' interests.

9.2   Integrity Systems, Moral Principles, and Trust

As argued in Chapter 7, integrity systems[7] are arguably the primary institutional vehicle available to ensure ethico-professional obligations are discharged and to combat crime and corruption (both being very serious forms of moral offence). Arguably, integrity systems have four principal aspects, at least potentially. First, they comprise enforceable laws and regulations, e.g., criminal codes. Second, they rely to some extent on markets. Markets serve multiple purposes, one of which is, I suggest, to incentivize ethical behavior, e.g., customers who are cheated by a supplier are unlikely to return, other things being equal. Third, there are reputational systems, of which more below. Finally, there are socio-moral norms, the moral principles that have been internalized by members of a social group and which – by virtue of being in part derived from the collective goods of institutions – motivate (in part) their behavior (see Chapter 2 Section 2.3). Ultimately, compliance with laws, and ethical incentives provided by markets and reputational devices, depend on a bedrock of widely accepted moral beliefs and other motivating moral attitudes, e.g., those definitive of the professions. Integrity systems seek to maintain and reinforce these motivating attitudes by, for example, training and education programs.

In relation to markets, integrity systems focus on removing or adjusting incentive structures that perversely promote unethical behavior (e.g., systems of remuneration in which liability does not track responsibility),

---

[7] See Miller, *Moral Foundations of Social Institutions*, chapter 6; Alexandra and Miller, *Integrity Systems for Occupations*.

and developing or reinforcing incentive structures that reduce unethical behavior (e.g., disclosure requirements).[8]

What of reputation and its relation to integrity systems? Reputation is importantly related to the discharging of moral obligations (virtue).[9] As we see later, deserved or warranted reputation can provide a nexus between self-interest (including the desire to be approved of) and virtue, and between (say) the financial self-interest of financial advisors and lenders, on the one hand, and due diligence, truthfulness, etc. in their dealings with investors and borrowers on the other.

Given this account of integrity systems, and our description of trust (Chapter 5 section 5.4.1), what is the relationship between moral principles, trust, and integrity systems? I have suggested that trust has a pivotal role to play in relation to compliance with moral principles, on the one hand, and integrity systems on the other.

With respect to such trust-dependent institutional obligations, integrity systems can only do so much. In particular, integrity systems cannot eliminate the vulnerability of promisees to promisors or of clients to professionals and, therefore, cannot obviate the need for trust. An integrity system can be designed and implemented to provide for sanctions against failure to discharge contractual obligations, to incentivize market actors not to cheat, and (by way of reputational devices) to incentivize members of occupational groups to aim for high ethical standards. However, it can neither eliminate the vulnerability of promisees, clients, and the like nor guarantee moral rectitude on the part of promisors, professionals, and so on: Hence the irreplaceability of trust.[10]

One feature of contemporary integrity systems is the increase in enforceable regulations and in ever more complex enforceable contracts in an attempt, at least in part, to do the job trust is (apparently) failing to do. However, as phenomena such as the legal "industry" of finding and exploiting regulatory loopholes and the practice of passing on the costs of corruption and fraud to consumers illustrate, the trust gap, supposing it exists, can never be successfully bridged in this manner. If finance companies cannot be trusted by their consumers to sell "safe" financial products, or financial advisors to give independent professional advice, then recourse

---

[8] Seumas Miller, "Institutions, Integrity Systems and Market Actors" in J. O'Brien (ed.), *Private Equity, Corporate Governance and the Dynamics of Capital Market Regulation* (Imperial College of London Press, 2007), pp. 297–327.

[9] Seumas Miller, "Financial Service Providers: Integrity Systems, Reputation and the Triangle of Virtue" in Dobos, Barry, and Pogge (eds.), *Global Financial Crisis*, pp. 132–157.

[10] See O'Neill, *A Question of Trust*, for a closely related point regarding accountability.

to regulations is unlikely by itself to deal adequately with the problem and may, instead, simply create additional costs; if employees cannot be trusted by their employers, or vice versa, then compliance and accountability mechanisms are not going to guarantee their honesty and, instead, may simply result in greater costs, albeit not necessarily only to the employers and/or employees themselves.

So integrity systems cannot replace trust. Moreover, integrity systems cannot guarantee moral compliance, more generally. Here I am speaking of the general reliance on others to comply with moral principles, e.g., not to murder, assault, rape, thieve, albeit such reliance takes us beyond the reach of trust in the sense under discussion at this point.

Let us now turn to a consideration of some of the main features of an integrity system for occupational groups, namely, codes of ethics and associated education programs, complaints and discipline systems, and ethics audits and ethics reputation indexes.

9.3   Codes of Ethics

Obviously, codes of ethics are concerned with ethics.[11] However, the terms "ethics" and "morality" are often used interchangeably. That said, some-times ethics is distinguished from morality. One way of making the distinction is as follows. Morality is about minimum standards of behavior and attitude. Do not kill the innocent, do not tell lies, do not steal or commit fraud. These are all minimum standards of behavior; they are moral principles. On the other hand – on this way of thinking – ethics is a wider notion. Ethics involves ideals and aspirations; it goes beyond mini-mum standards. A doctor who was competent and was not negligent might not be engaged in immoral behavior. Nevertheless, such a doctor might not be a good doctor. To be a good doctor implies doing more than merely complying with minimum standards. For example, a good doctor would have a caring attitude to his or her patients.

I will distinguish ethics and morality in this above-described way. So morality refers to minimum standards, while ethics refers to a wider field of value that embraces notions of what is good and worth aspiring to – ideals as well as minimum standards. Accordingly, codes of ethics will refer not

---

[11] For a useful introduction to codes of ethics see Margaret Coady and Sidney Bloch (eds.), *Codes of Ethics and the Professions* (Melbourne University Press, 1996). Earlier versions of the material in this section appeared in Seumas Miller, *Model Code of Principles of Ethics* (The Professional Standards Council of New South Wales and Western Australia, 2002), pp. 1–68; and Alexandra and Miller, *Integrity Systems for Occupations*, chapter 3.

only to moral principles, but also to ideals of the good. One important point to consider in this connection concerns punitive sanctions. Presumably, punitive (formal) sanctions – sanctions applied in the context of an appropriate complaints and discipline system – ought only to be deployed in relation to minimum standards (morality) but not in relation to ideals (ethics). A second important point concerns education. If ideals are to be realized then they need to be inculcated. If this is not to be done primarily by punitive sanctions, it will need to be done (at least in large part) by formal and informal education.

By presenting in an explicit form the basic ends (collective goods, in my parlance) of an occupation, the rights and duties of the members of the occupation, the constraints on their activity, the rights of clients, and so on, codes of ethics serve an educative purpose.[12] Knowledge of the code of ethics is knowledge of the ethical ideals and principles pertaining to that occupation, and members of the occupation can and ought to possess that knowledge. This knowledge is principally what is known as *practical*, as opposed to theoretical, knowledge. It is knowledge about how to do something, as opposed to knowledge concerning what is the case.

The knowledge expressed in a code is expressed in a condensed form. Accordingly, there is a need for additional explanatory material, e.g., regarding the nature and function of the specific occupation in question, and additional tools for applying this knowledge, e.g., a model of practical ethical reasoning. Moreover, this knowledge needs to be suitably contextualized in relation to specific concrete ethical problems that might be confronted by members of that occupational group. So there is also a need for supplementary case studies and the like.

Moreover, since this practical knowledge of ethical principles and ideals, and practical knowledge of their application, is not a static thing – ethical problems and the solutions to them undergo change – there is a need for ongoing revision of the code of ethics, ongoing education in relation to changes to the code of ethics, and especially ongoing education in relation to the application of the principles and ideals expressed in the code of ethics. The code of ethics, and associated ethical education, ought to be an important element in initial formal and informal education programs, and also in continuing education programs.

It is important to note that ethical codes not only have content; they are not simply documents that can be the objects of (practical) knowledge;

---

[12] For a useful discussion on functions of codes of ethics see Judith Lichtenberg, "What Are Codes of Ethics For?" in Coady and Bloch (ed.), *Codes of Ethics and the Professions.*

they also involve, or ought to involve, commitment on the part of the members of the occupation or organization in question.

The commitment in question is both personal and collective commitment. Each individual practitioner commits him or herself to the content of the code, or should do so. But each does so on condition the others do so; the individual commitments are interdependent, and therefore collective. Such interdependence of commitment to a common set of ideals and principles is in part constitutive of a self-conscious community of practitioners, and is a necessary condition for that community having an ethical culture. Accordingly, codes of ethics have as a purpose socio-ethical or cultural integration, as well as of education in the narrow individualistic sense.

In order that this commitment exists in some tangible form, there is a need at the very least for the individual members of the occupation or organization to participate in the establishment, and ongoing revision, of their code of ethics. Without such participation the code will not be a "live" document, and it will not be "owned" by the members of the occupational group or organization.

The process by which a code of ethics is drafted, or redrafted, ought to involve not only consultation regarding the basic principles and ideals, but also research into ethical problems confronted by members, and some attempt to have members ratify or otherwise indicate their acceptance of the code once it is finalized.

Codes of ethics prescribe and proscribe specific actions, and many of them attach sanctions to noncompliance. So, codes of ethics have a regulatory purpose, in addition to their educative and cultural integration purposes. Often the main regulatory role of a code of ethics is actually played by an associated code of practice. The code of ethics is a basic presentation of principles and ideals; the code of practice is a detailed description of the actions that are to be performed or not performed, and of the sanctions that attach to nonperformance. Be that as it may, here I want to elaborate on the notion of regulation and its relation to ethical behavior and to ethics education (formal and informal).

Regulation, like ethical education, ought to proceed in such a way as to secure compliance with appropriate moral principles, especially compliance with minimum standards, e.g., avoidance of criminal activity such as fraud, theft, eschewing of unfair practices, and so on.

Moreover, regulation of occupations involved in the market economy ought to promote an efficient, competitive market, and education likewise ought to promote this. However, regulation of itself, unlike education, is less able to promote pursuit of ideals, as opposed to conformity to minimum standards. This is not to say that the regulative and the educative roles of codes of ethics (and of codes of practice) are somehow independent of one another, or that they ought to be. Far from it. They ought to be interdependent and mutually reinforcing.

In contriving regulations, account ought to be taken not simply of the self-interested motivations of the relevant actors but also of their ethical motivations, including not only their sense of fairness and susceptibility to feelings of shame, but also their desire for the respect that goes with achievement of high ideals. This is a general truth that goes as much for codes of ethics and codes of practice as it does for laws and regulations.

Here it is worth bearing in mind that regulations, and the law more generally, are conformed with not only because they have sanctions attached but also because they are perceived to be fair and also rational in terms of the ends of the activity regulated. Compliance with unfair or irrational regulations can be very hard to achieve, even if heavy penalties attach to noncompliance. Indeed, it may be that the best regulatory strategies are ones in which the fairness and reasonableness of a regulation and the sanctions attaching to it mutually reinforce one another.[13]

Contriving and framing regulations gives rise to a wide array of quite specific ethical problems concerning the fairness of particular practices or reward systems, the ethical unacceptability of some conflicts of interest, and so on. Many of these are complex intellectual problems, and solving them involves not simply the identification of (often competing) ethical considerations but also the elaboration of new principles that give due weight to these ethical considerations. There is a need for systematic ethical reflection.

9.4 Complaints and Discipline Systems

In the previous section I pointed out that such codes ideally serve a number of purposes, identified as educative, integrative, and regulatory. The extent to which any actual code serves these purposes is partly a matter of its content and mode of development. But it also depends on the way in which it integrates with other elements of an overall occupational integrity system. Of particular importance here is the existence of a well-designed and functioning complaints and discipline system.[14] There is often a good deal of

---

[13] See Ian Ayres and John Braithwaite, *Responsive Regulation* (Oxford University Press, 1992).
[14] Earlier versions of the material in this section appeared in Alexandra and Miller, *Integrity Systems for Occupations*, chapter 4; and in Andrew Alexandra, Tom Campbell, Dean Cocking, Seumas Miller,

skepticism, if not downright cynicism, about codes of ethics, which are seen as "window dressing," among both the general public and members of the occupation itself. While there may be a number of reasons for this, arguably one important reason is the lack of effective responses to breaches of the standards laid down in codes.

Like a code of ethics, a complaints and discipline system serves a number of different purposes. As its name implies, there are two components to a complaints and discipline system: first gathering and classifying complaints (the complaint element), then assessing and responding to those complaints that are prima facie grounds for sanctioning a member of the occupation (the discipline element). An effective method for gathering complaints is a necessary condition for a fair discipline system; at the same time, complaints are more likely to be forthcoming if it is perceived that they will be taken seriously and responded to appropriately. Moreover, the complaint element can serve a number of valuable purposes in its own right, apart from providing the material on which the discipline element acts. These purposes include resolving grievances and gathering data to assist in policymaking. Like all the other elements of an occupational integrity system, the ultimate institutional purpose of a complaints and discipline system is to assist the members of an occupation achieve their ultimate institutional purpose, i.e., their collective end that is a collective good. While this claim is a truism, it is worth keeping in mind when considering the design and application of specific systems.

In relation to the purpose of detection of breaches of occupational standards, a distinction can be drawn between unsatisfactory conduct, on the one hand, and ethical misconduct, including corruption and criminality, on the other. Unsatisfactory conduct is conduct that falls short of the standard of competence and diligence that can reasonably be expected of a competent practitioner, as a consequence of carelessness or haste, for example. Misconduct, including corruption, describes more serious breaches of occupational standards. It might involve deliberate wrongdoing, as when a practitioner holds themselves out as possessing qualifications or competencies they do not have, or gives a client false information in order to win a commission or a promotion. It might also involve negligent or reckless breaches of occupational standards that the member should have known were likely to create substantial risks of harm or cost to others. Moreover, a pattern of behavior might constitute misconduct even though any single element in that pattern by itself would not. In the case of serious breaches,

and Kevin White, *Professionalization, Ethics and Integrity*, Report for the Professional Standards Council (2006).

the system may function to identify matters for criminal investigation by the police, sanction the member for disciplinary breaches, and/or direct them to provide restitution to those harmed by their actions.

A complaints and discipline system has an important role in gathering information for use by individual members of an occupation, occupational settings (such as businesses or public sector agencies), and the occupation as a whole. Data should be collected about the context, nature (e.g., conflict of interest, discourtesy), and frequency of complaints. Against the background of such data for the occupation as a whole (or relevant sub-groups thereof), information about individuals can be used to identify those who are "at risk" (who have, say, an unusual number of low-level complaints made against them) and action, such as professional development and/or monitoring, to be taken. Likewise, comparisons of similar occupational settings may reveal anomalous patterns of complaints (i.e., noticeably high or low compared to the norm) indicating the need for further investigation and, perhaps, action. The intelligence gathered through a complaints and discipline system is also an important source of information for an occupation's Ethics Audit (discussed in the next section.)

From the characterization of the institutional purposes of a complaints and discipline system outlined above, we can derive a number of general characteristics that such a system should possess. The overarching requirements are that the system is constructed in such a way as to achieve both procedural and substantive justice. That is, it should have fair, transparent, and effective procedures in place that are likely to reveal the truth concerning occupational (mis)conduct and deliver responses appropriate to that conduct.

Procedural justice, in this context, encompasses more than just the regulations governing the workings of disciplinary tribunals. It also includes the broader "user-friendliness" of the whole system, such as ease of access, speediness of dealing with complaints, support for participants, and so on, insofar as these affect the substantive justice of the way in which the system deals with wrongdoing. Most occupational associations have, at best, limited investigative powers and lack coercive powers, and depend on volunteers to sit on tribunals. Their complaints and discipline systems, then, are only likely to function effectively if their members, and those affected by members' actions, are willing to participate.

If (potential) complainants perceive that the complaint process is difficult or futile, or that they are likely to be met with hostility, they are obviously less likely to make or proceed with a complaint. That impinges on all the roles of the complaints and discipline system (e.g., it distorts information about occupational malfeasance, subverts proper norms regarding practitioner/client relationships, magnifies rather than resolves grievances, and so on.) Similarly, if members of occupations perceive that the system is unreasonably harsh (or unreasonably lenient) or selectively applied, they may be less inclined to participate in or support it.

9.5   Ethics Audits and Reputational Indexes

A key element in the establishment of effective integrity systems for occupations, and especially the professions, is the mobilization of professional reputation.[15] A high professional reputation is much sought after by members of the professions, and a low one to be avoided at all costs. Accordingly, there is an opportunity to mobilize this reputational desire in the service of promoting ethical standards. Here the aim is to ensure that professional reputation aligns with actual ethical practice, i.e., that a group or individual's high or low reputation is deserved. The way to achieve this is by designing appropriate integrity systems. Key elements of an integrity system track compliance with rules, e.g., accountability. The additional thought here is that key elements of an integrity system should track features of occupational groups that determine or should determine reputation. Most explicitly, a reputational index could be constructed whereby an ethics audit awards scores in relation to specific ethico-professional standards.

Deserved reputation represents an important nexus between self-interest and concern about others, and so, for our purposes here, between the self-interest of commercial occupational or associational groups and concern about consumers, clients, or the public generally. Here there are three elements in play: (1) reputation; (2) self-interest; and (3) ethical requirements, such as particular ethico-professional standards, but also more general desiderata such as client/consumer protection. Hence my reference to a triangle. The idea is that these three elements need to interlock in the following way.

First, reputation is linked to self-interest; this is obviously already the case – individuals, groups, and organizations desire high reputation and benefit materially and in other ways from it. Second, reputation needs to be linked to ethics in that reputation ought to be deserved; as already

---

[15] Alexandra and Miller, *Integrity Systems for Occupations*, chapter 5; Miller, "Financial Service Providers: Integrity Systems, Reputation and the Triangle of Virtue" in Dobos, Barry, and Pogge (eds.), *Global Financial Crisis*, pp. 132–157.

mentioned, the integrity systems are the means to achieve this. Third, and as a consequence of the two already mentioned links, self-interest is linked to ethics; given robust integrity systems that mobilize reputational concerns, it is in the self-interest of individuals, groups, and firms to comply with ethico-professional standards. I should also reiterate that self-interest is not the only or ultimate motivation for human action; the desire to do the right thing is also a powerful motivator for many, if not all people. Accordingly, the triangle is further strengthened by the motivation to do right.

In recent years, the notion of a Reputation Index has gained currency in a number of contexts, especially in business and academic circles. The term seems to have a number of different senses. Sometimes it is used to describe a way of measuring the reputation that an organization actually has: since reputation exists, so to speak, in the eye of the beholder. Actual reputation does not always match deserved reputation. Accordingly, sometimes the term is used to describe a way of calculating the performance of an organization on the basis of which its reputation should be founded.

The first step in the process is to determine a way of accurately measuring the ethical performance of individual or organizational members of occupational and industry groups; this is an ethics audit. Here I stress the importance of *objective* measures of ethical performance. The latter might include such things as results of consumer satisfaction surveys; gross numbers of warranted complaints and trends thereof; numbers of disciplinary matters and their outcomes; outcomes of financial, and health and safety audits (e.g., regarding electronic crime and corruption vulnerabilities). It would also include the existence of institutional processes established to assure compliance with ethico-professional standards, e.g., codes of ethics and conduct, financial and other audit processes, ethics committees, complaints and disciplinary systems, fraud and ethics units, professional development programs in ethics, ethics officers.

In addition to the ethics audit itself, there is a need for a process that engages with ethical reputation. Since ethical reputation should reflect the findings of the ethics audit, an ethical reputation audit should drive the relationship between *de facto* ethical performance (in effect, the deserved reputation) and actual reputation for ethical performance. The way to achieve this is by the participation of as many occupational and industry players as possible in ethics audits, and by the widespread promulgation of the results of their *de facto* ethical performance (as determined by the ethics audit), including in the media. Naturally, the results promulgated could be more or less detailed; they could, for example, simply consist in an overall rating as opposed to a complete description of the ethics audit results.

9.6 Conflicts of Interest

A fundamental ethical standard of particular relevance to professional reputation is the avoidance or management of conflicts of interest. Conflicts of interest are, of course, a potent source of ethical misconduct, indeed of corruption. Moreover, conflicts of interest are often not well-understood; this is so, at least in part, because determining whether or not something is a conflict of interest can be a difficult matter in need of sustained ethical analysis. Finally, and most importantly for our concerns here, conflicts of interest are intimately connected to questions of professional reputation. So much so that the avoidance of even the *appearance* of a conflict of interest can be an ethical requirement; it can be an ethical requirement by virtue of the damage it can do to the reputation of a practitioner, firm, or even an entire occupational group. Consider the reputational damage done to auditors when they appear to have a conflict of interest in undertaking well-remunerated consultative work for the very firms that they audit.

A conflict of interest occurs when a person or group's personal interest comes into conflict with their occupational duties, or when a person or group has two occupational roles, and the duties of one compete with the duties of the other.[16] For example, if a member of the tax office decided to adjudicate his own tax return, he would have a conflict between his personal self-interest and his fiduciary duty. Again, if an accountant happened also to be the manager of a football club, and as an accountant she was asked to audit the club's financial statements, she would have a conflict of interest.

In relation to role conflicts of interest it is important to distinguish what might be termed circumstantial conflicts of interest from structural conflicts of interest. The latter arise on an ongoing basis due to a structural feature of an occupation in an institutional setting. For example, financial planners who present themselves as offering independent financial advice but whose remuneration consists in large part in commissions paid by banks and other financial institutions who

---

[16] An earlier version of some of the material in this section appeared in Miller, Roberts, and Spence, *Corruption and Anti-Corruption*, chapter 8.

manufacture the financial products that the financial planners in question are selling to their clients.[17] Speaking generally, structural conflicts of interest are far more morally problematic than circumstantial conflicts of interests; after all, the latter are likely to occur only sporadically and to be less serious.

Conflicts of interest are conducive to ethical misconduct in a variety of ways, depending on the nature of the role of the person or group that has the conflict of interest. For example, a magistrate or police officer with a conflict of interest may fail to apply the law impartially, or a businessman who is a member of a local government body might vote to award himself a contract.

Sometimes it is hard to determine whether an apparent conflict of interest is real or not. And theoretically, a conflict of interest that is only apparent might not be problematic. However, often even the *appearance* of impropriety can be harmful to the reputations of persons and groups, and to the confidence that people need to have in practitioners and the occupations and institutions to which they belong. Accordingly, it is often very important to clarify and resolve *apparent* conflicts of interest, as well as to avoid real ones. Indeed, it may well be important to avoid even the appearance of a conflict of interest.

Further, the precise nature and boundaries of occupational roles should be clearly delineated and rendered perspicuous, for if this is not done then role confusion can arise, and with it the possibility of real or apparent conflicts of interest.

Before we proceed further, let us determine what a *conflict of interest* is. According to the "standard view":[18]

A conflict of interest is a situation in which some person *P* (whether an individual or corporate body) has a conflict of interest. *P* has a conflict of interest if and only if (1) *P* is in a relationship with another requiring *P* to exercise judgment on the other's behalf and (2) *P* has a (special) interest tending to interfere with the proper exercise of judgment in that relationship. The crucial terms in this definition are "relationship," "judgment," "interest," and "proper exercise."

The "relationship" required must involve one person trusting (or at least being entitled to trust) another to exercise judgment on his behalf. "Judgment" is the ability to make certain kinds of correct and reliable

---

decisions that require knowledge or skill. "Interest" is any influence, loyalty, concern, emotion, or other feature of a situation tending to make P's judgment (in that situation) less reliable than it ought to be. What constitutes a "proper exercise" of judgment is usually a matter of social fact; it includes what people ordinarily expect, what P or the group to which P belongs invites others to expect, and what relevant laws, professional codes, or other regulations require.[19]

What is generally wrong with a conflict of interest is that it renders one's judgment less reliable than it should be, and results in a failure to properly discharge one's duty. Generally, a conflict of interest can arise in at least one of two ways:

(1) Person (or persons) A has an individual (or collective) self-regarding interest that is in conflict, at least potentially, with his or her occupational duty, and therefore has the tendency to interfere with the proper exercise of A's judgment with regard to that duty.

(2) Person (or persons) A has two potentially competing occupational duties or roles that are in conflict with each other, at least potentially, and therefore one duty or role has the tendency to interfere with the proper exercise of A's judgment with regard to the other duty or role.

For example, there is a clear conflict of interest in the case of an accountant, Joe, who audits the financial statements of a club, and who is also the manager of that club. Consider the interest in the club that Joe has as the manager. Joe *qua* manager has an interest in maintaining the image of the club as financially viable. Now consider Joe's interest as an auditor in providing a true and fair statement of the club's financial situation. Joe's interest as a manager in maintaining the image of the club might have a tendency to make his judgment as auditor less reliable than it should be. Clearly there is a potential conflict of interest here, and one that arises from these two conflicting roles.

Crucially for our purposes in this work, conflicts of interest are conducive to corruption and other serious forms of ethical misconduct. For example, a police officer who also moonlights for a security firm faces a conflict of interest when called upon to investigate criminal allegations against the manager of the security firm. The police officer's personal interest in keeping his second job conflicts with the requirements of his role as a police officer, and may interfere with the proper exercise of his judgment in fulfilling his duty, as police officer, of upholding the law. He

[19] *Ibid.*

might be less zealous than he ought in his investigation of the criminal allegations against his boss. Again, a judge who presides over a criminal trial that involves his daughter as defendant in a rape case has a conflict of interest. Notice that the police officer in the first case, and the judge in the second case, may in fact not act corruptly; each may well intend to do his duty – by investigating the criminal allegation thoroughly (in the case of the police officer), or conducting the trial fairly (in the case of the judge); indeed, each may in fact discharge their duty. However, in each case the conflict of interest remains, and therefore there is at least an apparent inability to properly discharge their role requirements.

The above examples illustrate that although not every instance of a conflict of interest necessarily results in wrongdoing, nevertheless conflicts of interest are conducive to wrongdoing. Thus, it is best to avoid conflicts of interest; it is best, for example, that a judge with no familial connections to the defendant is appointed to the trial. In cases in which the conflict of interest is a minor one, and/or could only be avoided with great difficulty, it may be acceptable for the person with the conflict to disclose it without avoiding it. If so, disclosure might need to be backed up by some suitably rigorous process of accountability.

As we have already seen, many conflicts of interest involve a conflict between one's (individual or collective) self-interest and the requirements of the role that one occupies. Others involve a conflict between two different roles that one occupies. Still others involve a degree of role confusion that serves to mask a conflict of interest.

Conflicts of interest involving (individual or collective) self-interest are reasonably obvious, but what of *role conflicts*? By way of illustration, consider the following restrictions imposed in some organizations or professions: one cannot be both judge and advocate, or both editor and manager of advertising revenue of a newspaper, or both cashier-banker and manager of accounts payable and receivable in a large corporation. Underlying this institutional division of potentially conflicting roles is the *principle of the division and separation of responsibilities*. This principle is adhered to so that the proper exercise of one's judgment cannot be adversely affected by allowing one to occupy two potentially conflicting roles or functions. The role conflicts involve primarily a conflict between two roles, offices, or institutions. Traditionally, a Western democratic state is divided into distinct institutional "estates," for example, the government and the judiciary, whose purposes are by design supposed to remain separate and independent. The separateness and independence of these institutions from one another is designed to ensure a division of power, and also to ensure that potentially harmful structural conflicts of interest are avoided. Without this "separation of powers" we would have the intolerable situation in which a senior politician is the judge in a case involving a political opponent or in a case involving an adjudication in relation to the legality of a proposed government policy.

The most obvious way to deal with conflicts of interest that might result in corruption is to avoid them. In cases where there is a potential conflict between an institutional actor's self-interest and the duties of his institutional role, regulations requiring avoidance of these conflicts need to be introduced and some form of accountability mechanism established.

Role conflicts can best be avoided through a strict division of duties and responsibilities that does not allow one person to occupy both roles. For example, there is a traditional division of accounting responsibilities between the cashiering and banking functions on the one hand, and the accounts payable and receivable functions on the other hand.

In the case of accountancy firms, structural conflicts of interest might be avoided through the strict division and separation of the auditing and financial consultancy functions within the firm. However, this control may not be adequate to avoid conflicts of interest if fees from financial consultancy services far exceed auditing fees. One possible solution to this problem is to increase audit fees substantially so that they at least match those from financial consultancy services. If that is not possible, perhaps it should be impermissible for an accounting firm to provide auditing and consultancy services to the same client.

The potential structural conflict between the requirement for objectivity and impartiality in news reporting and editorial comment, on the one hand, and the commercial demands of advertising, on the other hand, might be avoided by having a strict division between those two functions in a media organization.

It is not always possible to avoid conflicts of interest. The next best solution is to disclose them. However, disclosure is only acceptable in the case of otherwise ethically acceptable practices. It would not be ethically acceptable for a politician to be a judge. Accordingly, disclosure would not be a solution to that conflict of interest.

On the other hand, the mandatory disclosure of advertorials as being in fact advertisements – and, therefore, in no sense to be regarded as sources of impartial and objective information – might be sufficient to eliminate the pretense that they are anything other than advertisements. In this particular type of conflict of interest, disclosure has almost the same effect as avoidance, for it eliminates the deceptive cloak and requires the advertorial to be seen for what it is – an advertisement.[20]

As we have seen, some *apparent conflicts of interest* can be as ethically problematic as real ones because of their potential to generate a loss of confidence in institutional processes, or a loss of trust in institutional actors. One way of eliminating these untoward effects of apparent conflicts of interest is disclosure. Often, full and frank disclosure reveals that the apparent conflict of interest is not a real conflict of interest, and this is sufficient to satisfy relevant parties that there are no grounds for loss of confidence or trust. Consider, in this connection, full disclosure of all donations to political parties (in conjunction with a cap on the size of all donations).

9.7 Conclusion

In this chapter I have outlined some of the main features of an integrity system for occupations (leaving aside the criminal justice system as such since it is dealt with elsewhere eg. in Chapter 7 and 8) and discussed each of these features in turn. The features in question are codes of ethics, complaints and discipline systems, and ethics audits and reputational indexes. Throughout, I have stressed the importance of integrating these various features in such a manner that they mobilize commitments to underlying social norms (felt moral principles and ethical values) and reinforce one another in the service of the collective ends of the particular occupational group in question. I have also discussed conflicts of interest and distinguished between circumstantial and structural conflicts of interest. Structural conflicts of interest are one of the main conditions conducive to corruption in occupational settings and, for that matter, in organizational settings.

---

[20] Davis, "Conflict of Interest," p. 593.

CHAPTER 10

Whistleblowing

In this final chapter of Part II, the focus is on an important element of anti-corruption and integrity systems that has come to the fore in recent times, namely, whistleblowing. As the recent disclosures concerning the law firm Mossack Fonseca, based in Panama (the so-called Panama Papers[1]), have dramatically revealed, whistleblowing can be a potent anti-corruption weapon. The disclosures came from an anonymous source who has "leaked" 11.5 million documents to two journalists, Bastian Obermayer and Frederik Obermaier, working for the Munich-based paper *Suddeutsche Zeitung*. The number of documents was so large that the two journalists sought assistance from the International Consortium of Investigative Journalists to sort, manage, and finally publish the findings globally and more or less simultaneously. This process involved journalists from eighty countries. The disclosures revealed that Mossack Fonseca had set up no less than 24,000 offshore companies. These "shell" companies have as one of their main purposes to mask the ownership of assets. Perhaps unsurprisingly, therefore, Mossack Fonseca's clients include dictators and drug dealers. A second important purpose is to avoid, if not evade, tax. In the British Virgin Islands and other so-called tax havens little or no tax has to be paid and, therefore, companies based in these havens can pay little or no tax, notwithstanding that the profits made by these companies were accrued in countries in which a substantial rate of tax has to be paid. Remarkably, setting up such offshore companies and using them to avoid tax is not typically unlawful; it is not tax evasion. Nevertheless, it self-evidently ought to be unlawful and the OECD is currently taking steps to bring it about that it is unlawful.[2] Importantly, this practice, unlawful or not, is corrupt. For it is a practice deliberately undertaken for the purpose

---

[1] Obermayer and Obermaier, *The Panama Papers*.
[2] OECD, "Base Erosion and Profit Sharing," www.oecd.org.

of avoiding taxes earned on profits in a given jurisdiction, and it has the predictable effect of undermining the institutional processes and purposes of legitimate tax regimes in those jurisdictions.

Naturally, the disclosure of information by whistleblowers is not normally on the vast scale of the Panama Papers. Moreover, unlike the publication of the Panama Papers, whistleblowing is sometimes unjustified or, at least, morally ambiguous. Indeed, there are a wide range of cases in which an employee discloses information without authorization from their employing organization. In some cases, disclosure of such information is manifestly unlawful and immoral, e.g., a corrupt intelligence officer's disclosure of sensitive information about a terrorist investigation to the terrorists under investigation in return for financial reward. In other cases, disclosure of such information, even if prima facie unauthorized, might, nevertheless, be lawful and morally required, e.g., the above-described Mossack Fonseca disclosures or a police officer's disclosure of information about a corrupt police chief's criminal activity to a police oversight body. In still other cases, the legality, and especially the morality, of the disclosure might be unclear, e.g., an intelligence officer's disclosure to the media of what he reasonably believes to be unlawful and immoral surveillance activity being conducted by his employing organization.

Famously, Daniel Ellsberg released the so-called Pentagon Papers to the *New York Times* newspaper, which published them in 1971.[3] Robert McNamara, a US Secretary of Defense during the Vietnam War, was responsible for a comprehensive analysis of US involvement in that war and Ellsberg worked on the project. Ellsberg developed the view that successive US administrations had lied about the war and, in particular, about the prospects of success. Moreover, he held that the American public had a right to know the details of this. The Nixon administration's reaction to this was extreme; indeed, its reaction involved unlawful activity, such as breaking into the Democratic Party Offices, leading to Watergate and the impeachment of Nixon.

Ellsberg disclosed information that the American public surely had a right to know. Moreover, it is unlikely that the disclosures would have seen the light of day if he had not gone to the media. Further, the disclosures, while damaging to the Nixon administration, in particular, did not involve unnecessary risk of harm to innocent third parties. For example, the

---

[3] Neil Sheehan, "Vietnam Archive: Pentagon Study Traces 3 Decades of Growing US Involvement," *New York Times*, June 13, 1971.

disclosures did not put the lives of US servicemen or other personnel at risk. Accordingly, Ellsberg's disclosures were evidently morally justified.

The recent disclosures of Edward Snowden are a different kind of case.[4] Snowden, a low-level private contractor to the US-based National Security Agency (NSA), ignored *prima facie* legal and moral confidentiality/secrecy obligations by engaging in unauthorized accessing, retrieving, and/or releasing of a large volume of confidential data from NSA to the press and, possibly, to foreign powers, e.g., China and Russia.[5] Snowden's activities are a major, indeed stunning, breach of institutional confidentiality and were enabled by the new information and communication technologies and, specifically, the existence of vast amounts of communicable, searchable, analyzable, stored data on a computer linked to a network. As such, his activities were prima facie not only unlawful but also, given that they predictably undermined institutional processes and purposes, corrupt.

However, release of some of this data to the press might be morally justified by the public's "right to know," e.g., the public's right to know that the NSA was engaged in an extremely large-scale collection process of the data of US and other citizens. In a liberal democratic polity, if the state engages in this kind of large-scale collection process without the knowledge and approval of the citizenry then, arguably, it goes beyond its remit and, potentially, undermines public trust in the government and its security agencies. In short, whereas the collection process may well be justified in itself, the manner in which it was implemented rendered it a *prima facie* corrupt process. That said, the release by Snowden of confidential data to foreign powers, e.g., China and Russia, if it has taken place, is a form of cyber-espionage. Moreover, it also constitutes *pro tanto* serious moral wrongdoing, since it potentially undermines legitimate security purposes and processes, and/or puts security personnel and others in harm's way. Whether or not it was morally wrong, *all things considered*, depends on the countervailing moral weight to be attached to Snowden's fulfilling the public's right to know about the NSA's data collection and related activities.

In this chapter I undertake three tasks. First (Section 10.1), I discuss the nature of whistleblowing with a view to differentiating it from other forms of unauthorized disclosure, e.g., leaking. Second (Section 10.2), I provide

---

[4] Glenn Greenwald, *No Place to Hide: Edward Snowden, The NSA and the Surveillance State* (London: Penguin Books, 2014).
[5] Tom Harper, Richard Kerbaj, and Tim Shipman, "British Spies Betrayed to Russians and Chinese," *Sunday Times*, June 14, 2015.

analyses of the moral principles of privacy and confidentiality, and differentiate these from the (arguably) non-moral principles of anonymity and secrecy (respectively). The principles of privacy and confidentiality have inherent moral weight – in a sense clarified below – and, as such, can underpin a requirement of nondisclosure. The same is not true of anonymity and secrecy. Rather, anonymity and secrecy only have instrumental value, if and when they have value at all. Finally (Section 10.3), I consider some of the arguments for and against different forms of unauthorized disclosure and do so in the context of the public's right to know, the integrity of institutions, as well as the principles of privacy and confidentiality.

10.1 Whistleblowing

To assist us in our attempt to provide an adequate definition of whistleblowing let us consider that paradigm of a whistleblower, Daniel Ellsberg, and try to pinpoint the key features of his activity as a whistleblower. Proceeding in this way, the first and most obvious feature of whistleblowing is that it involves making some alleged immoral, corrupt, and/or criminal activity a matter of public knowledge.[6] This means much more than voicing one's concerns to one or two individuals. Frequently, we tell spouses, friends, and members of our families about disturbing things that happen in the workplace because we wish them to understand and empathize with our feelings. Whistleblowing involves much more than this. It involves putting "information" on the public record in such a way that "the world," even if only potentially, can access it, and indeed, is likely to access it. The methods of achieving this are quite diverse, and consist of such communications as reports to a media outlet, book publications, revelations before a Parliamentary or Congressional Committee, and, more recently, material placed on the internet.

A further question that now arises concerns the position of the whistleblower in relation to the organization in which the corruption or wrongdoing is allegedly taking place. The whistleblower is most commonly a current or former employee of the organization whose activities are being exposed. Using this criterion, Ralph Nader, who exposed unsafe

---

[6] Earlier versions of the material in this section appeared in Alexandra and Miller, *Integrity Systems for Occupations*, chapter 4; and Miller, Roberts, and Spence, *Corruption and Anti-Corruption*, chapter 8. Many of the points made in that chapter were provided by Peter Roberts and this is reflected in the discussion here.

engineering practices in the US automotive industry, is not a whistle-blower because he was not an employee of the companies he criticized.

Let us now turn to the question of where the complaint is raised. In cases in which the information is published in the media, it is quite clear that the whistleblower is "going public." However, should an individual raise his or her concerns entirely within the organization, it is far from evident that this should be referred to as whistleblowing. For it would seem merely to be part of the "normal" practice within any ethically healthy organization, whereby an individual raises concerns and the management deals with them. At any rate, I will refer to this normal practice (as it ought to be, but frequently is not) as professional reporting or internal disclosure. This distinction becomes important when organizations ostensibly create mechanisms to accommodate whistleblowing but then put limits upon the public disclosure by individuals of their concerns. In these cases, it seems that the individuals involved are not whistleblowing at all, but are rather engaging in a formalized staff suggestion scheme or the like.

This distinction between internal and external disclosure can cause confusion, particularly in public sector institutions. When an individual raises his or her concerns with another public sector body – such as the Auditor-General or Ombudsman – in one sense the complaint has gone beyond being an internal management matter. However, if we conceive the agency to whom the individual belongs and the external public sector agency to whom the complaint has been referred as constituting parts of the same public sector organizational entity, then the individual is not engaged in whistleblowing. Specifically, the individual has not "made public" the alleged corrupt activity.

Implicit in the above discussion is that whistleblowing, properly understood, is restricted to corrupt, immoral, and/or criminal activity that is taking place in an organizational context. It is difficult to conceive of the act of "blowing the whistle" on behavior that is taking place in the family home or on the streets, such as a burglary or an assault.

A further crucial feature of whistleblowing is that the making public of the information is a deliberate act. Were the information to be revealed because an individual inadvertently left sensitive documents in a taxi, then no matter what effect the information had, the act could not be called "whistleblowing." This is because it was not done with the appropriate *intention*. For an action to count as whistleblowing it would normally need to be intended, and indeed deliberate, i.e., involving some form of prior reason-based decision.

Disclosure can be a form of preemptive defense; if so, does it constitute whistleblowing? The Sherron Watkins case highlights this dilemma.[7] As Vice President for Corporate Development at Enron, she was working directly under the Chief Financial Officer, Andrew Fastow, who was subsequently indicted for fraud. In August 2000, the wheels were starting to fall off the Enron enterprise, with the share price tumbling and CEO Jeffrey Skilling resigning. While it is not possible to determine with any certainty what motivated her, the circumstances strongly suggest that, in outlining her concerns to Kenneth Lay, she was simply seeking to distance herself from the wrongdoings at Enron rather than right this wrongdoing. People often have mixed motives, but her action would not count as whistleblowing if it turned out that her aim was not public disclosure in the public interest, but only self-protection.

Probably the most important feature of whistleblowing is its relation to some form of wrongdoing – typically unlawful activity. The whistleblower blows the whistle on wrongdoing. In this respect, whistleblowing differs from leaking. Information leaked does not necessarily pertain to wrongful or unlawful activity. Consider, for example, the leaking of embarrassing information.

However, the relationship between whistleblowing and wrongdoing is not always clear-cut. In many well-documented cases of whistleblowing, it is quite clear that some form of wrongdoing has occurred, and the whistle-blower has disclosed this wrongdoing to the public. However, in many other cases this is not so. Accordingly, there is an important distinction between instances in which the wrongdoing disclosed has actually occurred and cases in which the whistleblower has made a false allegation of wrong-doing based upon inference and limited knowledge. One of the character-istic features of whistleblowers is their strong belief in their cause, but strong beliefs are not necessarily to be equated with *true* beliefs. Accordingly, it is important to distinguish between whistleblowing in the primary sense of public disclosure of an *actual* wrongdoing and whistle-blowing in the secondary sense of public *allegations* of wrongdoing, where the allegations are not proven and may in fact be false.

Another key feature of whistleblowing is that the whistleblower puts the wrongdoing on the public record with the clear intention that some remedial action will be taken. Whistleblowers are not mere passive obser-vers of wrongdoing, but rather seek to right the wrongs that they observe. In most histories of whistleblowing, the individuals raise the matters with

---

[7] Dan Ackman, "Sherron Watkins had Whistle, but Blew it," *Forbes*, February 14, 2012.

their superiors in the hope that the wrong will be rectified, but it is not. Disillusioned with the management's response, they explore other avenues, and ultimately opt for public disclosure. By contrast, those who merely leak information do so for quite diverse motives (e.g., political self-interest) and typically their first option is public disclosure.

The final feature of whistleblowing is that the whistleblower is acting in a hostile environment and is under a real or potential threat of reprisal. Indeed, if the person contemplating the disclosure of wrongdoing does not believe that it is going to trigger some form of reprisal then, whether or not reprisal may in fact eventuate, it could reasonably be said that the person is not whistleblowing. Rather, he or she may simply be involved in a more or less routine complaints process, albeit one in which, as it turns out, there is conflict and even reprisal.

Here it is important to make a number of points. First, as indicated above, the whistleblower may be mistaken about the wrongdoing he or she believes has taken place. Second, there is a moral obligation on the part of the employee to disclose the kind of serious wrongdoing in question (assuming, of course, it has taken place). Each member of an organization has a moral obligation – an obligation held jointly with the other members – to contribute to the elimination or reduction of serious wrongdoing, including corruption, within the organization, notably by reporting such wrongdoing when it occurs. Third, any intentional and unjustified interference with the discharging of this obligation to report constitutes an act of corruption by virtue of being an attempt to undermine a morally obligatory institutional process. This is obviously the case where the process of reporting has been formalized and there is an explicit requirement to report. But it is also the case where the process is informal and implicit. For in the latter case, the moral requirement to report exists, even if this moral obligation has not been expressed in a law or regulation or policy statement.

The main elements of whistleblowing can be summarized as follows. The whistleblower is a member of an organization, and he or she deliberately places information about nontrivial wrongdoing on the public record, doing so for the purpose of having the wrongdoing stopped, and in the expectation that he or she may suffer some form of unwarranted interference and/or real or threatened reprisal.[8]

---

[8] See also F. Elliston, *Whistleblowing Research: Methodological and Moral Issues* (New York: Praeger, 1985), p. 15. For a detailed treatment of these issues see P. Roberts, A. J. Brown, and J. Olsen, *Whistling While They Work: A Good-Practice Guide for Managing Internal Reporting of Wrongdoing in Public Sector Organisations* (Canberra: ANU Press, 2011).

10.2   Privacy and Confidentiality

Whistleblowing is typically a disclosure of information that an organization, or member of such, has not disclosed and does not want disclosed. Such disclosure is, therefore, a breach of an organization's, or a member of an organization's, privacy or confidentiality. However, these notions of privacy and confidentiality are often not adequately distinguished from one another; nor are they always adequately distinguished from the notions of anonymity and secrecy. This is problematic since these are four different notions that have differential moral weight. Let me briefly discuss each of them and, in doing so, display their relationship to one another.[9]

The notion of privacy has proven to be a difficult one to explicate adequately.[10] Nevertheless, there are a number of general points that can be made. First, privacy is a moral right that a person has in relation to other persons with respect to (a) the possession of information about him/herself by other persons or (b) the observation/perceiving of him/herself – including of a person's movements, relationships, and so on – by other persons.

Second, the right to privacy is closely related to the more fundamental moral value of autonomy. Roughly speaking, the notion of privacy delimits an area, viz. the inner self; however, the moral right to decide what to think and do is the right to autonomy, and the moral right to decide *who to exclude and who not to* is an element of the right to autonomy. So the right to privacy consists of the right to exclude others (right to autonomy) from the inner self (the private sphere).

Third, a measure of privacy is necessary simply in order for a person to pursue his or her projects, whatever those projects might be. For one thing, reflection is necessary for planning, and reflection requires a degree of freedom from the intrusions of others, that is, a degree of privacy. For another, knowledge of someone else's plans can enable those plans to be thwarted. *Autonomy* – including the exercise of autonomy in the public sphere – requires a measure of privacy.

In the light of the above analysis of privacy, and especially its close relationships to autonomy, we are entitled to conclude that an extent of some kinds of privacy is a constitutive human good. As such, there is a

[9] An earlier version of the material in this section appeared in Seumas Miller and Patrick. Walsh, "NSA, Snowden and the Ethics and Accountability of Intelligence Gathering" in Jai Galliott (ed.), *Ethics and the Future of Spying: Technology, Intelligence Collection and National Security* (Abingdon-on-Thames: Routledge, 2015).

[10] Thomas Nagel, *Concealment and Exposure and Other Essays* (Oxford University Press, 2002).

presumption against infringements of privacy. That said, privacy can reasonably be overridden by security considerations under some circumstances such as when lives are at risk. After all, the right to life is, in general, a weightier moral right than the right to privacy. Thus accessing the financial records of a suspected terrorist, if conducted under warrant, is surely morally justified. Let us now turn to some notions that are closely related to privacy, namely, anonymity, confidentiality and secrecy.

Individual privacy is sometimes confused with anonymity but these are distinct notions. Anonymity is preserved when a person's identity in one context is not known in another. Consider the case of Jones, a respectable married man. In another context, Jones might be the anonymous client of a prostitute. Of course, Jones is "known" to the prostitute, indeed, intimately known. However, the prostitute does not know Jones in his home or work contexts and, likewise, his family and work colleagues do not know Jones in the context of the brothel. Again, consider Smith, a wealthy businessman. In another context, Smith might be an anonymous donor.

Anonymity can be a means to privacy (e.g., Smith wants to avoid publicity), or to avoid harm to oneself (e.g., the reputational damage that Jones might suffer if his visits to the brothel became known). Indeed, anonymity is vital in some situations, for example, an anonymous "tip-off" to police regarding a violent criminal who would kill such an informant if he knew their identity.

These examples demonstrate that sometimes anonymity is an instrumental good. But they equally reveal that it is not a constitutive human good. In this respect, anonymity is quite different from privacy. What of confidentiality?

The sphere of an individual's privacy can be widened to include other individuals who stand in a professional relationship to the first individual, for example, a person's lawyer or doctor. Moreover, morally legitimate institutional purposes give rise to confidentiality requirements with respect to information, for example, members of committees in relation to tender applications.

Law enforcement operations give rise to stringent confidentiality requirements, given what is often at stake, for example, harm to informants, the possibility that important investigations might be compromised. Military operations also give rise to stringent confidentiality requirements, such as "need to know" principles and legal prohibitions under official secrets legislation; again, the stringency of these requirements can be justified given what is often at stake, for example, harm to one's own combatants, and the possibility that military missions might be compromised.

At least in the case of security agencies, such as police, military, and intelligence agencies, a degree of compliance with principles of confidentiality is a constitutive institutional good in the sense that security agencies could not successfully operate without a high degree of confidentiality.

The other related notion of interest to us here is secrecy.[11] Secret information is not necessarily based on the moral right to privacy or on the principle of confidentiality. For unlike privacy and confidentiality, secrecy is a morally neutral or even pejorative notion. Thus person A can have a moral right to know person B's secrets and B have no grounds for nondisclosure, as might be the case if A is a police officer and B is an offender. Here B has a secret but it has no moral weight *qua* secret.

Secrecy implies that someone possessed of information does not want that information disclosed and that someone else has an interest in finding out the secret information. Secrecy is at home in contexts of conflict and fierce competition, for example, wars, organized criminality, and market-based companies. More generally, secrecy is at home in contexts of security (see next section).

Excessive secrecy undermines operational effectiveness; for example, the 1980 helicopter incursion by the USA into Iran to rescue hostages failed because secrecy prevented various helicopter crews from coordinating their activities. Moreover, high levels of secrecy can mask incompetence. For instance, the high levels of secrecy in relation to the actual intelligence in respect of the WMDs falsely thought to be possessed by Saddam Hussein masked the incompetent judgments of the US and UK political decision-makers based on that intelligence. High levels of secrecy can also mask corruption, as in the case of Mossack Fonseca, illegality, and human rights abuses, for example, in authoritarian regimes. Accordingly, by contrast with confidentiality, secrecy is not a constitutive institutional good.

I have distinguished privacy, anonymity, confidentiality, and secrecy, and argued that whereas privacy is a constitutive human good and confidentiality a constitutive institutional good, neither anonymity nor secrecy are constitutive goods but, at best, only instrumental goods. A final point concerns the relative moral weight of privacy and confidentiality. Here I make the point that sometimes confidentiality requirements can be

---

[11] Sissela Bok, *Secrecy* (New York: Random House, 1985).

overridden by the right to privacy and sometimes the reverse is the case. The NSA leaks by Snowden conveniently exemplify this tension. While the activities of the NSA were an infringement, if not a violation, of the privacy rights of individual US citizens and others, it is also the case that the leaks and subsequent publication in the media were an infringement, if not a violation, of the confidentiality rights of the NSA.

10.3 The Ethics of Unauthorized Disclosure: Security versus Right to Know

Thus far I have offered a definition of whistleblowing. I have also provided accounts of privacy and confidentiality according to which both of these notions have moral weight; each is a constitutive good. Whistleblowing is typically a breach of an organization's confidentiality and breaching an organization's confidentiality is a *pro tanto* moral wrong.[12]

However, unauthorized disclosure, whether in the form of whistleblowing or mere leaking, can in some circumstances be morally justified and, if so, typically by recourse to the public's right to know. By contrast, opponents of acts of unauthorized disclosure usually move beyond the claim that such acts are a breach of confidentiality: they invoke the moral value of security in some deeper or, at least, wider sense, e.g., that the breaches of confidentiality are a threat to national security. The general notion of security is somewhat inchoate, but it connotes something of greater moral weight than a mere breach of confidentiality per se; it implies that the breaches of confidentiality in question have further harmful consequences of some sort. For example, the moral weight attached to preserving confidentiality (as opposed to privacy) might be based on the harm likely to be visited upon a covert intelligence field agent by the group, organization, or nation that they will be regarded as having betrayed if their real identity is publicly exposed. In the light of the discussion above, we can now invoke the notion of institutional integrity. Confidentiality is a constitutive institutional good and, therefore, central to an institution's integrity. Thus, although the harmful consequences of particular serious breaches of confidentiality by institutional actors may vary considerably in terms of both their magnitude and type, they do have one thing in common; serious breaches of confidentiality tend to undermine

---

[12] I am assuming that it is a morally and legally legitimate organization. Breaching the confidentiality of the mafia is not a *pro tanto* moral wrong; indeed, it may well be a *pro tanto*, indeed all things considered, moral duty.

institutional integrity and, as such, are instances of corruption.[13] Accordingly, a fundamental moral dispute in this area concerns the right to know versus the institutional integrity. Under what circumstances should the one override the other? Here we need to get a clearer idea of the moral weight to be attached to each of these two values. Let us begin with the right to know.

10.3.1 Right to Know

The right to know is typically invoked in the context of the freedom of the press, which is in turn associated with and, in part, derivable from the freedom of speech – the latter being one of the fundamental human freedoms.[14] News media organizations have a particular role as an institution of public communication. Specifically, they have an institutional role as the free press in the service of the public's right to know – the role of the Fourth Estate alongside the executive, legislature, and judiciary within a liberal democracy.[15] Roughly speaking, the normative idea here is that in contemporary liberal democratic states, news media organizations – whether they are publicly or privately owned – have, or ought to have, as a fundamental institutional purpose the communication of information to the members of the public that the latter have a right to know.[16]

Respect for, and exercise of, this right to know is necessary in order for the free citizens of a democratic polity to govern themselves responsibly (albeit indirectly via an elected government). Moreover, this right to know goes hand in glove with individual freedom of speech. For it is only under conditions of free speech that the truths that the citizens have a right to know are likely to be communicated. The institutional purpose of the news media – the Fourth Estate – is in large part to see to it that the truths in question are *publicly* communicated. This role of the news media is especially important in mass societies in which word or mouth is an unreliable means of public communication, albeit in contemporary mass society social media have complicated matters in this area somewhat.

---

[13] Or at least are prima facie instances of corruption since it is possible that in some cases their perpetrators could not reasonably have known that they would, or tend to, undermine institutional integrity.

[14] John Stuart Mill's *On Liberty* (any edition) is the classic defense of individual freedom. See also A. Meiklejohn, *Political Freedom* (New York: Harper, 1960); F. Schauer, *Free Speech: A Philosophical Inquiry* (Cambridge University Press, 1982).

[15] Judith Lichtenberg (ed.), *Democracy and the Mass Media* (Cambridge University Press, 1990).

[16] Miller, *Moral Foundations of Social Institutions*, chapter 10.

Accordingly, the news media provide a public forum enabling communication by citizens, by interest groups, and by government and other institutions to the public at large, and enabling that communication to stand as a public record; this is the media as public forum. Second, the media, or at least members of the media such as journalists, have the task of unearthing and disseminating information of importance to the public; this is the media as investigator. Crucially, this includes information about governmental policies and actions that enables citizens to hold the government and its members to account. Snowden's disclosures published in *The Guardian* newspaper regarding the NSA's data collection practices (of which more below) are a case in point.

An important additional point touched on above concerns the boundaries of the public in question. In traditional accounts of the freedom of the press, the public is explicitly or implicitly taken to be the citizenry of a given liberal democratic nation-state; so the public forum is, in effect, the national forum. However, globalization has at the very least called this narrow notion of the public into question; there are now multiple publics, including a global public. In part, this is because there are global problems, such as climate change or international terrorism; the public interest in question is the interest of all or most of humanity. Thus the public forum is no longer always simply the national forum; it is also sometimes the international or global forum. Accordingly, one of the publics that the news media has a responsibility to serve by providing a forum has become humanity in general.

This completes our brief account of the fundamental liberal democratic moral value: the right to know. What of security, the value often seen to be in conflict with the right to know?

10.3.2 Confidentiality, Security, and Institutional Integrity

As argued above, confidentiality is a constitutive institutional good. In the case of security agencies, such as police, military, and intelligence agencies, it is easy to see why confidentiality is constitutive of their integrity. These agencies have security as their *raison d'etre* (collective good, in my parlance) and require a high level of confidentiality if their institutional purposes are to be achieved. However, the notion of security is a somewhat vague one.[17] Sometimes it is used to refer to a

---

[17] For an account of the notion of security see John Kleinig, Peter Mameli, Seumas Miller, Douglas Salane, and Adina Schwartz, *Security and Privacy: Global Standards for Ethical Identity Management in Contemporary Liberal Democratic States* (Canberra: ANU Press, 2011), chapter 2.

variety of forms of collective security, for example, national security (in the face of external military aggression), community security (in the face of disruptions to law and order), organizational security (in the face of fraud, breaches of confidentiality, and other forms of misconduct and criminality). Other times it is used to refer to personal physical security. Physical security in this sense is security in the face of threats to one's life, freedom, or personal property; the latter being goods to which one has a human right. Threats to physical security obviously include murder, rape, assault, and torture.

Personal (physical) security is a more fundamental notion than collective security; indeed, collective security in its various forms is in large part derived from personal security. Thus terrorism, for example, is principally a threat to national security precisely because it threatens the lives of innocent citizens. However, collective security is not simply to be identified with aggregate personal (physical) security. For example, terrorism might be a threat to the stability of a government and, as such, a national security threat, an example of which can be seen with the Islamic State's occupation of large parts of Iraq and Syria.

Aside from questions of the scope of security, for example, personal, organizational, national, there is the matter of the type of security. Here a distinction between informational and non-informational security might be helpful. Informational security is self-explanatory and basically consists of ensuring that privacy rights are respected and confidentiality requirements are being met.

Non-informational security pertains to physical or psychological harm to human beings, damage to physical "objects" (including the physical environment and artifacts), and certain forms of harm to institutional processes or purposes, for example, by means of corruption. Non-informational security is both a constitutive human good and a constitutive institutional good. After all, the lack of non-informational security evidently implies harm to persons and/or institutions.

It is widely accepted that both privacy rights and confidentiality requirements can be overridden by the needs of non-informational security. After all, the latter may involve saving lives, while the former might only involve some relatively unimportant disclosure of (private or confidential) information. It is perhaps less widely recognized that non-informational security can be overridden by privacy rights and confidentiality considerations. Examples here include ones such as intrusive surveillance of a suspected petty thief or accessing the confidential details of the location of a person under witness protection to interview him for a past minor crime. In the latter case the right to confidentiality is itself in the service of security, not so the right to privacy in the former case.

Aside from the *scope* and *types* of security there are various *contexts* of security. These include domestic law enforcement, international organized crime, counter-terrorism, war, cyberwar, trade "wars," and so on. These different contexts involve a variety of security concerns of differential moral weight; winning World War II was obviously of far greater importance than Australian farmers winning a commercial contract to supply live cattle to China. Intelligence-gathering needs to be understood in these various different contexts and the stringency of privacy rights and confidentiality requirements relativized to them. In domestic law enforcement, for example, there is a strong presumption in favor of the privacy rights of citizens, albeit these can be overridden in certain circumstances under judicial warrant. By contrast, in wartime military intelligence gathering is largely unfettered and the privacy rights of citizens curtailed under emergency powers. Moreover, the confidentiality rights of security agencies are increased under a "cloak of secrecy" and the privacy and confidentiality rights of the enemy suspended until cessation of hostilities. Counter-terrorist operations and so-called covert operations against hostile states with which one is not actually at war provide an additional problematic set of contexts.

10.3.3 Right to Know versus Security: Snowden and the NSA

In the light of this discussion of the moral right to know, institutional integrity, and the moral value of security what are we to make of the NSA leaks by Edward Snowden?[18] Is Snowden an heroic whistleblower, as some see him,[19] or a *de facto* foreign espionage agent guilty of treason, as others hold?[20] Speaking generally, these leaks were a breach of security in the sense that they infringed NSA confidentiality requirements and, indeed, US secrecy laws. As such, they undermined institutional integrity and, therefore, were acts of corruption, albeit apparently acts of noble cause corruption (assuming Snowden acted for the greater good, as he claims). However, the larger question is whether they undermined collective security in the stronger sense, for example, by compromising the legitimate

---

[18] Much of the material in this section is derived from Miller and Walsh, "NSA, Snowden and the Ethics and Accountability of Intelligence Gathering."

[19] Greenwald, *No Place to Hide*.

[20] Edward Jay Epstein, "Was Snowden's Heist a Foreign Espionage Operation?" *Wall Street Journal*, May 9, 2014.

intelligence-gathering activities of the USA and its allies, and by putting the lives of security personnel and, ultimately, citizens at risk.[21] On the other hand, there is the matter of the public's right to know. Surely the US citizenry had a right to know that this large-scale data collection was taking place. Moreover, the intelligence agencies, arguably, were acting outside their institutional remit and were themselves engaged in a corrupt practice, albeit one that may well be in itself morally justifiable. (An otherwise morally justifiable action might be corrupt if it has not been appropriately authorized, in this instance, democratically authorized (so to speak).) Indeed, assuming that the members of these agencies acted for the greater public good, their activity should perhaps be regarded as an instance of noble cause corruption (see Chapter 4). However, granted that the US citizens have a right to know, at least in general terms, about the data collection policies of their intelligence agencies and, indeed, have the right to approve or disapprove them, it does not follow that, objectively speaking, those policies should be allowed (or disallowed). So there are actually a number of issues here that need to be kept separate. First, there is the question of the institutional harm done by Snowden; this is in part a question about corruption and, specifically, the corrupt activity of an institutional actor, Snowden. Second, there is the question of whether the NSA acted outside its institutional remit; this is also in part a question about corruption, albeit on the part of those in positions of authority within the NSA and government. Third, there is the question of the justifiability of the NSA's bulk collection of data considered in itself, i.e., independent of whether it was, or needed to be, appropriately democratically authorized. Fourth, there is the question of the justifiability of Snowden's actions, all things considered. I have already suggested the answers to the first two questions. The now answer to the fourth question turns on the answer to the third question. I address this third question. I begin by trying to get a little clearer on some of the details.

As noted above, the NSA was engaged in the bulk collection of, in particular, the communication data of US and other citizens. The data in question was usually so-called metadata. Metadata does not include the content of telephone and other communications. Rather it is, for example, the unique phone number/email address of caller/recipient, the time of calls and their duration, and the location of caller/recipient. This collection of metadata generally consisted of the bulk collection of telephone data

---

[21] See A. Etzioni, "NSA: National Security vs. Individual Rights," *Intelligence and National Security*, 30 (2015), 100–136.

both for domestic and international calls. The development of data-mining and analytics techniques and technologies has resulted in faster and more efficient interception of telephone and other types of communications, the integration of this data with existing data, and the analysis thereof for intelligence purposes.[22] Intelligence agencies increased their focus on data mining and analytics technologies to extract new useable information from disparate data sources at the same time as non-state threat actors like terrorists were using multiple and more secure ways to communicate.[23]

After 9/11, the US Foreign Intelligence Surveillance Court (FISC) authorized the collection of bulk metadata allowing the NSA access to call records.[24] This was considered by government and the agency as the only effective way to continuously keep track of the activities, communications, and plans of foreign terrorists who disguise and obscure their communications and identities. Metadata security intelligence collection solutions such as those revealed in the Snowden leaks were also adopted because non-state actors (terrorists and transnational criminal syndicates) are using technological developments (in data processing, open source information, and commercially available encryption) to communicate, plan attacks, or conduct their own surveillance on national security and law enforcement authorities. Hence, intelligence agencies like the NSA had to exploit similar communications technology to track the "digital footprints" in multiple data feeds (metadata) – allowing them to respond more proactively to threat actor activities.

In addition to information about the metadata program, Snowden's revelations also included material about NSA's PRISM program, which allows the agency to access a large amount of digital information – emails, Facebook posts, and instant messages. The difference between metadata collection and PRISM is that the latter also collects the contents of those communications.

The collection of bulk metadata is morally problematic in that there is a presumption against the gathering of personal information on citizens by government officials, including law enforcement and other security personnel. This problem is evident in the metadata collection arising in the

---

[22] For a good discussion of the development of national security data mining capabilities in the United States after 9/11 see J. W. Seifert, *Data Mining and Homeland Security*, CRS Report RL31798 (Congressional Research Service, 2008).

[23] C. Joye and P. Smith, "Most Powerful Spy Says Snowden Leaks Will Cost Lives," *The Australian Financial Review*, May 8, 2014, 1 and 11.

[24] The FISC was established to provide judicial oversight of intelligence agencies (the NSA and FBI) seeking interception of communications of suspects.

Verizon and PRISM controversies. Verizon involved the collection by the NSA of the metadata from the calls made within the USA, and between the USA and any foreign country, of millions of customers of Verizon and other telecommunication providers, whereas PRISM involved the agreements between NSA and various US-based internet companies (Google, Facebook, Skype, etc.) to enable NSA to monitor the online communications of non-US citizens based overseas. While privacy laws tend to focus on the content of phone calls, emails, and the like, the Verizon episode draws our attention to metadata. It has been argued that since this data is not content its collection is morally unproblematic. To this it can be replied, first, that such metadata is collected to facilitate the communication purposes of callers/recipients and their telecommunication providers, and is consented to only for this purpose. Second, metadata enables the nonconsensual construction of a detailed description of a person's activities, associates, movements, and so on, especially when combined with financial and other data. The availability to security agencies of such descriptions is surely an infringement of privacy and, therefore, needs justification.

As we saw above, Verizon and PRISM have raised legitimate privacy concerns, both for US citizens and for foreigners, for example, in relation to metadata collection and analysis. Regarding metadata collection and analysis in the context of domestic law enforcement, the solution, at least in general terms, is evidently at hand; extend the existing principles of probable cause (or, outside the USA, reasonable suspicion) and the existing relevant accountability requirements, for example, the system of judicial warrants.

However, some of these privacy concerns pertain to foreign citizens. Consider the FISA (Foreign Intelligence Surveillance Act) Amendments Act of 2008. It mandates the monitoring of, and data gathering from, foreigners who are outside the USA by the NSA. Moreover, data gathered but found not to be relevant to the foreign intelligence gathering purpose of, say, counter-terrorism is not allowed to be retained. Importantly, however, there is no probable cause (or reasonable suspicion) requirement unless the person in question is a US citizen.

This is problematic insofar as privacy is regarded as a *human* right and, therefore, a right of all persons, US citizens or not. Moreover, these inconsistencies between the treatment of US citizens and foreigners are perhaps even more acute or, at least obvious, when it comes to the infringement of the rights to privacy and, for that matter, confidentiality of non-US citizens in liberal democratic states allied with the USA, for example, EU citizens.

Intelligence-gathering, surveillance, and so on of citizens by domestic law enforcement agencies is reasonably well defined and regulated, for example, in accordance with probable cause/reasonable suspicion principles and requirements for warrants; hence the feasibility of simply extending the law enforcement model to metadata collection within domestic jurisdictions.[25] However, this domestic law enforcement model is too restrictive, and not practicable, in relation to intelligence gathering from, for example, hostile foreign states during peacetime, let alone wartime.

The privacy rights of the members of the citizenry during wartime are curtailed under emergency powers, and the privacy and confidentiality rights of enemy citizens are almost entirely suspended. Military intelligence-gathering during wartime has few privacy constraints and, given what is at stake in all-out wars, such as World War II, this may well be justified. However, these are extreme circumstances and the suspension of privacy rights is only until the cessation of hostilities. Accordingly, this military model of intelligence-gathering is too permissive in relation to covert intelligence gathering from, for example, fellow liberal democracies during peacetime.

Intelligence-gathering activities, notably cyber-espionage, of the NSA do not fit neatly into the law enforcement model or the military model. At any rate, the question arises as to what is to be done in relation to cyber-espionage, in particular. On the one hand, the USA and its allies cannot be expected to defend their legitimate national interests with their hands tied behind their backs. So their recourse to (what is in effect) *cyber*-espionage seems justified. On the other hand, there is evidently the need for a degree of moral renovation of cyber-espionage as it is currently conducted.

10.4 Conclusion

In this chapter I have provided a definition of whistleblowing (as opposed to professional reporting) – a key feature of anti-corruption and integrity systems – and elaborated accounts of the key moral notions of privacy, confidentiality, institutional integrity, the moral right to know, and the moral value of security. In the light of these moral notions, I have discussed Edward Snowden's leaking of NSA confidential data to the press and distinguished this kind of whistleblowing from that of the likes of Daniel

---

[25] This is not to say that this is likely to happen. For example, new legislation in Australia and the UK might allow intelligence agencies to have access to metadata without a warrant.

Ellsberg and the anonymous whistleblower in the Mossack Fonseca dis-closures. Arguably, Snowden was morally justified in making known the NSA's bulk data collection processes to the public. The US public, in particular, had a right to know what its intelligence agency was doing in this area, given that it was engaged in going beyond its democratic remit in engaging in widespread infringements of the privacy rights of the US citizenry, i.e., the NSA was engaged in a form of corruption, albeit noble cause corruption. On the other hand, arguably the manner in which Snowden went about these disclosures, and perhaps the scale of the disclosures, was unnecessary in terms of what the public had a right to know, and harmful to the NSA in particular and to US security interests in general, i.e., Snowden was engaged in a form of corruption, albeit (again) noble cause corruption. Finally, Snowden's disclosures have evidently thrown into sharp relief a number of important ethical and policy dilemmas in relation to intelligence collection; dilemmas which to date remain unresolved.

PART III

Contexts of Corruption

CHAPTER 11

Market-Based Institutions

Part I (Chapters 1–6) of this book consisted of philosophical analyses of the key theoretical notions utilized throughout this work, namely, institutions, institutional corruption, institutional power, salient specific forms of corruption (bribery, nepotism, fraud, and abuse of authority), and collective institutional and moral responsibility. Part II (Chapters 7–10) consisted of an elaboration – in the light of the theoretical work in Part I – of anti-corruption systems or, more broadly, integrity systems, and some key institutional features thereof, notably investigations and whistleblowing. Part III (chapters 11–14) continues the applied emphasis of Part II but takes it in a somewhat different direction. The chapters in Part III consider both the nature of corruption in the light of institutional purpose (collective goods) and also anti-corruption measures. However, each of these chapters focuses on a particular institutional setting: market-based institutions (this chapter, Chapter 11), the banking and finance sector (Chapter 12), police organizations (Chapter 13), and political institutions (Chapter 14).

There is a widespread tendency to view corruption, at least in so-called developed nation-states, such as the USA, the UK, and other Western countries, as essentially a matter of a "few rotten apples." Unfortunately, there is both organizational and systemic corruption, if not grand corruption, in the developed nation-states as well as in the developing ones (not to mention so-called failed states). In relation to organizational corruption in the US corporate sector, Enron is a stand-out paradigm. In the context of the deregulation of the energy industry under the Reagan Administration, Enron became a cutting edge trading company dealing in a diverse range of goods and services, including natural gas, electric power, pollution permits, telecommunications, water, and Internet broadband. In the political climate of deregulation, free markets and profit maximization became Enron's religion.[1] New deals were struck in the pursuit of higher quarterly earnings, and to thereby drive Enron's stock up to the highest possible price; this allowed Enron's in-house deal-makers to claim huge profits for the company and justify large bonuses for themselves. Moreover, in this environment there was a powerful incentive to devise corrupt schemes designed to inflate profits and hide debt, and this is precisely what happened via the infamous Special Purpose Entities. Ultimately, of course, this house of cards collapsed.

In relation to systemic corruption involving thousands of companies in developed nation-states, as well as developing ones, consider the recent disclosures in the Panama Papers concerning the activities of Mossack Fonseca. As we saw in Chapter 10, Mossack Fonseca is a legal firm specializing in creating shell companies based in tax havens, such as the British Virgin Islands, for the purpose of enabling companies and individuals to avoid paying tax in the countries where they earned their profits. According to the Panama Papers, it has over 200,000 clients.[2] Remarkably, as already mentioned, this practice is legal, at least in the case of those firms and individuals whose initial profits were derived from legitimate businesses; albeit, apparently, many firms and individuals making use of Mossack Fonseca's services are criminals and criminal organizations. At any rate, to reiterate, the general point to be made here is that this extraordinarily widespread practice is a species of systemic institutional corruption; it is deeply corruptive of the tax regimes of multiple countries and ultimately deprives the citizens of these countries of billions of dollars of funds that ought to be available to provide infrastructure, services, etc. for them.

In relation to these and many other prevalent forms of organizational and systemic corruption, Marxist analyses of economic class structure and ideological superstructure are relevant. However, arguably these analyses are relevant only in a qualified form, since even such widespread systemic corruption calls for renovation of free-market institutions, and corporations in particular, rather than their abandonment.[3] One of the most obvious instances of a self-serving, class-based ideology is the much vaunted, but profoundly institutionally harmful, shareholder theory of value (of which more below). At any rate, our analysis of institutional corruption in the business and corporate sector needs to begin with the prevailing normative theories of markets and market-based institutions (Section 11.1). For it is such "theory" or, in some cases, pervasive ideology that first needs to be critiqued if

---

[1] Peter C. Fusaro and Ross M. Miller, *What Went Wrong at Enron* (Hoboken, NJ: John Wiley and Sons, 2002), p. 46.
[2] Obermayer and Obermaier, *Panama Papers*.   [3] Reich, *Saving Capitalism*.

institutional corruption in such institutions is to be successfully combated. Following this (Section 11.2), I provide my own normative teleological account according to which market-based organizations are (roughly speaking) multi-layered structures of joint action (see Chapter 1 Section 1.2) and market-based industries ought to have as their collective end the provision of an adequate and sustainable supply of a good or service at a reasonable price and of reasonable quality. Notice here the shift from single organizations to industries. In my view, it is the market-based industry as a whole, rather than the single organization per se, that is the primary locus of normative concern. The single organization is in large part merely part of the means to a larger (collective) end. In Section 11.3 I discuss three forms of institutional corruption: organizational, systemic, and inter-institutional. In Section 11.4 I discuss some anti-corruption strategies.

11.1 Normative Theories of Markets and Market-Based Institutions

11.1.1 Free-Market Fundamentalism

On one normative conception of markets, market actors act and ought to act in their self-interest and are entitled to do so on broadly libertarian grounds. In short, markets are, or ought to be, an expression of individual freedom (on the part of both buyers and sellers) and that is the end of the matter. On this radical free market conception, the normative structure of markets consists essentially in procedural requirements, notably free and fair competition. So there is no moral requirement that markets serve larger collective purposes, such as maximizing overall utility.

Such radical free market enthusiasts – market fundamentalists[4] – argue that any institutional purposes of markets ought to be subservient to or, indeed, ought to be merely an expression of, the freely made choices of market actors. Here there is often a conflation of organizations and individuals. Doubtless, the protection and promotion of individual freedom is a good thing, but large corporations are far from being individual human beings and, therefore, maximizing the freedom of the former is not necessarily maximizing the freedom of the latter. Indeed, the reverse is likely to be the case; increasing the freedom to act of large and powerful organizations often comes at the expense of the freedom of relatively powerless individuals, such

---

[4] George Soros, *The Crash of 2008 and What It Means: The New Paradigm for Financial Markets* (New York: Perseus Books, 2009) refers to such adherents as market fundamentalists and subjects them to sustained pejorative criticism.

as individual employees, consumers, and clients. The excesses of banks and other financial institutions in the Global Financial Crisis, and the consequent harm done to individual consumers, home-owners, retirees, investors, etc. graphically illustrate this point.

Moreover, this unqualified belief in free markets ignores the problem of the massively harmful effects of many free market practices, such as large-scale speculative trading, on nonparticipants in those markets; for example, the creation of cycles of bubble and bust that have undermined financial stability and significantly contributed to severe economic downturns. As J. S. Mill[5] and others of a liberal persuasion stress, it is good to exercise one's freedom of choice, but bad – and likely morally wrong – to cause harm to others in doing so. Moreover, many, if not most, large companies are not private sector firms in the sense required by the premise of this fundamentalist argument. Rather, they are corporations. And in any case, even private sector firms are in part constituted by legal, regulatory, and other institutional structures and, in particular, by the laws, regulations, conventions, etc. constitutive of the institutions of private property.

Corporations are the institutional creations of governments; they are not the preexisting market actors of the ideology of market fundamentalism. Governments have granted special *privileges* to corporations (notably, the limited liability of shareholders) for a good reason or, at least, ought to have done so.[6] The good reason for granting this privilege is that corporations will have the general institutional purpose of serving the community at large. The morally justifiable granting by governments of special privileges must serve *some* defensible social purpose. Libertarian theories often offer a contractualist account of corporations according to which, apparently, corporations have no prior institutional purpose other than that their owners (shareholders) decide upon. This argument ignores the special government-given privileges definitive of corporations.

Moreover, markets and market actors, including corporations, depend on infrastructure typically provided by governments, including not only communication and transport infrastructure but also educational, health, and security (e.g., police, military) infrastructure. Indeed, some market actors are in part constituted by infrastructure. For example, internet providers, such as Google, are in part constituted by the Internet. Again, financial markets, in particular, are in part constituted by financial

---

[5] J. S. Mill, *On Liberty*, (any edition).

[6] David Ciepley, "Beyond Public and Private: Toward a Political Theory of the Corporation," *American Political Science Review*, 107 (2013), 139–158.

infrastructure, such as interest rate and currency benchmarks, which provide public goods upon which market actors rely. At the core of competitive internet-based markets and financial markets is infrastructure serving collective purposes; the only question to be asked is whether it is doing so in an efficient, effective and fair manner.

Third, even if many companies are not directly dependent on governments, they typically rely on other institutions that are directly dependent on governments, such as banks. The banking system is dependent on governments in that, for example, they are dependent on banks of last resort, namely, central banks. In short, the freely acting, rationally self-interested, institutionally prior, human individual of the ideology of market fundamentalism is a myth, and a self-serving and socially harmful myth at that.

11.1.2 Other Normative Accounts

On a second normative conception, markets do serve, or ought to serve, larger collective purposes. This second normative conception is surely more plausible than the first, given the first denies, in effect, that markets have any institutional purpose at all. However, this second conception is a very broad church and it includes a number of quite different, indeed often opposing, normative "theories." In relation to markets in general, there is the appeal to the workings of the so-called "invisible"[7] hand; each market actor pursues their individual rational economic self-interest and, by means of the "invisible" hand, the common good is maximized. There are also normative theories of the corporation, such as the Shareholder Value Theory (SVT)[8] and Corporate Social Responsibility (CSR) theories.[9] SVT holds that the ultimate institutional purpose of corporations is to maximize profits and, thereby, maximize shareholder value. Since many financial institutions are corporations, their ultimate purpose must also, presumably, be to maximize profits and shareholder value. CSR theories canvass a wider range of

---

[7] My use of scare quotes is to imply that the so-called invisible hand is, and ought to be, more visible than sometimes assumed, especially to legislators, regulator, and industry leaders.

[8] See Milton Friedman, "The Social Responsibility of Business Is to Increase Its Profits," *New York Times Magazine*, September 13, 1970. For criticisms, albeit different from the ones I make here, see Lynn Stout, *The Shareholder Value Myth: How Putting Shareholders First Harms Investors, Corporations and the Public* (San Francisco: Berrett-Koehler, 2012). Importantly, Stout argues that there is no legal obligation on the part of CEOs and other managers to maximize shareholder value; this is a myth.

[9] For an elaboration and criticisms (again, different from the ones I make here) of these various theories, including CSR theories, see Robert Audi, *Business Ethics and Ethical Business* (Oxford: Oxford University Press, 2008). Some of these normative theories can be combined into hybrid accounts, e.g., SVT with the invisible hand view.

"stakeholders," such as employees, customers, and the community, and emphasize the so-called triple bottom line of "Profit, People, and Planet." However, none of these currently influential normative theories of the individual corporation or of the markets in which they compete are compelling.

The idea of the "invisible" hand mechanism, while important, needs to be put on a narrower and sounder footing than a general appeal to the amorphous notions of maximizing utility (however utility is understood, e.g., happiness, pleasure, preference satisfaction), optimizing welfare, or the like. Moreover, it is far from obvious that in all, or most, markets the pursuit of individual rational self-interest, even in the context of free and fair competition, actually maximizes overall utility. Consider, for example, occupational groups in the financial sector with fiduciary duties to their clients[10]: occupations such as banker, fund manager, financial planner, and so on. Evidently, the pursuit of individual rational self-interest, notably profit maximization, by the members of these occupational groups, far from maximizing overall utility, has been extraordinarily harmful to clients and highly damaging to the markets themselves.

For its part, SVT confuses (part of) the means (shareholder value) with the end (e.g., an adequate quantum of some good or service). Evidently, financial rewards, such as wages, executive remuneration, and dividends, are proximate, not ultimate, purposes; they are part of the reward system and, as such, the means to an end. The *raison d'etre* for the establishment of corporations or other business firms in a given sector is not to maximize shareholder dividends, much less to enrich corporate officers, but rather to provide an adequate and sustainable quantum of some good (e.g., houses) or service (e.g., legal services). The institutional purpose of banks, for instance, is to provide a secure place for depositors' funds, enable payments to be made, and the like. If a retail bank consistently fails to realize these latter purposes then it is failing as an institution, even if for some reason it continues to make a profit and, thereby, benefits shareholders. Again, the ultimate purpose of insurance companies is to provide insurance rather than to maximize shareholder dividends; the latter are a means to the former. If an insurance company makes a profit but consistently fails to pay out when it should, then it is failing as an institution; it is not providing actual (as opposed to promised) insurance, notwithstanding the benefits to shareholders. Moreover, SVT unacceptably narrows the list of

---

[10] Miller, "Trust, Conflicts of Interest and Fiduciary Duties," pp. 305–331.

stakeholders so that it consists only in shareholders;[11] remarkably, the interests of customers and clients, in particular, are omitted!

CSR theories, on the other hand, cast the net of stakeholders too wide and, thereby, dilute institutional purpose. CSR theories provide long lists of stakeholders, including not only shareholders, managers, employees, customers, and clients but also suppliers, other industry players, the environment, the wider society, and so on. No doubt, firms need from time to time to attend to a wide range of parties who are affected, positively or negatively, by their activities, as we all do. Certainly, they ought to avoid harming people and damaging the environment (and ought to provide compensation if they do). But the content of a normative theory of the corporation or of a particular industry or market cannot simply consist of a long list of affected parties, on pain of having provided little more than an unhelpfully general prescription to avoid harm and to be beneficent wherever possible. Aside from the absence of clear direction provided by such a prescription, it may tend to encourage window-dressing (e.g., minor charitable donations) at the expense of focused attention on what ought to be the core activity of an industry, and scrutiny of the manner in which that activity is undertaken. In short, CSR loses sight of the main game in any given industry: the producers or providers of the product or service and their customers or clients.

11.2   A Normative Teleological Account of Market-Based Institutions

In the light of the above deficiencies in prevailing normative accounts of markets and market-based institutions, I have proffered a general normative teleological theory and derived special normative theories. On this conception, which I have elaborated in detail elsewhere,[12] markets are social institutions and, as such, ought to serve collective ends and, specifically, generate collective goods. However, the collective goods in question are narrowly specified. It is not a matter of maximizing general utility, however defined, but rather of market actors competing with one another under conditions of free and fair competition and in doing so jointly producing an adequate and sustainable quantum of some specific good or service at a reasonable price and of reasonable quality. I stress that the goods or services in question have to be goods according to some objective standard including, but not restricted to, health and safety standards. For

---

[11] Or are at best rendered entirely subservient to the interests of shareholders.
[12] Miller, *Moral Foundations of Social Institutions*.

instance, a hitman provides a service and heroin traffickers a desired commodity; nevertheless, neither of these meet the required objective standards. The need for market actors to jointly produce an adequate supply of some (desirable) good or service is perhaps obvious in the case of the housing industry, the car industry, and in markets for agricultural goods. But it is no less true of other markets, such as financial markets. In the case of capital markets, the good in question is an adequate and sustainable supply of financial capital for investment by productive enterprises; in the case of pension funds, it is an adequate and sustainable quantum of funds to provide for workers post-retirement, and so on.

In the light of the above, it is clear that on the normative teleological account of social institutions, institutions, including market-based institutions, ought to achieve particular institutional purposes in the overall macro-institutional moral and legal framework setting in which they exist. Moreover, they do so by means of specific institutional structures and, for that matter, cultures. Accordingly, there are at least three salient *general* normative issues that arise, namely:

(1) *Institutional Purpose*: What *ought to be* the principal institutional purposes of the various markets and market-based industries? A pervasive ideology that identifies institutional purpose with the financial interests of one narrow category of stakeholders rather than with collective goods, as does the shareholder theory of value, is not only morally problematic in confusing means (reward structure, e.g., wages and salaries, dividends) with ends (collective goods), it is profoundly corruptive of institutions.

(2) *Institutional Means: (a) Structure, including Individual Rights and Duties*: Is the market-based industry or occupation in question structured so as to adequately realize its institutional purposes – its defining collective goods? For example, are there "too big to fail" institutions, as in the case of global banks? Is the structure of institutional rights (e.g., ownership rights), duties (e.g., fiduciary duties), and rewards (e.g., CEOs remuneration packages) morally acceptable and fit for institutional purpose? Or does it merely reward short-termism and encourage greed? (b) *Culture*: Is the organizational culture, e.g., so-called short-termism, morally problematic? More specifically, does it comply with relevant moral principles and is it conducive to the realization of the principal institutional purposes of the market-based industry in question?

(3) *Macro-Institutional Context*: What role ought the market or market-based industry or occupation in question play in the larger economic

order and, more specifically, what ought its institutional relationships be to relevant other institutions? For example, should Wall St. serve Main St.? Moreover, is there a tendency in contemporary settings for market-based institutions to "overpower" and corrupt (interinstitutional corruption), for example, public institutions such as government, e.g., via regulatory capture?

11.2.1 Institutional Purpose: Collective Goods

The basic normative question that needs to be asked of a business organization, market, or occupation, I suggest, is the same as for any social institution, namely: What *collective good(s)* does it exist to provide? Consider capital markets. The most salient – if not the only (see later) – collective good that capital markets exist to provide is an adequate and sustainable supply of capital at a reasonable price. I note the distinction between proximate and ultimate institutional purposes or ends: collective goods are the ultimate purposes of social institutions, but not necessarily their proximate purposes.

In the case of business organizations and markets, these collective goods include (1) the coordination of buyers and sellers of goods and services and (2) a quantum of a product or service sufficient to meet the relevant ongoing aggregate needs of the population in question.[13] Here Adam Smith's "invisible" hand mechanism is salient.[14] The outcome (a collective good) of the workings of the invisible hand is the ultimate purpose (collective end) of this institutional mechanism (e.g., an adequate supply of houses, or of auditing services, or of retirement savings, or of capital); profit maximization is the proximate end.

The existence of profit maximization adds a complication in the case of market-based organizations that is not present in the case of other social institutions. In the case of market-based organizations, but not necessarily other social institutions, there are *three* collective ends, namely: (1) the constitutive collective end, (e.g., the production of cars, the accumulation of depositor funds in banks, the accumulation of savings for investment, the accumulation of savings for future use); (2) the collective good (e.g.,

---

[13] For the developed version of the material in this section see Miller, *Moral Foundations of Social Institutions*, chapters 2 and 10. Some of the material in this section is drawn from that volume.

[14] Adam Smith, *The Wealth of Nations* (any edition). In fact the notion of an invisible hand, while famously attributed to Smith, is scarcely to be found in his writings. See Emma Rothschild and Amartya Sen, "Adam Smith's Economics" in Knud Haakonssen (ed.), *The Cambridge Companion to Adam Smith* (Cambridge University Press, 2006), p. 363.

transport, security of savings, investment of funds in infrastructure, income stream for retirees); and (3) profit maximization.

Notice that a constitutive collective end is not necessarily a collective good. Consider so-called toxic financial products, e.g., packages of sub-prime mortgages. The production of these financial products was the (realized) collective end of the members of investment banks. However, as it turns out, these products contributed significantly to the global financial crisis; they caused great harm to many groups, including ulti-mately to taxpayers when banks holding these "assets" were bailed out by governments. So the realization of this collective end was not a collective good; quite the reverse.

Moreover, we can now see that there are two potentially competing collective ends, namely, collective goods and profit maximization (in the case of corporations, profit maximization in order in turn to maximize shareholder value). By the lights of our account of social institutions, the claim must be that the pursuit of the collective end of profit maximization will, as a matter of contingent fact – and by virtue of the invisible hand – realize the collective good definitive of the social institution in question. Unfortunately, the empirical claim upon which the efficacy of the "invi-sible" hand is predicated is contestable and in some cases evidently false. For example, the reliance on wholly market-based mechanisms for the provision of investment funds for much-needed infrastructure in various countries, notably the USA and Australia, has evidently been a failure.[15]

11.2.2   Institutional Means: Structure, Rights, and Duties

Thus far we have focused on one dimension of the normative character of social institutions, namely, institutional purpose and, specifically, the collec-tive goods that institutions produce (or ought to produce). However, there are two other normative dimensions worthy of note here. First, there are the moral constraints on institutional activity. In this regard, institutional activity is no different from noninstitutional human activity; the prohibitions on murder, fraud, and theft, for example, constrain institutional activities.

Second – and more importantly for our concerns here – there is the structure of particular institutions, bearing in mind that institutional purpose ought to give direction to structure. At a general level, there is the question of whether an institution ought to be a market-based

---

[15] This is, of course, not to say that private sector partnerships with the public sector would not be effective in many instances.

institution at all. This ought not to be a question of ideology, but rather an empirical question; what structure, be it market-based or nonmarket-based, best realizes institutional purpose?

Here it needs to be noted that the distinction between market-based and nonmarket-based institutions is not necessarily a strict dichotomy; there is also the possibility of hybrid institutions: institutions that utilize the mechanism of the market but are not wholly market-based. As we have seen, compulsory retirement savings systems and financial benchmarks upon which capital markets depend are cases in point, and there are many others. But to reiterate: by the lights of our normative teleological account of social institutions, whether an institution ought to be wholly market-based, nonmarket-based, or a hybrid of both is a matter to be settled by recourse to collective goods: it is a matter of which of these three models most efficiently and effectively enables the collective good in question to be produced.

Further structural issues pertain to the size of market actors (e.g., "too big to fail" banks), structural conflicts of interest (e.g., ratings agencies that rate the financial products of investment banks, which in turn fund the ratings agencies), and regulators who are themselves "players in the game," e.g., the UK's Financial Conduct Authority pursues the particular interests of the City of London, potentially at the expense of other financial centers. Again, by the lights of my normative teleological account these matters of structure ought to be settled by recourse to the collective goods the markets in question, including global markets, ought to be realizing. "Too big to fail banks" are obviously unacceptable, given the threat they pose to the international financial system and, therefore, to the collective goods the system ought to be realizing. For the same reason, structural conflicts of interest need to be removed. Regarding regulators who are not impartial, the point to be made is that the collective good of a global financial market cannot merely be the interests of the City of London.

Third, there are, as already noted, a variety of *institutionally relative* moral rights and duties (as opposed to moral rights and duties that are logically prior to all institutions (i.e., natural rights and duties) or otherwise transcend particular institutions) that are derived at least in part from institutionally produced collective goods and, indeed, that are constitutive of specific institutional roles, e.g., the rights and duties of a fire officer or of a banker or of a fund manager or of a financial advisor or of an investor or of an inventor. These institutional rights and duties (which are also moral rights and duties) are constitutive of institutional roles and, therefore, are in part constitutive of the structure of specific institutions. And since the structure of an institution is, or ought to be, an important part of the means by which its institutional purposes are achieved, so it is that these institutional moral rights and duties are part of the means and hence, in part, derived from the institution's large purpose – its defining collective good. Thus debates about whether financial advisors ought to have the institutional right to charge commissions as opposed to, say, fees for services ought, on this view, to be settled in large part by recourse to the relative contributions of these two competing structures of occupational rights and duties to the larger institutional purpose (viz. efficient and effective provision of retirement savings). Again, debates about the ownership rights (e.g., patent rights) of individuals or companies who develop new products (e.g., new vaccines) ought to be settled in large part by recourse to the relative contributions of the competing ownership regimes to the larger institutional purpose (viz. provision of a sustainable supply of affordable, effective vaccines to the needy).

As we have seen, sometimes the end realized in joint action, including in multi-layered structures of joint action (organizational action), is not merely a collective end, it is also a collective *good*. (By *collective* good I simply mean that the good is collectively or jointly produced; I don't mean to imply that it is collectively or jointly consumed – it might be, and often is, individually consumed (see Chapter 1).) If so, then a joint right may well be generated. What is the relationship between joint moral rights and collective goods? The good is a realized collective end, and the participants in realizing that collective end, i.e., the contributors to the production of that good, possess a joint right to this collective good.

It is easy to see why these persons, and not some other persons, would have a right to such a good: they are the ones responsible for its existence, or continued existence. In this connection, consider the shareholders, members of the board of directors, managers, and workers (shareholders, officers, and employees) in a company that builds blocks of apartments that are sold for profit. Board members, managers, shareholders, and construction workers have a joint right to be financially remunerated from the sales of the apartments that they have jointly produced (albeit the amount of money to which each has an individual right may vary from one individual to another, depending on the nature and extent of their individual contribution). Moreover, if a component of the financial benefits to which they have a joint right is channeled into, say, a pension fund then they have a joint right to these funds (albeit, again, the amount of money to which each has an individual right may vary from one individual to another depending on the extent of their individual contributions over time). It is also clear that if one participating agent has a right to the good, then – other things being equal – so do the others. That is, there is interdependence of rights with respect to the good. The same point holds of workers (who provide labor), managers (who provide leadership), and investors (who provide capital): they have joint rights with respect to the financial benefits arising from the goods or services produced (e.g., whether in the form of wages, salaries, dividends).

Naturally, the remuneration is in many cases dependent on the specific legal contracts that have been entered into, including contracts of employment. However, these joint moral rights are not equivalent to, or reducible to, moral rights based on legal contracts. Rather, normatively speaking, these contracts presuppose the joint moral rights in question; it is because a construction worker, for example, has contributed (jointly with others) to the construction of the apartment buildings that he is morally entitled to a wage (whatever the legal situation might be). Moreover, this normative relationship between contracts and underlying joint moral rights is in evidence when it is claimed that a specific contractual payment was fair or unfair, for a contract might or might not reflect a person's contribution to the production of a collective good, depending on a host of contingencies (notably relationships of power). Consider in this connection the extraordinarily generous executive compensation packages on offer in some corporations, including investment banks that have had to be bailed out with taxpayers' money. In many cases, there is no correlation between executive compensation and contribution to the collective goods produced by the corporation or even to the profits generated by the corporation.[16]

11.2.3 Institutional Means: Culture

It is increasingly recognized by regulators and others that institutional culture is an important determinant of individual behavior.[17] However, these discussions are typically focused on unethical or illegal behavior and on the malign influence of culture, e.g., the culture of traders in recent cases of benchmark manipulation. What is missing from these deliberations is the relationship, or lack thereof, between culture (including both ethical and unethical dimensions of culture) and institutional purpose.

---

[16] Paul Gregg, S. Jewell, and Ian Tonks, *Executive Pay and Performance in the UK 1994–2002*, CMPO Working Paper Series No. 05/122 (Bristol: Centre for Market and Public Organisation, 2005).
[17] For example, Greg Medcraft, the former head of IOSCO, has stressed this point (e.g., "Corporate Culture and Corporate Regulation" – a speech given at the Law Council of Australia BLS AGM seminar in Melbourne on 20th November 2015).

Whether or not the members of some organization internalize the *desirable* ends and principles of an organization – as opposed to undesirable ones – is in part a matter of structure, e.g., eliminating structural conflicts of interest, but it is also in part a matter of institutional culture. Institutional culture is in turn dependent on the extent to which the collective moral responsibility[18] to achieve desirable ends, and eschew corrupt practices, is embedded in the organization by way of explicit institutional mechanisms (e.g., formal continuing education programs in professional ethics, whistleblower protection schemes, remuneration systems that do not encourage excessive risk taking) and implicit practices (e.g., managers who acknowledge their mistakes, employees who are unafraid to voice their concerns).

If, on the other hand, the prevailing ethos or culture of an organization, and perhaps even ideology of central elements of a sector, downplays desirable institutional goals and other ethical considerations in favor of the pursuit of individual self-interest then it should hardly surprise when individual self-interest overrides compliance with ethical principles, even ones enshrined in the law. This is no doubt especially the case in a context of high temptation and opportunity, on the one hand, and low risk of detection and conviction, on the other, e.g., LIBOR manipulation by bank traders motivated by large bonuses in a context of an oversight body with a structural conflict of interest.

11.3 Corruption in Markets and Market-Based Institutions

In the Introduction I distinguished between inherently corrupt organizations, such as the mafia, and organizations that engage in corrupt behavior, e.g., Enron. In this context, Mossack Fonseca provides an interesting case. On the one hand, unlike the mafia or drug cartels, its core activity, i.e., setting up offshore companies, is not unlawful. On the other hand, its core activity, as we saw above, is inherently corruptive of tax regimes in particular. Arguably, therefore, it is an inherently corrupt organization rather than merely an organization that engages in corrupt activity.

We can also distinguish between corrupt organizations and corrupt industries, e.g., some monopolistic markets in which competition is nonexistent and, as a result, prices are exorbitant. The efficiency and effectiveness of markets relies on free and fair competition. No doubt determining what constitutes free and fair competition in various diverse contexts is a difficult matter. However, a market-based industry dominated by a single

---

[18] Miller, "Collective Moral Responsibility: An Individualist Account."

organization that exercises its economic power to set exorbitant prices and drive out competition is not a free and fair market whatever else might be said for it. Other things being equal,[19] by virtue of their exercise of economic power, monopolies tend to undermine markets. In general, as is well-known, power tends to corrupt; as a corollary, monopolies tend to be corruptive of markets.

As our examples demonstrate, these various distinctions apply to market-based occupations, organizations, and markets; they pertain to the corruption of businesses and markets themselves. However, in addition to the corruption of businesses and markets, there is the potential corruption *by* market-based actors of other institutions; interinstitutional corruption (so to speak). Corruption by market-based organizations of the news media in its role as the Fourth Estate is a case in point (see Chapter 14 Section 14.3).

There are, of course, other sets of distinctions that could be invoked in relation to the identification and analysis of institutional corruption in market-based industries. For example, Robert Reich has usefully distinguished[20] what he calls the five building blocks of capitalism. From the perspective of this work, these building blocks are five important components of the overall structure of the institution of market-based industries. As such, they do not include the institutional purpose, or rather purposes, of market-based industries, i.e., their collective ends (collective goods).[21] I have argued in this work and elsewhere that in general terms the collective end of market-based industries is to provide an adequate and sustainable quantum of some good or service at a reasonable price and of reasonable quality. On this view, each of these structural components ought to be evaluated and, indeed, designed or redesigned, in large part in the light of its contribution to institutional purposes, i.e., its contribution to the relevant collective goods produced by the market-based industry in question. At any rate, the five structural components in question are ownership rights, e.g., copyright, patents; market power, e.g., monopolies, oligopolies; contracts, e.g., between buyers and sellers of goods, services, labor and capital; bankruptcy, e.g., who gets what when a business fails; enforcement of laws and regulations, e.g.,

---

[19] Monopolies can, of course, be constrained by regulation and the use of intrusive state power.

[20] See Reich, *Saving Capitalism*, chapters 2–9.

[21] Reich himself favors a democratic proceduralist normative account rather than a teleological one because he thinks abstract notions of the public good are unhelpful. However, my own account avoids such unhelpfully abstract notions in favor of specific goods and services. See Reich, *Saving Capitalism*, p. 82.

liabilities, punishments. Each of these structural components is potentially subject to deliberate and self-serving interference of a kind that undermines the institutional purposes of market-based industries. Reich and others have demonstrated the great extent of this interference, i.e., of institutional corruption of market-based industries in the USA and elsewhere.[22] I do not have the space to consider each of these structural components in my discussion of corruption in market-based industries, useful as this exercise would be. Rather I will utilize the distinction between organizational and market-based industry corruption.

11.3.1   Corruption of an Organization: Enron

The collapse of Enron illustrates the nexus between power and corruption within a large corporation. The corrupt practices, including the creation of Special Purpose Entities to hide liabilities and offer a misleading picture of Enron's finances to investors, were the creatures of the CEO, CFO, and other members of the management team. It was their position of authority within the organization that enabled the existence of corruption on such a large scale and with such devastating consequences.

Enron also evidences the role of structural conflicts of interest in facilitating corruption. These conflicts of interest included that of the Chief Financial Officer (CFO) and those of those remunerated by bonuses for attracting new business. Traditionally, the CFO is the executive officer within an organization who is entrusted with ensuring that it operates with financial discipline and propriety. However, in a business environment where investors expect, and managers require, increased earnings in every financial quarter, CFOs come under pressure to "cook the books" and make them look better than they are in reality.[23] CFOs can come to have two potentially conflicting roles; (1) the traditional role of policing the integrity and accuracy of the accounts and financial statements of a company, and (2) the contemporary "role" of making sure that the quarterly earnings of the company look the best that they can, and even at times assisting this outcome by recourse to some "creative" accounting. This conflict of roles creates, in turn, a conflict of interest that has the tendency, at least potentially, to interfere with the proper exercise of the CFO's fiduciary duty of ensuring the integrity and accuracy of the company's

---

[22] Reich himself holds that these processes of interference are not corruption on the grounds, apparently, that they are more subtle than bribes (Reich, *Saving Capitalism*, p. 83). But, as I have argued throughout this work, the notion of corruption Reich relies on here is far too narrow.

[23] Dave Lindorff, "Chief fudge-the-books officer," www.salon.com, February 20, 2002.

financial statements; a duty entrusted to him by the board of directors and shareholders of the company. Andrew Fastow's dual role as CFO of Enron and manager of the Special Purpose Entities (SPEs), such as LJM (see Section 9.6), involved a serious conflict of interest; one which Fastow, as the company's financial watchdog, should have avoided.

Enron's in-house dealmakers launched new deals irrespective of the risks involved. They did so in order to boost quarterly earnings and the value of Enron stock, and thereby enable themselves to claim huge profits for the company, and, as a consequence, earn large bonuses for themselves. These dealmakers had an interest in earning immediate big bonuses for themselves through risky deals. This interest was in conflict, at least potentially, with their fiduciary duty to enhance the earnings of the company in real terms and over the long term; that is, not simply by means of short-term paper profits.

Naturally, such corruption is not only dependent on the power of the offenders, it is also dependent on their immorality; the Enron CEO and CFO, for example, had few moral scruples, and little concern for the welfare of Enron's shareholders and employees. So the existence of this power/corruption nexus points to the importance of robust social norms: commitment and compliance on the part of individuals to socially engendered moral principles. However, social norms by themselves are not enough; they are necessary, but not sufficient. As argued in Chapter 7, an additional necessary condition for combating corruption is adequate institutional accountability mechanisms. In the case of Enron, such mechanisms included inadequate auditing controls.

In the absence of accountability, mechanisms in relation to the powerful, hierarchies based on patronage, rather than merit, tend to develop, and thus benefits, such as promotion, are distributed on the basis of "loyalty" to the powerful, including complicity in corrupt schemes, rather than on the basis of merit, e.g., high-quality performance. Nor does this point pertain only to government. It holds equally for other organizational settings, such as large corporations. Indeed, this claim has been argued persuasively by Robert Jackall[24] in relation to large US corporations in particular. When the notion of democracy is discussed, it is normally done so in the context of government. However, the power/corruption nexus provides good reason for democratizing many other institutions, including corporations.

[24] Jackall, *Moral Mazes*.

II.3.2   *Markets, Monopolies, and Corruption*

Notwithstanding the pervasive rhetoric in favor of "free markets" and against "big government," many of the most important market-based industries in the USA and globally are monopolistic or oligopolistic in character and, as such, noncompliant with the fundamental principles of free and fair competition and in need of more stringent, rather than less stringent, regulation. This is not to say that there is a need for more regulation; rather what is called for is so-called "smart" regulation, and in many cases strong regulation, including the break-up of monopolies and oligopolies, is required.

According to Reich (who echoes many others):

> Many of the corporations that have gained dominance over large swathes of the economy in recent years have done so by extending their domains of intellectual property [large pharmaceutical companies, such as Pfizer, and large biotech corporations, such as Monsanto]; expanding their ownership of natural monopolies, where economies of scale are critical [large cable operators, such as Comcast]; merging with or acquiring other companies in the same market; gaining control over networks and platforms that become industry standards [large internet based companies, such as Amazon and Google]; or using licensing arrangements to enlarge their dominance and control. Such economic power has simultaneously increased their influence over government decisions about whether such practices should be allowed. All this has hobbled smaller business.[25]

The question that arises at this point is why governments have not intervened to reform these markets in a manner that curbs the excessive market power of certain market actors in monopolistic and oligopolistic market-based industries. Why have governments not introduced robust anti-trust legislation? Evidently, part of the answer is that the corporations in question have become so powerful that they can effectively lobby legislators not to enact the required anti-trust legislation. Certainly, the corporations in question spend very large amounts of money lobbying legislators and, in particular, providing millions of dollars to their election campaigns. I return to this issue in Chapter 14. Here I reiterate the point that the deliberate and self-serving interference by market actors of a kind that undermines the institutional purposes of market-based industries, such as blocking or thwarting anti-trust legislation, constitutes institutional corruption.

---

[25] Reich, *Saving Capitalism*, p. 30.

11.4   Anti-Corruption Strategies for Market-Based Industries

In relation to the establishment of anti-corruption strategies for corruption in market-based industries, I suggest that there are four main steps as well as a raft of smaller ones. In relation to the latter, see, for example, Chapter 9. As we have seen, normatively speaking, market-based organizations are multi-layered structures of joint action engaging in free and fair competition within a market in order to realize collective goods consisting of an adequate and sustainable supply of some good or service at a reasonable price and of reasonable quality. Therefore, government and industry bodies ought to intervene to ensure that market-based industries are in fact achieving this purpose. Accordingly, the first main step is for this larger institutional purpose to be enshrined in relevant legislation, e.g., corporations law, and done so at the expense of the prevailing ideology of maximizing shareholder value.

Second, and as a corollary of this, robust anti-trust legislation needs to be introduced in market-based industries suffering from monopolistic or oligopolistic distortions, i.e., lopsided market power relationships, with a view to "downsizing" overly powerful market actors and breaking up overly powerful horizontally structured conglomerates. Other legislation relevant to the problem of overly powerful market actors concerns intellectual property, e.g., a patent system that drives up the prices of basic medicines and foodstuffs.

Third, corporations ought to be required to put in place a more democratic structure that is more reflective of the actual contributions made by shareholders, managers, and workers in the overall context of what is in reality, and not simply according to my joint action model, an essentially cooperative enterprise. Here substantial worker representation on boards of directors and worker ownership of some meaningful percentage of shares are useful starting points.

Fourth, a more effective enforcement regime needs to be more widely introduced and acted upon. Such a regime needs to include criminalizing corporations per se and introducing more stringent criminal and civil liability provisions for directors and managers, i.e., the so-called directing mind and will of the company. Crucial in all this is regulatory activity that fixes responsibility, and ultimately liability, for harm done. For example, in the context of an increase in corporate crime, and the tendency for corporations to simply treat fines as a business cost, Fisse and Braithwaite have advocated the strategy of so-called enforced accountability. Enforced accountability consists of strengthening and restructuring corporate criminal liability in such a way as to enforce internal disciplinary measures against offending individuals.[26] A second example is Tomasic and Bottomley's suggestion that partnership-like liability rules be placed on the boards of public companies, so that members of boards become jointly and severally liable for the actions of any particular director.[27] A third example is the strategy whereby third parties, such as legal and accountancy firms, are held liable for managerial impropriety in virtue of the fact that they assisted the impropriety and, more importantly, the fact that they have deep pockets.[28]

Such strategies raise important ethical questions in relation to the collective moral responsibility of corporations and subgroups of corporations, as distinct from the individual moral responsibility of particular human beings. However, my account of collective moral responsibility as joint moral responsibility is helpful here since it underwrites such strategies, supposing they are efficacious. On my account, while it may be entirely legitimate to ascribe *legal* liability to nonhuman entities, such as corporations, it is only human beings that are properly speaking *moral* agents. So, my starting position in relation to the notion of collective or joint responsibility is that while individual human beings have moral agency, and therefore moral responsibility, corporations and other institutions do not. This position has been argued for in detail elsewhere.[29] Suffice it to say here that corporations are not agents because they do not possess mental states, such as intentions and beliefs. But if they are not agents, then they are not moral agents, and therefore they cannot be held morally responsible. I say all this notwithstanding the fact that *in law* they can be held to be agents, to perform actions, and to be liable. For it simply does not follow from the fact that corporations can be held legally liable that they have moral responsibility. Accordingly, my rejection of the notion of corporate moral responsibility is consistent with embracing, for example, Fisse and Braithwaite's above-mentioned strategy of enforced accountability.

On my teleological normative conception we can conceive of corporations as consisting of a set of jointly participating individual agents. It follows that the directors, managers, and employees (and, for that matter,

---

[26] Brent Fisse and John Braithwaite, *Corporations, Crime and Accountability* (Cambridge University Press, 1994).

[27] R. Tomasic and S. Bottomley *Directing the Top 500* (Allen and Unwin, 1993) p. 174.

[28] Paul Finn, "The Liability of Third Parties for Knowing Receipt or Assistance" in Donovan Waters (ed.), *Equities, Fiduciaries and Trusts* (Toronto: Carswell, 1993).

[29] Miller "Collective Moral Responsibility: An Individualist Account".

shareholders, albeit there are complications here) of a corporation can be held jointly morally responsible for many of their actions, namely their joint actions. For example, all the members of a production team could be held jointly responsible for the existence of the new car that their individual actions jointly produced. Moreover, fairness dictates that the members of that production team be rewarded, at least in part, on the basis of the economic success of this new car, and conversely, penalized if it should turn out to be defective in some way.

Of course, the fact that a corporation is hierarchically structured and consists of specialized spheres of individual, as well as joint, activity has implications for ascriptions of moral responsibility. On the one hand, directors and other managers – the so-called directing mind and will of a corporation – may well be in large part morally responsible for the actions of their subordinates, insofar as those subordinates are acting under the instructions of these managers. Correspondingly, employees in the lower echelons have diminished individual and collective responsibility for corporate policies and procedures. The upshot of this is that managers and employees, taken together, have collective (joint) moral responsibility for behavior in compliance with corporate policies and procedures. (Naturally, here as elsewhere, agents who share in the collective responsibility for some activity may have differential degrees of responsibility, e.g., a given manager may have a greater degree of moral responsibility than a lower echelon employee.)

However, it is a contingent fact that corporations are extremely hierarchical; indeed, it is a contingent fact that in some corporations, far from being involved in the decision-making process, workers within a corporation are the victims of exploitation or coercion. If so, those workers whose tasks contribute to the collective ends of the corporation have not themselves adopted those ends. But – ideally, at least – employees freely undertake their work in order to secure the collective end of a productive enterprise and thereby to receive their reward. Moreover, the existence of corporations in which workers are powerless is presumably in itself morally abhorrent. Accordingly, this would be an argument for greater democratization of corporations and greater protection of individual rights, such as autonomy, in workplace settings. Once again, the result of such a process of democratization and increase in individual autonomy would be to drive corporations toward the joint enterprise model that I am putting forward for consideration with its accompanying benefits in terms of corruption reduction.

11.5 Conclusion

In this chapter I have discussed and rejected a number of prevailing normative theories of market-based industries and elaborated my own teleological normative account, according to which the collective end (collective good) of market-based industries is the provision of an adequate and sustainable supply of some good or service at a reasonable price and of reasonable quality. Given this account, and my analysis of institutional corruption (Chapter 3), I have identified a number of important forms of institutional corruption in market-based industries (at the organizational and industry levels) and exemplified some of these. Finally, and in light of the discussions of anti-corruption and integrity systems in Chapters 7–10 and of collective responsibility in Chapter 6, I have suggested a number of general anti-corruption measures for market-based organizations and industries.

CHAPTER 12

Banking and Finance

The massive economic, social, political, and other harms caused by the Global Financial Crisis, the Sovereign Debt Crisis, and the Great Recession have generated considerable scrutiny of financial markets and financial institutions, notably banks, and a variety of defects have been identified.[1] These include structural problems (e.g., "too big to fail"[2] systemically important financial institutions), regulatory inadequacies (e.g., enabling regulatory arbitrage), criminal and unethical behavior indicative of corrupt cultures (e.g., benchmark manipulation), and short-termism (e.g., in equity markets). Accordingly, a wide variety of structural, regulatory, and culture-change reforms have been proposed and, in some cases, implemented.[3] These include increased capital ratios for banks, splitting retail/investment banking conglomerates into utilities and market-based investment only institutions,[4] providing government with the legal power to convert bank debt into equity,[5] simplifying and harmonizing the regulatory architecture, redesigning oversight bodies and increasing their investigative and other powers, overhauling the administrative arrangements and methodologies in relation to

---

[1] Garnaut, *The Great Crash of 2008*; G. Gilligan and J. O'Brien (eds.), *Integrity, Risk and Accountability in Capital Markets: Regulating Culture* (Oxford: Hart Publishing, 2013); I. MacNeil and J. O'Brien (eds.), *The Future of Financial Regulation* (Oxford: Hart Publishing, 2010); Dobos, Barry, and Pogge (eds.), *Global Financial Crisis: Ethical Issues*; N. Morris and David Vines (eds.), *Capital Failure: Rebuilding Trust in Financial Services* (Oxford: Oxford University Press, 2014).

[2] See, for example, US Attorney-General Eric Holder's answers to the Senate Judiciary Committee as reported in A. Sorkin, "Realities behind Prosecuting Big Banks," *New York Times*, March 12, 2013.

[3] Financial Services Authority, *Turner Review: A Regulatory Response to the Global Banking Crisis* (London: FSA, 2009).

[4] Perhaps in accordance with the so-called Volcker Rule, originally within the Dodd-Frank Wall Street Reform and Consumer Protection Act, but subsequently watered down.

[5] Financial Stability Board, "FSB announces policy measures to address systemically important financial institutions (SIFIs) and names initial group of global SIFIs," www.fsb.org, November 4, 2011.

financial benchmarks, strengthening the licensing requirements of financial institutions and occupations, banning "unsafe" financial products (e.g., various complex derivatives), curtailing executive remuneration, realigning the incentive arrangements for fund managers with the long-term interests of savers and companies, introducing legally based fiduciary duties for financial service providers, drafting codes of ethics and embedding educational and other professionalization processes, and so on and so forth.

Whatever the virtues of many of these suggested reforms – and, arguably, their main shortcoming is their failure to be implemented in the face of opposition from powerful financial interests[6] – they do not for the most part address the matter of institutional *purpose*. Institutional purpose has tended to be neglected in the reform process.[7] However, as argued in Chapters 7 and 11, it is one of the principal tasks of those who regulate markets, principally legislators and regulators, to ensure that the ultimate institutional purposes of markets, be they financial or otherwise, are in fact achieved.

The notion of institutional purpose in play here is normative: the purposes that financial markets and financial institutions *ought to have*. Naturally, these purposes vary, or ought to vary, from one kind of financial market to another and from one kind of financial institution to another. Thus the institutional purpose of equity markets is not the same as that of foreign exchange markets. Again, the institutional purpose of pension funds is not the same as that of banks, and that of retail banks not the same as that of investment banks. Moreover, if one looks, for example, at the objectives of many regulators of financial markets one typically finds only limited aims, e.g., to reduce crime and protect consumers, and procedural concerns, e.g., to promote competition and efficiency. There is little or no reference to the ultimate institutional purposes or ends of particular financial markets. Accordingly, there is a pressing need for an

---

[6] See, for example, Seumas Miller, "'Trust me. . .. I'm a (systemically important) bank!': Institutional corruption, market-based industries and financial benchmarks," *Law and Financial Markets Review*, 8 (2014), 322–325.

[7] This is not always the case. For example, Mark Carney, Governor of the Bank of England, implicitly recognizes institutional purpose in Mark Carney, "Inclusive Capitalism: Creating a Sense of the Systemic," *Inclusive Capitalism Conference*, London, May 27, 2014, and at the time of writing there is a somewhat belated discussion in Australia whether or not the purpose of Australia's compulsory retirement scheme (superannuation) ought to be specified and enshrined in law (Corporations Act 2001), and specified, in particular, as the purpose of providing an adequate income stream for retirees as opposed to, say, a pool of savings for investment by government or savers. Even an institution that was designed and constructed by government did not have its institutional purpose specified and agreed upon. See, for example, Joanna Mather and Sally Rose, "Low tax sought for $2.5m super," *Australian Financial Review*, 11 (2016), 6.

adequate *general* normative account or "theory" of financial markets, and for adequate *special* normative "theories" of particular financial markets, e.g., equity markets.

In this chapter I apply my teleological normative account of institutions in general, and market-based institutions and occupations in particular, to financial markets. More specifically, I apply my account to recent widespread institutional corruption in the banking sector, capital markets, financial benchmarks, and financial service providers, and propose a variety of anti-corruption measures.

12.1 Banks

On my teleological account, both organizations and markets are essentially complex multi-layered structures of joint action and, as such, have collective ends that are also collective goods.[8] Financial institutions, such as banks, are no different from any other social institution in this respect; that is, there is a need to identify collective ends that are collective goods and, as such, provide the *raison d'etre* for their existence. However, evidently in the case of the banking sector, as elsewhere in the financial system, the prior fundamental ethical question as to the ultimate institutional purposes (collective goods) of this sector remains unanswered or is, at least, contested. Yet, as argued above, without an answer to this question, governments, regulators, and policymakers cannot give appropriate rational direction to the banking sector.

On the teleological account of the market mechanism there is an outcome that ought to be aimed at, if not necessarily by all market actors, certainly by legislators, regulators and, I suggest, responsible representatives and members of the industry. The latter are well aware of the market as a whole and the need to regulate and, if necessary, redesign and restructure it to achieve desirable outcomes.[9] To this extent, the "invisible" hand is to an important extent visible. Moreover, normatively speaking, this outcome is, to reiterate, a collective end that is also a collective good.

---

[8] Earlier versions of the material in this section and the following one appeared in Seumas Miller, "Capital Markets and Institutional Purposes: The Ethical Issues' in Lisa Herzog (ed.) *Just Financial Markets* (Oxford University Press, 2017); Miller, "'Trust me.... I'm a (systemically important) bank!': Institutional corruption, market-based industries and financial benchmarks"; Seumas Miller, "The Global Financial Crisis and Collective Moral Responsibility" in Andre Nollkaemper and Dov Jacobs (eds.), *Distribution of Responsibilities in International Law* (Cambridge University Press, 2015), pp. 404–433; Miller, "Global Financial Institutions, Ethics and Market Fundamentalism"; Miller, *Moral Foundations of Social Institutions*, chapter 10.

[9] There is, of course, often disagreement in relation to specific regulatory and other proposals.

Further, it is an end that is realized by the market as whole and not simply by a single market actor. I argued in Chapter 11 that the collective end in question is an adequate and sustainable supply of some good or service. Moreover, the good or service in question should be of reasonable quality and available at a reasonable price.

If this is correct, then there are a number of questions to be addressed in relation to any given market or market-based institution, including financial institutions such as banks. First, is the product or service actually a good, normatively speaking; is it worthy of production? Presumably, as is the case with unsafe foodstuffs, "innovative" financial products that are, nevertheless, unsafe ought not to be produced. Second, is the good or service offered at a reasonable price? The oligopolies in banking in the UK, EU, Australia, and elsewhere are problematic in this regard. Third, is the supply sustainable? Short-termism driven by the desire to maximize profits as reflected in quarterly returns is a problem in terms of this long-term yardstick.[10] Fourth, is the quantum of the good or service in question adequate? Here we can distinguish between different segments of a consumer or client group; specifically, we can distinguish between high-income earners, middle earners, and low-income earners. The housing market, for example, would be inadequate if it only provided a stock of expensive mansions affordable by high-income earners; likewise, a housing mortgage market that did not cater for low-income earners.

Moreover, on my normative teleological account, financial rewards such as wages, executive remuneration, and dividends are proximate, not ultimate, purposes; they are part of the reward system and, as such, the means to an end. The end in question on this account is, of course, the provision of an adequate and sustainable supply of some good or service (of reasonable quality and at a reasonable price).

Let me now turn directly to the matter of the institutional purposes of banking. I do so from the standpoint that the ultimate institutional purpose of the banking and finance sector is to provide for the needs of the nonfinancial productive sector and, ultimately, the aggregate rights-based needs of human beings (as opposed to, say, corporations). Normatively speaking, banking and finance are a derivative second order form of economic activity. In short, Wall Street exists or, at least, ought to exist, to provide for the needs of Main Street. Thus the institutional purpose of capital markets is to provide an adequate and sustainable

---

[10] John Kay, *Kay Review of UK Equity Markets and Long Term Decision-Making* (London: UK House of Commons, 2013).

quantum of capital at a reasonable interest rate (directly or indirectly) for the productive sector. Again, the institutional purpose of derivatives markets (e.g., swaps, options, futures) is to mitigate risk (provide financial insurance), often, admittedly, for actors in the financial sector, but not only for them because financial stability is a necessary condition for the productive sector to function effectively.[11]

On this normative teleological account, it is of the first importance to specify the specific institutional purpose or purposes of the banking sector. I take it that core institutional purposes of the banking sector are the provision of the following[12]:

(1) secure locations for depositors to deposit and withdraw their funds;
(2) payments system;
(3) an adequate supply of reasonably priced loans of reasonable quality (i.e., based on safe assets) for homeowners and for small- and medium-sized businesses (SMBs or SMEs).

Following John Kay's terminology, let us refer to institutions that have these purposes as narrow banks.[13] According to Kay, in recent times "retail savings institutions metamorphosed from the purpose of meeting routine financing needs of everyday banking into function that were treated as profit centres in their own right."[14] Kay goes on to argue that narrow banks should be regarded as utilities. Currently existing retail/investment banking conglomerates should be split into utilities and market-based investment-only institutions. Moreover, narrow banks, and only narrow banks, should be deposit-taking institutions with depositor's funds guaranteed.

Viewed from this perspective, an important question arises in relation to speculative trading, e.g., speculative trading on currencies, commodities, and derivatives. Arguably, speculative trading is for the most part a market-based method of redistributing funds from one party to another. Moreover, large-scale speculative trading can create bubbles that burst and lead to stock market crashes, banking collapses, unemployment, shortages, and/or overpriced goods and services, and so on. Perhaps, therefore, speculative trading ought to be curbed, e.g., by placing limits on

---

[11] It is an empirical question as to whether or not they actually achieve this purpose. Clearly, so-called toxic financial products did the reverse.
[12] John Kay, "Should We Have Narrow Banking?" in *The Future of Finance: The LSE Report* (London: London School of Economics and Political Science, 2010).
[13] Kay might not have had this precise set of purposes in mind; no matter for my purposes here, e.g., perhaps not the business loans.
[14] *Ibid.*, p. 224.

speculative positions in commodity markets. (We return to the issue of speculation below.) At any rate, the point to be made here is that high-risk activities, such as speculative trading, are highly problematic for deposit-taking institutions. Hence, the soundness of Kay's recommendation that such activities not be allowed in narrow banks.

A further issue in the global banking sector pertains to institutional structure. As already noted, an important macro-institutional feature of the global banking sector is the phenomenon of global financial institutions that are "too big to fail." Thus there were a number of bailouts of major banks and other financial institutions following the decision in 2008 to allow Lehman Brothers to fail; a decision that is thought to have virtually brought the international financial system to its knees. Importantly, for our concerns here, the phenomenon of banks that are "too big to fail" has morphed into the phenomenon of banks that are "too big to regulate." For example, there is the recent money-laundering case of the multinational bank, HSBC.[15] HSBC received a US$1.9 billion fine for failing to have in place effective anti-money laundering measures and for failing to conduct due diligence on some of its account holders. Criminal negligence not-withstanding, HSBC retained its license to operate, having in effect been deemed by the regulators "too big to fail." However, the inference that is being drawn from HSBC's retention of its license in these circumstances is that it is, in effect, too big to regulate.

According to the Financial Stability Board,[16] there are twenty-nine systemically important financial institutions; in effect, twenty-nine institutions that are too big to fail and, therefore, too big to regulate or, at least, to regulate effectively. Evidently, corruption, instability, and other harms arising from commercial competition between the investment arms of banks in a market context in which there is an overriding imperative to maximize profit and in which many of these banks are "too big to fail" looks to be too great to be overcome, other than by substantial institutional redesigning and restructuring. This would involve splitting the investment from the retail arm of banks to form two separate institutions, as recommended by Kay – or, at the very least, iron-clad segregation within one institution, if that is possible – and "downsizing" banks "too big to fail" and, therefore, "too big to regulate." A market in which an individual market actor cannot fail is a contradiction in terms and is, in

---

[15] J. Treanor and D. Rushe, "HSCB to pay 1.2 billion pounds over Mexico scandal," *The Guardian*, December 10, 2012, available at www.theguardian.co.uk.

[16] Financial Stability Board, "FSB announces policy measures to address systemically important financial institutions."

any case, intolerable in the global banking sector, given what is at stake, namely, global financial stability.

12.2   Capital Markets

As noted above, the Global Financial Crisis, the Sovereign Debt Crisis, and the Great Recession – which recession appears to be continuing in one form or another at the time of writing, at least in Europe, Japan, and in some of the so-called emerging economies, such as Brazil – has revealed various deficiencies in equity markets, in particular. These include short termism (driven by the desire to maximize profits as expressed in quarterly returns),[17] an excess of purely speculative trading of shares, and massive and harmful capital outflows (e.g., from developing economies). These deficiencies have been exacerbated by the advent of high-speed trading[18] and unregulated so-called dark pools.[19]

According to Kay, for example, the decline of major British companies, such as ICI and GEC, was in large part a consequence of the replacement of the conception of the corporate executive not as efficiently and effectively managing a producer of goods and services but rather as a "meta-fund manager, acquiring and disposing of a portfolio of businesses rather as a fund manager might view a portfolio of shares."[20] Kay goes on to say, "The central issues for this Review [Kay Review of Equity Markets] arise from the replacement of a financial services culture based on trust relationships by one based around transactions and trading. We can see that shift in the management preoccupations of ICI and GEC, and in the development of a market place in which hedge funds and high frequency traders account for a majority of turnover on the London exchange even though they hold an insignificant proportion of the stock."[21]

As already emphasized, by the lights of my teleological normative account of social institutions, capital markets have as their institutional purpose (collective good) to provide an adequate and sustainable supply of financial capital to (especially nonfinancial) productive firms at a reasonable cost. Moreover, the productive firms in question are ones that meet

---

[17] John Kay, *Kay Review of UK Equity Markets and Long Term Decision-Making*.
[18] Michael Lewis, *Flash Boys: Cracking the Money Code* (London: Penguin, 2014).
[19] Thomas Clarke, "High Frequency Trading and Dark Pools: Sharks Never Sleep," *Law and Financial Markets Review*, 8 (2014), 342–351.
[20] John Kay Speech at *Kay Review of UK Equity Markets and Long Term Decision-Making* launch, Department for Business Innovation and Skills, London, July 23, 2012, p. 9.
[21] *Ibid.*

aggregate human needs (e.g., for food, clothing, shelter), including, indeed especially, in impoverished countries where these needs are greatest.

Capital markets characterized by short termism and dominated by speculative trading are at odds with this collective good since such markets are not focused on long-term investment in productive firms. Moreover, as Kay indicates, these untoward features of capital markets have infected even the management of the firms themselves. In short, the tail (Wall Street) is now wagging the dog (Main Street).

Ironically, the problem is compounded by free markets. For example, the absence of control over capital outflows enables massive and harmful inflows and outflows of capital from one economy to another based on speculation, e.g., on fluctuations in commodity prices, currencies, and interest rates and, in particular, on the likely actions of other traders, rather than a consideration of the likelihood of the long-term productivity of firms. Here, as elsewhere, the groups most harmed tend to be the less well-off.

There is a raft of reforms that has been suggested to deal with these deficiencies in capital markets. These range from redesigning corporate governance structures and regulating "dark pools," through to the reintroduction of capital controls under some circumstances and innovative proposals such as a radical extension of the concept of Special Drawing Rights to create a new global reserve currency to help stabilize global financial markets and make reserves available for investment in productive enterprises in impoverished countries.[22]

As noted above, an important macrostructural feature of the global financial sector pertains to the legislators and regulators. National governments and regulators have an ambiguous role in relation to global financial markets, for national governments and their regulators are to some extent partisan, and (understandably) seek to look after the interests of their own banking sector (e.g., the "City" in the case of UK regulators). This is especially the case if, as in the case of the UK, the finance and banking sector is of major importance to the economy as a whole. Moreover, in the absence of a uniform set of global regulations and a single global regulator with real authority, regulators operating at a national level can be played off against one another by multinational corporations. Evidently, there is a need to redesign the global regulatory structure to deal with this problem. John Eatwell has suggested that a World Financial Authority should be established on the grounds that the domain of the regulator should be the same as the domain of the market that is regulated.[23] This is surely correct, at least in theory. However, it faces prodigious practical difficulties, such as from nation-states unwilling to cede authority to such a body. Eatwell, however, has argued that it is possible to establish such a body, given the degree of mutual self-interest in play.

At any rate, the general point to be stressed here is that any such proposals need to be adjudicated by recourse to institutional purpose: Are they efficient and effective in relation to the realization of the collective good that should be provided by capital markets?

12.3 Financial Benchmark Manipulation

Recent revelations of financial benchmark rigging, e.g., of LIBOR (a globally important benchmark on which trillions of dollars of financial transactions are based), by many, if not most, of the leading global banks, indicate that the problems in the global banking sector not only continue post the GFC, but are systemic. As argued throughout this work, institutional corruption is both a moral notion and a causal or quasi-causal notion. That it is a moral and not merely a legal notion is evident from the fact that corruption can exist in the absence of laws proscribing it.[24] For example, until very recently it was not unlawful to knowingly make false LIBOR submissions for financial gain. Nevertheless, such manipulation of financial benchmarks is, and always was, a paradigm of corrupt activity; hence it has been criminalized, albeit belatedly. Corruption is a causal notion since an action is corrupt only if it corrupts something or someone. Thus an action, e.g., manipulation of foreign exchange rates for financial gain, is an action of institutional corruption by virtue of having a *corrupting effect* on an institutional process or purpose, e.g., undermining the process of determining median foreign exchange rates.

Benchmarks, such as LIBOR, are instances of such mechanisms.[25] Other examples are voting to elect a candidate to political office, use of money as a

---

[23] John Eatwell, "The Challenge Facing International Financial Regulation," Speech given at Queens College, Cambridge, 2000, pp. 1–20; John Eatwell and Lance Taylor, *Global Finance at Risk: The Case for International Regulation* (New York: New Press, 2000).

[24] Miller, *Moral Foundations of Social Institutions*, chapter 5. See also Lawrence Lessig, "America: Compromised Studies in Institutional Corruption," 2014–2015 Berlin Family Lectures, University of Chicago.

[25] Earlier versions of the material in this section appeared in Miller, "'Trust me. . .. I'm a (systemically important) bank!': Institutional corruption, market-based industries and financial benchmarks"; Miller "The Global Financial Crisis and Collective Moral Responsibility"; and Seumas Miller, "The

medium of exchange and, more generally, exchange systems such as markets for goods and services. Joint institutional mechanisms[26] (chapter 1 section 1.3) consist of (a) a complex of differentiated but interlocking actions (the input to the mechanism); (b) the result of the performance of those actions (the output of the mechanism); and (c) the mechanism itself. In the case of LIBOR, the inputs are the interest rate estimates submitted by the banks. So there is interlocking and differentiated action (the various inputs of the submitters). Further, there is the process applied to the inputs (the mechanism). This mechanism consists in averaging the various submissions.[27] The application of the mechanism (the averaging process) to the input (the submissions) yields an output: the LIBOR interest rate for some currency over some period.

Note the following important points regarding this joint institutional mechanism, assuming it is working as it should and realizing its normative institutional purposes, i.e., if it is not malfunctioning or corrupted. First, that there is a result is (in part) constitutive of the mechanism. The result, i.e., the particular interest rate arrived at (LIBOR), is not aimed at by each or any of the banks; after all, none of the banks can predict the result, let alone bring it about by aiming at it. Nevertheless, each of the banks has a common end (more precisely, a collective *epistemic* end[28]), namely that the average interest rate – whatever that is – will be produced by this mechanism.

Second, the generation of an interest rate by this mechanism serves a further institutional purpose that is the *raison d'être* of the mechanism (and, as such, in part constitutive of it), namely, that of providing a *benchmark* interest rate upon which various institutions and individuals can rely. So at one level of description the result of the application of the mechanism is simply an interest rate arrived at by averaging, but at another level of description this interest rate is a benchmark. This ultimate benchmarking purpose is itself a collective end of the joint institutional

Corruption of Financial Benchmarks: Financial Markets, Collective Goods and Institutional Purposes," *Law and Financial Markets Review*, 8 (2014), 155–164.

[26] Miller, *Social Action*.

[27] The averaging process is somewhat more complex than simple averaging since some of the highest and lowest submitted rates are excluded from it. However, this is a sufficient description for our purposes here.

[28] More precisely, there is a two-stage process, the first stage of which is the production of LIBOR, the second stage of which is its communication and acceptance by numerous institutions and individuals as a credible benchmark. The collective end is an epistemic one since it consists in an item of knowledge (ideally). For more on this see Miller, *Moral Foundations of Social Institutions*, chapter 11 and "Joint Epistemic Action: Some Applications".

mechanism, but one aimed at not just by the bankers but also by those who use LIBOR to set their own interest rates. That any one of the interest rates in question serves as a benchmark is an end that is realized not simply by the banks generating it via their submissions, but also by other institutions and individuals using it as such. Absent the participation of both parties (or categories of party), LIBOR would cease to exist.

Third, and needless to say, providing false submissions, or otherwise seeking to manipulate the results of the mechanism, is a matter of moral significance, given its important institutional purpose and the consequent trust placed in it by so many. This point has been reinforced by the Wheatley Review's recommendation that noncompliance, e.g., by intentionally making false submissions, be a criminal offence.

The institutional purpose of financial benchmarks, such as LIBOR and WM/Reuters' reference rates, is the production of a public good in the economist's sense of non-rival and non-excludable goods – but also, and importantly for our purposes here, a collective good, in my sense – albeit one the production of which was until recently unregulated.[29] Moreover, these public goods that are also collective goods are produced by *cooperative* rather than competitive action, e.g., the cooperative action of submitters in the case of LIBOR. So benchmarks are not produced by market actors engaged in competition as, for example, prices are. Financial benchmarks are not simply prices consequent upon supply and demand but which no-one is actually aiming at; rather, they are the aimed at average or median (or other numerical relationship) calculated on the basis of recorded transactional data or judgments thereof. Moreover, they are calculated, promulgated, and relied upon as a public and collective good, i.e., as a mutually known benchmark upon which market actors can rely. Accordingly, they constitute financial infrastructure underpinning market activity in the finance sector but not produced by market actors acting as market actors. Moreover, as recent revelations have made abundantly clear, financial benchmarks constitute infrastructure that is vulnerable to corruption by market actors. Significantly, the various manipulations of financial benchmarks in question have involved collusion between banks and have implicated senior bank staff; so the matter cannot simply be dismissed as a case of "a few rotten apples."

On the view proffered in this work of collective responsibility as joint responsibility, collective responsibility is ascribed to individuals. Each

---

[29] Miller, "The Corruption of Financial Benchmarks: Financial Markets, Collective Goods and Institutional Purposes."

member of the group is individually morally responsible for the outcome of
the joint action. However, each is individually responsible, jointly with the
others; hence the conception is relational in character. Thus in the case of a
million dollar bank heist, each member of the gang is responsible jointly
with the others for the theft of the million dollars because each performed
his contributory action in the service of that collective end (the theft of the
million dollars).

On this kind of relational view, the various relevant bank submitters,
traders, and/or managers involved in some particular episode of LIBOR
interest-rigging can be ascribed collective moral responsibility for this
particular corrupt action and for any (personal and/or institutional)
harm that might result from it. As we have seen in relation to the
LIBOR scandal, the network of joint actions and omissions can be quite
wide and complex without necessarily involving all, or even most, bank
personnel. Moreover, some joint actions or omissions might be of greater
moral significance than others, and some individual contributions, e.g.,
those of senior bank managers, of greater importance than others. Further,
the cumulative damage done by an ongoing series of such episodes of
corrupt action by numerous bank personnel from different institutions and
on multiple occasions might conceivably also be sheeted home to the entire
large group, albeit there are various barriers to the ascription of collective
moral responsibility in large groups in which each member only makes a
small causal contribution.

Importantly, and as noted by the Wheatley Review,[30] there is a collective
institutional responsibility on the part of LIBOR submitters to provide
well-founded, truthful submission and, thereby, arrive at correct LIBOR
rates. It was this collective *institutional* responsibility – and, given the
moral significance in terms of the resulting harm, breach of trust, etc.
collective *moral* responsibility – which those who engaged in false submissions failed to discharge and, in so failing, corrupted the LIBOR process.
What is remarkable is that pre-Wheatley it was probably not a legal offence
to engage in LIBOR interest-rate rigging; evidently, bank robbery was
regarded as one thing, but robbery by bankers quite another.

It goes without saying that the response to benchmark corruption needs
to be a process of institutional redesign resulting in an independent
administrator of the benchmark, an appropriate governance structure for
the administrator, a reliable methodology for calculating the benchmark
rates, and stringent oversight and disciplinary powers in relation to would-

---

[30] Wheatley Review op. cit.

be manipulators.[31] However, there is a further point that needs to be pressed home and that has apparently gone unnoticed by IOSCO and by financial commentators. Since financial benchmarks constitute infrastructure productive of public goods that are also collective goods by means of cooperative action rather than competitive market-based activity, the most appropriate institutional vehicle to administer financial benchmarks is a utility or quasi-utility rather than a market actor. Indeed, in performing this function an administrator is, in effect, a utility or quasi-utility and should be treated as such and funded accordingly, e.g., by taxes levied on users. The ongoing revelations of systematic corruption of financial benchmarks by market actors merely serve to underline the need for an independent utility to perform this function. Moreover, as with other market actors operating without the full discipline of the market, benchmark administrators that are themselves market actors have an accountability gap; a gap that will need to be bridged by additional and intrusive regulatory apparatus. This is a further reason to abandon the fiction that the institutional mechanisms for the provision of financial benchmarks are essentially markets.

12.4 Financial Service Providers

In the overall context of the GFC and the EU Sovereign Debt Crisis, the financial planning industry in the USA, the UK, Australia, as elsewhere in the finance sector, ethical issues have in recent times come to the fore.[32] Consider in this connection the selling of "exotic" financial products, such as CDOs (collateralized debt obligations) to unsophisticated investors, and various Ponzi schemes in which financial advisors played a crucial role in recruiting investor-victims.

Professionalization is evidently a large part of the proposed solution to identified problems in the financial planning industries. Here we need to make some general points about professionalization and integrity systems.

---

[31] IOSCO, International Organization of Securities Commissions, *Principles for Financial Benchmarks: Final Report* (Madrid: International Organization of Securities Commissions, 2013), available at www.iosco.org.

[32] Earlier versions of the material in this section appeared in Miller, "Capital Markets and Institutional Purposes: The Ethical Issues'; Miller, "Trust, Conflicts of Interest and Fiduciary Duties: Ethical Issues in the Financial Planning Industry in Australia" in Morris and Vines (eds.), *Capital Failure: Rebuilding Trust in Financial Services* (Oxford: Oxford University Press, 2014), pp. 305–331; Miller, "The Global Financial Crisis and Collective Moral Responsibility"; Miller, "Global Financial Institutions, Ethics and Market Fundamentalism"; Miller, *Moral Foundations of Social Institutions,* chapter 10 the following:

Professionalization is perhaps thought of as a set of closely related processes rather than a single, unitary process; the process of professionalization cannot be a "one size fits all" affair. The professionalization of journalists, for example, cannot mean the same thing as it does for lawyers, given the potential problems posed for freedom of the press by the establishment of a regulatory authority. More specifically, it is not self-evident that the members of all occupations that are professions, or should professionalize, have or should have a fiduciary duty, e.g., journalists arguably should not.

Professionalization in the sense in use here is simply the process, or processes, by means of which an occupation lacking the features characteristic of a profession – the features listed in Chapter 9 Section 9.1– is transformed into an occupation that has those features; or, at least, the process by means of which such an occupation comes to have most of those features. Professionalization in this sense is decidedly not the process by means of which an occupation acquires various trappings of the professions for the purposes of achieving a higher status, more institutional power, and greater financial and other rewards than otherwise might be forthcoming.

Professionalization in our favored sense can be an important component of an integrity system for an occupation, assuming that occupation is one that ought to be a profession. Here we need to bear in mind that many occupations are not, and ought not ever to become, a profession. Let us assume, then, that in the evolving financial sector there is a need for a profession of financial advisors, i.e., a professionally accredited occupational group possessed of expert knowledge, professional independence, and with a fiduciary duty grounded in the vulnerability of the needy, e.g., retirees, and so on. If so, and given the problems identified in the financial planning sector, e.g., conflation of sales and advisory roles, there is good reason to think that professionalization can function as an important component in building an overall integrity system for financial advisors.

That said, it should also be emphasized at the outset that professionalization is only one component in the construction of such an integrity system; it would be illusory, I suggest, to think that it could provide the complete solution to all the problems. Specifically, what I referred to earlier as the macro-institutional context, e.g., of the financial products and services industry, needs to be attended to when focusing on micro-occupational reform, e.g., of the occupation of financial advisor.

Further – and, again, notwithstanding the general contribution that professionalization might make to occupational "integrity" – it is important to maintain a distinction between those occupations that have a distinctive role as key elements of an integrity system (e.g., auditors), and those who have obligations the discharging of which it is a purpose of the integrity system to ensure (e.g., the corporations whose financial records are audited). Different occupations have different roles in relation to integrity systems: auditors are "gatekeepers" in the sense of independent scrutineers of financial health, lawyers have an important role in relation to ensuring understanding and compliance with the law (e.g., on the part of their corporate clients/employers), and so on (this is "gate-keeping" in a different sense).

Naturally, in one sense the members of an occupation, profession, or institution are themselves both part of the integrity system and simultaneously actors with obligations the discharging of which it is a function of the integrity system to ensure. However, the truth of this general point does not obviate the need to identify the precise role each relevant occupation ought to play in an integrity system for (say) financial services and, therefore, what professionalization ought to consist of for each of these occupations. Here, as elsewhere, the devil is to some extent in the detail. For example, a financial advisor who was a member of a fully professionalized occupational group of financial advisors would be entirely independent of financial product manufacturers. Moreover, such a professional would presumably not only have a detailed understanding of any relevant financial product and of the desirable economic purposes served by that product, but would also take him or herself to have a professional and moral obligation to provide advice to clients, licensees, financial product manufacturers, regulators, and, for that matter, the public at large with respect to the risks attached to specific financial products; indeed, such a professional advisor would, if he or she deemed it to be appropriate, strongly recommend – perhaps via the professional association – that certain financial products be banned as serving no useful economic purpose and as likely to do serious harm. Such a professional financial advisor would indeed be part of the overall integrity system for the financial products and services industry, and would be providing that "ethics" service as part and parcel of their professional role as a financial advisor and not, this should be stressed, as a "white knight" engaged in supererogatory good works. If members of the medical profession keep quiet about the deficiencies of certain drugs and, indeed, continue to prescribe them, should this not be regarded as a breach of their professional moral obligations? Likewise, if lawyers are principally engaged in finding and exploiting loopholes for their well-heeled clients, and without regard to the larger purposes of the law in their particular legal sphere – as has evidently recently been the case in various sectors of the corporate and financial sectors – surely they are breaching their professional moral obligations in relation to the larger purpose of the administration of justice (and irrespective of whether or not they have breached any particular law). Moreover, surely their fellow lawyers – again perhaps via the relevant professional association – should be doing something about this.

The establishment of a legally based fiduciary duty and the banning of certain forms of conflicted remuneration are important contributions to building occupational "integrity" among financial advisors, both directly and indirectly (via professionalization). The likelihood of these intentions at the micro-occupational level being successful depends in part, I suggest, on some larger issues concerning the macro-institutional framework; an institution and, therefore, an institutional framework, itself comprising purpose(s), structure, and culture(s).[33] What is the macro-institutional framework in which the envisaged process of professionalization is to take place? What impact, if any, are the legislative changes going to have on that institutional framework?

More specifically, are vertically integrated structures of financial product manufacturers, financial advisory licensees, and financial advisors likely to undergo any functional (i.e., in terms of their *de facto* institutional purposes), structural and/or associated cultural changes and, if not, what are the implications for the success or otherwise of the envisaged process of professionalization of financial advisors?

I have suggested that integrity systems are the principal institutional vehicle for promoting ethical conduct and combating crime and corruption. If this is right, then it ought to be instructive to view any proposed process of professionalization of financial advisors through the lens of an appropriate integrity system for this occupation. How does legislation and this professionalization process complement and complete(?) an appropriate integrity system?

Legislation and the envisaged professionalization process, more generally, ought to address the various dimensions of an integrity system identified in Chapters 7 and 9 with respect to the motive, capacity and opportunity to engage in corruption, including macro-structural reform, deterrence focused regulation, market incentives, reputational incentives, and underlying, widely accepted, moral beliefs and attitudes. Moreover, as well as functioning as a part of the (so to speak) external integrity system for financial advisors it provides for a new set of (so to speak) internal obligations constitutive of the role of the financial planner; so in a sense it seeks to build integrity both from without and from within.

In relation to the regulatory dimension of the integrity system for financial advisors, what is most salient is, of course, legislation that

---

[33] See Miller, *Moral Foundations of Social Institutions*, Introduction.

provides a regulatory framework conducive to professionalization. Naturally this legislation needs to be enforceable, and regulatory authorities need to be provided with enhanced powers to revoke the licenses of those who fail to comply with the new requirements and to ban individual advisors who fail to meet their professional obligations.[34]

Crucially, there is a need for a number of quite specific measures expressly designed to contribute to the process of transformation of an occupation formerly composed essentially of sales personnel into a profession comprising purveyors of high-quality, independent, financial advice. To reiterate: these measures include the creation of a (legal) fiduciary obligation and a ban on various forms of conflicted remuneration in favor of a *bona fide* fee-for-services model.[35] The list of conflicted remunerations is lengthy, but it ought to include such ones as commissions to financial advisors emanating (ultimately) from the financial product manufacturers with respect to whose products the advisors are giving their advice.

In relation to underlying, widely accepted, moral standards and values, a process of understanding and internalization of ethico-professional standards and values by individual financial advisors is envisaged. Hence, there is a focus on codes of ethics and, relatedly, on professional ethics awareness raising, training, and education, including through professional bodies. To this extent, there is an attempt to specify and communicate professional obligations and values and, in doing so, to tap into the underlying, widely accepted, and preexisting general moral standards and values of the institutional actors in question.

As far as reputational incentives are concerned, there is a need for a plan to utilize reputational devices as an additional and complementary layer of the overall integrity system for the occupation. For example, a reputational index (comprised of objective indicators of ethical "health") could be constructed, an ethics audit conducted (by an independent body) – the results of which would give a comparative picture of the various firms in the industry – and these results promulgated.[36] Given the sensitivity of many actors in the financial services industry to reputational risks, notably

---

[34] FOFA Bill No. 1 Items 2–4. ss. 913B(1)(b), 913B(4)(a), and 915C(1)(aa) (license cancellation); FOFA Bill No. 1 Items 5–7. ss. 920A(1)(ba), 920A(1)(d), 920(1)(da), and 920A(1)(f) (banning of individuals).

[35] By *bona fide* I mean one that excludes all conflicted remuneration including links between advice given and transactions made, as in so-called asset-based fees. See later in the text of this final section.

[36] For further details on this and other reputational devices see Alexandra and Miller, *Integrity Systems for Occupations*, chapter 5. See also Miller, "Financial Service Providers: Integrity Systems, Reputation and the Triangle of Virtue" and "Financial Service Providers, Reputation and the Virtuous Triangle."

lack of trust on the part of customers/clients in the independence of financial advisors, the absence of reputational devices would be a significant omission.

However, it is in the area of (so to speak) market-induced "integrity" at what I have referred to as the macro-institutional level that is typically the greatest source of concern. This is not to deny that there are the standard market incentives and disincentives in place that (respectively) encourage ethical behavior and discourage unethical behavior especially, but not exclusively, among independent financial advice providers. These incentives do exist and they are strengthened by the proposed greater emphasis on appropriately communicated disclosure, enhanced financial literacy of consumers/clients, and the like.

Nevertheless, market incentives and disincentives are heavily influenced by the particular (as it were) macro-institutional structure of the market in question and, in the case of the many financial service industries, that structure is characterized by a small number of large, vertically integrated, organizations. Moreover, functionally these organizations are market actors driven by the profit motive. It follows that the pervasive culture in these organizations will be reflective of this function and structure. The question that arises at this point in the discussion is whether or not the process of professionalization of financial advisor is likely to be substantially diluted and/or diverted in important respects in the institutional setting. In short, is the macro-institutional environment likely to derail the micro-occupational agenda?

I conclude this chapter my making some specific points that give some substance to these worries.

(1) If a financial advisor's business is owned by, or otherwise associated with, a financial product manufacturer, such as a bank, insurance company, or fund manager, then there is the potential for a conflict between the financial advisor's commitment to that product manufacturer and the requirement to act in the interest of their client. This is a conflict of roles. Likewise, if the financial planner's fee for services is linked in some way to a product transaction (e.g., if the investment recommended by the advisor increases by x% then the fee increases by x%), then there is a potential conflict between the advisor's interest and the client's interest.[37] This is conflicted remuneration.

---

[37] FOFA bans such fees on borrowed amounts only (FOFA Bill No. 2 ss. 964B-G). Various commentators have suggested multiple conflicts of interest remain post FOFA. See, for example, D. Kingsford Smith, "Insider the FOFA Deal: Success of the Experiment Depends on Extent and Quality of Implementation," www.clmr.unsw.edu.au, date unknown.

(2) There is a question mark in relation to the *ability* of financial advisors to discharge their professional obligations, as opposed to any direct ethical concerns in relation to conflicts of interest and/or fiduciary obligations. As stated above, professionals are distinguished in part from other occupations by virtue of the possession of a body of expert knowledge, and financial planners ought to be required to have tertiary training. However, in the absence of any requirement that financial advisors have an understanding of the *full* array of competing financial products available in the market (or perhaps even of the ones they are familiar with, should they be complex "exotic" products), are individual financial advisors likely to be in a position to satisfy adequately the financial needs of their clients, i.e., to provide unbiased advice based on a complete, or near-complete, detailed understanding of the available products?

(3) Given that many, if not most, financial planning businesses in some jurisdictions are owned by, or otherwise associated with, financial product manufacturers, there is a question as to whether the culture of members of the occupation of financial advisor will shift from, so to speak, a sales-based culture to the culture of a profession. Would substantial impetus provided by legislation and associated professionalization processes be decisive? Of particular importance here will be the growth in the relative numbers of genuinely independent financial planning businesses.

12.5 Conclusion

In this chapter I have applied my normative teleological account of social institutions (including multi-layered structures of joint action and joint institutional mechanism) to financial markets. In doing so, I have distinguished the general normative "theory" of financial markets from special normative "theories" of particular financial markets and their constitutive market-based institutions. The applications in question were in respect of the banking sector, capital (specifically, equity) markets, financial benchmarks (a species of joint institutional mechanism), and the financial planning industry. I identified corruption in these financial markets and mentioned various proposed anti-corruption or more broad-based integrity measures. I argued that these instances of institutional misconduct constituted corruption, and these remedies were remedies principally by the lights of the (normatively understood) institutional purposes of these financial markets and market-based institutions.

CHAPTER 13

Police Organizations

Elsewhere[1] I have elaborated my teleological normative account of policing according to which police organizations have as their fundamental purpose to protection of legally enshrined, enforceable, moral rights, including property rights and other institutional rights. In doing so, I have also explicated the notion of order, as in law and order, in terms of its contribution to the protection of moral rights. In this work I have emphasized the central role of police organizations as part of anti-corruption and integrity systems and, most obviously, as a critical component of the criminal justice system (which is the single most important anti-corruption system within a modern polity). It almost goes without saying that police corruption is deeply problematic, given the critical anti-corruption role of police organizations. By comparison with banking and finance institutions, there is very little confusion or controversy with respect to the fundamental purposes of police organizations crime fighting and combating corruption; few doubt that these are important purposes of police organizations, even if they hold that they have other important purposes.[2] Moreover, the various forms of police corruption are not, in general, contested. For this reason, in this chapter my emphasis is on the nature of police corruption and how to combat it rather than on defending my account of the institutional purposes of police organization.[3]

---

[1] Miller and Blackler, *Ethical Issues in Policing*, chapter 1; Miller and Gordon, *Investigative Ethics* chapter 1; Miller, *Moral Foundations of Social Institutions*, chapter 9; and Miller, *Corruption and Anti-Corruption in Policing*, chapter 1.

[2] *Ibid.*

[3] Earlier versions of the material in this chapter appeared in Miller, *Ethical Issues in Policing*; Miller *Corruption and Anti-Corruption in Policing*, chapters 4 and 5; Miller, "Integrity Systems and Professional Reporting in Police Organisations," *Criminal Justice Ethics* vol. 29, no. 3 2010, pp. 241–257.

13.1 Integrity Systems for Police Organizations

As argued in Chapter 9, occupations, including professions and quasi-professional groups, such as police officers, are defined in terms of the basic purposes that they ought to serve, as well as by their constitutive activities.[4] The different purposes and activities of different professions generate differences in required moral character. Thus it is because the police must track down and arrest criminals that police officers need to have a disposition to be suspicious, a high degree of physical courage, and so on. In entering into a particular profession, individuals accept professional obligations. As we saw in Chapter 6, some of these obligations are also moral obligations. The moral obligations are different from and additional to the moral obligations these professionals had before entering the profession. For example, if a police officer fails to intervene in an attempted burglary, she has not only failed to do what her profession requires, she has also failed to do what morality now requires of her. So, it seems, in undertaking a particular profession, an individual is obligated to possess or develop a specific moral character in order to be able to discharge the profession's distinctive moral obligation.

At least two things seem to follow from this account of the moral character of a member of a profession, or at least of the moral character of police officers. First, the fact that a police officer is deficient in some character trait that is highly morally desirable in members of some other profession, or in some specific private role, would not necessarily count against the officer *qua police officer*. For example, we can contrast a sexually promiscuous police officer with a sexually promiscuous husband, wife, or Catholic priest. If the police officer restricts his sexual activities to his private life and does not, for example, pursue work colleagues or others he deals with in his capacity as a police officer then, arguably, his sexual promiscuity has no bearing on his fitness to discharge his role. Matters are entirely different for husbands, wives, and Catholic priests.

Second, the fact that a police officer is deficient in some character trait might well count against that officer, even though the trait in question is

---

[4] There is a dispute as to whether policing ought to be regarded as a profession or a craft. I suggest that police are an emerging profession. At any rate, at the very least they should be regarded as a quasi-profession to distinguish them from occupations that require little or no specialized training and knowledge. However, these controversies make no difference to the points I am making here since elsewhere I have defined policing according to this teleological conception and this conception does not depend on police being accorded the status of a profession. See Miller and Blackler, *Ethical Issues in Policing*, chapter 1. On the notion of a profession see Alexandra and Miller, *Integrity Systems for Occupations*, chapter 1.

not necessary for, or highly desirable in, members of most *other* occupations, or in most *private* roles. Consider physical courage. This is necessary for police officers, but presumably not for academics and accountants. Indeed, a character trait might be a virtue in a police officer but a *vice* in members of most other professions – and even in most private roles. Suspiciousness might qualify as such a trait. The same constant looking about for wrongdoing that makes a good detective might make someone a bad husband or wife.

A further point about moral character might follow from the nature and purposes of policing. This concerns moral character conceived in general terms, as distinct from specific character traits. Perhaps the minimum standards of integrity, honesty, courage, loyalty and so on demanded of police officers ought to be higher than for many, even most, other occupations. After all, police have extraordinary powers that are not given to others, including the power to take away for limited periods the liberty of their fellow citizens. Moreover, police are subject to moral temptations to an extent not typically found in other occupations. Consider detectives working in drug-law enforcement: they are exposed to drug dealers prepared to offer large bribes just to have an officer do nothing. Arguably, the conjunction of extraordinary powers with enhanced temptations justifies setting higher minimum standards of moral character for police than for members of many other professions.

As argued throughout this work, maintaining and enhancing the integrity of a profession is partly a matter of attending to the *structure, purpose*, and *culture* of the organizations in which professional practitioners are housed. Consider structure, both legal and administrative. In an organization that needs to possess integrity, such as a police organization, the administrative processes and procedures in relation to, for example, promotion or complaints and discipline, should embody relevant ethical principles of fairness, procedural justice, transparency, and the like. Now consider purpose. In a police organization that possesses integrity, the organizational goals actually pursued should align closely with the morally legitimate purposes of the profession of policing, such as justice and the protection of human rights, including the rights to life and liberty.[5] Finally, consider culture. In an organization that needs to possess integrity, such as a police organization, the pervasive ethos or spirit, that is, the culture, should be, for example, conducive to high performance, both technically and ethically, and supportive in times of need, but intolerant of serious

---

[5] Miller and Blackler, *Ethical Issues in Policing*, chapter 1.

incompetence and misconduct. Naturally, the nature and influence of culture can, and arguably should, vary from one type of organization to another, depending in part on the nature of the work of the occupational group housed within that organization. Police organizations, for example, are characterized by a culture in which a high level of loyalty can be expected.

As noted in Chapter 7, in looking at options for promoting integrity and combating ethical failure by professionals, it is very easy to look and opt for some kind of "magic bullet" solution, such as increasing penalties or giving more intrusive powers to investigative agencies. Consider the integrity testing of police officers. Does this practice actually reduce police corruption? Or does it rather increase levels of distrust between, say, management cops and street cops and, thereby, compound the problem of the so called blue wall of silence, whereby street cops (in particular) protect their corrupt colleagues?[6] Perhaps random integrity testing in relation to minor ethical misconduct is problematic in this respect, whereas targeted integrity testing in relation to serious forms of corruption is much less so because it is widely accepted by police officers. The findings of an empirical attitudinal study of Victoria Police officers seem to confirm that this is the case.[7]

In attempting to determine the causes of unethical professional practices, there are a number of preliminary questions that need to be addressed. One set of questions pertains to the precise nature of the unethical practice at issue, and the context in which it occurs. What practices are involved? Minor gratuity taking? Theft from burgled premises? Excessive force? Fabricating evidence? What is the motivation? Is it greed? Is it a (possibly misplaced) sense of justice (so-called, noble cause corruption[8])? Are there, for example, some compelling practical facts that explain the practice, say, a belief that the only way to secure convictions of serious drug offenders involves the use of unlawful methods? What other pressures, such as a lack of resources, might explain the unethical practice in question? Another set of questions concerns the extent of the corruption or unethical practice: Is it sporadic or continuing, restricted to a few "rotten apples" or widespread within the police department?[9] Here, as

---

[6] See, for example, Jerome Skolnick, *Justice without Trial: Law Enforcement in a Democratic Society* (New York: Macmillan, 1977), p. 58.

[7] Seumas Miller, Steve. Curry, Ian Gordon, John Blackler, and Tim Prenzler, *An Integrity System for Victoria Police: Volume 2* (Canberra: Centre for Applied Philosophy and Public Ethics, 2008).

[8] See chapter 4 and Miller, "Noble Cause Corruption Revisited" in Villiers and Adlam (eds.), *A Safe, Just and Tolerant Society: Police Virtue Rediscovered.*

[9] Miller and Blackler, *Ethical Issues in Policing*, chapter 5.

elsewhere, rhetoric is no substitute for evidence-based conclusions, difficult though it may be to provide the latter.

Integrity systems for police organizations can and do vary. However, such systems ought to have at least the following components or aspects[10]:

- an effective, streamlined complaints and discipline system;
- a comprehensive suite of stringent vetting and induction processes reflective of the different levels of risk in different areas of the organization;
- a basic code of ethics and specialized codes of practice – for example, in relation to the use of firearms – supported by ethics education in recruitment training, and ongoing professional development programs;
- adequate welfare support systems, for example, in relation to drug and alcohol abuse, and psychological injury;
- intelligence gathering, risk management and early warning systems for at-risk officers, for example, officers with high levels of complaints;
- internal investigations, that is, the police organization takes a high degree of responsibility for its own unethical officers;
- proactive anti-corruption intervention systems, for example, targeted integrity testing;
- ethical leadership, for example, promoting police who give priority to the collective ends definitive of the organization rather than their own career ambitions; and
- external oversight by an independent, well-resourced body with investigative powers.

As the foregoing points suggest, a key element in an integrity system for police organizations is an organization-wide, intelligence-based, ethics risk-assessment process. This involves good intelligence and an organization-wide ethics risk-assessment plan and – based on good intelligence and the risk-assessment plan – the identification of corruption/rights violations/ethical misconduct risks in the police organization. Ethical risks in a contemporary police organization might include risks in many, if not most, of the following areas:

- data security, notably electronic data;
- drug investigations, given the massive funds involved and the absence of victims who might complain;

---

[10] Seumas Miller and Tim Prenzler, *An Integrity System for Victoria Police: Volume 1* (Canberra: Centre for Applied Philosophy and Public Ethics, 2008).

- excessive use of force;
- informant management, given that many informants are themselves criminals; and
- infiltration by organized crime.

Other areas of concern in many police organizations are the ethical risks stemming from severe stress among police officers and the inability of managers to identify and respond effectively to severe stress in their subordinates; noble cause corruption, in which officers break the law to achieve good outcomes, for example, by doctoring statements and even fabricating evidence; political and/or media and/or police hierarchy pressure for results, or even actual interference in high profile investigations, thereby compromising the investigative process and (potentially) its outcome.

Once ethical risk areas have been identified, preventive countermeasures need to be put in place. These countermeasures should track the identified risks. Some countermeasures and the risks that they track include the following.

- In relation to data security: segregation of, and controlled access to, internal affairs databases; audits of data base access.
- In relation to drug investigations: early warning systems, for example, profiles of at risk officers/locations/high-risk areas; intelligence-driven targeted integrity testing of individuals/locations; audits of drug squads and forensic laboratories.
- In relation to excessive use of force: complaints-driven investigations informed by intelligence, for example, a high number of complaints of excessive use of force.
- In relation to informant management: accountability mechanisms such as documentation naming the informant, ensuring that a police officer with an informant has a supervisor who meets with the officer and the informant, having a supervisor who monitors the police officer's dealings with the informant, and recording all payments (including electronic transfers, to prevent theft).
- In relation to infiltration by organized crime: stringent and constantly updated vetting procedures (especially for officers in sensitive areas), ensuring adequate supervision of all officers, and monitoring and utilization of intelligence data bases (including criminal associations).
- In relation to stress: ensuring adequate supervision of all officers; introduction of stress management tools.

- In relation to all of the above: ongoing ethics training based on identified risks in specific roles.

Having discussed integrity systems for police organizations in general terms, I turn now to a historically important challenge that faces police organizations, namely, professional reporting bearing in mind the distinction made in Chapter 10 between whistleblowing (external disclosure, e.g., to the media), and professional reporting (internal disclosure). My concern here is principally with professional reporting.

13.2   Professional Reporting and Police Culture

Organizational integrity systems, including integrity systems for police organizations, rely heavily on the members of organizations to report the ethical misconduct of their colleagues and, in the case of criminal offenses, to be prepared to provide sworn evidence against them. Historically, police officers have been very reluctant to "rat" on their corrupt colleagues, and this reluctance has been explained in large part in terms of police culture[11] and, specifically, the above-mentioned "blue wall of silence."[12]

Police culture is a complex phenomenon and one much-commented on. Moreover, we need to distinguish the sociological description of police culture from the ethical or, more broadly, normative analysis of it. According to Robert Reiner, a sense of "mission" is a defining characteristic of police: "it's a sect, it's like a religion, the police force," "you're 'ordained' as a policeman, so to speak";[13] "it is important in understanding police work that it is seen as a mission, a worthwhile enterprise, not just another job."[14] "The core of the police outlook is this subtle and complex inter-mingling of the themes of mission, hedonistic love of action and pessimistic cynicism."[15] Brian Chapman refers to Balzac's notion of policing as the noblest profession, because in their person police play the roles of soldier, priest, and artist.[16] But, Chapman suggests, there are moral dangers associated with these roles:

The policeman, like the civil servant, the judge, and the soldier, is preconditioned to accept the doctrine of the golden end, the doctrine of the Jesuits, the *raison d'être* of the health of the Republic, of St Ignatius, of

---

[11] See, for example, Robert Reiner, *The Politics of the Police* (Brighton: Harvester, 1985), chapter 3, "Cop Culture."

[12] See, for example, John Kleinig, "The Blue Wall of Silence: An Ethical Analysis," *International Journal of Applied Philosophy*, 15 (2001), 1–23.

[13] Reiner, *The Politics of the Police*, p. 245.   [14] *Ibid.*, p. 85.   [15] *Ibid.*, p. 91.

[16] Brian Chapman, *Police State* (London: Pall Mall Press, 1970).

Bismarck, and of Gaugin. The policeman like the soldier does not flinch from force, since contact with violence, as well as with human stupidity, is part of his professional life. The danger inherent in this doctrine for the policeman is that, if unchallenged, in the end the soldier may have to sacrifice the women and children, the priest the Jews, and the artist his family.[17]

Social scientists have documented how police officers inducted into a police culture of this sort can begin to see many of the situations that they confront as so-called Dirty Harry scenarios. The police officer comes to believe that he has to dirty his hands by unlawful use of force, deceit, or fabrication of evidence in the service of a higher end ("mission") of justice. The Clint Eastwood film *Dirty Harry* embodies this way of thinking: Inspector Harry Callaghan tortures a psychopathic killer to try to determine the whereabouts of the girl the killer has taken hostage, and does so with the apparent approval of cinema audiences. The point to be stressed here is a variant on the one made by Chapman above, namely, the inherent potential of this police sense of mission to lead police to believe that at least on some occasions they can disregard, or even think that they are somehow above, the law.

As noted earlier, a feature of police culture is the strong sense of loyalty felt by police officers to one another. Police work is inherently dangerous and requires a high level of cooperation and trust, particularly among street police. So it is unsurprising that police culture is characterized in part by a strong sense of solidarity among police officers. Moreover, at least in many large metropolitan police services, this solidarity goes hand in glove with an "us versus them" mentality in respect of both the public and police management. The public are often thought by police to misunderstand, dislike, and/or fear the police; after all, it is the public who are being policed and in urban crime-ridden areas it may be difficult for the police to separate offenders from ordinary law-abiding citizens. Police managers are often thought by street police to be unsupportive, untrustworthy, and punitive; after all, it is the managers who are policing the police and in police organizations with an acknowledged corruption problem street police are likely to be especially distrustful of the police managers who are under political pressure to be seen to be doing something about the corruption.

Numerous inquiries into police corruption have noted that police officers typically expect other police officers not to report them, even

[17] *Ibid.*, p. 103.

when they have engaged in criminal acts and notwithstanding the legal requirement that they do so. This "blue wall of silence" depends in part on the feelings of loyalty that I have been describing. Perhaps it also draws support from the feeling among many police officers that at times they are justified in breaking the law, whether by failing to report corruption or by engaging in (at least) noble cause corruption. Many police officers interviewed in the aforementioned recent Victoria Police study said that they would be very reluctant to report a minor assault by a police officer on an offender if the offender had been provocative or had otherwise "deserved it," notwithstanding that the assault in question was a criminal act.[18]

Police solidarity can often be a virtue. It enables officers to cooperate with one another and to stand solid in the face of danger, for example, to successfully discharge their responsibilities in relation to crowd control or when two police officers "on the beat" confront a violent offender. It also reinforces the individual capacity for physical courage, including a preparedness to die in the service of others. And it generates a willingness to help other police when they most need help. But such solidarity can also be a vice. Historically, in many police organizations solidarity has manifested itself in a willingness to elevate organizational interests above those of the public, including by tolerating corruption in the ranks. Notoriously, police have engaged in cover-ups of the crimes of fellow officers. Such cover-ups represent examples of the immorality that solidarity can bring about.

As mentioned earlier, one dimension of police culture is the schism between street cops and management cops and, more specifically, between street cops and internal affairs investigators.[19] This aspect of police culture can have profound implications for the effectiveness of the police organization. If there is an "us-them" attitude between lower and upper echelon employees, an organization is hardly likely to perform at optimum levels of efficiency and effectiveness. For example, it is conducive to a punitive culture in which minor ethical misconduct on the part of subordinates, once exposed, is harshly punished – often following an Internal Affairs (IA) investigation in the service of a police management hell-bent on demonstrating a tough anti-corruption stance to its political masters and the public at large – when a remedial/development response would be far more appropriate. Naturally, such a punitive culture reinforces the "blue wall of silence," particularly among lower echelon police officers.

---

[18] See Miller et al., *An Integrity System for Victoria Police: Volume 2*, and Kleinig, "The Blue Wall of Silence."

[19] E. Reuss-Ianni and F. A. J. Ianni, "Street Cops and Management Cops: The Two Cultures of Policing" in *Control in the Police Organisation* ed. Maurice Punch (London: MIT Press, 1983).

It might be argued in response to this, and by way of supporting punitive management action, that it is often very difficult to convict experienced police officers of serious forms of corruption. They have a thorough knowledge of criminal law and police investigative methods, and the evidentiary threshold for conviction – that is, beyond reasonable doubt – is high. Accordingly, the argument runs, management may need to settle for less and should do so. Hence it is allegedly justifiable to relentlessly pursue, and harshly punish, officers for relatively minor ethical misconduct, that is, noncriminal, disciplinary matters. After all, they are known to have committed serious criminal offences – albeit this cannot be proven – and the evidentiary threshold (e.g., on the balance of probabilities) is much lower for disciplinary matters; so success is far more likely.

This argument is highly problematic. For one thing, in the absence of good evidence, the supposed "knowledge" on the part of management or internal affairs investigators of the corrupt activities of certain officers is questionable; accordingly, there is a real danger of taking excessively punitive action against officers who are innocent or who have at most engaged in minor ethical misconduct. For another thing, even in the case of those officers who are engaged in criminal activity, disciplinary action that is short of termination does not remove the problem. Indeed, it may exacerbate it, for example, by alerting the officers in question to the fact that they are under scrutiny.

Although the structure, purpose, and culture of an institution provide a framework within which individuals act, these dimensions do not fully determine the actions of individuals. There are a number of reasons for this. For one thing, rules and regulations cannot cover every contingency that might arise, and laws, norms, and ends need to be interpreted and applied. For another thing, culture is not necessarily fully determinative of action, or even the dominant factor in play. Not only is there available space within the institutional framework and occupational culture for a degree of individual autonomy, but also changing circumstances and unforeseeable problems make it desirable to vest individuals, including individual police officers, with discretionary powers.

Notwithstanding the malign influence of certain aspects of police culture in many police organizations, the moral courage of individual police officers can enable them to resist encroachments on the exercise of their autonomy. The image of a pervasive, monolithic, and dominant attitude and action determining culture is only ever partly true. Moreover, there is a range of responses to the malevolent aspects of police culture, including reducing the opportunities for corruption and introducing an elaborate system of detection and deterrence. As discussed above, such responses constitute part of the overall integrity system. However, they are not sufficient.

Reliance on detection and deterrence alone bypasses the issue of moral responsibility which lies at the heart of corruption. In the last analysis the only force strong enough to resist corruption is the moral sense – the motivating belief in doing what is right and avoiding doing what is wrong. If most police officers, including members of departments of internal affairs and of the police hierarchy – the ones who investigate corruption – do not for the most part have a motivating belief in avoiding doing what is illegal or otherwise immoral, no system of detection and deterrence, no matter how extensive and elaborate, can possibly suffice to control corruption. The motivating belief among police officers in doing what is right can be reinforced by ensuring a just system of rewards and penalties within the police organization itself. Unjust systems of promotion, unreasonably harsh disciplinary procedures for minor errors, unfair workloads, and so on, are all deeply corrosive of the desire to do one's job well and to resist inducements to do what is illegal or otherwise immoral.

The belief in doing what is right can be reinforced by ensuring an appropriate system of command and control – appropriate, that is, to the kinds of responsibilities that attach to the role of police officer. It may be that very hierarchical militaristic/bureaucratic systems of command and control are inappropriate in most areas of modern policing, given the nature of the police officer's role. Police officers have considerable powers – including the power to take away people's liberty – and they exercise those powers in situations of moral complexity. It is inconsistent to give people a position of substantial responsibility involving a high level of discretionary ethical judgment and then expect them to mechanically and unthinkingly do what they are told.

The belief in doing what is right does not exist independently of the habit of reflection and judgment on particular pressing ethical issues. Aside from anything else, one can do what is right only if one knows what is right and there are multiple morally grey areas in policing. Accordingly, the belief in doing what is right can be reinforced by ensuring that ethical issues in police work, including the ethical ends of policing itself, are matters of ongoing discussion and reflection in initial training programs, further education programs, supervision, ethics committees, and in relation to ethical codes. Since the belief in doing what is morally right, and the attendant capacity for ethical reflection and judgment, including in relation to the moral ends of policing, are in fact important in policing – far more important than in many other professions – ethical discussion and deliberation ought to have a central place in policing.

The belief in doing what is right can be reinforced by utilizing the intrinsically collective nature of policing, and, in particular, by stressing that police officers are collectively (jointly) responsible for controlling corruption. It is a mistake to undermine police solidarity and loyalty, leaving isolated individuals who are responsible only for their own actions and who do what is right only because they fear to do what is wrong. It is equally a mistake to rely wholly on the individual heroism of the likes of Frank Serpico.

It is obvious that police officers are collectively responsible for ensuring that the moral ends of policing are realized. Law enforcement, order maintenance, and so on cannot possibly be achieved by individual police officers acting on their own. As already noted, policing is a cooperative enterprise. However, police corruption undermines the proper ends of policing. Such corruption, moreover, depends in part on the complicity or tacit consent of fellow officers. So controlling police corruption is a collective responsibility. It follows that not only is loyalty to corrupt officers misplaced, it is an abrogation of duty. Collective responsibility entails a culture of selective loyalty – loyalty to police officers who do what is right, but not to those who do what is wrong. The loyalty of police officers is warranted only by those who embody the ideals of policing, and in particular by those who are not corrupt. Indeed, collective responsibility also entails such actions as police reporting corrupt fellow officers, and support for, rather than opposition to, well-intentioned officers who report police corruption.

The collective effort to ensure that the fundamental institutional purposes (collective goods) of policing are pursued will contribute to their internalization by police officers. More important, such a collective effort will ensure that police officers identify with those purposes so that self-respect, as well as the respect of others, depends on the pursuit of those purposes and on opposition to corruption. This amounts to a change in police culture, but not one that is at the expense of loyalty per se or of the commitment to cooperation and assistance to fellow officers that underpins it.

Of course, it is one thing to provide a coherent account of what police culture *ought* to be, and quite another to change it and, specifically, to break down the "blue wall of silence" and bring about a culture that is intolerant of corruption and encourages professional reporting of corruption. However, the provision of such a coherent normative account is a necessary first step, and designing the various elements of an integrity system – including reduction of opportunities, accountability mechanisms, ethics education programs – is an important second step.

An important aspect of the process of developing a culture that is intolerant of corruption involves rationality, as opposed to morality or legality. I suggest that developing such a culture presupposes that the conditions exist under which it is rational for individual police officers to report their corrupt colleagues, and not simply deemed to be legally or morally obligatory for them to do so. It is this issue that I explore in the final section, with particular reference to the relationship between professional reporting and internal affairs investigations.

13.3 Professional Reporting and Internal Affairs Investigations

In the discussion thus far, I have suggested that police culture is not necessarily a pervasive and monolithic social force that is the dominant determinant of the attitudes and actions of police officers in all police organizations. Many of the classic features of police culture are principally features of police serving in large, metropolitan, bureaucratic, and hierarchical organizations. Moreover, between and within even these organizations there are significant attitudinal and behavioral differences in respect of police corruption. I have further suggested, in effect, that police culture is in large part a rationally and morally legitimate response to the operational policing environment and, as such, cannot be, and ought not to be, jettisoned in its entirety. I now suggest that police culture, not being the pervasive, monolithic, and dominant force that it is often presented as being, is a malleable phenomenon; in principle, it can be changed and, in particular, its malignant features can be curtailed, even if they cannot be removed entirely.

Curtailment depends on a number of things, notably designing and implementing appropriate integrity systems. However, in the context of an appropriate overall integrity system, curtailment typically depends in part on adjusting the incentive structures in place so as to make compliance with the dictates of malignant features of police culture much less rational than it otherwise would be. (This is perhaps most obvious in the case of the deterrence mechanisms that are a necessary feature of most integrity systems.)

Unfortunately, in dysfunctional, corruption-riddled police organizations compliance on the part of any given police officer with the malignant features of police culture may be quite rational. This is not to say that the malignant features of police culture are an irresistible force. Far from it; these features of police culture are by no means the only important factors at work, and compliance, though rational, is not the only choice available. However, it is to say that the particular configuration of factors in play is such that these malignant features of police culture end up being the decisive factors at work. Accordingly, the challenge facing those seeking to design an appropriate integrity system is how to bring it about that these malignant features of police culture cease to be the decisive factors at work; it is not necessarily, at least in the first instance, a matter of directly removing these features.

Here I want to narrow my focus and explore, in particular, an apparently important relationship between reluctance on the part of police to report corrupt fellow officers, on the one hand, and the quality of internal affairs investigations, on the other. Good, though by no means decisive, empirical evidence of this relationship has been provided in the Victoria Police study.[20] The relevant parts of the study comprise a survey of ethical attitudes, an analysis of all internal affairs corruption investigations files over a five-year period, and the conducting of some seventy focus groups of serving police officers (circa 500 police officers out of a police force of 9000). Moreover, the evidence for this relationship is further strengthened by the consideration that it has an intuitively rational structure to it.

The first point to be made here is that in well-ordered liberal democratic states, such as Australia, the majority of police officers in many, if not most, contemporary police organizations are evidently not themselves corrupt and do not engage in ongoing corrupt activities. For example, although the 1990s Wood Royal Commission into police corruption in the New South Wales Police Force in Australia found systemic corruption, it was largely limited to groups of detectives functioning in the area of illicit drug investigations and specific local area commands in which there was an endemic drug problem, for example, the King's Cross red light area in Sydney. Moreover, evidence from the Victoria Police study indicated that the majority of police officers in Victoria Police and, presumably, similar police organizations, strongly desire to rid their organization of corruption and criminality. A further finding of the Victoria Police study was that the majority of police officers believe that they morally (and not simply legally) ought to report/provide evidence in relation to the minority of corrupt colleagues.

[20] Miller et al., *An Integrity System for Victoria Police: Volume 2.*

Notwithstanding this belief that they ought to report and provide evidence in relation to their corrupt colleagues, most police officers are apparently unwilling to report their corrupt colleagues; this was a further finding of the Victoria Police study. How can this be so?

Certainly, there is nothing illogical or even atypical in this. People often have moral beliefs that they are unwilling to act on, notably when it is not in their self-interest to do so or when there are other felt moral considerations in play such as feelings of loyalty. Unsurprisingly, it turns out that the attitudes and, therefore, the culture of Victoria Police are a complex and differentiated phenomenon: evidently there is a strong and widespread belief that corrupt police morally ought to be reported – including because it is unlawful not to do so – but there is a contrary feeling that it is or might be disloyal to do so. This contrary feeling is an attitudinal barrier to reporting corrupt fellow officers, especially at the lower end of corruption or in relation to noble cause corruption. In the context of my attempt here at explication of the rational structure underlying police action (or, at least, inaction) this attitudinal barrier can usefully be thought of as a presumption against reporting corrupt colleagues. Considered on its own, this presumption might well be overridden by the belief among police that police corruption (at least in its more serious forms) ought to be reported. However, there is a third consideration in play, namely, the irrationality of reporting corrupt colleagues. Evidently, this third consideration is the decisive one. Let me explain.

According to the empirical evidence provided in the Victoria Police study, one important aspect (I do not say it is the only important aspect) of the rational structure of the situation is as follows:

Conclusion (c): Police officers (junior and senior) are reluctant to provide evidence in relation to corrupt officers because (for the reason that):

Premise (a): Police *believe* that internal investigations are unlikely to result in convictions and/or termination and that they are, in any case, often management-driven witch-hunts of innocent police or of police who have, at most, engaged in minor ethical misconduct;

Premise (b): If honest police officers report/provide evidence in relation to corrupt officers and those officers are exonerated and remain in the force, then the police culture is such that their own careers will suffer from the stigma of having sided with a punitive management/internal affairs department and "ratted on" their colleagues (who are widely believed to have been innocent or at least only guilty of a minor infraction).

Of course, the fact that their exonerated colleagues are widely believed to be innocent, or at most guilty of only a minor infraction, is a function in large part of police culture. The loyalty of fellow police officers ("one's brothers") surely demands a strong presumption in favor of one's innocence or, at the very least, a presumption in favor of the offense in question being an understandable breach of a legal or ethical principle. (The breach may be regarded as understandable because the principle in question is a minor one or because the circumstances were such that compliance was not unproblematic or some-such.)

Notice, however – to return to the rational structure of (a) and (b) therefore (c) above – that police culture (the "blue wall of silence") gets traction here only on the assumption that police believe that internal investigations are unlikely to result in convictions and/or termination of corrupt officers, and that there will be, as a consequence, a widespread view that the officers investigated were not guilty of any serious offense, but merely the victims of a punitive management/internal affairs department.

The widespread belief of police in many police organizations that internal investigations are unlikely to result in convictions and/or termination of corrupt officers is not without rational foundation. Historically, internal investigations in many, if not most, large metropolitan police organizations – including, until recently, Victoria Police – have as a matter of *fact* (and not simply of officers' beliefs) had relatively little success; certainly, they have typically resulted in low rates of conviction and/or termination of officers under investigation. Moreover, again historically, in many, if not most, large metropolitan police organizations, police who inform on other police are as a matter of *fact* "sent to Coventry", if not subjected to harassment, by their colleagues, and in many cases their careers have been ruined. So police officers' beliefs in this respect are well founded.

The lack of success of internal police investigations is, of course, in part dependent on the reluctance of police officers to provide evidence regarding their corrupt colleagues. There is also reluctance on the part of police to become internal investigators; solidarity dictates that investigating allegations of corruption against one's fellow officers is unlikely to be an attractive role, and highly unlikely to be preferred to the role of investigating alleged offenders who are not police officers. At any rate, for this and other reasons internal investigators are unlikely to be high-quality investigators and, even if they are, their investigations of fellow police officers may well manifest a lack of commitment or be otherwise flawed. Yet internal investigations need to be of the highest quality, given that the people under investigation are themselves police and, therefore, familiar with police investigative methods.

One of the flaws to be found in many internal investigations is a breach of confidentiality that has compromised the investigation. Such breaches of confidentiality are themselves acts of corruption and yet they have often taken place with impunity. But again this is reflective of the malignant features of police culture; a culture of being reluctant to ensure that suspected corrupt police are brought to book, whether those police are the ones who engaged in the original act of corruption or those who sort to protect them by engaging in the secondary act of corruption, for example, a breach of confidentiality.

So there is a vicious circle in operation: the "blue wall of silence" undercuts the efficacy of internal investigations, which in turn reinforces the "blue wall of silence." However, the point I want to stress here is that – in *these* circumstances – it would be irrational of police officers to report, or provide evidence in relation to, their corrupt colleagues. For, on the one hand, they reasonably believe that this will not result in the conviction/ termination of these corrupt officers and, on the other hand, they reasonably believe that it will ruin their own careers. Moreover, the irrationality of reporting corrupt colleagues is, I suggest, the decisive factor in determining their action (or at least inaction). They believe it is morally wrong not to report their corrupt colleagues (at least in serious cases), feelings of loyalty notwithstanding; however, they believe that no good will come of it but only harm to themselves.

What is the way out of this impasse? There is a need for the following countermeasures. First, internal affairs departments ought to investigate only criminal matters and serious disciplinary matters that warrant termination. (And perhaps the difficulty of terminating police also needs to be looked at, for example, by recourse to Loss of Commissioner Confidence provisions, although there are procedural rights issues in this area.[21]) Other ethical misconduct ought to be regarded as a management/remedial issue. The latter is important partly as a means of reducing the possibility that initial minor ethical lapses on the part of new recruits will come to be regarded, by the offending officers themselves as well as others, as fatal moral compromises that forever impugn their integrity and prevent them from ever reporting the serious ethical misconduct of their corrupt colleagues.

---

[21] Loss of Commissioner Confidence provisions exist in a number of Australian police services, including Victoria Police and New South Wales Police.

Second, the rate of internal investigations convictions/terminations needs to be improved to a high level of success. In the first instance (that is, in the context of reluctance on the part of officers to inform on their corrupt colleagues), this can be partly achieved by

(1) increasing the quality of internal investigations (e.g., by head-hunting high-quality investigators), increasing data security measures (e.g., the use of "sterile corridors," the stringent vetting of IA personnel, including administrative staff), audits of investigations, and adequate resourcing of IA departments;

(2) the use of well-resourced proactive anti-corruption strategies, for example, targeted integrity tests, intrusive surveillance methods that do not rely heavily on the willingness of police to provide evidence regarding corrupt colleagues; and

(3) recourse to well-resourced external oversight bodies with an independent investigative capacity, especially in relation to serious corruption in the upper echelons of a police organization.

Third, the stigma attached to being an internal investigator and to reporting, or providing evidence against, corrupt police needs to be reduced by

(1) normalizing the role of internal investigator, for example, by making two years as an internal investigator mandatory for all police investigators seeking promotion to senior investigative positions;

(2) instituting measures to protect (physically and career-wise) those who provide evidence against corrupt colleagues, for example, the implementation of internal witness protection programs and transparent promotion processes; and

(3) introducing ongoing tailormade ethics education programs that sensitively and squarely address the issues of police culture, internal affairs investigations, and professional reporting.

In short, it needs to become rational, and not simply legally and ethically mandated, for police officers to report, and provide evidence in relation to, their corrupt colleagues. Given that most police officers are not themselves corrupt and believe that they morally ought to report or provide evidence in relation to their corrupt colleagues, they will do so – or at least are more likely to do so – if conditions are created under which it will be rational for them to do so; that is, if it works for them and brings rewards rather than punishment. These conditions will include the following.

A reasonable number, and a high rate, of convictions/terminations of corrupt police officers as a result of a well-resourced, high-quality, internal

investigations department focused only on criminal and serious disciplinary matters, and operating in the context of

(1) the normalization of the role of internal investigator; and
(2) the felt duty on the part of most police to report/provide intelligence/
     evidence regarding criminal/corrupt colleagues in knowledge that if
     they do:
     (a) the persons in question are likely to be convicted/terminated; and
     (b) they themselves will suffer no harm or adverse career consequences.

These specific conditions are consistent with, and conducive to, a defensible police culture that is fit for institutional purpose – one in which
loyalty is felt to be owed to police officers who embody the ideals and
legitimate ends of policing, but not to corrupt colleagues. Such a police
culture is likely in turn to facilitate the emergence of these specific
conditions.

Naturally, these recommendations in relation to internal investigations
and professional reporting are only one piece in the puzzle; I am not
suggesting that they constitute a panacea. Indeed, I earlier elaborated a
detailed set of key elements of an integrity system for police organizations.
More generally, I am suggesting that in combating police corruption more
attention needs to be paid to the rational structure underlying individual
police decision-making and the ways in which it might be adjusted (and, in
a sense, less emphasis placed on police culture as a standalone determining
factor). However, the rational structure in question is not the familiar one
of rational self-interested actors unmoved by morality or by irrational (or
non-rational) social forces; police are clearly moved by a complex mix of
individual self-interest, moral beliefs, and cultural factors.[22] Combating
corruption in policing, as elsewhere, involves in part unearthing this
rational structure and devising ways to adjust it so that self-interest,
moral beliefs, and cultural factors work together to promote ethical conduct and reduce corruption rather than the reverse.

13.4   Conclusion

In this chapter I have identified some of the main causes of police corruption and outlined an integrity system for police organizations. Given the
importance of professional reporting to reducing and preventing corruption in police organizations, and the entrenched culture-based opposition

---

[22] I do not mean to imply that these three categories are mutually exclusive.

to such reporting within many police organizations (the so-called blue wall of silence), I have analyzed the ethical underpinnings of professional reporting and police culture. In the final section I discussed the all-important relationship between professional reporting and internal affairs investigations and, in particular, the circumstances in which professional reporting might become rational (as well as moral) from the perspective of individual police officers, e.g., the circumstance that internal investigations were widely believed to be both fair and efficacious.

CHAPTER 14

Government

As we have seen, according to my individualist, teleological theory of social institutions, the ultimate justification for the existence of human institutions, such as government, the education system, the economic system, the criminal justice system, and their organizational elements, is their provision of some collective good or goods to the community.[1] Moreover, these collective goods are, normatively speaking, the collective ends of institutions, and as such they further specify prior social norms that govern, or ought to govern, the constitutive roles and activities of members of institutions, and conceptually condition the deontic properties (institutional rights and duties) that attach to these roles. Thus, a police officer has certain deontic powers of search, seizure, and arrest, but these powers are justified in terms of the collective good – the protection of legally enshrined, enforceable moral rights, let us assume – that it is, or ought to be, the role of the police officer to maintain. It is also worth reiterating that there is no easy rights-versus-goods distinction. Human rights certainly function as a side constraint on the behavior of institutional actors. But equally, the securing of human rights and other moral rights can be a good that is aimed at by institutional actors.

Further, a defining property of an institution is its institutional purpose or, on other accounts, its function (see Chapter 1). Thus a putative institutional entity with deontic properties, but stripped of its institutional purpose or substantive function, typically ceases to be an institutional entity, at least of the relevant kind; would-be surgeons who cannot perform surgery are not surgeons. Equally, would-be police officers who are incapable of conducting an investigation, or who cannot make arrests or exercise any form of authority over citizens, are not really police officers. Here, by "substantive function" I have in mind the specific defining collective ends

[1] The material from the opening two sections is derived from Miller, *Social Action*, chapter 3; and Miller, *Moral Foundations of Social Institutions*, chapter 12.

of the institution or profession (or other occupation). In the case of institutions, including professions, the defining ends will be collective ends that are collective goods; they will not in general be merely desired ends or ends that an individual could realize by his or her own action alone (albeit, the means/end chain terminating in these collective ends consists in large part in individual actions directed at individual ends). In short, in this work the assumed normative theory of institutions is my *teleological* theory. Moreover, as noted earlier, institutions in general, and any given institution in particular, require *empirically informed* normative teleological theories.

Thus far, I have generally spoken in terms of the theory of institutional action where institutions have been taken to be different and separate organizations (or organizations of organizations). Accordingly, as is the case with other institutions, insofar as the occupants of political offices intentionally (or negligently) perform actions (in their institutional capacity) that undermine legitimate political processes, persons (*qua* political actors), or purposes (collective goods), then they are engaged in political corruption. Moreover, as argued in Chapter 3, institutional actors, including government officials, can perform acts of corruption notwithstanding that these acts are lawful.[2] So politicians who support policies only because bribed to do so, or who use their office to provide jobs for their relatives and friends (nepotism), or who are responsible for the arbitrary arrest and imprisonment of their political opponents (abuse of authority) are engaged in political corruption (as well as human rights violations), and this is so even if these actions happen not to be unlawful in the jurisdictions in question.

So far so good; however, as noted in the discussion of institutional webs of interdependence in Chapter 1 Section 1.8, there is also a need for a theoretical account of the *interrelationships* between different institutions and such interrelationships bring with them the potential for political corruption. There is some evidence that in recent decades in the Western liberal democracies, public sector institutions have been unacceptably weakened as a consequence of policies coming under the banner of so-called economic rationalism. Such policies include the so-called light touch regulation and deregulation in the finance sector leading to "too big to regulate" retail and investment conglomerate financial institutions previously disallowed (see Chapter 12), the privatization of law enforcement agencies and prisons, and the outsourcing by government of administrative functions and computing services. Moreover, institutional actors, such as legislators and regulators as

---

[2] Indeed, in some cases, they might even be acts that ought not to be unlawful.

well as self-interested powerful market actors acting via their lobbyists and utilizing, for instance, political campaign contributions,[3] have acted jointly to weaken or otherwise undermine the institution of government or, in many cases, have failed to act jointly to arrest processes weakening and undermining government, so – given their institutional responsibilities in this regard – they can, at least in principle, be held collectively (i.e., jointly) morally responsible for at least some of this institutional damage to government. Further, given that their actions or omissions in this regard were not coerced, it evidently follows that the actions and omissions in question were corrupt. I note that in all likelihood the process in question of weakening and undermining the institution of government was in large part a process of institutional corrosion (see Chapter 3 Section 3.1). However, it also seems unlikely that it was not also in part a process of institutional corruption, given the role played by deliberate lobbying, political campaign contributions, and related activities of powerful collective self-interests. Here the processes of corrosion and corruption have in all probability reinforced one another.

More specifically, the doctrine of institutional separation in the context of an interlocking framework with a common purpose(s) (collective goods) has to an extent been undermined, notably in the USA, as a consequence of a form of interinstitutional gridlock, whereby one institution (or branch of government) seeks to thwart or impede another rather than cooperate with it. Consider in this connection the obstructionism of the Republican-dominated House of Representatives in respect of the policies of President Obama's administration. A related, albeit in one respect contrasting, phenomenon is one in which one of these institutions (or branches of government) engages in institutional overreach, or even overpowers another institution, undermining the second institution. Arguably, in the USA the so-called war on terrorism provided a pretext for executive overreach vis-à-vis the legislature.[4] Naturally, temporary interinstitutional gridlock or minor, episodic institutional overreach may not be intended and may simply be an unwanted side-effect of (respectively) fiercely competitive processes or excessive zeal in the pursuit of legitimate institutional purposes. If so, then such activity may not qualify as corruption. However, if institutional actors are collectively morally responsible for ongoing institutional gridlock, or institutional overreach, that seriously undermines the

---

[3] Lawrence Lessig, "Institutional Corruptions," *Edmond J. Safra Working Papers*, March 15, 2013, available at www.ethics.harvard.edu/lab; Reich, *Saving Capitalism*.

[4] John W. Dean, *Broken Government: How Republican Rule Destroyed the Legislative, Executive and Judicial Branches* (New York: Penguin, 2007).

functioning of the political institutions in question, then their actions potentially constitute a form of political corruption and not merely a form of corrosion of political institutions.

As far as the *nature* of the relationship between institutions is concerned – and, therefore, the various webs of institutional interdependence and, in some cases, chains of collective institutional responsibility (see Chapter 6 Section 6.2.1) – on my teleological account this is to be determined primarily on the basis of the extent to which the differential defining collective ends of institutions are complementary rather than competitive, and/or the extent to which they mesh in the service of higher-order collective ends. In this connection, consider the complementary ends of the institutional components of the criminal justice system, viz., the police (a collective end to gather evidence and arrest suspects), the courts (a collective end to try and sentence offenders), and the prisons (a collective end to punish, deter, and rehabilitate offenders). Again, consider the complementary (collective) ends of the legislature, the executive, and the judiciary in the liberal democratic state.

However, the point also needs to be made that social institutions are not necessarily to be understood as the constitutive elements of a holistic, e.g., organicist, conception of a society. For one thing, many social institutions are trans-societal or trans-national, e.g., the international financial system. For another thing, the *de facto* and normative reach of many social institutions, such as universities and many media organizations, goes beyond the society or nation in which they are located.

In times of institutional crisis, or at least institutional difficulty, problem-solving strategies and policies for reform need to be framed in relation to the fundamental ends or goals of the institution or set of complementary institutions; which is to say they need to be contrived and implemented on the basis of whether or not they will contribute to transforming the institution or institutional structure in ways that will enable it to provide, or better provide, the collective good(s) that justify its existence.

14.1 Government as a Meta-Institution

As far as the institution of government is concerned, I note three important respects in which it is to be distinguished from many other institutions. First, government is a *meta-institution*. We have seen that many social institutions are organizations or systems of organizations. For example, capitalism is a particular kind of economic institution, and in modern times capitalism consists in large part in specific organizational forms – including multinational corporations – organized into a system. I have also noted that some institutions are meta-institutions: they are institutions (organizations) the principal activities and purposes of which consist in organizing other institutions. The most important meta-institution is government; governments enact laws, and develop and implement policies, in respect of the activities of other institutions, as well as of individual citizens. Indeed, the tasks of a contemporary government consist in large part in organizing, including designing and redesigning, other institutions (both individually and collectively). Importantly, governments have as a collective end to see to it that other institutions realize their specific collective ends, e.g., that market-based institutions compete under conditions of free and fair competition. Hence, other things being equal, government officials who intentionally (or negligently) promote or fail to prevent monopolies or oligopolies may well be in part collectively morally responsible for institutional corruption of the markets in question (see Chapter 11). These officials may also be responsible for political corruption insofar as they have culpably failed to discharge their own institutional responsibilities and, as a consequence, the purposes of these political institutions are undermined. Again, government officials who are culpable in a context of regulatory capture by corporations may be engaged in political corruption.

More generally, governments have as a collective end to see to it that other institutions considered as a totality function in the interests of the community as a whole: the public good (or public interest) – in the sense of the common good of the polity rather than in the economists' sense of non-rival and non-excludable goods. Unlike most of the definitive collective ends of other institutions, the collective end (the public good) of, at least, liberal democratic governments is extremely vague and underspecified. Accordingly, whether or not they have engaged in corruption, as opposed to simply having formulated bad policy, is in many cases extremely difficult to determine; indeed, in many cases there will be no determinate answer to that question. Nevertheless, the public good is to a considerable degree specified both by prior specific, natural rights of the citizenry that such governments are morally required to protect, and by the much less vague content of the collective ends of the institutions that such governments regulate. Thus failure on the part of legislators to make provision for adequate funding for the judiciary may well constitute political corruption, and a policy of legislators to interfere in police investigations is almost certainly corrupt. Moreover, as we saw in Chapter 1 Section 1.7, citizens have a joint right to political participation, e.g., by voting and standing for political office, and political participation is both a collective end-in-itself and a collective good of systems of government, and certainly of liberal democracies. Accordingly, individual or collective actions on the part of legislators that undermines this collective good by, for instance, stripping citizens of their voting rights is likely to constitute corruption (in addition to being a rights violation).

In their important role as meta-institutions, governments enact legislation and policy not only in respect of each institution considered on its own but also in respect of the appropriate degree of cooperation and even integration between institutions, including the interface between private and public institutions, and in respect of hybrid institutions, such as in the financial and security areas. Here a range of institutional design questions arise for contemporary liberal democracies. Ought retail banks to be split from investment banks, provided with government-backed depositor guarantees, and be transformed into public utilities? Ought there be, for example, correctional facilities owned by corporations? What is the appropriate relationship between police organizations and the anti-fraud units of corporations? More generally, have market-based institutions, and especially multinational corporations, come to possess a degree of institutional power that is inconsistent with the degree of institutional power that governments must possess if governments are to discharge adequately their institutional purposes?

In addition, governments have as a collective end the maintenance and renovation of the framework of the moral rights of the citizenry, including an array of natural rights, such as the right to life and the right to freedom of thought, and political rights. As we have seen, these political rights are joint rights of citizens to political participation and comprise rights to choose the government, stand for political office and, in a broad sense, determine the legislative and policy agenda of the government. The exercise of these joint rights constitutes the so-called public will. Naturally, there can be considerable tension between the public will and the public good more narrowly construed (voters can get it wrong), and between both of these and individual moral rights (the tyranny of the majority).

The role of government is potentially fraught insofar as individual moral rights are potentially, and often actually, at variance with the exercise of government power (as opposed to government authority). Accordingly, there is a grave threat of political corruption in this area: specifically, abuse of authority (abuse of power) on the part of politicians. An important structural corrective to this threat is the separation of institutional powers, including an independent judiciary, an independent media and police organizations possessed of investigative independence (of which more below). Indeed, these latter institutions are key components of the overall integrity system for governments. Needless to say, the independence in key respects of these institutions from government is itself potentially, and sometimes actually, at variance with the exercise of government power (as opposed to government authority). Here again there is a grave threat of political corruption in the form of abuse of authority (abuse of power) on the part of politicians. The single most important institutional impediment to this latter process of political corruption is democracy albeit, as the rise of demagogues demonstrates, democracy is far from being a panacea. The power of the meta-institution of government needs to be constrained by the citizenry at large via democratic institutions; citizens can vote to replace politicians who abuse their authority by violating the rights of citizens or by undermining the independence of other institutions, such as the judiciary, the media (Fourth Estate), or the police.

Here I note that since many social institutions are not society- or nation-specific, the role of governments in terms of regulation and coordination of another institution is not necessarily bilateral (so to speak) or even one-to-many. It may be that many governments need to be involved in the regulation and coordination of a single social institution, e.g., the global capital market system.

Naturally, in claiming that governments are meta-institutions I do not want to deny that governments ultimately govern individual citizens, for certainly they do. As I stated above, governments govern individual citizens *directly*, e.g., by means of the criminal laws against assault. However, in large part contemporary governments also govern individual citizens *indirectly* via some other institution, e.g., qua employees of a corporation, or via the tax office or the police. Indeed, the edifice of laws enacted by successive governments in respect of the actions of individual citizens, whether qua citizens or qua institutional actor of some sort, is itself an institutional arrangement that intercedes between government and citizen.

A second important property of governments is their vulnerability to collective acceptance; a point stressed in Chapter 2. There is a reason for the vulnerability of institutional authorities, especially political authorities. In the special case of institutional authorities, deontic properties are *ontologically dependent* on collective acceptance: no collective acceptance, no deontic properties. The point here is not simply that, say, rulers cannot *exercise* their right to rule if their right to rule is not collectively accepted. Rather, speaking generally, a ruler does not even possess a *right* to rule unless she is able to exercise authority over her subjects. This seems to be a general feature of the deontic properties of those in authority (whatever kind of authority they might possess) and of political authorities in particular.

I note that this point concerning the vulnerability of political institutions by virtue of their ontological dependence on collective acceptance needs to be distinguished from consent-based theories of government, e.g., the representative theory of liberal democratic government. The latter is a specific normative theory of one species of government; the former is a property of all governments, consent-based or otherwise.

I further note that this dependence of political institutions on collective acceptance is a double-edged sword. It is, of course, a good thing insofar as it constitutes a potential brake on the excesses of authoritarian governments. On the other hand, it can lead to the emasculation of the institution of government to the point at which the polity becomes a so-called failed state comprising factions engaged in internecine conflict. An important counterweight to the emasculation of government is an informed, rational, and reflective citizenry committed to the collective good(s) as an end and to the institution of government as a necessary means to the realization of this end. Unfortunately, as Plato long ago observed, corrupt governments are conducive to the rise of demagogues, and demagogues facilitate the further corruption of the institution of government and, additionally, corrupt the citizenry, whose irrationality and ignorance they exploit. Arguably, Vladimir Putin, the President of Russia, and, for that matter, Donald Trump, the recently elected President of the USA, are cases in point.

A third important property of government is its use of coercive force and, specifically, the normative claim that government is entitled to a monopoly on the use of coercive force on pain of a return to the state of nature. Here we do not have to accept Hobbesian contractarianism or other unpalatable forms of authoritarianism. For what is uncontroversial is that contemporary liberal democratic governments govern largely by way of *enforceable legislation* and could not do otherwise. (What is also uncontroversial is that there are moral limits on governmental power, and the moral legitimacy of governments – and therefore their right to legislate and to use coercive force to enforce the law – depends in part on their respecting those limits. I return to this latter point below.)

In the discussion of police institutions (Chapter 13), I suggested that the principal collective end of police organizations was the protection of justifiably enforceable, legally enshrined, moral rights. The requirement that the justifiably enforceable moral rights be legally enshrined ties the institution of the police to the institution of government and, in particular, to the legislature. The police exist in part to enforce the laws the government introduces and, specifically, those laws that embody justifiably enforceable moral rights.

However, there are many laws that do not appear to embody justifiably enforceable moral rights. Many of these laws prescribe actions (or omissions), the performance (or non-performance) of which provides a social benefit. Consider the laws of taxation. The benefits provided by taxation include the provision of roads and other services to which arguably citizens do not have a basic moral right, and certainly not a justifiably enforceable moral right. On the other hand, taxes also enable the provision of benefits to which citizens do have justifiably enforceable moral rights, e.g., medicine for life-threatening diseases, basic welfare, and so on. Certain legally enshrined moral rights are justifiably enforced by police, as are laws that indirectly contribute to the securing of these rights. The moral rights in question are justifiably enforceable moral rights. But, to reiterate, there are many laws that are not of this sort. Many of these latter laws are fair and reasonable, and the conformity to them enables collective goods to be provided. But what is the justification for their enforcement by police? I will shortly argue that the fact that they provide collective benefits, and/or that they are fair and reasonable, does not of itself provide an adequate justification for their enforcement. Perhaps consent to the enforcement of just and reasonable laws that enable the provision of collective benefits provides an adequate moral justification for such enforcement. Here there is an issue with respect to the degree and type of enforcement that might be in this way justified; deadly force may not be justified, even if it is consented to in relation to fair and reasonable laws that enable collective benefits to be provided. Moreover, as is well-known, there is a problem in relation to consent. Evidently, there is not in fact explicit consent to most laws, and the recourse to tacit consent seems not to offer a sufficiently strong and determinate notion of consent.

At any rate, I want to make two points here in relation to what is nothing more than a version of the traditional problem of the justification for the use of coercive force by the state to enforce its laws.[5] First, self-evidently, there is no obvious problem in relation to the enforcement of laws that embody *justifiably enforceable* moral rights, including human rights. Moreover, there may well be other laws that can justifiably be enforced (up to a point) on the grounds that not only are they fair,

---

[5] See Ronald Dworkin, *Laws Empire* (Oxford: Hart Publishing, 1998), p. 190. There are questions here in relation to the *exclusive* right of the State to enforce moral rights. Arguably, the State only has an exclusive right to punish, but not an exclusive right to enforce in the narrow sense of protection against rights violations.

reasonable, and productive of social benefits, but in addition citizens have consented to their enforcement (up to that point).

Second, I want to suggest that, notwithstanding our first point, there are fair, reasonable, and socially beneficial laws with respect to which enforcement is not morally justified. Further, there may not be an adequate justification for enforcement of some of these laws, even if enforcement were to be consented to. The reason for this is that the nature and degree of enforcement required to ensure compliance with these laws – say, use of deadly force – is not morally justified.[6] Certainly, recourse to deadly force – as opposed to non-deadly coercive force – is not justified in the case of many unlawful actions; specifically, unlawful actions not regarded as serious crimes. Indeed, this point is recognized in those jurisdictions that have made it unlawful for police to shoot at many categories of "fleeing felons." It is more often than not now unlawful, because immoral, to shoot at (say) a fleeing pickpocket.

It follows from the above that there are moral limits on government, and they are of two general kinds. First, there are those limits that exist by virtue of the *contingent fact* that citizens have not authorized (legitimately consented to) the government to act outside those limits. Hence a democratic government cannot, or ought not to, embark on a protracted war without the consent of the citizenry. (This is consistent with a government acting in self-defense in the context of an unexpected armed attack and, then, seeking and gaining retrospective authorization to do so.) If it does so, it is going beyond what it has been authorized to do. It is abusing its authority and, therefore, engaged in institutional corruption. Second, there are those (theoretically more restricted) limits that exist by virtue of the inalienability of some basic moral rights, such as the right to life and the right to freedom; these limits exist because governments *could not be authorized* by their citizens to exceed them. Thus there is no circumstance in which a liberal democratic government could legitimately be authorized to enslave some or most of its citizenry, e.g., if a majority or even all of the citizens consented to enslavement this would not provide a legitimate authorization. Clearly, if the members of a government were morally responsible for large-scale rights violations, such as enslavement, then the government in question would be, thereby, an illegitimate government. However, the point to be stressed in the context of this work is that the members of such a government would also be engaged

---

[6] This is consistent with there being a moral obligation to obey these laws; we are speaking here of the justification for the *enforcement* of such laws. For an account of the moral justification for obeying the law, see Miller, *Social Action*, pp. 141–151. See also David Luban, *Lawyers and Justice* (Princeton University Press, 1988), chapter 3.

in institutional corruption; specifically, political corruption. Let us explore further the concept of political corruption.

14.2 Political Corruption

Dennis Thompson discusses the case of Charles Keating, a property developer, who for many years generously contributed to the election and reelection campaigns of various politicians on the rise, and then called on his indebted political friends – five senators – to do him a big favor in return.[7] Government investigators were about to seize the assets of a subsidiary (Lincoln Savings and Loans) of a company owned by Keating and he wanted the senators to cause the regulatory authorities to back off. To that end, Keating instigated two meetings between the regulators and five senators who had been recipients of his generosity. Although upon completion of their audit the San Francisco regulators, under the direction of the Chair of the Federal Home Loan Bank Board, Edwin J. Gray, had recommended that Lincoln be seized, Gray was replaced as chairman and the investigation transferred to Washington for a new audit; an outcome much to Keating's liking. However, in April 1989, two years after Keating's meetings with the senators, the government seized Lincoln, which declared bankruptcy. In September 1990, Keating was charged with forty-two counts of fraud. Lincoln's losses amounted to $3.4 billion and many of its elderly investors individually suffered substantial financial losses. Federal regulators filed a $1.1 million civil racketeering and fraud suit against Keating, accusing him of diverting Lincoln's deposits to his family and to political campaigns.

As Thompson[8] points out, the Keating case involved (1) the provision, or at least the appearance of the provision, of an improper service on the part of legislators (the senators) to a constituent (Keating), viz. interfering with the role of a regulator (Gray) on behalf of Keating, (2) a political gain in the form of campaign contributions (from Keating to the senators), and (3) a link, or at least the appearance of a link, between (1) and (2), viz. the service being offered *because of* the political gain. Accordingly, the case study involves at least the appearance of corrupt activity on the part of the senators. Moreover, I agree with Thompson that such an appearance might be sufficient for institutional corruption, in that (a) damage has been done to a political institution by virtue of a diminution in public trust in that institution, and (b) the senators ought to have known that their actions

---

[7] See Miller et al., *Corruption and Anti-Corruption*, chapter 3.
[8] Dennis F. Thompson, *Ethics in Congress: From Individual to Institutional Corruption*, p. 37f.

might have this effect, and therefore they ought not to have performed those actions.[9] Moreover, this institutional corruption resulted from the appearance of a conflict of interest, albeit in the context (as it turned out) of Keating's fraudulent activities, the collapse of a major financial institution, and the subsequent damage done to elderly investors. As legislators, the senators have a duty to provide a service to their constituents. However, the appearance of a conflict of interest arises when legislators use their office to provide a questionable "service" to a person upon whom they are, or have been, heavily reliant for campaign contributions.

A related kind of conflict of interest – and attendant corruption – in government involves the improper extension of a political role; as such, it is a species of institutional overreach. Consider, in this connection, a case of alleged corruption involving the Prime Minister of Italy, Silvio Berlusconi. It appears that his government used its political power to introduce a controversial new law that would allow defendants to seek the transfer of their trial from one court to another, if *they* felt the first court was likely to be biased against them. Berlusconi's lawyers indicated that they would avail themselves of the "legitimate suspicion" law to have their client's trial on charges of bribing Roman judges to be moved from Milan (where it is felt that the court would be biased against Berlusconi) to Brescia (where Berlusconi enjoys widespread political support). There was a suspicion that the new law was deliberately introduced by Berlusconi's government in order to assist his defense against charges of corruption, and thereby enable him to escape prosecution. The attempt by the Italian Government to introduce the legitimate suspicion law can be seen as a case where the legislative role has been used to improperly interfere with the judicial function. If so, this amounts to political corruption of a judicial process, viz. the process of determining what matters should be heard in what courts.

Lawrence Lessig has claimed that the USA's democratic electoral process is institutionally corrupt.[10] Lessig argues that although US citizens as a whole participate in the election of, say, the President of the USA, nevertheless, the outcome is not *wholly* dependent on these US citizens as it should be in a bona fide democracy. For the outcome is also dependent upon a small group of "Funders" who bankroll particular candidates in the election and without whose funding no potential candidate could hope to win office; after all, elections are hugely expensive. Since these funders are in no way

---

[9] *Ibid.*, pp. 42–43.   [10] Lessig, "Institutional Corruptions."

representative of the US citizenry, I agree that democracy in the USA is corrupt in the respect identified by Lessig.[11]

In respect of the above three cases and analyses by Thompson or Lessig I say the following: First, Thompson's account of institutional corruption is too narrow. It is a description of one species of institutional corruption only, albeit an important one. As the Berlusconi example demonstrates, political corruption can be motivated by personal gain (including to avoid just punishment) and not merely for political gain. Nor can Thompson rename such corruption, "individual corruption." For Berlusconi's actions, if successful, would have been a case of abuse of authority by a Prime Minister acting jointly with other senior members of the government (albeit, in the service of his personal gain[12]) and, as such, corruptive of the institution of the government. Moreover, as noted above, it would also have been corruptive of the institution of the judiciary. In keeping with my own account of institutional corruption and, specifically, of political corruption, the motives for political corruption are multiple, diverse, and not restricted to political gain; indeed, private and political gain are often inseparable in practice, especially in the case of corrupt government leaders. What counts is that the action (or omission) is performed by an institutional actor in his/her capacity as an institutional role occupant (e.g., legislator) and that he or she intended, knew, or should have known that it would undermine (or was an action of a kind that tends to undermine) an institutional process (e.g., judicial process), person (qua institutional actor), or purpose (collective good) (see Chapter 3).

Second, and consistent with what Lessig claims, the moral responsibility for the institutional corruption of the US democratic electoral process is a species of *collective* moral responsibility understood as joint responsibility. (I note that this is a relational individualist account; so ultimately, it is individuals who are fully morally responsible for their own contributory actions or omissions, but often only partially responsible (jointly with others) for the outcomes of these joint actions or joint omissions to which they contributed – see Chapter 6.) For one thing, both the candidates themselves and their funders know, or should know, that they are participating in the undermining of the US democratic electoral process.[13] Moreover, there is the additional and already

---

[11] I note that the recent success, albeit ultimate failure, of Bernie Sanders in the US Democratic Party primaries in relying only on small donations and the ultimate success of a billionaire (not necessarily dependent on large donations from other billionaires), i.e., Donald Trump, has complicated the picture somewhat.

[12] As well as perhaps their personal and political gain, given his leadership role.

[13] It is not a necessary condition for an action to be an act of corruption that its performer knows that the action complies with my definition of corruption.

mentioned, deliberate and mutually beneficial causally connected processes of campaign financing (by and traceable to, for instance, individual members of Big Parma or Wall St. who, for example, authorized the funds in question) and institutionally damaging legislation (by, and traceable to, individual legislators who voted for this legislation). Again, this institutionally damaging process is known to the participants, or should be known to them. Indeed, at least in the case of the relevant members of the corporations in question, these individuals – in financing particular political candidates and/or parties – intended (via their lobbyists) to influence legislators to enact institutionally damaging legislation (albeit, perhaps not under that description), and in doing so pursued their corporate (and individual) self-interests at the expense of the integrity of the political institutions of their country. Further, clearly the members of the US government could change the campaign financing system, if they jointly chose to do so, and thereby combat the corrupting effect of the Funders under current arrangements. For instance, election funding could be capped at a certain level and elections could be required to be publicly funded. In short, an anti-corruption regime in respect of US campaign financing could be established, if the legislators had the will to establish it. Additionally, an independent well-resourced, national anti-corruption commission with intrusive powers to investigate breaches of this new campaign financing regulation and other forms of political corruption could be established.

Third, however, Lessig's claim regarding the relationship between dependence corruption and institutional processes is problematic. Lessig states that there can be instances of "dependence corruption" regardless of the institutional processes necessary for the institution to fulfill its purpose, whereas Thompson, for instance, holds that we need to refer to such processes if we are to determine whether a dependency is improper (and, therefore, corrupt).[14] By the lights of my teleological normative account of institutions (and, by extension, presumably Thompson's own broadly teleological account) a dependency is corrupt only if it undermines institutional purposes, either directly or indirectly via undermining actual (legitimate) institutional processes (or, in the case of my account if not Thompson's, by undermining persons *qua* institutional role occupants). Moreover, corruptors who are institutional role occupants use their institutional position in order to perform the actions that corrupt or, at least, have a tendency to corrupt. For instance, once elected US members of Congress might provide a service to large funders of their election campaigns – a service that non-funders do not

[14] Thompson, "Two Concepts," 12.

get. This dependency of members of Congress on large funders undermines institutional purpose in two main ways. First, the public will a collective good has been undermined since, as Lessig points out, the funders can in effect restrict entry into political office. Second, the public interest also a collective good has been undermined, since the actions of the members of Congress now tend to track private interests, specifically those of large funders, rather than the public interest. Accordingly, whether or not a dependency is improper is to be determined *ultimately* by recourse to institutional purpose (understood in terms of collective goods) and, since institutional purposes do not exist in a vacuum, by recourse to those institutional processes that are effective or defective in relation to realizing that purpose and that meet (or fail to meet) other desiderata, notably moral constraints (and, in particular, institutionally embodied moral constraints). In the US Congress example, the campaign financing processes are defective. In short, surely we need to have recourse to both institutional purposes and the processes (or, at least, the rights and duties constitutive of institutional roles)that realize (or fail to realize) those purposes if we are to determine whether or not an action or set of actions is corrupt. I note that some defects in institutional structures might consist merely in the absence of a process rather than a defective process per se. If so, it is at least conceivable that institutional purposes are being undermined by fully compliant institutional actors and yet no existing process should be replaced or adjusted; rather there is a need to design and implement a new process without making any other changes. However, even in such a case there will be institutional processes and roles that are incorrectly assumed, or perhaps insincerely claimed, to be the means to realize the institutional purpose; an institutional purpose cannot simply be a thought bubble bereft of any concrete institutional vehicle for its realization. Moreover, the processes to be designed and implemented, the ones that *ought to be* in place, are processes that realistically could be in place, given the larger extant structure of the institution in question; so there are structural as well as teleological institutional constraints on even entirely new processes.

14.3   Political Corruption and the Media

Let us now turn finally to the role of the media in political corruption, bearing in mind the important role the media plays in the interface between the government and the citizenry in liberal democracies understood as deliberative democracies in the minimal sense that the citizenry are reasonably well-informed, well-intentioned, and reflective. We have thus far focused on the corrupt actions of political office holders and the need for them to be held to account by the independent institutional components of the overall integrity system, e.g., the judiciary, criminal investigative agencies, and the Fourth Estate. However, the citizens have an institutional role in a democracy, e.g., *qua* voters. As we saw in Chapter 1, citizens have joint moral and institutional rights to participate in democratic political institutions, but they also have joint moral and institutional obligations, notably to ensure that they are adequately informed and to comply with the outcomes of properly conducted elections. Indeed, the citizenry is a crucial component of the integrity system for governments alongside, as mentioned above, independent institutions (the judiciary, Fourth Estate, etc.). Accordingly, a question arises as to the extent to which members of the citizenry are corrupted and/or corruptors. More specifically, does the media in a given polity have a corrupting effect on the institutional relationship between the government and the citizenry? That relationship is a complex one. At one level, the government stands in a relationship of authority vis-à-vis the citizenry; at another level, the government is authorized by the citizenry. So the relationship is one of public trust; the citizenship entrusts the government with authority to govern for the collective good and not to overreach or otherwise abuse its authority.

As argued in Chapter 11, being mere institutional instruments, market-based organizations *per se* can easily be used to serve harmful purposes, e.g., corporations that produce and sell tobacco or armaments. Moreover, as noted in Chapter 11, those social institutions that produce a collective good that is identical (at least in part) with their constitutive collective end can suffer a process of corrosion or corruption once they are "privatized," or otherwise transformed into predominantly market-based enterprises. Arguably, some organizations within the print and electronic media sector in the USA, UK, and elsewhere are cases in point. Clearly, media agencies purporting to provide impartial and objective news and analysis, yet who are under the thumb of authoritarian regimes such as in the case of China, for example, are failing to achieve their avowed institutional purpose by virtue of the institutional overreach of government and are, therefore, institutionally corrupt at least to some degree, whether they be public or private sector agencies.

Because the mainstream media, including what I will refer to as tabloid TV, is pervasive – 75 percent of the discretionary (nonwork, nonsleep) time of Americans is spent watching TV[15] – it profoundly influences, directly or indirectly, the institutions of public communication and, thereby, social attitudes and public policy. Most print and electronic media organizations

---

[15] A. Gore, *The Assault on Reason* (New York: Penguin, 2007), p. 6.

in Western nations are commercial businesses, i.e., business institutions.[16] However, these organizations also have a particular role as an institution of public communication. Specifically, they have an institutional role as the free press in the service of the public's right to know: the role of the Fourth Estate alongside the executive, legislature, and judiciary within a liberal democracy. Moreover, in the case of the print and electronic media – at least in its role as a public communicator of news and comment – its existence as a business corporation is, or ought to be, subservient to, indeed, an instrument serving its institutional function as the Fourth Estate. As argued above, business organizations in competitive markets are not ends in themselves but ought to be viewed purely instrumentally; this is certainly so in the case of the print and electronic media in respect of their role as public communicators of news and comment.

Here it is important to reaffirm the distinction between the *de facto* ends of the media and the ends that it ought to have. Perhaps the principal end of the mainstream media in the USA is in fact to provide entertainment and make profits for corporations rather than function as the Fourth Estate. There are a number of considerations in support of this empirical claim. First, much of mainstream media news and comment is "sound-bites," dumbed-down reports, sport, celebrity "news," infotainment, advertorials, and the like; the content lacks descriptive breadth or analytical depth, and it typically appeals to the lowest common denominator. In short, much of the news content of the mainstream media is a form of entertainment, including "selling" a consumerist-oriented way of life.

Second, there is a high degree of concentration of ownership in the mainstream media. The mainstream US media, including news and comment, is in large part owned by large corporate conglomerates for which news is simply one commercial product, e.g., the parent company of the mainstream news-provider NBC is General Electric.[17]

Third, mainstream media enterprises are often simply components of large corporate conglomerates and most have close institutional relationships with corporations outside the media. According to Elliot Cohen, citing a recent US university-based research study, "only 118 people compose the membership on the boards of directors of the ten big media giants. These 118

---

[16] Earlier versions of the material in this section appeared in Seumas Miller, "Freedom of the Press," *Politikon*, 22 (1995), 24–36; and Miller, *Moral Foundations of Social Institutions*, chapter 6.

[17] Elliot Cohen (ed.), *News Incorporated: Corporate Media Ownership and Its Threat to Democracy* (New York: Prometheus Books, 2005), p. 18.

individuals in turn sit on the corporate boards of 288 national and international corporations."[18]

Finally, there is evidently an unhealthy relationship between these media enterprises and political institutions (the US government and US political parties, in particular). Consider the blatant and one-eyed partisanship displayed by "shock jock" political commentators, such as Sean Hannity of Fox TV and Steve Bannon. Indeed, Bannon was recently appointed by President-Elect Donald Trump as his chief strategist and senior counsel.

From the perspective of a free press in the service of the public's right to know (the Fourth Estate), each of these four considerations is very troubling. Taken in combination they call into question the independence of these media enterprises and their journalists, and the truth, objectivity, and balance of the news reports that they disseminate.

One specific political consequence of the current state of these corporate media institutions relates to US elections. As Al Gore says:

> Since voters still have the real power to elect their leaders, those who wish to exchange wealth for power must do so, in part, by paying for elaborate public relations campaigns to try to shape the opinions of the millions who spend so much time watching television. At times it seems as if a genuine democratic conversation is taking place, but it flows mainly in one direction – from those who have raised enough money to buy the television advertising to those who watch the ads and have little effective means for communicating in the opposite direction.[19]

The housing of journalists, editors, and commentators in large media corporations and corporate conglomerates has evidently compromised the role of the media as an independent communicator. Consider in this connection Bill O'Reilly, the host of Fox TV's *The O'Reilly Factor*. O'Reilly's comments placed a right-wing "spin" on events and do not even attempt to respect the canons of objective argument; indeed, even his factual claims are suspect.[20] Indeed, the disregard for the facts is now apparently so widespread in the channels of public communication that large numbers of members of the citizenry have been conditioned to the point that they no longer seem to regard truth-telling as of fundamental importance in matters political. Certainly, Donald Trump's disregard of the truth and practice of blatantly lying (e.g., regarding President Obama's birthplace) failed to halt his march to the Presidency. Indeed,

---

[18] Elliot Cohen and B. W. Fraser, *The Last Days of Democracy: How Big Media and Power-Hungry Government Are Turning America into a Dictatorship* (New York: Prometheus Books, 2007), p. 14.
[19] Gore, *Assault on Reason*, p. 78.   [20] Cohen and Fraser, *Last Days of Democracy*, p. 83.

although this is presumably intended to be hyperbole, according to Francis Fukuyama we live in a "post fact world."[21] If so, then political culture in the USA and elsewhere has been profoundly corroded, if not corrupted, and those in the media who are in part morally responsible for this state of affairs are corruptors by the lights of our definition.

As already noted, the general justification for the existence of the media as a public forum is that members of the public – or at least their representatives or spokespersons – have a moral right to address the public at large. In this connection, the recent arrival of the Internet and of social media is important. These technologies enable a very large number of people to have access to very large audiences. On the other hand, they are not immune to interference and censorship, e.g., with the complicity of the search engine giant Google, the authoritarian Chinese government employs tens of thousands of people to police Chinese citizens using the Internet by intercepting their communications, shutting down websites, etc.[22] Moreover, recent policy decisions in the USA threaten to undermine Internet freedom by refusing to maintain its status as a "common carrier" akin to telecommunication systems such as telephone networks; common carriers are open to all, and control of communications rests entirely with users.[23] Nor does an unregulated Internet and unfettered social media necessarily provide a solution to these problems. For, as recent publication of falsehoods regarding Hilary Clinton and others on Facebook during the US presidential elections demonstrates, the Internet and social media are open to abuse and require regulation. Moreover, social media, in particular, does not supplant the need for a public forum for the citizenry of a given polity as a whole, as opposed to a wide variety of forums for diverse, segmented, partisan groups.

The upshot of this discussion is that there is a need to renovate the Fourth Estate to ensure that it can discharge its institutional role. Evidently, there is a need for a well-funded and independent public broadcaster (along the lines of the original conception of the British Broadcasting Corporation (BBC) in the UK and Australian Broadcasting Corporation (ABC) in Australia) with a remit to provide objective, impartial, and balanced (albeit, not necessarily neutral) news and comment; moreover, traditional distinctions in this area, e.g., between news and comment, and between both and advertorials, need to be resurrected. Monopolistic or oligopolistic media organizations need to be downsized. There is also a need to legislate to ensure editorial independence from media proprietors.

---

[21] Francis Fukuyama, "The Emergence of a Post-Fact World."   [22] *Ibid.*, p. 219.
[23] *Ibid.*, p. 218.

Relatedly, there is a need to ensure an appropriate degree of independence of journalists from editors. Finally, an independent and well-funded Fourth Estate monitoring and oversight agency needs to be established with powers to investigate breaches of editorial and journalistic independence.

14.4 Conclusion

In this chapter I have elaborated an account of the institution of government as a meta-institution: an institution that gives direction to and regulates other institutions. When members of governments legislate in a manner that undermines the institutional processes and purposes of other institutions for purposes of political or personal gain then, other things being equal, it is likely that the legislators in question are engaged in political corruption. Integrity systems for liberal democratic governments comprise an array of independent or quasi-independent institutions, including the judiciary and the police. Importantly, however, governments are accountable to the citizenry, notably via democratic elections. In this regard, and notwithstanding the rise of social media, the role of the Fourth Estate, as the provider of a public forum for the citizenry as a whole (rather than as segmented audiences of social media), as a source of informed, balanced, and objective news and comment, and as an investigator, is crucial since citizens need to be reasonably well-informed, well-intentioned, and reflective if they are to discharge their own role as citizens adequately in a liberal democratic polity. Moreover, the corruption of the citizenry is itself far from being a remote possibility, especially in the context of weakening social norms and the absence of a commitment to the collective good. In this connection, a central problem is the existence of corruption in the media in respect of its critical role as an interface between government and the citizenry in facilitating deliberative democracy. Accordingly, I have made some suggestions regarding an integrity system for the Fourth Estate.

Bibliography

Ackman, D., "Sherron Watkins had Whistle, but Blew it" *Forbes*, February 14, 2012.

Acton, Lord, *Essays on Freedom and Power* (London: Skyler J. Collins, 2013).

Alexandra, Andrew, "Dirty Harry and Dirty Hands" in Coady, Tony, James, Steve, Miller, Seumas, and O'Keefe, M. (eds.), *Violence and Police Culture* (Melbourne: Melbourne University Press, 2000).

Alexandra, Andrew and Miller, Seumas, "Needs, Moral Self-Consciousness and Professional Roles" *Professional Ethics,* 5 no. 1–2 (1996), 43–61.

Alexandra, Andrew and Miller, Seumas, *Integrity Systems for Occupations* (Aldershot: Ashgate, 2010).

Alexandra, Andrew, Campbell, Tom, Cocking, Dean, Miller, Seumas, and White, Kevin, *Professionalization, Ethics and Integrity*, Report for the Professional Standards Council (2006), pp. 1–185.

Audi, Robert, *Business Ethics and Ethical Business* (Oxford University Press, 2008).

Ayres, I. and Braithwaite, John, *Responsive Regulation* (Oxford University Press, 1992).

Bachrach, P. and Baratz, M. S., *Power and Poverty: Theory and Practice* (Oxford University Press, 1970).

Banfield, E., *The Moral Basis of a Backward Society* (New York: Free Press, 1958).

Bayles, M. D., "Professional Power and Self-Regulation" *Business and Professional Ethics Journal,* 5 (1986), 26–46.

Behr, P. and Witt, A., "Visionary's Dream Led to Risky Business" *Washington Post*, July 28, 2002.

Below, A., *In Praise of Nepotism: A Natural History* (New York: Doubleday, 2003).

Billingsley, R., Nemitz, T., and Bean, P. (eds.), *Informers: Policing, Policy and Practice* (Cullompton, Devon, 2001).

Bok, Sissela, *Secrecy* (New York: Random House, 1985).

Bovens, Mark, "Analysing and Assessing Accountability" *European Law Journal*, 13 (2007), 447–468.

Bowden, *Killing Pablo* (London: Atlantic Books, 2001).

Boylan, Michael, *Basic Ethics* (Upper Saddle River, NJ: Prentice Hall, 1999).

Bratman, Michael, *Shared Agency* (Oxford University Press, 2014).

Bronitt, Simon and Roche, Declan, "Between Rhetoric and Reality: Socio-Legal and Republican Perspectives on Entrapment" *International Journal of Evidence and Proof*, 4 (2000), 77–106.

Brown, M. F., *Criminal Investigation: Law and Practice*, 2nd edn. (Boston: Butterworth-Heineman, 2001).

Carney, Mark, "Inclusive Capitalism: Creating a Sense of the Systemic" Inclusive Capitalism Conference, London, May 27, 2014.

Carson, T. L., "Bribery" in Becker, L. C. and Becker, C. B. (eds.), *Encyclopaedia of Ethics*, 2nd edn. (London: Routledge, 2001).

Chapman, Brian, *Police State* (London: Pall Mall Press, 1970).

Ciepley, D. "Beyond Public and Private: Toward a Political Theory of the Corporation" *American Political Science Review*, 107 (2013), 139–158.

Clarke, Thomas, "High Frequency Trading and Dark Pools: Sharks Never Sleep" *Law and Financial Markets Review*, 8 (2014), 342–351.

Coady, C. A. J., "Dirty Hands" *Encyclopedia of Ethics*, 2nd edn. (London: Routledge, 2001).

  Messy Morality: The Challenge of Politics (Oxford University Press, 2008).

Coady, M. and Bloch, S. (eds.), *Codes of Ethics and the Professions* (Melbourne University Press, 1996).

Cohen, Elliott (ed.), *News Incorporated: Corporate Media Ownership and Its Threat to Democracy* (New York: Prometheus Books, 2005).

Cohen, Elliott and Fraser, B. W., *The Last Days of Democracy: How Big Media and Power-Hungry Government Are Turning America into a Dictatorship* (New York: Prometheus Books, 2007).

Cohen, Howerd, "Overstepping Police Authority" *Criminal Justice Ethics*, 6 (1987), 52–60.

Copp, David, "Collective Moral Autonomy Thesis" *Journal of Social Philosophy*, 38 (2007), 369–388.

Davidson, Donald, "Freedom to Act" in Honderich, T. (ed.), *Essays on Freedom of Action* (London: Routledge and Kegan Paul, 1973).

Dean, J. W., *Broken Government: How Republican Rule Destroyed the Legislative, Executive and Judicial Branches* (New York: Penguin, 2007).

DeGeorge, Richard, *Competing with Integrity* (New York: Oxford University Press, 1993).

DeGeorge, Richard, *Nature and Limits of Authority* (University of Kansas Press, 2000).

Delattre, Edwin, *Character and Cops*, 2nd edn. (Washington, DC: AEI Press, 1994).

Dobos, N., Barry, C., and Pogge T. (eds.), *Global Financial Crisis: The Ethical Issues* (London: Palgrave Macmillan, 2011).

Duff, R. A., *Answering for Crime: Responsibility and Liability in the Criminal Law* (Oxford: Hart Publishing, 2007).

Dunfee, T. W. and Warren, D. E., "Is Guanxi Ethical? A Normative Analysis of Doing Business in China" *Journal of Business Ethics*, 32 (2001), 191–204.

Dunnighan, C. and Norris, C., "The Detective, the Snout and the Audit Commission: The Real Costs in Using Informants" *Howard Journal of Criminal Justice*, 38 (2005), 67–86.

Dworkin, Gerald, *The Theory and Practice of Autonomy* (Cambridge University Press, 1988).

Dworkin, Ronald, *Laws Empire* (Oxford: Hart Publishing, 1998).

Eatwell, John and Taylor, L., *Global Finance at Risk: The Case for International Regulation* (New York: New Press, 2000).

Eitan, N., Hoerel, C., McCormack, T., and Roessler, J., *Joint Attention: Communication and Other Minds* (Oxford University Press, 2005).

Elliston, F., *Whistleblowing Research: Methodological and Moral Issues* (New York, Praeger, 1985).

Epstein, E. J., "Was Snowden's Heist a Foreign Espionage Operation?" *Wall Street Journal*, May 9, 2014.

Erskine, Toni, "Assigning Responsibilities to Institutional Moral Agents" *Ethics and International Affairs*, 15 (2001), 67–85.

Etzioni, Amitai, "NSA: National Security vs. Individual Rights" *Intelligence and National Security*, 30 (2015), 100–136.

Fan, Y. "Guanxi's Consequences: Personal Gains at Social Cost" *Journal of Business Ethics*, 38 (2002), 371–380.

Ferguson, C., "Heist of the Century: Wall Street's Role in the Financial Crisis" *The Guardian*, May 20, 2012.

Financial Services Authority, *Turner Review: A Regulatory Response to the Global Banking Crisis* (London: FSA, 2009).

Financial Stability Board, "FSB announces policy measures to address systemically important financial institutions (SIFIs) and names initial group of global SIFIs," www.fsb.org, November 4, 2011.

Finn, Paul, "The Liability of Third Parties for Knowing Receipt or Assistance" in Waters, D. (ed.), *Equities, Fiduciaries and Trusts* (Toronto: Carswell, 1993).

Fischer, J. M. (ed.), *Moral Responsibility* (London: Cornell University Press, 1986).

Fisse, Brent, and Braithwaite, John, *Corporations, Crime and Accountability* (Cambridge University Press, 1994).

Frankfurt, H. G., "Three Concepts of Free Action" in Fischer, J. M. (ed.), *Moral Responsibility* (London: Cornell University Press, 1986).

Freiberg, Arie, *The Tools of Regulation* (Sydney: Federation Press, 2010).

French, Peter, "The Corporation as a Moral Person" *American Philosophical Quarterly*, 16 (1979), 207–215.

Friedman, Milton, "The Social Responsibility of Business Is to Increase Its Profits" *New York Times Magazine*, September 13, 1970.

Fukuyama, Frances, *Trust: The Social Virtues and the Creation of Prosperity* (London: Penguin Books, 1996).

Fusaro, P. C. and Miller, R. M., *What Went Wrong at Enron* (Hoboken, NJ: John Wiley and Sons, 2002).

Garnaut, Ross, *The Great Crash of 2008* (Melbourne University Press, 2009).

Gert, Bernard, *Common Morality* (Oxford University Press, 2007).

Giddens, S., *The Constitution of Society: Outline of the Theory of Structuration*, (Cambridge: Polity Press, 1984).

Gilbert, M., *On Social Facts* (Princeton University Press, 1989).

Gilligan, G. and O'Brien, J. (eds.), *Integrity, Risk and Accountability in Capital Markets: Regulating Culture* (Oxford: Hart Publishing, 2013).

Gore, A., *The Assault on Reason* (New York: Penguin, 2007).

Grabosky, Peter, Smith, R., and Dempsey, G., *Electronic Theft: Unlawful Acquisition in Cyberspace* (University of Cambridge Press, 2001).

Green, L., *The Authority of the State* (Oxford University Press, 1989).

Green, S. P., *Lying, Cheating and Stealing: A Moral Theory of White Collar Crime* (Oxford University Press, 2006).

Greenwald, G., *No Place to Hide: Edward Snowden, The NSA and the Surveillance State* (London: Penguin Books, 2014).

Gregg, P., Jewell, S., and Tonks, I., *Executive Pay and Performance in the UK 1994–2002*, CMPO Working Paper Series No. 05/122 (Bristol: Centre for Market and Public Organisation, 2005).

Griffin, James, *On Human Rights* (Oxford University Press, 2008).

What Can Philosophy Contribute to Ethics? (Oxford University Press, 2015).

Harfield, Clive, "Police Informers and Professional Ethics" *Criminal Justice Ethics*, 31 (2012), 73–95.

Harfield, Clive and Harfield, Karen, *Covert Investigation*, 3rd edn. (Oxford University Press, 2012).

Harper, T., Kerbaj, R., and Shipman, T., "British Spies Betrayed to Russians and Chinese" *Sunday Times*, June 14, 2015.

Harre, Rom, *Social Being*, 2nd edn. (Oxford: Blackwell, 1993).

Heidenheimer, A. J. and Johnson, M. (eds.), *Political Corruption: Concepts and Contexts*, 3rd edn. (Piscataway, NJ: Transaction Publishers, 2001).

Hindess, Barry, "Good Government and Corruption" in Larmour, P. and Wolanin, N. (eds.) *Corruption and Anti-Corruption* (Canberra: Asia-Pacific Press, 2001), pp. 1–10.

Identity Theft Resource Center, *Aftermath Study: What Victims Have to Say about Identity Theft* (The Identity Theft Resource Center, 2015), available at www.idtheftcenter.org.

IOSCO, International Organization of Securities Commissions, *Principles for Financial Benchmarks: Final Report* (Madrid: International Organization of Securities Commissions, 2013), available at www.iosco.org.

Jackall, Robert, *Moral Mazes* (New York: Oxford University Press, 1998).

Joye, C. and Smith, P., "Most Powerful Spy Says Snowden Leaks Will Cost Lives" *The Australian Financial Review*, May 8, 2014.

Kay, John, "Should We Have Narrow Banking?" in *The Future of Finance: The LSE Report*. (London: London School of Economics and Political Science, 2010).

Kay Review of UK Equity Markets and Long Term Decision-Making (London: UK House of Commons, 2013).

Kingsford Smith, D., "Insider the FOFA Deal: Success of the Experiment Depends on Extent and Quality of Implementation," www.clmr.unsw.edu.au.

Kleinig, John, *Ethics in Policing* (Cambridge: Cambridge University Press, 1996).
  "The Blue Wall of Silence: An Ethical Analysis" *International Journal of Applied Philosophy*, 15 (2001), 1–23.
  "Rethinking Noble Cause Corruption" *International Journal of Police Science and Management*, 4 (2002), 287–314.
Kleinig, John, Mameli, P., Miller, S., Salane, D., and Schwartz, A., *Security and Privacy: Global Standards for Ethical Identity Management in Contemporary Liberal Democratic States* (Canberra: ANU Press, 2011).
Klitgaard, Robert, *Controlling Corruption* (Los Angeles: University of California Press, 1988).
Klitgaard, Robert, Maclean-Abaroa, R., and Lindsey Parris, H., *Corrupt Cities: A Practical Guide to Cure and Prevention* (Oakland, CA: ICS Press, 2000).
Klockars, C. B., "The Dirty Harry Problem" reprinted in Blumberg, A. S. and Niederhoffer, E. (eds.), *The Ambivalent Force: Perspectives on the Police* (New York: Holt, Rinehart and Winston, 1976).
Kung, Hans, *Global Responsibility: In Search of a New World Ethic* (New York: Crosswords, 1991).
Ladd, J., "Philosophical Remarks on Professional Responsibility in Organizations" *International Journal of Applied Philosophy*, 1 (1982), 58–70.
Lambsdorff, J. G., *The Institutional Economics of Corruption and Reform: Theory, Evidence and Reform* (Cambridge University Press, 2007).
Lessig, Lawrence, "Institutional Corruptions," *Edmond J. Safra Working Papers*, March 15, 2013, available at www.ethics.harvard.edu/lab.
Lessig, Lawrence, *Republic, Lost: How Money Corrupts Congress – and a Plan to Stop It* (New York: Twelve, 2011).
Lewis, M., *Flash Boys: Cracking the Money Code* (London: Penguin, 2014).
Lichtenberg, Judith (ed.), *Democracy and the Mass Media* (Cambridge University Press, 1990).
Lichtenberg, Judith, "What Are Codes of Ethics For?" in Coady, M. and Bloch, S. (eds.), *Codes of Ethics and the Professions* (Melbourne University Press, 1996).
Lindorff, D., "Chief fudge-the-books officer," www.Salon.com, February 20, 2002.
List, C. and Pettit, P., *Group Agency* (Oxford University Press, 2011).
Luban, David, *Lawyers and Justice* (Princeton University Press, 1988).
Lukes, Steven, *Power: A Radical View*, 2nd edn. (London: Palgrave Macmillan, 2005).
Machiavelli, N., *The Prince*, any edition.
MacNeil, I. and O'Brien, J. (eds.), *The Future of Financial Regulation* (Oxford: Hart Publishing, 2010).
MacNeil, I., Wotherspoon, K., and Taylor, K., *Business Investigations* (Bristol: Jordan Publishing, 1998).
Mandiant Intelligence Centre, *APT1: Exposing One of China's Cyber Espionage Units* (Washington, DC: Mandiant Intelligence Centre, 2013), available at http://intelreport.mandiant.com.
Matherm, J. and Rose, S., "Low tax sought for $2.5m super" *Australian Financial Review*, 11 (2016).

May, Larry, *Sharing Responsibility* (University of Chicago Press, 1992).

McCormack, G., *The Emptiness of Japanese Affluence* (Sydney: Allen and Unwin, 1996).

Medcraft, G., "Extending the Regulatory Perimeter: Mapping the IOSCO Agenda" *Law and Financial Markets Review*, 8 (2014), 95–97.

Meiklejohn, A., *Political Freedom* (New York: Harper, 1960).

Mellema, G., "Collective Responsibility and Qualifying Actions" *Midwest Studies in Philosophy*, 30 (2006), 168–175.

Miller, Kaarlo and Tuomela, R., "We-intentions" *Philosophical Studies*, 53 (1988), 115–137.

Miller, Seumas, "Joint Action" *Philosophical Papers*, 11 (1992), 275–299.

"On Conventions" *Australasian Journal of Philosophy*, 70 (1992), 435–445.

"Freedom of the Press" *Politikon*, 22 (1995), 24–36.

"Collective Responsibility" *Public Affairs Quarterly*, 15 (2001), 65–82.

"Collective Moral Responsibility: An Individualist Account" *Midwest Studies in Philosophy*, 30 (2006), 176–193.

"Against the Moral Autonomy Thesis" *Journal of Social Philosophy*, 38 (2007), 389–409.

"Is Torture Ever Morally Justifiable?" *International Journal of Applied Philosophy*, 19 (2005), 179–192.

"What Makes a Good Internal Affairs Investigation?" *Criminal Justice Ethics*, 29 (2010), 30–41.

"Police Detectives, Criminal Investigations and Collective Moral Responsibility" *Criminal Justice Ethics*, 33 (2014), 21–39.

"Integrity Systems and Professional Reporting in Police Organizations" *Criminal Justice Ethics* vol. 29 no. 3 2010, 241–257.

"The Corruption of Financial Benchmarks: Financial Markets, Collective Goods and Institutional Purposes" *Law and Financial Markets Review*, 8 (2014), 155–164.

"'Trust me.... I'm a (systemically important) bank!': Institutional corruption, market-based industries and financial benchmarks" *Law and Financial Markets Review*, 8 (2014), 322–325.

"The Global Financial Crisis and Collective Moral Responsibility" in Nollkaemper, A. and Jacobs, D. (eds.), *Distribution of Responsibilities in International Law* (Cambridge University Press, 2015), 404–433.

"Social Norms" in Holmstrom-Hintikka, G. and Tuomela, R. (eds.), Synthese Library Series, *Contemporary Action Theory* (Dordrecht: Kluwer, 1997), vol. II, pp. 211–229.

"Noble Cause Corruption Revisited" in Villiers, P. and Adlam, R. (eds.), *A Safe, Just and Tolerant Society: Police Virtue Rediscovered* (Winchester, UK: Waterside Press, 2004).

"Concept of Corruption" in Zalta, E. N. (ed.), *Stanford Encyclopedia of Philosophy*, Fall 2005 edn.

"Institutions, Integrity Systems and Market Actors" in O'Brien, J. (ed.), *Private Equity, Corporate Governance and the Dynamics of Capital Market Regulation* (Imperial College of London Press, 2007), pp. 297–327.

"Individual Autonomy and Sociality" in Schmitt, F. (ed.), *Socialising Metaphysics: Nature of Social Reality* (Lanham: Rowman&Littlefield, 2003), pp. 269–300.

"Noble Cause Corruption in Politics" in Primoratz, F. (ed.), *Politics and Morality* (Basingstroke: Palgrave Macmillan, 2007), pp. 92–112.

"Financial Service Providers: Integrity Systems, Reputation and the Triangle of Virtue" in Dobos, N., Barry, C., and Pogge, T. (eds.), *The Global Financial Crisis: Ethical Issues* (London: Palgrave Macmillan, 2011), pp. 132–157.

"Trust, Conflicts of Interest and Fiduciary Duties: Ethical Issues in the Financial Planning Industry in Australia" in Morris, N. and Vines, D. (eds.), *Capital Failure: Rebuilding Trust in Financial Services* (Oxford: Oxford University Press, 2014), pp. 305–331.

(ed.), *Ethical Issues in Policing* (Wagga Wagga: Keon, 1997).

Social Action: A Teleological Account (Cambridge University Press, 2001).

Model Code of Principles of Ethics (The Professional Standards Council of New South Wales and Western Australia, 2002).

The Moral Foundations of Social Institutions: A Philosophical Study (New York: Cambridge University Press, 2010).

Corruption and Anti-Corruption in Policing: Philosophical and Ethical Issues (Dordrecht: Springer, 2016)

"Joint Epistemic Action: Some Applications" *Journal of Applied Philosophy,* published online February 2016

Miller, Seumas and Blackler, John, "Restorative Justice: Retribution, Confession and Shame" in Braithwaite, J. and Strang, H. (eds.), *Restorative Justice: From Philosophy to Practice* (Aldershot: Ashgate Press, 2000).

Ethical Issues in Policing (Aldershot: Ashgate, 2005).

Miller, Seumas and Gordon, Ian, *Investigative Ethics. Ethics for Police Detectives and Criminal Investigators* (Hoboken, NJ: Wiley Blackwell, 2014).

Miller, Seumas and Makela, Pekka, "The Collectivist Approach to Collective Moral Responsibility" *Metaphilosophy*, 36 (2005), 634–651.

Miller, Seumas and Prenzler, Tim, *An Integrity System for Victoria Police: Volume 1* (Canberra: Centre for Applied Philosophy and Public Ethics, 2008).

Miller, Seumas and Walsh, Patrick, "NSA, Snowden and the Ethics and Accountability of Intelligence Gathering" in Galliott, J. (ed.), *Ethics and the Future of Spying: Technology, Intelligence Collection and National Security* (Abingdon-on-Thames: Routledge, 2015).

Miller, Seumas, Roberts, Peter, and Spence, Edward, *Corruption and Anti-Corruption: A Study in Applied Philosophy* (Saddle River, NJ: Prentice Hall, 2005).

Miller, Seumas, Curry, Steve, Gordon, Ian, Blackler, John, and Prenzler, Tim, *An Integrity System for Victoria Police: Volume 2* (Canberra: Centre for Applied Philosophy and Public Ethics, 2008).

Moffit, A., *A Quarter to Midnight: The Australian Crisis – Organised Crime and the Decline of the Institutions of State* (Sydney: Angus and Robertson, 1985).

Moore, Michael, S., *Causation and Responsibility: An Essay in Law, Morals and Metaphysics* (Oxford University Press, 2009).

Morris, N. and Vines, David (eds.), *Capital Failure: Rebuilding Trust in Financial Services* (Oxford University Press, 2014).

Morriss, Peter, *Power: A Philosophical Analysis* (Manchester University Press, 2002).

Nagel, Thomas, *Concealment and Exposure and Other Essays* (Oxford University Press, 2002).

Nagel, Thomas, *The Last Word* (Oxford University Press, 1997).

Noonan, J. T., *Bribes* (New York: Macmillan, 1984).

Nye, Joseph, "Corruption and Political Development: A Cost-Benefit Analysis" *American Political Science Review*, 61 (1967), 417–427.

O'Neill, Onora, *A Question of Trust: Reith Lectures for 2002* (Cambridge University Press, 2002).

Obermayer, B. and Obermaier, F., *The Panama Papers: Breaking the Story of How the World's Rich and Powerful Hide Their Money* (London: Oneworld, 2016).

OECD, Organisation for Economic Co-operation and Development, "Base Erosion and Profit Sharing," www.oecd.org/ctp/beps.htm.

Parsons, Talcott, *On Institutions and Social Evolution* (Chicago University Press, 1982).

Pearson, Z., "An International Human Rights Approach to Corruption" in Larmour, P. and Wolanin, N. (eds.) *Corruption and Anti-Corruption* (Canberra: Asia-Pacific Press, 2001), pp. 30–61.

Pei, Minxin, *China's Crony Capitalism: The Dynamics of Regime Decay* (Harvard University Press, 2016).

Phongpaichit, P. and Piriyarangsan, S., *Corruption and Democracy in Thailand* (Chang Mai: Silkworm Books, 1994) (1996 edition).

Pogge, Thomas, *World Poverty and Human Rights* (Cambridge, UK: Polity Press, 2008).

Pope, J. (ed.), *National Integrity Systems: The TI Source Book* (Berlin: Transparency International, 1997).

Pritchard, M. S., "Bribery: The Concept" *Science and Engineering Ethics*, 4 (1998), 281–286.

Raz, Joseph, (ed.), *Authority* (New York University Press, 1990).

Reich, R. B., *Saving Capitalism: For the Many Not the Few* (New York: Alfred A. Knoff, 2015).

Reiner, Robert, *The Politics of the Police* (Brighton: Harvester, 1985).

Reuss-Ianni, E. and Ianni, F. A. J., "Street Cops and Management Cops: The Two Cultures of Policing" in Punch, M., *Control in the Police Organisation* (London: MIT Press, 1983).

Roberts, Peter, Brown, A. J., and Olsen, J., *Whistling while they work: A good-practice guide for managing internal reporting of wrongdoing in public sector organisations* (Canberra: ANU Press, 2011).

Rose-Ackerman, S., *Corruption and Government* (Cambridge University Press, 1999).

Rothschild, E. and Sen, Amartya, "Adam Smith's Economics" in Haakonssen, K. (ed.), *The Cambridge Companion to Adam Smith* (Cambridge University Press, 2006), pp. 319–365.

Saks, M. J., "Explaining the Tension between the Supreme Court's Embrace of Validity as the Touchstone of Admissibility of Expert Testimony and Lower Courts' (seeming) Rejection of Same" *Episteme*, 5 (2008), 329–331.

Sampford, Charles, Smith, R., and Brown, A. J., "From Greek Temple to Bird's Nest: Towards a Theory of Coherence and Mutual Accountability for National Integrity Systems" *Australian Journal of Public Administration*, 64 (2005), 96–108.

Sanger, D. E., Barboza, D., and Perlroth, N., "Chinese Army Unit Is Seen as Tied to Hacking against US" *New York Times*, February 18, 2013.

Schauer, F., *Free Speech: A Philosophical Inquiry* (Cambridge University Press, 1982). *Profiles, Probabilities and Stereotypes* (Cambridge: Harvard University Press, 2003).

Schmitt, F., "Joint Action: From Individualism to Supraindividualism" in Schmitt, F. (ed.), *Socializing Metaphysics: The Nature of Social Reality* (Lanham: Rowman and Littlefield, 2003), pp. 129–166.

Schoeman, F., *Responsibility, Character and the Emotions* (Cambridge University Press, 1987).

Searle, John, *The Construction of Social Reality* (New York: Free Press, 1995). *Intentionality* (Cambridge University Press, 1983).

Seifert, J. W., *Data Mining and Homeland Security*, CRS Report RL31798 (Congressional Research Service, 2008).

Sharman, J. C., *The Despot's Guide to Wealth Management: On the Interntional Campaign against Grand Corruption* (Ithaca, NY: Cornell University Press, 2014).

Sheehan, N., "Vietnam Archive: Pentagon Study Traces 3 Decades of Growing US Involvement" *New York Times*, June 13, 1971.

Sinnott-Armstrong, W., "Entrapment in the Net" *Ethics and Information Technology*, no. 1, 1999, p. 99.

Skolnick, J., *Justice without Trial: Law Enforcement in a Democratic Society* (New York: Macmillan, 1977).

Smith, G., Button, M., Johnson, L., and Frimpong, K. (eds.), *Studying Fraud as White Collar Crime* (London: Palgrave Macmillan, 2011).

Sorkin, A., "Realities behind Prosecuting Big Banks" *New York Times*, March 12, 2013.

Soros, George, *The Crash of 2008 and What It Means: The New Paradigm for Financial Markets* (New York: Perseus Books, 2009).

Stiglitz, Joseph, *Making Globalisation Work: The Next Steps to Global Justice* (London: Penguin, 2006). *The Great Divide: Unequal Societies and What We Can Do* (New York: W. W. Norton, 2016).

Stout, Lynn, *The Shareholder Value Myth: How Putting Shareholders First Harms Investors, Corporations and the Public* (San Francisco: Berrett-Koehler, 2012).

Szigeti, Andras, "Are Individualist Accounts of Collective Moral Responsibility Morally Deficient?" in Konzelmann-Ziv, A. and Schmid, H. B. (eds.), *Institutions, Emotions and Group Agents: Contribution to Social Ontology, Studies in the Philosophy of Sociality 2* (Dordrecht: Springer, 2014).

Thompson, Dennis F., "Moral Responsibility and Public Officials: The Problem of Many Hands" *American Political Science Review*, 74 (1980), 259–273.

"Two Concepts of Corruption: Individual and Institutional" *Edmond J. Safra Working Papers*, 16 (2013) available at SSRN: http://ssrn.com/abstract =2304419 or http://dx.doi.org/10.2139/ssrn.2304419.

Ethics in Congress: From Individual to Institutional Corruption (Washington DC: Brookings Institution, 1995).

Tomasic, R. and Bottomley, S., *Directing the Top 500 (Allen and Unwin, 1993).*

Treanor, J. and Rushe, D., "HSCB to pay 1.2 billion pounds over Mexico scandal" *The Guardian*, December 10, 2012.

Wainwright, T., *Narconomics* (London: Ebury Press, 2016).

Walzer, Michael, "Political Action: The Problem of Dirty Hands" *Philosophy and Public Affairs*, 2 (1973), 160–180.

Spheres of Justice: A Defense of Pluralism and Equality (New York: Basic Books, 1983).

Weber, Max, "Politics as a Vocation" in Gerth, H. and Wright Mills, C. (eds.), *From Max Weber: Essays in Sociology* (London: Routledge, 1991), 77–128.

Economy and Society: An Outline of Interpretive Sociology (New York: Bedminster Press, 1968), 77–128.

Wells, J. T., *Fraud Examination: Investigation and Audit Procedures* (New York: Quorum Book, 1992).

Wiggins, David, "Claims of Need" in Wiggins, David, (ed.), *Needs, Values, Truth: Essays in the Philosophy of Value*, 2nd edn. (Oxford: Blackwell, 1991), pp. 6–11.

Wood, J. J., *Final Report: Royal Commission into Corruption in the New South Wales Police Service* (Sydney: NSW Government, 1998).

Zimmerman, Michael, "Sharing Responsibility" *American Philosophical Quarterly*, 22 (1985), 115–122.

Index